THE CONFEDERATE STATES MARINE CORPS:

THE REBEL LEATHERNECKS

By

Ralph W. Donnelly

Foreword

by

Brigadier General Edwin H. Simmons, USMC (Ret)

WHITE MANE PUBLISHING COMPANY, INC.
1989

This revised edition is based on Ralph W. Donnelly's privately printed limited edition three volume history of the Confederate States Marine Corps published between 1973 and 1983.

E
596
.D66
1989
June/1998

This White Mane Publishing Company, Inc., book
was printed by:
Beidel Printing House, Inc.
63 West Burd Street
Shippensburg, PA 17257

In respect to the scholarship contained herein, the paper used in this book meets the guidelines for permanence and durability of the Committee on Production Guidelines for Book Longevity of the Council on Library Resources.

For a complete list of available publications, please write:
White Mane Publishing Company, Inc.
P.O. Box 152
Shippensburg, PA 17257

Library of Congress Cataloging-in-Publication Data

Donnelly, Ralph W.
    The Confederate States Marine Corps / by Ralph W. Donnelly;
foreword by Edwin H. Simmons.
        p.   cm.
    Rev. ed. of: The history of the Confederate States Marine Corps.
1976.
    Includes bibliographical references.
    ISBN 0-942597-13-3 : $24.95
    1. Confederate States of America. Marine Corps.   2. United
States--History--Civil War,   1861-1865--Campaigns.   I. Donnelly,
Ralph W. History of the Confederate States Marine Corps.
II. Title.
E596.D66   1989   89-24824
973.7'42--dc20   CIP

PRINTED IN THE UNITED STATES OF AMERICA

TABLE OF CONTENTS

APPENDICES

PLATES AND ILLUSTRATIONS

LIST OF TABLES

FOREWORD

This book puts into one convenient volume a virtual lifetime of scholarly inquiry on the part of the author, Ralph W. Donnelly. *Rebel Leathernecks* is a good title, conjuring up, as it does, the thought of Marines in Confederate gray serving in a brave if small way at the apex of the struggle, afloat and ashore. That, in fact, is the way it was.

How Ralph Donnelly, a portly, pleasant, now elderly man, who sees the world through very thick glasses and was once a school teacher and an insurance man, became so immersed in the history of the Confederate Marines is itself an interesting story.

He remembers reading as a child some of the old-time books on the war including one, which he still has, by a Mrs. C. Emma Cheney called *Young Folks History of the Civil War*. Although born and raised in Washington, D.C., at a time when it was still pretty much a southern city, his family was not Secessionist in its inclinations. His grandfather, as a private in Company A, 1st New Jersey Infantry, had worn blue and had lost an eye and took a bullet in the chest during his first skirmish on Little River Turnpike in October 1861. Taken prisoner he languished in Libby Prison in Richmond until released in the spring of '62. He, Ralph's father, and Ralph's brother are all buried in Arlington Cemetery.

Ralph's interest in the Civil War grew slowly through high school and college. His specific interest in the Confederacy developed before World War II during his study of American political science in graduate school at Catholic University. In those years he was a junior high school teacher in Montgomery County, Maryland, and Washington, D.C. During the war he did his bit as a research analyst with the Office of Strategic Services. After the war he switched to the insurance business and worked for different firms in various places until 1967 when he joined the U.S. Marine Corps as a civilian historian. He was with the Reference Section, Historical Branch, History and Museums Division of Headquarters, Marine Corps, until his retirement in 1975 after which he moved to Washington, North Carolina, where he continues to remain very active in historical and genealogical work.

In the early 1950's he had joined both the Washington Civil War Roundtable and the American Military Institute. Membership in both these organizations brought him into contact with some great Civil War historians, including, most notably, Bruce Catton.

In the meantime he had been learning his way around the Confederate records in the National Archives. One evening at a meeting of the Roundtable he was asked what he might have learned about the Confederate States Marine Corps and he had to confess, very little.

His curiosity piqued, he began looking into the Confederate Marines. He found that almost nothing had been published on them. J. Thomas Scharf in his monumental *History of the Confederate States Navy* (1887) had given only four pages to the gray-clad Marines. Most of the few articles that had been published were derived from brief mentions in the Navy *Official Records*. Ralph began to look for more information and thus began his fascination with the Southern corps of Marines.

A first product was an article on the uniforms of the Confederate Marines in *Military Collector & Historian* in the spring of 1957. Other articles and papers followed. In 1973 he self-published his *Biographical Sketches of the Commissioned Officers of the Confederate States Marine Corps*. This was followed in 1976 by *The History of the Confederate Marine Corps* and in 1979 by his *Service Records of Confederate Enlisted Marines*. All three of these were paperbacks in essentially monograph format and with typescript text.

Rebel Leathernecks is a polished new edition of *The History of the Confederate States Marine Corps*. "Definitive," "seminal," and "classic" are effusive, much over-used, words. In the case of *Rebel Leathernecks*, however, they are well-justified. There may be further refinements to the history of the Confederate Marines, but the great body of scholarship has been accomplished by Ralph Donnelly.

Edwin H. Simmons
Brigadier General
U.S. Marine Corps (Retired)

Mount Vernon, Virginia
29 July 1989

Chapter I

ORGANIZATION OF THE
CONFEDERATE STATES MARINE CORPS

The Confederate States Marine Corps in its organization and contemplated use was designed to be a counterpart of the United States Marine Corps. One of the earliest acts of the Confederate Congress was a law that all the United States laws for Marines, not inconsistent with Acts of the Confederate Congress, were declared adopted and applicable to Confederate Marines.[1]

It is inevitable in studying the Confederate Marine Corps that comparisons be made with the United States Marine Corps and the respective Navies they were designed to serve.

The pre-war size of the U.S. Marine Corps varied, but it was in the neighborhood of an over-strength infantry regiment plus a headquarters staff. The report of the Marines' Adjutant Inspector dated November 2, 1860, gave the strength of the Corps as 1,775.

Table 1

Pre-War Strength of U.S. Marine Corps: November 2, 1860

Officers	63
Non-comms. at Headquarters*	4
1st Sergeants	46
Sergeants	63
Corporals	139
Musicians	28
Drummers	39
Fifers	37
Boy learners of music	9
Privates	1347
Aggregate	1775

* The noncommissioned officers at Headquarters were a Sergeant Major, a Quartermaster Sergeant, a Drum Major, and a Fife Major.

1

The 63 officers of the U.S. Marine Corps were commissioned as follows:

Colonel Commandant		1
General Staff:		
Major, Adjutant and Inspector	1)	
Major, Paymaster	1)	
Major, Quartermaster	1)	
Captain, Asst. Quartermaster	1)	4
Lieutenant Colonel		1
Majors		4
Captains		13
First Lieutenants		20
Second Lieutenants		<u>20</u>
		63[2]

Replacements for separated and retired officers as well as newly created billets led to the appointment of 63 new second lieutenants from April 1861 through April 1865. The needs of the Corps speeded up the promotion process to such an extent that 13 second lieutenants appointed on November 25, 1861, were promoted to first lieutenant the next day.

The peak strength of the U.S. Marine Corps during the war was February 28, 1865, when 90 officers (including five retired but recalled for active duty) and 3,791 enlisted men were carried on the rolls for a total of 3,881.

As of 1861, the U.S. Navy consisted of 1,457 officers and 7,600 men authorized, a total of 9,057. Based on the peacetime figures, the U.S. Marine Corps was about 20% of the size of the U.S. Navy.

The Confederate States of America established its provisional government at Montgomery, Alabama on February 4, 1861. Three days after Jefferson Davis was inaugurated on February 18, an act to establish the Navy Department became effective with the President's signature.

Plans were made by the new office of Secretary of the Navy Stephen R. Mallory for the creation of a Navy and a Marine Corps. Working hand-in-hand with the Congress, a budget was prepared March 12, 1861, which contemplated a six-company battalion of Marines commanded by a major.[3] An Act of Congress on March 16, 1861, formalized this budget and provided for a headquarters consisting of a major, a quartermaster, a paymaster, an adjutant, a sergeant major, and a quartermaster sergeant. It also provided specifically for six companies, each consisting of a captain, a first lieutenant, a second lieutenant, four sergeants, four corporals, two musicians, and 100 men. This provision for companies was an innovation suggestive of the British Marine Corps rather than that of the United States. Although a major (battalion commander) was provided for in the Act of March 16, 1861, the executive functions of the Corps were originally exercised by Secretary of the Navy Mallory. Mallory's supervision of details extended from issuing orders to officers directly to approving the appointment of the orderly (or first) sergeant for Captain Van Benthuysen's company.

Under the Act of March 16, the ratio of officers (commissioned and noncommissioned) to privates was 11 to 100, or roughly 1 to 9. Since this was a regular unit, the high professional character of the officers was preserved by the application of the principle of appointment rather than resorting to the debilitating volunteer principle of the election of officers by the men.

After the enlargement of the Confederacy by the secession of the Upper South (Virginia, Arkansas, Tennessee, and North Carolina) and the outbreak of hostilities, the Corps was enlarged by the amendatory Act of May 20, 1861, which authorized a Corps of 46 officers and 944 enlisted men. Although a company organization was not prescribed in the Act, the ranks and ratings provided for were similar to those authorized for an Army ten-company regiment.

The new law provided for a colonel, a lieutenant colonel, a major, a quartermaster (major), and adjutant (major), a paymaster (major), a sergeant major, a quartermaster sergeant, and two [principal] musicians. The Colonel Commandant, Lloyd J. Beall, was appointed May 23, 1861, three days after the reorganization Act of May 20 was approved. The lieutenant colonel and the line major did not accept their appointments until the next month. These were obviously meant to constitute the staff of the Corps. This was confirmed by the Secretary of the Navy in a communication to the Comptroller of the Treasury on February 20, 1862, in which he stated, "The Paymaster, Quartermaster, and Adjutant of the Marine Corps, are staff officers, and are entitled to the same pay and allowances as the General Staff of the Army." The Act provided 10 captains, 10 first lieutenants, 20 second lieutenants, 40 sergeants, 40 corporals, 10 drummers, 10 fifers, and 840 privates for the line of the Corps, but no reference was made to organization by companies.[4] Disregarding the musicians, the ratio of officers (commissioned and non-commissioned) to privates was improved to 12 to 84, or 1 to 7.

This improved ratio was in accord with the suggestion of the Secretary of the Navy in his report of April 26, 1861, that another second lieutenant be added to each company. The frequent use of Marines in small detachments was cited as justification for the additional officer.

The use made of the Marine Corps dictated further organizational changes, and on August 14, 1862, the Colonel Commandant wrote to Secretary Mallory:

> Having found by experience that the peculiar service of marines requires a larger proportion of noncommissioned officers and musicians than the land service, from the fact that the Corps is liable to be divided up into small detachments as guards on board of ships and at naval stations, and that these guards are not complete without one or two noncommissioned officers and a musician to each, I have the honor to present for your recommendation to Congress the following amendment to the act above cited: That the act of Congress reorganizing the Marine Corps, approved May 20, 1861, be so amended as to allow the Corps of Marines 60 sergeants, 60 corporals, 20 drummers, 20 fifers, and 2 principal musicians, the principal musicians each to receive the pay and allowances of a sergeant-major.[5]

The colonel's suggestions were incorporated in the Act of September 24, 1862, which increased the non-commissioned officer strength of the Corps by an additional 20 sergeants and 20 corporals. The Act also added 20 drummers and 20 fifers to the previously authorized ten of each as well as clarifying the position of the two musicians with the regimental staff as "Principal Musicians."[6] This made, at least on paper, each company consist of 84 privates, six musicians, six corporals, six sergeants, and four officers. Disregarding the musicians, the ratio of officers (commissioned and non-commissioned) to privates was further improved to 16 to 84, or 1 to 5¼.

The Confederate Marine Corps was never recruited up to its authorized strength, but did show a gradual increase while the battle-worn, disease-plagued, and detail-depleted Army regiments were reduced progressively to almost company strength. In 1861 the Corps had an estimated strength of 350 officers and men which probably increased to about 500 in 1862. The Corps' strength was up to 560 by 1863, and to 571 as of October 31, 1864. It probably never exceeded 600 at any one given time, yet there were about 1,200 different enlisted men on the rolls at one time or another.

The Confederate Navy had under 700 commissioned and warrant officers in late 1864, and the total enlisted strength as of October 31, 1864, was 3,674. So the Confederate Marine Corps at the end of October 1864 was slightly more than 13% for the size of the war-time Navy of which it was a component part. True, it never achieved its authorized strength and had to be content with no more than 60%, but that was acceptable for the size navy it was serving. For that matter the Navy itself never seemed to have enough men. The war-time U.S. Marine Corps amounted to less than 7% of the size of the Federal Navy (less than 3,900 in the Marine Corps compared with about 59,000 naval personnel), a drop from its pre-war 20%.

The post of Corps Quartermaster was a subject of some legislative tinkering in 1861. The original Act of March 16, 1861, prescribed that there be both a quartermaster and a quartermaster sergeant. The Act provided further that it was the duty of the Corps Quartermaster to visit the different posts where portions of the Corps might be stationed as often as necessary for the proper discharge of his duties. The Act of May 20, 1861, continued these duties adding that the post of quartermaster should carry the rank of major.

The first quartermaster of the Corps was Samuel Z. Gonzalez, a former U.S. Naval Storekeeper, who resigned from the Warrington Navy Yard, Pensacola, Florida, at the time of that state's succession. He was appointed as of April 3, 1861, but resigned shortly afterwards effective September 13, 1861. His duties were performed for a brief time by Captain John D. Simms, and then on November 6, 1861, all property and funds belonging to the Marine service in Gonzalez' possession were ordered turned over to Lieutenant Adam N. Baker, detailed as Acting Quartermaster to the Marine Battalion at Pensacola,

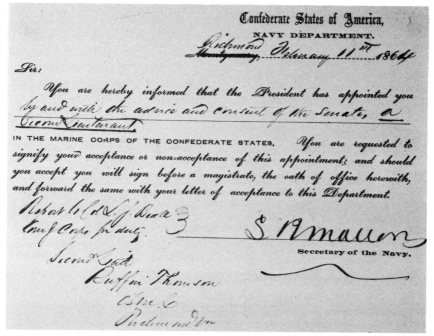

Type of Confederate States Marine Corps Commission actually used.
From the RUFFIN THOMSON PAPERS, Southern Historical Collection, University of North Carolina Library, Chapel Hill, N.C., by permission.

but this came to an end with Baker's desertion from the service shortly thereafter on November 13, 1861.

A bill to dispense with the office of Corps Quartermaster was introduced on December 5, 1861, in the Confederate Provisional Congress, read the first and second times, and referred to the Committee on Naval Affairs. On December 11, Colonel Beall sent his objections to Secretary of the Navy Mallory in a letter in which he outlined his concept of the duties of the quartermaster as well as those of the paymaster:

> Sir: I have the honor to return herewith a copy of a bill before Congress to abolish the office of quartermaster to the marines and to devolve the duties of that office upon the paymaster of the Corps.
>
> I feel satisfied from my experience that the passage of this bill by Congress would impair the efficiency of the Marine Corps and prove detrimental to the interest of the Government. This Corps, being, as it were, isolated from the other military branches of the service, should be complete within itself, and with this view Congress has organized it and made a distinct appropriation for its support. The duties of quartermaster of the Marine Corps combine those of commissary of subsistence and ordnance officer, besides all those that relate to the procuring, safe-keeping, and the distribution of clothing. The quartermaster is required to give bonds for the faithful performance of these duties and for a strict accountability of the funds placed in [his] hands. Without such an officer it would frequently be necessary to entrust public money to officers who have given no security for its faithful disbursement.
>
> I consider the duties of paymaster entirely incompatible with those of quartermaster, inasmuch as his time is periodically employed in making payments at points where the marines may be stationed, in paying the officers monthly by correspondence, and in settling the accounts of discharged marines. These duties require him to be fixed in position, when not engaged in making his periodical payments, and would prevent him from giving that attention to the duties of quartermaster that their importance requires.
>
> It is true that in the Army there are no paymasters, but it has been found necessary to detail quartermasters to perform their duties alone. Besides, in the Army there are not only commissaries of subsistence but officers detailed especially as ordnance officers and for the purpose of procuring clothing material and having it made up.

In conclusion, I beg leave to remark that the Marine Corps is now embarrassed with a want of clothing, in consequence of being for some time past without a quartermaster.[7]

On December 23, 1861, Mr. C. M. Conrad of the Committee on Naval Affairs reported the bill back with the recommendation that it be tabled and that the Committee be discharged. This was agreed to, and on the next day President Davis nominated Algernon S. Taylor, Captain, C.S.M.C., as quartermaster. His nomination was approved February 7, 1862, with an effective date of December 4, 1861.

The South's surplus of naval officers and the need for utilizing their training brought about a Congressional Act authorizing the President to confer temporary rank and command on Navy officers doing duty with Army troops. These officers were highly useful and almost the sole source of experience in handling large guns. This Act omitted to authorize similar temporary rank and command for Marine officers, and an amendatory Act rectifying the omission was passed by Congress and approved under the date of February 5, 1862.[8]

An act of justice was the Act of April 11, 1863, which made special provision for those Confederate Navy and Marine officers who had resigned from the U.S. Navy or Marine Corps on account of secession and who had been arrested and imprisoned as a consequence of their resignation. The Act provided that they should receive leave of absence and pay for the term of their imprisonment up to the time of their appointment in the Confederate Navy or Marine Corps.[9] Existing records show that Thomas S. Wilson received $561.00 for the period from August 22, 1861, to February 28, 1862. John R. F. Tattnall was paid $317.30 for the period from October 6, 1861, to January 21, 1862. Robert Tansill received $813.40 for the period from August 24, 1861, to January 19, 1862.

Once the Marine Corps got under way, it become necessary to establish a headquarters staff. Colonel Beall requested legislation on December 17, 1861, to provide for a headquarters clerk, considered indispensable for the proper keeping of the books, records, and returns of the Corps. The Secretary of the Navy on March 6, 1862, authorized the employment of a writer for the Commandant's office with the pay and allowances of a sergeant major ($60 per month). John L. Adams had been employed in January in anticipation of the written approval. Several months later his salary was raised to $1,000 per year.

The budget for 1863 provided for a salary of $1,500, but the Secretary of the Navy refused to pay the increase until Congress passed permanent legislation. This was done, and the President signed the Act on April 30, 1863, providing for a clerk to the Commandant of the Marine Corps and another to the Quartermaster. The annual compensation was not to exceed $1,500 each.[10]

In November 1863, the Budget estimates for the first half of 1864 included a salary item of $750 for a quartermaster's clerk. Elsewhere the budget provided compensation for a regimental sergeant major and a regimental quartermaster sergeant at $21 a month each (the same as line sergeants) as well as for two civilian clerks, one each to Headquarters and the Paymaster, at $125 a month ($1,500 a year). Pay vouchers of the Corps Paymaster for the second half of 1864 reflected the increasing inflation of the times. Clerk John L. Adams was paid $333.33 a month ($4,000 a year) during a period when Quartermaster Sergeant Benedict Howard received only $24.80 a month.

Table 2

THE STAFF OF THE CONFEDERATE STATES MARINE CORPS

Colonel Commandant	Lloyd J. Beall	5/23/61 for the war
Lieutenant Colonel	Henry B. Tyler	6/18/61 for the war
Major	George H. Terrett	6/20/61 for the war
Quartermaster (Major)	Samuel Z. Gonzalez	4/3/61 to 9/13/61
Quartermaster (Actg.)	John D. Simms	c. 10/20/61
Quartermaster (Actg.)	Adam N. Baker	11/6/61 to 11/13/61
Quartermaster (Major)	Algernon S. Taylor	12/4/61 for the war
Paymaster (Major)	Richard T. Allison	5/10/61 for the war
Adjutant (Major)	Israel Greene	8/14/61 for the war
Sergeant Major	Edwin Wallace	2/1/64 to 7/25/64
Quartermaster Sergeant	Wm. H. Robinson	c. 11/1/62
Quartermaster Sergeant	Benedict Howard	1864
Principal Musician (2)	No record of any appointments	
Headquarter's Clerk	John L. Adams	1/ /62 thru 12/31/64
Paymaster's Clerk	No record of any appointment*	
Quartermaster's Clerk	John W. Slaughter	c. 11/1/61 to c. 8/ /63
Quartermaster's Clerk	Wm. F. Phillips, Jr.	c. 8/ /63 to c. 12/ /64

* Private Arthur Hayne Beall, son of Colonel Beall, was assigned to duty with the Paymaster upon enlistment in October 1864. On November 27, 1864, he was discharged from the Corps upon being appointed an Acting Midshipman in the C.S. Navy.

Several years passed before efforts were made to secure a Sergeant Major for the Corps. Adjutant Greene forwarded Colonel Beall's request in January 1864 for Captain Meiere in Mobile to try to procure a suitable man for the post. Meiere then placed an advertisement in the Mobile *Advertiser and Register* which

which read, in part:

> Wanted . . . . ALSO—A thoroughly drilled, sober and intelligent Man for the position of Sergeant Major of the Confederate States Marine Corps. Apply immediately at the MARINE BARRACKS, on Commerce street, below Church.[11]

Several applications were received in response to the advertisement, but Captain Meiere was most impressed by an application from an Edwin Wallace, late of the Royal Marines and the son of a Sergeant Major of the Royal Marines. Wallace had been born in the Service, educated at the Duke of York Military School in London, and appeared to be fully qualified. Meiere then requested Admiral Buchanan to either transfer Wallace to the Marine Corps or to discharge him to permit his enlistment, believing that his appointment would ". . . greatly add to the efficiency of the military branch of the Navy."[12]

By General Order dated February 1, 1864, at Mobile, Private Edwin Wallace was promoted to Sergeant Major of the Confederate States Marine Corps.

A week later, on February 8, 1864, Wallace left Mobile for Drewry's Bluff outside Richmond. Meiere at this time expressed his regrets that he had not obtained permission to retain Wallace for a month or two as his command ". . . would have been much benefited by his instruction." Meiere wrote a complimentary statement concerning Wallace's knowledge of all the different drills, sword exercises, his habits, neatness, and respectful demeanor. He remarked that some "brushing up" in company drill and in the giving of orders as prescribed in Hardee's Tactics was wanted, but expressed confidence this could be soon corrected.

But something apparently went wrong. By March 27, 1864, Captain Meiere was replying to Colonel Beall's inquiry as to what promises had been made to Sergeant Major Wallace on his enlistment. Meiere responded that no promises whatever had been made, but that he had been told he would probably be comfortably fixed at Drewry's Bluff as he could have his wife with him, as some of the other men did, subsequent to his enlistment. The disagreement was apparently deep seated as the records show that Wallace was reduced to the ranks on July 25, 1864, and deserted on July 30, 1864.

The Headquarters of the Marine Corps in Richmond was located on the 4th floor of Mechanics' Institute, on 9th Street between Main and Franklin, in 1862, and was apparently moved to 115 Broad Street, formerly occupied by Swords & Thaw, Dry Goods, between 8th and 9th Streets, by January 1863.

The 115 Broad Street address was given as the office of the Corps Quartermaster in May 1862. Mail was handled through a post office box, and letters addressed to officers at this box would be forwarded to them wherever located. In October 1862 this box was #961; in July it was #1100.

One feature of the Marine Corps system established by the Confederate Government that is rarely mentioned, and which was probably more of a theory than an accomplished fact, was that of the "Invalid Corps." The Invalid Corps was a means by which individuals who were physically unsuited for combat duty could be retained for limited service and receive regular pay.

The original Act of February 17, 1864, applied to all officers, non-commissioned officers, musicians, privates, and seamen who had or might become disabled by wounds or other injuries or disease contracted in line of duty. The Invalid Corps was placed under the Secretary of War even though the Act referred to "seamen," but Marines were not specifically mentioned. The Act of June 7, 1864, extended the provisions of the original act to Marine Corps enlisted men by specific reference. These men now became eligible for retirement to the Invalid Corps. The amending act also vested the assignment to duty of members of the Navy and Marine Corps Invalid Corps in the Secretary of the Navy rather than in the Secretary of War as provided in the original act.[13]

The Act of January 16, 1865, providing one complete suit of uniform clothing for officers of the Army, Navy, and Marine Corps, included officers of the Invalid Corps below the rank of brigadier general in the Army or captain in the Navy.[14]

These acts were followed by the Act of January 27, 1865, which permitted the provisions of the Invalid Corps Act to be extended to enlisted personnel of the Navy or Marine Corps who had or who might resign or receive an honorable discharge in ignorance of the Act. It also gave the President (with the advice and consent of the Senate) the power to reappoint to his former rank any meritorious disabled officer who had resigned prior to the Act, or in ignorance of it. The exercise of this permission was limited to those who could present a medical certificate of disability, and, if the officer as assigned to active duty, he would rank from the date of assignment to such duty. It further provided that retired officers would receive half pay except when on active duty when they would receive the full pay and allowance appropriate to their rank.[15]

Late in 1864, a petition reported signed by nearly all of the officers of the Marine Corps was sent to the President asking to have the Corps transferred to the Army and increased to a brigade of three regiments. One of these three regiments was to be designated as "Marine Infantry," and from it the Secretary of War would obtain the guards requisitioned by the Secretary of the Navy. This must have been the change alluded to by Lieutenant Thomson who wrote, ''We are making an effort to have our organization changed now if we succeed we will be placed upon a more respectable footing than now . . .''[16]

The proposal reached the floor of the Confederate Congress on February 6, 1865, when Senator William A. Graham of North Carolina (who had been the U.S. Secretary of the Navy, 1850-'52) submitted the following resolution:

> *Resolved,* That the Committee on Naval Affairs be instructed to inquire into the expediency of transferring the Marine Corps, or so much thereof as may not be required for urgent duty in that branch of service, to the Army, for such length of time as the condition of the public defense may require.[17]

But the Journal records show that no time was lost in burying the proposal since two days later the Committee on Naval Affairs was discharged from further consideration of the resolution.

This movement probably had its root in the relative inactivity of the Marine Corps and the great need for increasing the strength of the Army. The possibility of promotion should the Corps be expanded to a brigade probably had an appeal to some. After all, no officer originally commissioned as a captain or a higher rank received a permanent promotion during the entire war, and only a few enjoyed temporary Provisional Army commissions at a higher grade. It was rumored in March 1865 that Marine Major George Hunter Terrett, who held a Provisional Army commission as a colonel, would be promoted to brigadier general, but nothing came of it. This would have been turning the clock back as Terrett had been a brigade commander immediately before the first battle of Manassas [Bull Run], being replaced by James Longstreet who was in turn followed by Ambrose P. Hill.

NOTES AND REFERENCES

Chapter I — Organization of the Confederate States Marine Corps.

1. *Provisional and Permanent Constitutions of the Confederate States* (Richmond, Va.: Tyler, Wise, Allegre and Smith, Printers, 1861), 104: Sec. 9, No. 70, An Act to Provide for the Organization of the Navy, approved March 16, 1861.

2. *Annual Report of the* [U.S.] *Secretary of the Navy for 1860,* 383-385; report of the Adjutant & Inspector, U.S.M.C., to the Commandant, U.S.M.C., dated November 2, 1860.

3. U.S. Navy Department, *Official Records of the Union and Confederate Navies in the War of the Rebellion* (30 vols. and index; Washington, D.C., 1894-1922), Series II, vol. 2, 45: #4, Estimates of pay of officers, noncommissioned officers, musicians, and privates of the Marine Corps for the year ending the 4th February, 1862. This source cited hereafter as *N.O.R.* with Series I understood. Roman numerals "II" will precede *N.O.R.* to indicate Series II.

4. C.S. Navy Department, *Register of the Commissioned and Warrant Officers of the Navy of the Confederate States, to January 1, 1863* (Richmond, Va.: Macfarlane & Fergusson, 1862), 35. Also Microcopy 625, Roll 412, *Area File # 7,* p. 458, U.S. National Archives: S. R. Mallory to Lewis Cruger, Navy Dept., Richmond, February 20, 1862.

5. II *N.O.R.* 2, 251: Col. Lloyd J. Beall, C.S.M.C., to Secretary of the Navy S. R. Mallory, Richmond, Va., August 14, 1862.

6. James M. Mathews, *Public Laws of the Confederate States of America passed at the second session of the First Congress; 1862* (Richmond: R. M. Smith, Printer to Congress, 1862), 60.

7. II *N.O.R.* 2, 116-117: Col. Lloyd J. Beall, C.S.M.C., to Secretary of the Navy S. R. Mallory, Richmond, Va., December 11, 1861.

8. James M. Matthews (ed.), *The Statutes at Large of the Provisional Government of the Confederate States of America* (Richmond: R. M. Smith, Printer to Congress, 1864), 5th Session, Provisional Congress, Chap. LXVI, 258.

9. W. W. Lester and William J. Bromwell, *A Digest of the Military and Naval Laws of the Confederate States, from the Commencement of the Provisional Congress to the End of the First Congress Under the Permanent Constitution* (Columbia: Evans and Cogswell, 1864), paragraph 583, 209-210.

10. James M. Matthews (ed.), *Public Laws of the Confederate States of America passed at the third session of the First Congress; 1863* (Richmond: R. M. Smith, Printer to Congress, 1863), Chap. LVI, 132.

11. Mobile *Advertiser and Register,* Friday, January 22, 1864, 2:5. Also in editions for January 24, 2:6, and January 30, 2:5.

12. MS. *Day Book of the Commanding Officer, C.S.M.C., Mobile, Ala.* [Letter Book, October 8, 1862 - June 7, 1864], 215. This source cited hereafter as *Mobile C.O. Day Book.*

13. James M. Matthews (ed.), *Public Laws . . . 1st Session, 2d Congress* (1864), Chap. XXI, 260.

14. U.S. War Department, *The War of the Rebellion: A Compilation of the Official Records of the Union and Confederate Armies* (128 vols. and atlas; Washington, D.C., 1880-1901), Series IV, Vol. 3, 1033. This source cited hereafter as *O.R.* with Series I understood. Roman numerals "II," "III," or "IV" will precede *O.R.* to indicate Series II, III, or IV. Also in Charles W. Ramsdell (ed.), *Laws and Joint Resolutions of the Last Session of the Confederate Congress (November 7, 1864 - March 18, 1865) Together with the Secret Acts of Previous Congresses* (Durham: Duke Univ. Press, 1941), 16.

15. Ramsdell, *op. cit.,* 27-28.

16. Lt. Ruffin Thomson, C.S.M.C., to "Dear Pa," Drewry's Bluff, Va., November 3, 1864, Papers of Ruffin Thomson, Accession 3315, Southern Historical Collection, University of North Carolina. This source cited hereafter as *Thomson Pp., SHC, UNC.*

17. U.S. Senate, 58th Congress, 2d Session, Document 234, *Journal of the Congress of the Confederate States of America, 1861 - 1865* (7 vols.; Washington, D.C., 1904), IV, 523. Cited hereafter as "C.S. Congress *Journal.*"

Chapter II

THE FIRST YEAR

The first recruiting done for the Confederate Marine Corps was at the original seat of government, Montgomery, Alabama, by the first officer appointed in the Corps, Captain Reuben T. Thom. Thom recruited some 27 or more men in Montgomery between March 25, the date of his commission, and April 29, 1861. Four days after Thom's commissioning two more captains of Marines (George Holmes and Andrew J. Hays) and three lieutenants (Calvin L. Sayre, Becket K. Howell, and Henry L. Ingraham) were appointed with commissions dating from March 29, 1861. Captain Alfred C. Van Benthuysen was commissioned to rank from the following day, March 30, 1861, and was ordered immediately to New Orleans on recruiting duty under Captain George Holmes.

Recruiting efforts then shifted to the port city of New Orleans. Existing records indicate enlistments were first made there around April 10, 1861, by Captains Holmes and Van Benthuysen. Captain Thom followed and recruited between May 23 and June 29, 1861. On admittedly incomplete records, we find that at least 194 men were recruited between April 10 and June 29, 1861.

Table 3

Recruitment of Marines at New Orleans: April 10 - June 29, 1861

Recruited by:	Co. A	Co. B	Co. C	Co. F	Total
Captain George Holmes	33	2	5	1	41
Captain A. C. Van Benthuysen	0	113	0	0	113
Captain Reuben Thom	0	0	34	0	34
Not given	1	0	5	0	6
Total	34	115	44	1	194

Even so, enlistment was considered slow and was excused on the grounds that both the states of Alabama and Louisiana were recruiting in the same towns at the same time.

Lieutenant Henry Laurens Ingraham, C.S.M.C., arrived in Pensacola, Fla., from Montgomery on the morning of April 3, according to newspaper accounts. Five days later he was reported as having a few Marines with him (probably some of the 10 recruited at Montgomery in March) and planning to organize a large corps. The same paper reported the appointment of Samuel Z. Gonzalez, late U.S. Navy Storekeeper, as Quartermaster with the rank of major in the Marine Corps of the Confederate States.

Upon the recruitment of sufficient men at New Orleans to constitute a company, Capt. Van Benthuysen's company (soon to be known as Company B) was organized on April 23 with the appointment of three sergeants, four corporals, and two musicians. First Sergeant Charles Scott's appointment dated back to April 15. The *Daily Picayune* reported the next day, April 24, that a company of 95 Marines recruited by Capt. Van Benthuysen would leave for Pensacola that afternoon by the Mobile boat. Twenty of Van Benthuysen's Marines were being left in New Orleans to form part of the crew of *Sumter*.[1]

Available records show that 95 men were enlisted by Van Benthuysen on or before April 23 at New Orleans, and that none were recruited by him for a period of nine days, probably when he was at Pensacola. His recruiting resumed on May 3, 1861.

The Pensacola correspondent of the New York *Herald* wrote his paper on April 26:

> Captain Van Benthuysen's corps of Confederate States marines, about eighty strong, reached this city this evening from New Orleans and Mobile, via Hall's Landing. They passed other troops on the way, and reached here in good condition. The corps was recruited mostly from the United States army in Texas, artillery and infantry. They are the first instalment of regular Confederate States Marines that have arrived here.[2]

This suggestion that the Confederate Marines had been recruited from U.S. Army troops has not been confirmed by other sources, but it was a possibility. A total of 319 enlisted men deserted from the 1st and 3rd Infantry, 2nd Cavalry, and 1st and 2nd Artillery in Texas from February through April 1861.[3] Although, it has been thought these men entered units organized in Texas.

While not too much is known of the background of the men enlisted at these first recruiting centers, one phase of the story is unveiled by the statements of seven of the deserters picked up by the Federals in Florida in October 1861. Of these men, four claimed Pennsylvania as their home, two claimed New York, and the seventh hailed from Indiana. No statement is given for two others in the party. The presence of Northern men in the Confederate Marine Corps was explained by the simple and logical fact that they were steamboat men on the Mississippi stranded and out of a job by the approaching hostilities and faced with the alternatives of enlisting, being imprisoned, or starving. These men characterized their fellow Marines as largely Northern or foreign born and estimated that some 200 of the 250 in the three companies serving in the Pensacola area would desert at their first opportunity.[4]

While these men may have been completely honest in explaining how they happened to join the Corps and why they deserted, they misjudged their comrades as to the probability of desertion for the heavy per cent they forecast failed to materialize.

Secretary of the Navy Mallory reported to President Davis on April 26 that a company of 100 Marines (Captain Van Benthuysen's company) had been assigned to a heavy battery confronting Fort Pickens, off Pensacola, and the men were being actively drilled in the use of heavy guns as well as in the use of small arms.

Secretary Mallory wrote Captain Van Benthuysen the next day (April 27):

> Your dispatch, announcing your arrival at Pensacola with Seventy enlisted marines, was received this day.
>
> You will turn the men over to Capt. Thom and proceed to N. Orleans, enlist the remainder of your Company, and return to Pensacola to command them.
>
> Two Sergeants and a Corporal will be turned over to you by Captain Thom, and you will transfer them to Captain Holmes to aid the recruiting service.[5]

The New Orleans *Delta* reported to its readers that as of April 27, 1861, a contingent of 109 Marines was serving with the left wing (Colonel Adley H. Gladden commanding) of the Army assembled around Pensacola, and the Warrington Navy Yard. With Captain Thom at Pensacola it is probable that the difference in the number of Marines present between Van Benthuysen's recruits and the 109 mentioned represented the recruits enlisted at Montgomery by Thom.

Recruiting continued back in New Orleans for both the Navy and the Marine Corps. A naval atmosphere was created by the use of the steamship, *Star of the West*, as a receiving ship at the Navy Yard at Algiers, opposite New Orleans. In use before being commissioned, she was re-christened the C.S.R.S. *St. Philip* and became an official unit of the new Confederate Navy on May 4, 1861, under the command of Midshipman Comstock. Captain Van Benthuysen returned from Pensacola about this time and by the middle of the next week was reported as having a second contingent of some 150 Marines ready to leave for duty before Fort Pickens. Actually this second group went off under the command of Lieutenant Becket K. Howell.

Captain Van Benthuysen was apparently considered the senior Marine officer at Warrington (adjacent to Pensacola) as of May 17. On that day Secretary of the Navy Mallory, performing the functions of the Marine Corps commandant, sent the following instructions to the Captain from the Navy Department at Montgomery:

> Clothing and uniforms are ordered [?] at New Orleans for the Corps at Warrington. You are enjoined to see that the Marines are so instructed and drilled in the use of their arms as to make them efficient soldiers in the shortest time. During the hot weather early morning and late evening drills should be observed. You can procure all the arms required from the Ordnance officer on duty at Warrington.
>
> You will urge the completion of the tents at the earliest moment, and in the mean time you will select and prepare an appropriate place for an encampment, bearing regard to health, shade and water,—and obtain the Commanding General's permission to occupy it.
>
> The health of the men must be studied,—and upon the arrival of a superior officer you will report these orders to him.[6]

Within a short time the Pensacola Marines were drawing assignments. An early assignment was one of those non-sensational yet thoroughly essential jobs that Marines everywhere are called upon to perform, that of maintaining a property guard. For example, a detachment went to guard naval property at the Farnsworth depot on the railroad. This guard was reduced on June 8, 1861, to a minimum of one "competent non-commissioned officer and two privates," and the balance of the detachment sent to rejoin the battalion at the Navy Yard. Five men of Company B were still guarding the naval stores on the railroad as late as December 31, 1861.

Shipboard duty came up on June 19, 1861, when General Braxton Bragg ordered that a commissioned officer [Second Lieutenant David G. Raney, Jr.] and 12 men be detailed from the Marines as a guard on the Steamer *Time* in the Pensacola harbor, replacing a detachment of Alabama volunteers. Company B furnished a corporal and 10 privates to this guard. When a Marine Guard (possibly a replacement) was relieved on November 17, 1861, the Marine officer in charge was Lieutenant Wilbur F. Johnson.

A Harbor Police was organized about this time to patrol Pensacola harbor. One or more small boats were assigned to this duty, and the Marines were called upon to furnish crews. In the beginning, Company B furnished 13 men for this duty, carrying them on the muster roll as on "Daily Duty."

But the opportunity for sea duty was not being overlooked. Back in New Orleans progress was being made toward placing the C.S. Steamer *McRae* and the C.S.S. *Sumter* in commission. A draft was made upon the Marines stationed at Pensacola for the guard for the *McRae*, and an order was issued on June 27, 1861, for Lieutenant Richard H. Henderson, one sergeant, two corporals, and 20 privates, selected from the "best instructed men of that corps," to proceed immediately to New Orleans and report to the Commanding Officer of the C.S. Steamer *McRae*.[7] These men were furnished by Captain Van Benthuysen's company, later Company B.[8]

During the same month Lieutenant Howell was preparing a Marine Guard for service on the *Sumter*. The Navy officers were all present and the crew had been "shipped" by May 24, 1861. Presumably they were quartered on the *Star of the West* (the C.S.R.S. *St. Philip*) until received on board the *Sumter* on June 3. A clothing bill for the contingent indicates the guard for the *Sumter* totaled 21 Marines, consisting of Lieutenant Howell, three noncommissioned officers, and 17 privates.[9] This figure is confirmed on the payroll of the *Sumter* covering the period of April 1 through September 30, 1861. The Marines composing the guard detailed for the *Sumter* were apparently a challenge to Lieutenant Howell as well as to Commander Raphael Semmes, the commanding officer. Semmes, in describing the guard, commented: "The Marines being mostly foreigners, Germans, are the most indifferent set of men I have in the ship. It is very difficult to 'lick them into shape.' " In view of the last names of the men, one wonders why Semmes referred to them as "Germans"; their names seem to be largely English and Irish.

Prior to 1861, the U.S. Government was engaged in the early stages of the construction of a fort on Ship Island, an island located in the Gulf of Mexico about 12 miles south of Biloxi, Mississippi. On May 22, 1861, the Cutter *Morgan* (formerly the Revenue Cutter *Lewis Cass*) acting under the orders of Col. William J. Hardee landed men who destroyed various wooden buildings and the lighthouse structure. Major General David E. Twiggs almost immediately decided to occupy and fortify the island. While awaiting some heavy guns to mount on Ship Island, he reported on June 18 that he had assembled some troops at Mississippi City, Mississippi (near Gulfport).

Captain Edward Higgins, a member of General Twiggs' staff and formerly an officer of the U.S. Navy, approached Lieutenant Alexander F. Warley, of C.S.S. *McRae*, with a request for men to implement a planned expedition down the lake to capture the Federal launches which had been conducting raids in Mississippi Sound.

Warley hesitated as he was not the captain of *McRae*, but Higgins persisted and told Warley he only needed his men for 36 hours. Captain Huger was away on a visit for several days, leaving Warley in command temporarily.

Finally Warley consented to join the expedition, and "made a clean sweep of all hands, carrying off even the captain's cook, steward and servant, all our young officers, all the marines, and last [but] not least, the surgeon . . . ." "Away we went, with a crew of 80 sailors, landsmen and boys, some twenty marines and a sergeants' squad of men my friend [Capt. Higgins] had procured from the Louisiana regulars."[10]

Somewhere during the move, an additional 35 Marine recruits under Captain Reuben T. Thom, then recruiting in New Orleans, were added to the expedition. These men, joined with the 20 Marines from *McRae,* gave Captain Thom some 55 Marines under his command which went ashore on Ship Island.

The expedition left New Orleans on July 5, 1861, under the over-all command of Captain Higgins, with Captain A. L. Myers in command of the steamer *Oregon,* and the steamer *Swain,* under Lieutenant A. F. Warley. Both ships were reported to be manned, at least in part, by the crew of *McRae*. Failing to encounter any of the Federal launches, Captain Higgins decided to occupy Ship Island.

The ships stopped first at Bay St. Louis to fill sand bags to protect the boilers, and to complete related chores, then left at 9 A.M. on Saturday, July 6. After arriving at Ship Island, 140 men were put on shore at 4 P.M. on July 6 along with the 8-inch gun, a 32-pounder, and two small howitzers under the command of Lieutenant Warley.

Three days later, on July 9, Warley's men exchanged fire with the U.S.S. *Massachusetts* and drove her off. Warley had high praise for Thom, commenting: "Where work was to be done there was the captain [Thom] to be found and his men working as I never saw raw recruits work before."[11]

Warley's command of sailors and Marines was relieved by three companies of the 4th Louisiana Volunteers under Lieutenant Colonel H. W. Allen and was back in New Orleans on July 10 to rejoin *McRae*. Thom's 35 recruits were probably then sent to join the Marine battalion at Pensacola. Thom continued his recruiting efforts in Mobile during August and the first half of September 1861, presumably completing his company organization.

Warley was fortunate as his command suffered no casualties and General Twiggs' headquarters issued a general order of thanks and appreciation which may have restored Warley to Captain Huger's good graces.

GENERAL ORDER.
Confederate States of America   )
Headquarters Department No. 1   )
New Orleans, La., July 12, 1861.)

The Major General commanding this ·department, thankfully acknowledges the valuable and efficient services rendered by the officers, seamen and marines of the C.S. Navy, on the late expedition which resulted in placing Ship Island in our possession, and driving off the vessels stationed there. Their gallantry in volunteering for the service, the prompt manner in which they executed it, the patience and cheerfulness with which they submitted to labor and exposure, and the coolness and courage displayed by them in the action with the enemy, call for his unqualified admiration. To Lieutenant commanding. T. B. Huger, of the Confederate Steamer McRae, for his hearty cooperation in allowing his officers and men to join the expedition, the Major General tenders his special thanks.

By order of Major General Twiggs.

EDWARD HIGGINS,
Captain La. Artillery C. S. A., and Aid-de-Camp.[12]

About this time Secretary of the Navy Mallory was reporting to President Davis that "Recruiting for the Marine Corps is progressing, and it is stationed at the Pensacola forts, cooperating with the army under General Bragg."

The first Marine Corps staff officer to report to Pensacola for duty was Major Samuel Z. Gonzalez, the Corps Quartermaster. A former U.S. Navy storekeeper, he was appointed as of April 3, 1861. He cleared General Bragg's headquarters on June 28 and was assigned to duty with the Marine battalion serving in Colonel A. H. Gladden's Third Brigade.

The commanding officer of the Marine battalion at Pensacola, Lieutenant Colonel Henry B. Tyler, reported to General Bragg for duty and was assigned to "join the detachment of his corps" with the Third Brigade on July 26, 1861. Tyler was an experienced Marine officer with 38 years' service and had just resigned as the Adjutant and Inspector of the U.S. Marine Corps on May 2, 1861. But his resignation was not accepted, and he was recorded in Federal records as "Dismissed" as of May 4, 1861. His Confederate Marine commission dated from June 18, 1861. Tyler was the temporary commander of Bragg's Third Brigade by September 1, 1861. His service at Pensacola probably terminated on December 10, 1861, when he went on leave for 30 days.

Colonel Lloyd J. Beall, just resigned as a U.S. Army major and paymaster on April 22, 1861, had ben appointed as the commanding officer of the Corps on May 23, 1861, in Montgomery, two days after Congress adjourned. Beall was a West Point graduate of 1830 and had been at the Academy for a time with Jefferson Davis who had graduated in 1828. The two had been second lieutenants in the First Infantry from July 1, 1830, until March 4, 1833. Major George H. Terrett, the third ranking officer of the Corps, and lately a captain and brevet major, U.S. Marine Corps, was commissioned on June 20, 1861. Terrett served first as a colonel in the Provisional Army of Virginia and as a brigade commander in the Alexandria-Manassas area from at least April 29 until after the battle of Manassas on July 21, 1861. Then he apparently reported directly to Marine Headquarters in Richmond where he found no particular need for his services in the Corps at that time. It was not until June 19, 1861, that the new Adjutant, Major Israel Greene, entered the Confederate Marine Corps.

The Corps came in for criticism early in September. A detail of nine enlisted men sent out in a rowboat at Pensacola on harbor patrol on the night of the 8th failed to report back on the morning of the 9th. General Bragg immediately issued an order requiring the Commanding General of the Second Brigade to regulate and control this patrol duty and publically stated: "The desertion, from this service to the enemy, of a whole boat's crew of Marines on duty under the orders of a private, reflects great discredit on the discipline and management of that organization."[13] He even complained to the Adjutant General of the Army about the incident, charging "gross neglect on the part of the officer in charge of this service in not sending an officer in command on such a duty."[14]

A Board of Officers appointed by General Bragg to investigate the disappearance of those men reported they had been "captured by the enemy." But, as we have already seen, they were actually deserters, and the fulminating Bragg, his Board to the contrary, had sized up the situation correctly.

At 3:30 A.M. on the morning of September 14, 1861, some 100 Federal officers, sailors, and Marines, made a raid by small boats into Pensacola harbor with the objects of destroying the Confederate schooner *Judah* and spiking a large gun in battery at the southeast end of the Navy Yard.

The *Judah* was moored by the wharf under the protection of the battery manned by Captain Van Benthuysen's company of Confederate Marines. In spite of a desperate resistance on the part of the crew of the *Judah*, the Federals succeeded in taking possession of the schooner and in burning her to the water's edge. Two men made their way to the 10-inch Columbiad on the wharf, shot down the single Marine sentry, spiked the gun, and brought off its tompion as a trophy.[15] Bragg was of the opinion that the deserters of September 8 led the raid, but these men appear to have been kept in custody and sent North, being finally released at Fort Hamilton, New York, on October 10, 1861.[16]

Although Federal Marines participated in the raid, the attacking party apparently withdrew before the Confederate Marines from the battery reached the scene of action. Armed conflict between the two Marine Corps was narrowly missed.

An escaped slave reported that 30 Confederates, "principally Marines under the command of H. B. Tyler, late adjutant of our Marine Corps," had been killed in this attack on the Pensacola Navy Yard, but the available Confederate records fail to substantiate this rumor.

In mid-September another draft was made upon the Corps at Pensacola, this time for an entire company. Captain George Holmes and his Company A were ordered on September 18 to proceed to Savannah, Georgia, ". . . and report for duty without delay to Flag-Officer Josiah Tattnall, Commanding the C.S. Naval forces on the coasts of South Carolina and Georgia."[17] The company moved promptly and was in camp at Savannah by September 20 as on that day Captain Holmes requisitioned a cord of wood for a company of 70 enlisted men. The transfer of Holmes' company left Van Benthuysen's and Thom's companies, less detachments, still on duty at Pensacola with a reported strength of 12 officers and 196 enlisted men.

This conforms to a statement made to Federal authorities by Private Almond Rice, one of the party of nine deserters who failed to return from patrol duty in Pensacola harbor on the night of September 8, 1861, that there were three companies of Marines at the Warrington Navy Yard amounting to some 250 men. (This was prior to the departure of Holmes' company.)

During the months of August, September, and October, efforts had been made by Captain Andrew J. Hays to recruit a Company D for the Marine Corps at the Mississippi River port of Memphis, Tennessee. His efforts could hardly be termed highly successful since, according to incomplete and scattered records, he obtained only 28 men. Lieutenant George P. Turner was endeavoring at the same time to recruit in Mobile for Captain Hays' Company D with but little success.

In a tit-for-tat type of warfare, although somewhat belatedly after the destruction of the *Judah*, the Confederates made a return stab on October 9, 1861, against the camp of the 6th New York Volunteers ("Billy" Wilson's Zouaves) on Santa Rosa Island, about four miles from Fort Pickens. General Richard H. Anderson assembled a force of available Army troops and a detachment of Navy officers and Marines under Captain Brent. Two Marine officers, Lieutenants Calvin L. Sayre and Wilbur Johnson, served as volunteer aides to General Anderson and were complimented for rendering "active and efficient assistance throughout the whole of the operations."

". . . Lieutenant Sayre, while fearlessly using his revolver with effect, had his thigh bone shattered just above the right knee by a musket-ball, and, being left upon the ground, fell into the hands of the enemy." Sayre was disabled for active field duty thereafter as a result of this wound, but it was General Bragg's opinion that "he would make an active and efficient beaureax officer." Paroled, he was later exchanged and ordered on various staff and bureau assignments with the Army.

Lieutenant Johnson escaped being wounded and received the commendation of General Anderson who said of him, ". . . the ardor and intrepidity of Lieutenant Johnson, while deserving especial notice, give promise of this young officer's future success and distinction."[18]

The Marines were not assigned to any of the three provisional battalions organized by General Anderson, and the inference is that they were held in reserve, possibly on the boats used to ferry over the Army troops. The consolidated casualty list for this action shows no Marines killed or wounded other than Lieutenant Sayre serving on the General's Staff.[19] In the absence of official reports, recourse must be made to other accounts. The Petersburg *Express,* in reporting the arrival of Thom's Company C from Florida, credited them with having participated in the Santa Rosa battle. Years later, published accounts of the war service of W. G. Huddleston, a one-time member of Thom's Company C, claimed he was wounded on Santa Rosa Island by the explosion of a shell.

Captain Van Benthuysen's company of Confederate Marines served a battery consisting of one 10-inch Columbiad on the stone wharf inside the Warrington Navy Yard. The battery had been constructed by the Marines "in a handsome and efficient manner," according to General Bragg.

When the Federal bombardment opened on the morning of November 22, the Marine battery withheld its fire until positive orders were received. General Richard H. Anderson ascribed the failure to reply immediately to the misconstruction of an order given at the time of the Santa Rosa expedition. After firing only two shots, General Anderson sent a "Cease firing" order, fearing to provoke heavy enemy fire which might damage the steamer *Time* lying at the wharf.

The Marine Corps' participation in this bombardment was best told by Captain Van Benthuysen's report. This report, found in the form of a corrected draft, was not available to the editors of either the Army or Navy *Official Records* who were forced to footnote General Anderson's report with the cryptic and unsatisfying comment, "Not found." This is the text of the report:

Van Benthuysen Battery
Navy Yard nr. Pensacola, Fla.
Nov. 26th/61

Thos S. Mills
Captn., & A.A.G.

Sir:

At 10 A.M. on the 22nd the enemy opened fire. Some of the shot fell in the yard.

I immediately placed by Battery and everything in readiness for action.

I received orders from Genl. Anderson at 11 A.M. to reply.

I fired 2 shots directing them at the Fort.

Shots	Length of fuze	Elevation	Point of Bursting
1st	5 inch	11⁰	On Parapet
2d	Over 5 inch	"	Short of fort

I then received orders from Genl. Anderson to cease firing: which I did.

The Enemy directed many shots at the Battery. Left Wing of Yard and the Steamer Time. They seemed to use many descriptions of missiles: All failing in their object.

My Battery altho. an open one, owing to the skill in its erection, presented so perfect a Barrier, that I met with not a single casualty, as regards men, magazine or gun.

The firing of the enemy was on that day extremely accurate. Shot after Shot falling about the Battery & Stmr Time.

The enemy ceased firing at about 9 P.M., a heavy rain falling.

At 10 A.M. on the 23rd I recd. orders through Capt. Thos. S. Mills, A.A.G., to reply if the enemy commenced firing. And, to do so about once an hour. The enemy opened fire at 10 1/2 A.M. I replied immediately. Being the first battery to do so on our side. Many shots from their Rifle Battery, were very accurate; grazing the top of my Embankment. Altho I fired 20 shots that day and succeding night, there were not near so many fired at me, as the day before.

The following is a statement of my shots the effect of any Shots being 20 for the day & night.

Shots	Length of fuze	Elevation	Where Struck
1	5 1/3 in.	11°	Burst short of Fort
2	"	12°	" " " "
3	"	"	" " " "
4	6 in.	12 1/2°	Centre of Fort
5	Over 6 in.	12 1/3°	" " "
6	about 6 in.	"	Short
7	6 in.	12 1/2°	Short
8	6 1/3 in.	12 1/2°	Centre of Fort
9th	"	"	" " "
10th	6 1/2	"	" " "
11th	"	"	" " "
12th	6 7/10	12 1/3°	Glacis
13th	"	"	Over wall
14th	"	"	At and over wall
15th	6 8/10	"	Centre of Fort
16th	6 9/10	12 3/4°	Proper range
17th	6 9/10	12 3/4°	Proper range
18th	"	"	" "
19th	7	"	Glacis
20th	"	"	Wall

The enemy did not cease firing till about 2 1/2 A.M. on the 24th. The Company fired from only one or two Batteries toward the _____ shot were directed at the Navy Yard and My Battery.

Nor did I cease until after he had done so. But fired the last two shots. I then ceased, it being about 4 A.M. The Colorado having moved to the left of my Battery, I immediately raised the Embankment on that side several feet.

I have not met with a single casualty during the entire action, nor has my battery.

I take occasion to report to you the excellent conduct of my men.

I take pleasure in saying that Lt. Henderson and Lt. Hyams merit great praise for their cool and gallant conduct: it being the first time of their being under fire.

> I am, Sir, very respectfully
> Yr. obt. servt.
> A. C. Van Benthuysen
> Captn. Marine Corps
> Comm dg Battery[20]

Captain Thom's company of marines was in the Navy Yard at the time the bombardment began, but was among the troops withdrawn from the Yard. While standing near the north wall and supposedly out of action, a shot penetrated the walls and among those wounded by the flying brick were two of Thom's Marines.[21]

Several days after the November 22-23 attack on Pensacola, the Secretary of the Navy asked General Bragg for the release of another company of Marines. This time orders from the Colonel Commandant called for the transfer of Captain Thom's Company C,[22] but the order, dated the 26th, did not specify the destination or the nature of the new assignment.

The day after Captain Thom's company was ordered away, General Bragg made various transfers to Van Benthuysen's Company B which was remaining at Pensacola. Included in these transfers were some 19 men recruited by Captain Andrew J. Hays and by Lieutenant George P. Turner for Company D along with several other men soon to be discharged for disability. It was probably at this time that Thom's company received 15 men originally recruited by Captain Hays in Memphis, Tennessee. Several days later, on December 3, 1861, Captain Hays was ordered to duty with nine new companies of Mississippi volunteers, remaining on Army duty for the remainder of the war. The men intended for Company D to be commanded by Captain Hays seem to have been distributed between Companies B and C and their company organization abandoned.

The scheduled departure of Company C irked Bragg and brought forth this acid comment (which incidentally reveals the company's destination) directed to Adjutant General Cooper:

> Captain Thom's company of Marines, 100 men, leaves today [November 29, 1861] for Virginia, by request of the Secretary of the Navy. This is the third draft made on me, and while it gives me great pleasure to discipline and instruct his men, the Secretary must excuse me for declining any longer to furnish him arms, &c. It is a depleting process I cannot stand.[23]

And so it was. The arms, accoutrements, ammunition, and camp equipage drawn by the company from the stores of the Army of Pensacola were ordered returned before the departure of the company. Then, undoubtedly much to the dyspeptic Bragg's disgust, and reflecting upon the discipline and instruction that it had gven him such "great pleasure" to impart, the arms were found to be in poor shape. A general order was issued commenting on the "gross and unpardonable neglect by officers and men" of the weapons which had resulted in many being "seriously damaged, some entirely ruined." The officer or soldier who by neglect or intention destroyed the efficiency of a gun was characterized as being as harmful to his country as though he had abandoned the weapon to the enemy on the battlefield, and Bragg promised to disarm any such careless company in the future and "turn over their guns to better men."[24]

At the time of the detachment of Thom's company from the Army of Pensacola, Col. Beall requested that Marine detachments for the steamers *Patrick Henry* and *Jamestown* be organized from Thom's company and sent on to Richmond while the remainder would report to Flag-Officer Forrest at the Gosport Navy Yard, near Norfolk. It was this last detachment that ultimately went on board C. S. S. *Virginia* (late *Merrimack*). It was requested that the company have its full complement of officers with the sick or absent being replaced. Upon arrival of the *Virginia's* detachment at the Gosport Yard, they were sent on board *United States*, serving as a Receiving Ship.[25]

The company's arrival at Petersburg, Va., was the subject of a news story in the Petersburg *Express* around December 5, 1861,

> It is a splendid company of men, numbering 110—all active, young, and able-bodied. They have been on duty at Pensacola for the last eight months, and have participated in the two recent engagements there, viz: The Santa Rosa battle, and the engagement with Fort Pickens. A portion of them will be detailed to man the Patrick Henry, and the balance of them proceed to the Merrimac. Their commander

gives them the character of being the most desperate fighting men in the South, and woe be to the luckless Yankees that engage them. Captain Thom, we believe, is a native Virginian—from Fredericksburg, or vicinity.[26]

Another group desertion took place on December 21, 1861, from Captain Van Benthuysen's company stationed at the battery on the Navy Yard wharf. A group of six men quickly spiked the two guns of the battery (evidently one had been added since the November bombardment), jumped into a waiting boat, and rowed rapidly across the harbor to Fort Pickens. Only one shot was fired by a sentinel. They reached Fort Pickens, just twelve minutes away, before the alarm was spread to the other batteries. They had been able to enlist the sentinel on guard over the battery to join them.[27] This helped prevent an alarm and made a successful get-away possible.

Colonel Harvey Brown, U.S.A., at Fort Pickens, shipped the men north on the U.S. Steamer *Rhode Island* to Philadelphia. From there they were transferred to Fort Lafayette in New York Harbor. Within several days all had taken the oath of allegiance and had been released. One of these men was from Massachusetts, one from Wisconsin, one from Maine, and three from New York. All told the same story of being Northerners trapped in New Orleans by the outbreak of the war and being compelled by economic necessity to join the Confederate service.[28]

Remaining on duty at Woolsey, Florida, (then a village to the north and immediately adjoining the Navy Yard) after the transfer of Companies A and C, and the disbanding of Company D, was Captain A. C. Van Benthuysen's Company B which at the end of the year consisted of five officers and 79 men present and 27 absent. Of those absent, 20 were assigned to the *McRae* on the New Orleans Station and five were guarding naval stores on the railroad. By February 1, 1862, only a "Detachment C.S. Marines" of unknown strength was still on assignment to Brigadier General Sam Jones' Army of Pensacola.

The departure of Thom's Company C on November 29, 1861, from Pensacola for Virginia left just Van Benthuysen's Company B at Pensacola. On February 12, 1862, Company B was ordered to Mobile for naval service. They left two days later by train. Upon arriving at Mobile, a detachment was employed for a time as a Marine Guard on the Receiving Ship *Dolman* and on the gunboat *Florida*. Service on *Florida* (later *Selma*) was brief as her log carries the comment, "On the 2nd [of March] transferred the guard of ten Marines to Capt. Van Benthuysen of the C.S. Marine Corps."[29] Some Marines of Company B had been left behind at Pensacola under the command of Lieutenant R. M. Ramsey who witnessed the disability discharges of a group of eight Marines on or about February 24th. He signed their papers as "Lt Comdg Co." He was then under orders to bring all the stores under his charge as Acting Quartermaster to Mobile, closing out the Marine presence at Pensacola.

The assignment of Van Benthuysen's company to Mobile was of short duration for they were sent to Virginia almost immediately. A future Marine officer, Ruffin Thomson, encountered them in Richmond the night of March 9 and left a word picture in a letter home:

> . . . there being no hotel there, I had to pass the night in a car surrounded by a company of marines just ordered from Pensacola. They spake the "rich Irish Brogue." My pocket was not picked. All that have been victims of Richmond rascality agree they would rather risk their pocketbooks in their [the Irish Marines'] hands than with a Richmond hotel keeper.[30]

On March 11, 1862, just two days after the *Monitor-Merrimack* [Virginia] engagement, Van Benthuysen's company reported for naval service at the Gosport Navy Yard.

A detachment of Van Benthuysen's company managed to get captured during the summer of 1862. The major clue to this capture is the official notice of the exchange of "Capt. A. C. Van Benthuysen's Marines" as published in Special Order 191, paragraph 3, item 10, A. & I.G., dated August 16, 1862. The most probable locale of this surrender was New Orleans in April 1862, and the reference was probably to the Marine Guard of the *McRae* which was a detail from Van Benthuysen's company. We do know that in June 1862 Navy Paymaster John W. Nixon, formerly of New Orleans, was in Jackson, Mississippi, engaged in settling the accounts from New Orleans and had been directed to pay the paroled men on his books up to the date of their transfer to Paymaster Ware at Mobile.

Marine Paymaster Richard T. Allison wrote Lieutenant James R. Y. Fendall, C.S.M.C., (at Mobile?) on August 17, 1862, concerning payments due various Marines and commented, apropos to the above "By this time, I presume, all the paroled marines have been released. But of this you will hear from the Adjutant." The final transfer of Marines' accounts from Paymaster Nixon at Jackson, Mississippi, was not reported to the Navy Department until November 15, 1862.

NOTES AND REFERENCES

Chapter II — The First Year.

1. New Orleans *Daily Picayune*, Supplement, Wed., April 24, 1861, 5:5.

2. Washington *Evening Star*, Tues., May 7, 1861, 2:4, "Pensacola Affairs."

3. Richard P. Weinert, Jr. "The Confederate Regular Army," *Military Affairs*, vol. 26, no. 3 (Fall 1962), 100.

4. II *O.R.* 2, 96-97: statements of Almond Rice, John Matthews, Samuel Benham, B[enjamin] F. Lidy, Ovid P. Reno, and John Harmon. Confederate records give Reno's name as "Renault." Almond Rice did return to his home in Angelica, N.Y., and does not seem to have taken any further part in the war. He had two brothers in the Federal service, Robert and Charles. Rice married late in life, being past 49 years old, and apparently lived out an otherwise uneventful life in Angelica.

   Benjamin F. Lidy (Lighty) returned to York County, Pa., when released as did Ovid P. Reno where they were friends and neighbors for years after the war. One of Lidy's sons married a daughter of Ovid P. Reno. Reno served as a corporal, Co. K, 188th Pennsylvania Volunteers. He died Sept. 14, 1910, and Lidy in 1912. Both are buried in the Bethel Methodist Cemetery, Chanceford Township, York County, Pa., near Shenks Ferry on the Susquehanna.

5. Secretary of the Navy S. R. Mallory to Capt. Van Benthuysen, Montgomery, Ala., April 27, 1861, in Papers of Capt. Alfred C. Van Benthuysen, Louisiana Historical Association Collection, MSS. Dept., Special Collections Division, Tulane University Library. Cited hereafter as *Van B. Pp.*

6. *Loc. cit.,* Secretary of the Navy Mallory to Capt. Van Benthuysen, Montgomery, Ala., May 17, 1861.

7. G.O. 70, H.Q. Troops C.S. near Pensacola, Fla. (Bragg), June 27, 1861, *Entry 265, R.G. 109,* U.S. National Archives.

8. Payroll for Capt. Van Benthuysen's company, C.S.M.C., for April-June 1861, dated June 30, 1861, *Van B. Pp.*

9. Papers relating to the C.S.S. *Sumter,* C.S.N. Miscellaneous Papers, Accession 438, Portfolio #10, Manuscripts Division, Library of Congress. Now on microfilm.

10. Warley's story is to be found in Microcopy #1091, *Subject File of the C.S. Navy,* Roll 13, frames 667-673.

11. *O.R.* 53, 708-709: report of Lt. A. F. Warley, C.S.N., to Capt. E. Higgins, C.S.A., New Orleans, July 10, 1861.

12. New Orleans *Daily Picayune*, Sat., A.M., July 13, 1861, 2:3. See also "A Naval Brush at Ship Island" in the *Daily Picayune* for July 11, 1861 (also in P.M. edition for July 10); also under "The City" column, "The Fight at Ship Island" in the same issue.

13. S.O. 227, H.Q. Troops C.S. near Pensacola, Fla. (Bragg), Sept. 9, 1861, *Entry 265, R.G. 109,* U.S. National Archives.

14. *N.O.R.* 16, 675: Brig. Gen. Braxton Bragg to A.G.C.S. Army, H.Q. Troops C.S. near Pensacola, Fla., Sept. 16, 1861.

15. *Ibid.,* 670-672: report of Flag-Officer Wm. Mervine, U.S.N., U.S. Flagship *Colorado*, Sept. 15, 1861.

16. II *O.R.* 2, 96-97.

17. S.O. 237, para. 1, H.Q. Troops C.S. near Pensacola, Fla. (Bragg), Sept. 18, 1861, *Entry 265, R.G. 109,* U.S. National Archives.

18. *O.R.* 6, 463: report of Brig. Gen. Richard H. Anderson, C.S.A., Oct. 23, 1861.

19. Microcopy #836, *C.S. Army Casualties,* Roll 1, "Florida: Santa Rosa Island," frames 180-183, U.S. National Archives.

20. Report of Capt. A. C. Van Benthuysen, Nov. 26, 1861, *Van B. Pp.*

21. *O.R.* 6, 495: report of Brig. Gen. Richard H. Anderson, Nov. 28, 1861.

22. G.O. 131, para. 1, H.Q. Army of Pensacola (Bragg), Nov. 26, 1861, *Entry 265, R.G. 109,* U.S. National Archives.

23. *O.R.* 6, 772: Maj. Gen. Braxton Bragg to Adjt. Gen. S. Cooper, C.S.A., Nov. 29, 1861. An edited version is also printed in *N.O.R.* 16, 854.

24. G.O. 133, H.Q. Army of Pensacola (Bragg), December 1, 1861, *Entry 265, R.G. 109,* U.S. National Archives.

25. Col. Lloyd J. Beall, C.S.M.C., to Gen. Braxton Bragg, H.Q., C.S.M.C., Richmond, Va., November 20, 1861, *C.S.N. Subject File, OV, R.G. 45,* U.S. National Archives.

26. "Company of Marines" from the Petersburg *Express* reprinted in the Washington, N.C., *Dispatch,* c. December 17, 1861, 4:1.

27. Record of Events, Muster Roll for Co. B, C.S.M.C., for November-December 1861, *Van B. Pp.*

28. II *O.R.* 2, 229, 341, and II *O.R.* 3, 205.

29. Record of Events, Muster Roll for Co. B, C.S.M.C., for Nov. 1, 1861-Feb. 28, 1862, *Van B. Pp.* Also *Log of C.S.S. Florida* (later *C.S.S. Selma*) for March 1-8 [1862], p. 6, Accession 1542, Southern Historical Collection, University of North Carolina.

30. Ruffin Thomson to "Dear Pa," near Richmond, March 10, 1862, *Thomson Pp.,* Southern Historical Collection, University of North Carolina. This observation was called to my attention by Major Don Gardner, U.S.M.C., who did his M.A. thesis in 1973 on *The Confederate Corps of Marines* at Memphis State University.

Chapter III

MARINES IN VIRGINIA

An oft-quoted story based on the statement of J. Thomas Scharf, the widely known historian of the Confederate Navy, credited Richmond as being the focal point for the concentration of many former U.S. Marine Corps officers and about 100 ex-enlisted U.S. Marines in May 1861. These men, according to Scharf's version, became the nucleus of the Confederate States Marine Corps in the Virginia area. But his version does not conform to the facts relating to the early organization of the Corps as detailed in the preceding chapter.

The Marine Corps activities in Virginia in 1861 were basically in the Norfolk area and originated with the Gosport Navy Yard affair of April 20, 1861. Existing records show that First Lieutenant Adam N. Baker, U.S.M.C., attached to the Norfolk naval station, resigned at the time the Gosport Yard was changing hands, and Captain Jabez C. Rich, U.S.M.C., deserted from the *Pennsylvania* at Norfolk. A Private Heilman [Julius F. Heileman] U.S.M.C., who refused to help defend *Pennsylvania,* was sent ashore by Lieutenant Commanding Donaldson. Heilman later served as a Junior Second Lieutenant in the Henrico (Virginia) Artillery and as a sergeant in the Richmond Fayette Artillery.

One of the stories concerning the Gosport Yard that has practically disappeared with time is that "a sergeant of Marines named Myers, knowing what was to take place, and not wishing to be carried off with his company, set fire to the barracks before the appointed time, and endeavored to escape in the confusion. He succeeded, but was shot at several times while scaling the walls."[1] In partial confirmation of this story, Captain Charles Wilkes, U.S.N., reported officially that the Marine barracks had *by some accident* caught fire at an early hour [probably 2 A.M.].

This must have been the same Myers who had been an orderly sergeant in the Marine detachment stationed in the Navy Yard, but, as a Virginian, had been unwilling to be in arms against his State and had managed to remain behind when the *Pawnee* and *Cumberland* left the Gosport Yard. William Lamb, of Norfolk, Virginia, recommended to the Governor of Virginia on May 2, 1861, that

Sergeant Myers, late of the U.S. Marine Corps, be commissioned a captain in the service of the State. He did become the captain of a company of Virginia Volunteers organized in Portsmouth which became Company E, Sixth Virginia Infantry, but the company had a short life, falling victim of too strict discipline.[2]

The United States Marine detachments at the Gosport Navy Yard were not a source of recruits for the Confederate Marine Corps as the U.S. Marine Corps records show that just two men deserted on April 20, 1861. These have been identified as sergeants in Captain Thom's company of Confederate Marines who enlisted at Montgomery, Alabama, on April 27, 1861. Strangely enough, neither Myers nor Heilman [Heileman] were reported as deserters.

It was a Virginia State Marine Corps which had its beginning in the Norfolk area in the spring of 1861, not the Confederate States Marine Corps.

Captain Robert B. Pegram, Virginia Navy, received orders from Governor John Letcher of Virginia on April 18, 1861, to proceed to Norfolk and there assume control of the naval station with authority to organize naval defenses, enroll and enlist seamen and marines, etc. Lieutenant Adam N. Baker, who had just resigned from the U.S. Marine Corps, was immediately appointed a captain in the Virginia Marine Corps. As such, on the 22nd (?) he received orders from Yard Commandant French Forrest to "at once open a Rendezvous for men for the Marine Corps of Virginia," and to appoint the proper noncommissioned officers.

The Virginia State Ordinance of April 27, 1861, provided for a Navy of 2000 seamen and marines with their officers, the sailors being enlisted for three years and the marines for five, but the number actually enlisted has not been determined.

Shortly thereafter J. Otey Bradford (U.S. Naval Academy, 1857-'59) was appointed a lieutenant in the Virginia Marine Corps, and on May 12 he was ordered to report for duty on board the Frigate *United States*, serving as receiving ship in the Gosport Yard. On May 23 Captain Jabez C. Rich (formerly of the U.S. Marines) was assigned to duty at the Craney Island battery. Other Virginia Marine Corps officers, in addition to the U.S. Marine Corps officers coming South, included Lieutenants Andrew Weir (formerly a lieutenant in the U.S. Navy) and C. Miles Collier (also found as "Colyer").

The number of enlisted Virginia Marines must have been small for on June 7, 1861, Commander Thomas T. Hunter was ordered to Raleigh, North Carolina, to try to secure "100 Minnie Rifles or muskets for the use of the Marine Guards" of the Norfolk Naval Station.[3]

The conversion of the Steamer *Yorktown* in Richmond into a naval vessel brought about an order on July 10, 1861, transferring all the seamen, ordinary seamen, landsmen, and Marines on the Receiving Ship *United States* in Gosport to the *Yorktown* (soon to be known as the *Patrick Henry*). Seven enlisted Marines, presumably just transferred from Virginia State to Confederate service, went on board the *Patrick Henry* on July 13, 1861, but were transferred about three weeks later on August 4 to the *Jamestown*.

On June 4, 1861, the Richmond *Daily Examiner's* correspondent, "Seaboard," at Portsmouth was writing that serious consideration was being given to converting Captain John E. Deans' Portsmouth National Greys company into Marines. It was felt in Portsmouth that there was an immediate need for a nucleus for building this essential arm of defense. The tentative plan was to place part of the company on board the Virginia Receiving Ship as a Marine Guard and retain the remainder on duty as a police guard for the Navy Yard. The transfer of the Virginia Navy to the Confederate States four days later on June 8 made it unnecessary to convert Captain Deans' company, and it became Company H of the Third Virginia Infantry on July 12, 1861. This company had been ordered to the Gosport Navy Yard on April 21, 1861, and remained there doing guard duty until August when it received orders to rejoin its regiment. The Norfolk County Rifle Patriots (Company F, 41st Virginia Infantry, Captain William H. Etheridge) were transferred to the Navy Yard during the latter part of May 1861 where they did guard duty while the ironclad *Virginia (Merrimack)* was being built. In March 1862, after the arrival of Captain Van Benthuysen's company of Confederate Marines, this company left the Navy Yard and joined its regiment at Sewell's Point.

The affiliation of Virginia with the Confederate States made the maintenance of a separate military and naval force unnecessary, and steps were soon taken to assimilate the Virginia forces into those of the Confederacy. The Committee of the Virginia Governor's Advisory Council, consisting of John J. Allen, Francis H. Smith, and M. F. Maury, reported that President Davis was willing "to accept the services of the officers, seamen, and Marines of the Virginia Navy as troops of Virginia now in service for the war." Acting on this information, the Advisory Council of the State of Virginia then advised the Governor to issue a general order transferring to the authority of the Confederate States all the officers, seamen, and Marines of the Provisional Navy of Virginia. This was done by General Order #25 dated June 8, 1861.[4]

The transfer of the Virginia Navy to the Confederate States on June 8, 1861, was not without complications for the Virginia Marine officers. Not all the officers of the Virginia Navy (and Marine Corps) were transferred to Confederate service, but just those who had resigned from the U.S. Navy in consequence of the secession of Virginia or of any of the Confederate States and who were fit for active service. Virginia officers who had not resigned from the U.S. Navy on account of the secession or who were not regarded as fit for active service were not commissioned in the Confederate service. This restriction would not affect Jabez C. Rich or Adam N. Baker who were entitled to their Confederate Marine commissions. Baker accepted his Confederate Marine commission on June 6, 1861, and hence was not involved in the transfer of Virginia Marines to Confederate service. These conditions did leave Lieutenants Andrew Weir, C. Miles Collier, and J. Otey Bradford without Confederate commissions.

On July 23, 1861, both Captain Rich and Lieutenant Weir were dismissed from the service of Virginia for inefficiency,[5] but Captain Rich was in a position to accept a commission in the Confederate Marine Corps which he did on October 26, 1861.

On August 2, Congress asked the Secretary of the Navy to report on the reception of officers of the Provisional Navy of Virginia into the Confederate Navy. Shortly afterwards, Second Lieutenant J. Otey Bradford of the Virginia Marine Corps serving on board the C.S. Steamer *St. Nicholas* at Fredericksburg, Virginia, wrote a letter dated August 19, 1861, presenting his dilemma to G. W. Munford, Secretary of the Commonwealth of Virginia. Bradford complained that although the Confederate Navy Department issued him orders, they refused to pay him either pay or travel money upon submitting his vouchers and orders. He had run out of personal funds and requested guidance for presenting a claim.[6]

The fact that some of the Virginia Marine officers had not been accepted by the Confederacy led to a remonstrance from Captain John R. Tucker, C.S.N., on August 22, 1861, to Hon. C. M. Conrad, Chairman of the Naval Affairs Committee, that although the Confederate Navy Department did not recognize Virginia Marine officers on their rolls for pay, it was issuing orders to such officers. Tucker's avowed intent in writing the letter was to attract attention to an area which probably needed legislation. The Secretary of the Navy acknowledged that the order from the Confederate Navy Department was a mistake and against the instructions of the Department.[7] However, with the commissioning of the remaining Virginia Marine officers in other services, the questions became moot.

On November 22, 1861, the mechanics in the Gosport Yard were organized into companies of "smallarms men" of fifty men each, and one company in each week was to undergo drill for one hour before sunset. Three days later Captain John D. Simms of the Confederate Marine Corps was detailed to command and drill them.

Captain Thom's Company C was sent from Pensacola to Virginia on November 29, 1861. They arrived at the Gosport Yard the evening of December 7, 1861, and were sent on board the Receiving Ship *United States*.[8] This was the first body of Confederate Marines in Virginia. This company was designed primarily to be the Marine Guard for that naval innovation, the C.S.S. *Virginia*, more commonly known today as the *Merrimack*. Some of these same men were assigned to the C.S.S. *Jamestown* and to the C.S.S. *Patrick Henry*. Pending assignment to a naval vessel for active duty, Captain Thom and Lieutenant Thomas Peter Gwynn were ordered to the Receiving Ship *United States* in the Gosport Yard on December 9, 1861. Thom was to command the Guard on the *United States*.

The ironclad *Virginia* was commissioned for service at Norfolk on February 17, 1862, and the available Marines at Norfolk were assigned to her. At the time she was launched, according to an eyewitness, the only officer of the *Virginia* present was her Marine Guard commander, Captain Thom.

Commander John R. Tucker, commanding the C.S.S. *Patrick Henry*, apparently wrote the Navy Department about the same time requesting the assignment of some additional Marines to his ship for Captain Franklin Buchanan, then in charge of the Office of Orders and Detail, wrote him, "There are no marines to send to you. The guard of the *Merrimack,* now *Virginia*, takes all those in Norfolk."[9] Either this request was for Marines in addition to those already on board the *Patrick Henry* or else his request was honored shortly afterwards.

Captain Thom had some 54 Marines on the *Virginia* (two sergeants, two corporals, one musician, and 49 privates), and on board the *Jamestown* were 20 more Marines (one sergeant, one corporal, and 18 privates) from Company C under the command of Lieutenant James R. Y. Fendall. The *Patrick Henry's* guard, originally under the command of Lieutenant Richard H. Henderson, consisted of 24 enlisted men (one sergeant, one corporal, and 22 privates) who came on board on December 7, 1861. They were a detachment from Captain Thom's Company C, and Captain J. N. Barney of the *Jamestown* referred to them in a letter dated February 14, 1862, concerning the pay of his Marines, writing:

> Some of the men have had no money since they enlisted. They were not paid when transferred to this ship, at the request of their officer, with the understanding that they would be paid on their arrival at Richmond. The marines of the same company sent to the Merrimac & Patrick Henry have both received some money, and I hope that when Mr. Morgan comes down he will be prepared, if not

to pay them off to the end of last quarter, at least to give some fifteen or twenty dollars each . . . .[10]

Little official mention was made of the participation of Marines in the engagements in Hampton Roads on March 8-9, 1862, other than Admiral Buchanan's report. "The Marine Corps was well represented by Captain Thom, whose tranquil mein gave evidence that the hottest fire was no novelty to him."[11] The part played by the Marines in these engagements is implied rather than stated in the various accounts of the battles. The casemated *Virginia* offered no opportunity for the Marines to perform their accepted function of smallarms men engaged in sharpshooting, in boarding, or in repelling boarders. It seems more probable that the Marines were utilized in manning the ten big guns of the converted *Merrimack*. The ship had two pivot guns, one fore and one aft, commanded by Lieutenants Charles Simms and John T. Wood. Of the eight broadside guns, Midshipman Henry H. Marmaduke and Boatswain Charles H. Hasker each commanded one. Lieutenants John R. Eggleston and Walter R. Butt each commanded a gun. Lieutenant Hunter Davidson is reported to have commanded "guns" (two?). Buchanan's report states that one of his [Thom's] guns was served effectively and creditably by a detachment of the United Artillery of Norfolk under the command of Captain Kevill. By elimination, Thom probably commanded one gun in person, and his Marines may have manned several guns.

In the absence of a specific official report on the services of the Marines on board the *Jamestown* (2 guns) during the engagements in Hampton Roads on March 8-9, we turn to a letter written by Lieutenant Commanding J. N. Barney to his Marine officer, First Lieutenant J. R. Y. Fendall, on the occasion of Fendall's transfer from the *Jamestown*.

> C.S.S. Jamestown
> James River 29 April 1862

1st Lt. J. R. Y. Fendall
    C.S.M.C.

Sir

I regret that our official connection should be severed by the order detaching you from this ship, and I desire before parting to express to you my appreciation of the zeal & attention to your duties which you have uniformly shown while under my command. When you brought the Marine guard on board you were given charge of one of the great guns with the handling of which neither you or your men were acquainted. Devoting yourself with energy & application to the subject you very soon brought your men to an excellence & thoroughness of drill highly creditable to your self and to them. In the action of the 8th & 9th of March the coolness, rapidity, & _____ [precision?] with which your gun was handled was noticed by me as well as a matter of remark with the officers of the ship. In my report to Flag Officer Buchanan of those engagements I stated that "every officer & man did his whole duty; exhibiting a zeal & courage worthy of the cause in which we are engaged." This applies with full force to the Marine Guard.

Wishing you every success in life, I am,

Very truly yours
J. N. Barney Lt. Comd.[12]

A copy of this letter was forwarded to the Confederate Marines' Headquarters to be made a part of Fendall's record.

Captain Van Benthuysen's Company B of Confederate Marines arrived at the Gosport Navy Yard on March 11, 1862, two days after the engagements in Hampton Roads. Van Benthuysen then served as commander of the Marine Guard at the Gosport Yard with Lieutenant Gwynn filling in for him temporarily in mid-March when Van Benthuysen went on leave. On March 19, Captain John D. Simms was ordered to the command of the Marines at Gosport. Company B's tenure at the Gosport Yard was short-lived as the Yard was evacuated by the Confederate forces on the night of May 9-10, 1862.

The failure of the Virginia troops to take Fort Monroe in April of 1861 gave the Federal forces a toehold on the peninsula lying between the York and James Rivers. The Confederate forces managed to contain the Federals by the Yorktown-Warwick line until the spring of 1862. This was backed by a second defensive line at Williamsburg centered on Fort Magruder. A third line, unfortified, but nevertheless to prove effective, was the line of the Chickahominy River. The York River was denied the Federals by the Confederate batteries at Yorktown and across the river at Gloucester Point. The use of Hampton Roads and the James River was denied the Federals by the ponderous, yet effective, *Virginia* whose very life depended on her base at the Gosport Navy Yard at Norfolk.

Federal pressure led to the evacuation of Yorktown on the night of May 3. On the 4th, a reconnaissance up the York River by U.S.S. *Chocura* and U.S.S. *Corwin* revealed the river was open as far as West Point, the effective head of navigation. The Confederate Army was forced to make a rapid retreat to the Chickahominy River to prevent being cut off from Richmond by Federal troops being landed from transports in the vicinity of West Point.

The Confederate forces fought a delaying action at Williamsburg in a soaking rain on May 5 in order to give the lead divisions and the trains a chance to make their way to the Richmond area. On the afternoon of May 6, word reached General Joseph E. Johnston that the expected Federal transports and their protecting gunboats were at the head of the York River and were disembarking troops in the vicinity of Eltham Plantation. After permitting the Federal troops to move inland away from the protection of the Navy's guns, the Confederates turned them back on May 7. But by then the entire Confederate Army on the Peninsula had concentrated around Barhamsville, eliminating the possibility of using the York River as an avenue for Union troops to cut in between the Confederate Army and Richmond. Johnston had neatly extricated his forces from a springing trap and none too soon.

Only the *Virginia* stood between the Northern Navy and an advance up the James River right to the wharves of Richmond. The weak batteries on the James at Rock Wharf and Hardin's Bluff offered no real obstacle; the only backstop to the *Virginia* that offered any hope was Drewry's Bluff.

Although warned of the impending evacuation of Norfolk, Captain Josiah Tattnall, commanding the *Virginia*, was not prepared for its sudden abandonment by General Benjamin Huger's troops on the night of May 9-10. As a result of a council of war the day of the 9th, Tattnall had been led to believe he would have at least ten days to prepare only to be faced with *un fait accompli* on the morning of May 10 without any notice from Huger.

After lightening ship during the day of May 10 in order to cross the river shoals on the way up river to Richmond, Tattnall was stunned by word from his pilots that without strong easterly winds to pile up water in the river, it would be impossible to ascend the James.

Without a base, unable to retreat up the James, and with the ship so lightened as to ride too high in the water to be fought, there was no choice left but to destroy the *Virginia*. Ramming her aground at Craney Island, she was set afire and blew up at 4:58 A.M. on the morning of May 11, 1862.

About eight miles below Richmond on the south bank of the James River so located on a bend of the river as to command an approach into the bend for some distance is Drewry's Bluff. The river is narrowest at this point, making it easier to put in obstructions. As early as March 20, 1862, President Davis had reported to the House of Representatives that Drewry's Bluff which had "intimate relations with the defenses proper of the city" of Richmond had been chosen as the place to locate obstructions in the river against such vessels as the *Monitor*. The battery and the river obstructions were being constructed under the direction of Lieutenant Charles T. Mason of the Army Engineers.

But there had been no sense of urgency about fortifying Drewry's Bluff. General R. E. Lee had requested on April 4 that a 10-inch columbiad, with barbette carriage, be sent to Drewry's Bluff. The need for workmen everywhere with the most pressing and important posts being just a matter of conjecture, made for a shortage of workmen at Drewry's Bluff, and the War Department had this called to its attention by the Chief Engineer of Defenses of City of Richmond, Thomas H. Wynne, on April 29, 1862. The estimated time for completing the river obstructions at this date was three months. It was reported as late as May 9 that there were but three guns in battery.

The mounting of the first three guns at Drewry's Bluff by Captain Augustus Drewry's Southside Artillery was supervised by Colonel Robert Tansill "who wore the full Regimentals as Colonel of Artillery."[13] Tansill had just come south after release from Fort Warren, Massachusetts, used as a Federal prison, and brought with him over 28 years of experience as a U.S. Marine officer and enlisted man. He had accepted a commission as a captain of Confederate Marines on January 22, 1862, but had resigned it on February 15, 1862, to accept his commission as a colonel of artillery.

Unable to cope with the Federal ironclads, the C.S.S. *Jamestown* and C.S.S. *Patrick Henry* retreated up the James River to Drewry's Bluff. Here the *Jamestown* was sunk to complete the river obstruction. Her two guns were taken ashore and placed in position on the Bluff. Three guns from the *Patrick Henry* were also added to the defenses at the Bluff, one a solid shot eight-inch gun, and two rifled 32-pounders. The officers and crews of the *Jamestown* and the *Patrick Henry* went ashore to man these guns. This was probably on May 10 as General Lee wrote General Joseph E. Johnston that day that several naval guns had been mounted in addition to the three already there and that every exertion was being made to render the obstructions effective and the battery as formidable as possible.[14]

The crew of the *Virginia* reached Richmond by train from Suffolk, a fitting conclusion to their twenty-two mile march from Craney Island outside Norfolk to Suffolk, on May 12 after the destruction of that vessel, and were then sent down the James River to Drewry's Bluff to supplement the crews of the *Jamestown* and the *Patrick Henry*. The officers were ordered the next day to report for duty with their men to Commander Farrand, C.S.N., at Drewry's Bluff. The locale of activity for Thom's and Van Benthuysen's companies of Marines had now shifted to Richmond and the nearby Drewry's Bluff. Almost immediately they were to see active service, half sea duty and half field duty by nature, in the defense of Richmond.

The Federal gunboats, relieved of the fear of any attack by the fearsome *Virginia*, headed up the James River toward Richmond. It was not an easy trip, and the commanders of the gunboats all complained of the harassing small-arms fire from the rifle pits along the banks of the river. Lieutenant John C.

8-inch Columbiad in position at Drewry's Bluff commanding the James River.
Picture taken in April 1966 by Ralph W. Donnelly.

Beaumont of the U.S.S. *Aroostook* commented that they ". . . proceeded up the river, under a sharp fire of musketry from both banks, to which I replied occasionally with howitzers and small arms."[15] The *Port Royal* complained of rifle bullets piercing the bulwarks, and Captain George U. Morris had a personal reason to complain as a minie ball gave him a severe flesh wound in the right leg. Commander John Rodgers, commanding U.S.S. *Galena*, reported rifle pits lining the banks manned by sharpshooters who annoyed the gunners. (This function was the main service performed by the Marines, i.e., the pinning down of the enemy's gunners and riflemen.) Rodgers observed that these sharpshooters would hinder the removal of obstructions in the river unless driven away by a cooperating land force. This set the pattern for much of the work along the James River for the remainder of the war. *Galena* suffered heavily, some 13 killed and 11 wounded (one mortally), from the combined small-arms and artillery fire.[16]

The vessels found that when they got in close to the fortifications on Drewry's Bluff they were unable to elevate their guns sufficiently to reach the Confederate guns emplaced perhaps 60 feet above them. As long as the ships' guns kept up a steady fire, few Confederate shots were fired in return, but whenever the North's fire slackened, the guns on the Bluff were remanned and a vigorous fire resumed. Harassed by musketry from the rifle pits on the banks of the river, and unable to make a noticeable impression against the earthworks of Drewry's Bluff, the squadron was forced to give up the effort and retire downstream. The consensus of the Navy officers was that it would take Army troops operating on the land in conjunction with the naval squadron to eliminate Drewry's Bluff.

These so-called "sharpshooters" who caused the Federal gunboats such irritation included a two-company battalion of Confederate Marines under Captain John D. Simms. Simms, an experienced, battle-wise, former U.S. Marine officer, had participated in the capture of the San Cosme Gate to Mexico City on September 13, 1847, and in the storming and destruction of the Canton Barrier Forts in China in November 1856.

On May 16 Captain Simms made the following report to Colonel Lloyd J. Beall:

> Drewry's Bluff Battery
> May 16th 1862
>
> Colonel,
> I have the honor to make you the following report. On the 15th inst. the enemy's gunboats having made their appearance near the battery at Drury's Bluff, I stationed my command on the bluffs some two hundred yards from them to act as sharpshooters. We immediately opened a sharp fire upon them, killing three of the crew of the Galena certainly, and no doubt many more. The fire of the enemy was materially silenced at intervals by the fire of our troops.
>
> It gives me much pleasure to call your attention to the coolness of the officers and men under the severe fire of the enemy. The companies comprising my battalion were commanded by Capts. Van Benthuysen and Meiere.
>
> Very Respectfully
> Jno. D. Simms
> (Signed)   Capt. C.S. Marines
> Commd'g[17]

Captain Julius Ernest Meiere, who had succeeded Captain Thom in the command of the Marine Guard of the *Virginia*, commanded Company C in this engagement while Captain Van Benthuysen commanded his own Company B.

So close did this squadron have to come to the banks of the river that Lieutenant John Taylor Wood, C.S.N., called out to an officer in the pilot house of the *Monitor* as they were retreating: "Tell Captain Jeffers [commanding the *Monitor*] that this is not the way to Richmond."[18]

The introduction of Confederate Marines in the Richmond area brought calls for recruits in the Richmond papers. A rather gruesome and bloodthirsty advertisement appeared in the *Daily Examiner* early in May 1862. Designed to encourage recruiting in the Confederate Marine Corps, it enlarged upon the participation of the Marines by commenting, "In the late naval engagements in Hampton Roads, there were about one hundred marines, who had the pleasure of witnessing the departure, and expediting the journey of three or four hundred Yankees on their way to 'Davy Jones' locker.' " Repeat performances were virtually guaranteed new recruits.[19]

At the same time official recruiting notices were calling for able-bodied men for the Marine Corps to serve at naval stations and on board iron-clad gunboats and such renowned ships as the C.S.S. *Virginia* (the *Merrimack*). The advertisements made a particular point of asking for men suitable for appointment as noncommissioned officers as well as for a few boys as learners of music (enlistment subject to their parents' consent). Captain George P. Turner signed as Recruiting Officer with his office in the basement under the Quartermaster's Office, 115 Broad Street, Richmond. The Petersburg *Express* was requested to copy the advertisement and send its bill to A. S. Taylor, Quartermaster, Marine Corps, at the same address.

During the summer of 1862, probably in July, Captain George Holmes' Company A was transferred from Savannah, Georgia, to the Richmond area to join Companies B and C to form a three-company battalion at Camp Beall, Drewry's Bluff. With the concentration of these three companies as a field battalion at Drewry's Bluff and the location of the Navy Department and Marine Corps Headquarters in Richmond, the Richmond area became the center of Confederate Marine Corps activities for the remainder of the war. The Marine Corps duties in Savannah were taken over by the newly organized Company E, commanded by Captain John R. F. Tattnall.

The Marine camp, known as Camp Beall, was an area within the confines of the Post of Drewry's Bluff. The Marine battalion originally camped in tents in the summer and fall of 1862, but steps were taken with the approach of winter to construct wooden barracks. The Marines themselves furnished the labor, and while the actual construction was going on, drilling was suspended, and military duty cut to guard duty. As late as November 23, 1862, Lieutenant Henry L. Graves was writing that the winter quarters were not yet completed, but he was

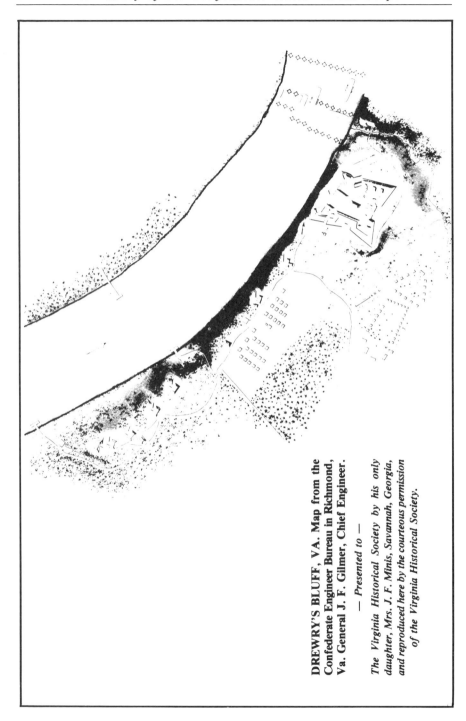

DREWRY'S BLUFF, VA. Map from the Confederate Engineer Bureau in Richmond, Va. General J. F. Gilmer, Chief Engineer.

— Presented to —

The Virginia Historical Society by his only daughter, Mrs. J. F. Minis, Savannah, Georgia, and reproduced here by the courteous permission of the Virginia Historical Society.

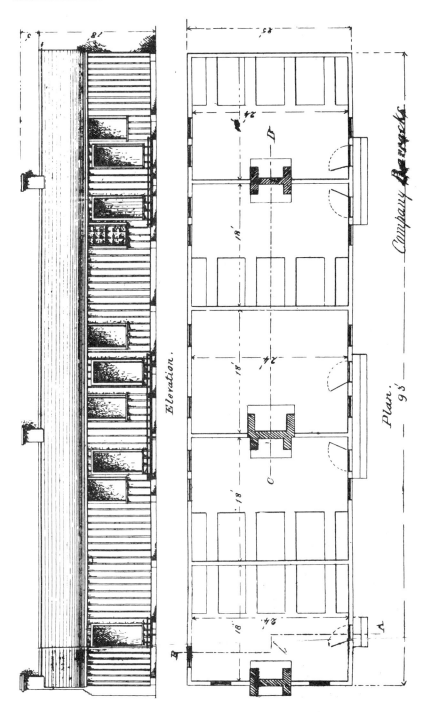

Plans for company barracks to be constructed at Drewry's Bluff, Va.

This sketch is from the Charles Tayloe Mason Papers by permission of the Virginia Historical Society.

Sketch of the Confederate Marine camp at Drewry's Bluff, Va., made by Frank Vizetelly in the summer of 1862 and published in the *Illustrated London News* **for November 15, 1862.**
This picture is reproduced from the Collections of the Library of Congress.

DRURY'S BLUFF, A CONFEDERATE POSITION ON THE JAMES RIVER, NEAR RICHMOND, VA.

Artist's sketch of Drewry's Bluff and river obstructions as seen coming up the river.

From *FRANK LESLIE'S ILLUSTRATED FAMOUS LEADERS AND BATTLE SCENES OF THE CIVIL WAR (N.Y., 1896), 362.*

comfortable in his tent. He had dug down some three or four feet into the ground and had the sides walled up closely with plank. The tent itself was stretched over as a roof. Wind proof and with little dampness, he considered it comfortable for sleeping.[20]

The date of the completion of the barracks is not certain, but on January 3, 1863, Secretary of the Navy Mallory was scheduled to pay an official visit to the camp at Drewry's Bluff. The whole battalion was ordered out to receive him with the officers dressed in full uniform and the men under arms. The suggestion is that this visit was in the nature of "showing off" the newly completed Marine barracks.

The command of Drewry's Bluff was given to Captain Sidney Smith Lee on May 15, 1862, the day the Federal Naval Squadron was turned back, and he supervised the strengthening and expansion of the defenses at the Bluff into a permanent fort. In November 1862, the Navy Department ordered a board of Navy officers to ". . . examine carefully all the guns at Drewry's Bluff under the command of Captain Lee, their character and positions, the magazines, hotshot furnaces, the river obstructions at that point, and the defenses generally, including the seamen and marines, and report thereon as early as practicable."[21] Earthworks were expanded, emplacements were made for field guns, and the entire outer perimeter stretched out over a mile while the inner works were improved and the construction of barracks, magazines, etc., continued as became a permanent post. Cabins were constructed for the housing of the midshipmen attached to the Confederate Naval Academy which functioned on board the C.S.S. *Patrick Henry* anchored in the James River at the foot of Drewry's Bluff.

The establishment of the post at Drewry's Bluff soon attracted a number of people, particularly the families of men assigned there. In addition to the barracks built for the garrison troops, by mid-1863, neat log-houses were built for the families of the garrison and the refugee ladies and children from Norfolk and Portsmouth, creating a small village. A hotel was soon in operation and doing a good business; a post-office was established with twice daily contact with Richmond, and in October 1863, a Masonic Lodge was established with an initial membership of 25. Considered an attraction were the gardens cultivated by members of the garrison which supplied them with an abundance of excellent vegetables.

A chapel was built for the post, and visiting ministers from the city occupied the pulpit on Sundays. Adjacent to the chapel was a cemetery, but the wooden markers have long since disappeared. At certain times today, the indentations of the graves can still be discerned. The death notice of a small child who died at the bluff after a long illness appeared in the Richmond *Sentinel* of

August 31, 1864. The child, the youngest of E. R. and Julia A. Y. Johnson of Norfolk, was named Rebellion Virginia Chicora Davis Johnson.

Communication with Richmond was by means of the Steamer *Schultz*, Captain Hill, which left her wharf at Rocketts in Richmond every afternoon at 3 o'clock and returned at 6:15 P.M. The fare for the round trip was just one dollar (soon raised to two dollars). By October 1863, the excursion schedule for *Schultz* was changed to leaving her Richmond wharf at 10:30 A.M. and leaving the Bluff for her return trip at 1:30 P.M. Occasionally trips had to be cancelled when *Schultz* was used as a flag of truce boat.[22]

During the Chancellorsville Campaign of May 1863, Major Francis W. Smith's artillery battalion stationed at Drewry's Bluff and most of the crew of the C.S.S. *Richmond* were sent to the city of Richmond to man the defenses. News reached the Bluff on May 4 of a Federal cavalry raid (Stoneman's) against the rear and flank of Lee's army. The Marines at the Bluff were sent out on picket, but the threat failed to materialize. The pressure was relieved on May 10 when the news of a costly victory at Chancellorsville arrived, accompanied by the evaporation of the threat of the cavalry raid. Distance, time, and a possible failure on the part of the Federals to appreciate Drewry's Bluff as a keystone of the Richmond-Petersburg defense line counted heavily in the Confederates' favor. Weaker on the land side, as usual with forts commanding water, Drewry's Bluff was to exercise command over the Richmond-Petersburg sector until circumstances finally forced its abandonment. It had the dual responsibility of closing the water approach to Richmond and of protecting the railroad link from Richmond to Petersburg and the South.

May 1864 brought an emergency situation on the Richmond-Petersburg line, and once again Drewry's Bluff acted as an anchor in the center of the tenuous and sorely pressed line.

The Army of Northern Virginia had its hands full trying to contain the Federal Army of the Potomac in the Wilderness in bitter battles on the fifth and seventh of May followed by the Battle of Spotsylvania on May 8. To meet this menace, the Richmond-Petersburg line had been stripped of all the troops that could possibly be spared. Troops were ordered to Virginia from the South Atlantic coast to cover this weak area.

The Army of the James under General Benjamin Butler was thrown into this otherwise quiet sector south of the James River while a cavalry column under Brigadier General August V. Kautz left Suffolk, both having the prime objective of severing the railroad connection between Richmond and the South. The senior Confederate officer in the area with headquarters at Petersburg was Major

General George E. Pickett with but one regiment, and it was only by the piece-meal assembly of units arriving from the south and the transfer of troops from the north bank of the James over the pontoon bridge near Drewry's Bluff, beginning on May 6, that the Federal thrusts were blunted. Not too soon, however, were they stopped to prevent Kautz's cavalry cutting of the railroad by the destruction of the Stony Creek bridge, the Nottoway bridge, and the track torn up at Jarrett's station. Even Butler's troops scored a limited success with some 300 to 500 yards of track being torn up and with three telegraph lines being cut.

The first troops from the south to reach the Drewry's Bluff area early on the morning of May 6 were 300 men of the 21st South Carolina Infantry of Hagood's Brigade. When they reached Petersburg on their way north, General Pickett permitted them to continue north on the cars. They detrained about 5 A.M. after entering the outer works of Drewry's Bluff and awaited events.

A member of the 21st South Carolina recalled later:

> Along the railway between Petersburg and Richmond the command was marched to Drewry's Bluff. We formed in a line of breastworks, a detachment of marines on our left. These marines were from the gunboats in the James River. The writer [Henry K. DuBose], on the left of Company B came into elbow touch with this pattern of soldiery, as they stood at attention, like statues in their close fitting fighting jackets, erect with their pieces at carry, ... They did present the appearance of holiday soldiers on dress parade well groomed and fed, they did not appear as if they would prove very reliable in case of attack . . . . [23]

The disparaging remark of the South Carolinian remained untested as his unit moved out that afternoon to participate in the engagement at Port Walthall Junction, about ten miles south of Drewry's Bluff, but the Marines apparently remained at their stations at the Bluff.

May 6 and 7 marked the engagements at Port Walthall Junction and Chester Station. A farther advance by the Federals brought them closer to Drewry's Bluff. By the morning of May 9, the Federal troops were within two or three miles of the trenches outside of Drewry's Bluff. General Seth Barton, C.S.A., sent orders to Major Terrett, C.S.M.C., commanding at Drewry's Bluff, to be in readiness to meet the enemy immediately. The Federal nearness to Drewry's Bluff was reported promptly to both Secretary of the Navy S. R. Mallory and to Corps Commandant Beall.

The Marines were reported in readiness and in position in the defensive trenches at the close of the day on May 9. Sounds of heavy firing in the direction of Port Walthall had reached Drewry's Bluff, but the immediate sector was quiet.

The need for all available troops to meet the Federal movement brought forth the following telegram from Major Terrett to the Secretary of the Navy at "12:30.", May 9th:

> If you can possible spare the two Marine Guards at the Navy Yards please send them immediately. They number about 60 men and should be of incalculable service here.[24]

These sixty men would have made a sizeable reinforcement to the Post at Drewry's Bluff as the tri-monthly return of the Post dated May 10 showed just 17 officers and 309 men actually present for duty. These were presumably Major Francis Smith's Artillery battalion and the battalion of Confederate Marines.

For the next several days messages were relayed through Drewry's Bluff, but the action was elsewhere in the field. Sheridan's cavalry left Beaver Dam, Virginia, on May 10, heading towards Richmond with Jeb Stuart's cavalry in hot pursuit. There was little left to defend Richmond other than the Local Defense units of office clerks and factory workmen and a few units of heavy artillery on permanent assignment to the Richmond defense batteries. The decimated troops of the Maryland Line were encamped outside the town of Hanover Junction. Stuart's cavalry reached Yellow Tavern on the 11th where it engaged with Sheridan's force, slowed his advance, but lost General Stuart mortally wounded.

Two brigades of troops at Drewry's Bluff were recalled back across the James River on the 12th to go to Richmond to meet Sheridan who was between the outer and intermediate defense lines of Richmond.

Shortly after noon on May 12 (Thursday), First Lieutenant Fergus MacRee, C.S.M.C., Adjutant of the Post of Drewry's Bluff, advised Secretary Mallory that the enemy was immediately in front of the fort and skirmishing with small arms had commenced. Major Terrett was reported "in the trenches," which was apparently a reference to the earthworks forming part of the outer perimeter. After the first flurry, skirmishing with small arms and artillery fire broke out again in the afternoon. The part played by the Confederate Marines as a unit is obscure, and but little reference has been found to their participation. A biographical sketch of Lieutenant Francis H. Cameron, C.S.M.C., remarks that he took a conspicuous part in Butler's defeat at Drewry's Bluff, having command of the left wing of the Confederate skirmish line, but the exact date is not given.[25]

On the 13th, the so-called outer works of Drewry's Bluff were carried by the 3d New Hampshire and the 55th Pennsylvania Regiments, aided in no small measure by the fire power from their Spencer repeating rifles.

On the 14th the Commanding Officer at Drewry's Bluff was ordered to hold his command under arms that night in anticipation of an attack from the enemy. By the 16th the battles of Proctor's Creek and Drewry's Bluff drew to a close, and the Post at Drewry's Bluff began receiving and forwarding by boat to Richmond the prisoners taken over those days. Drewry's Bluff had withstood the test of the Federal Army in 1864 as it had that of the Federal Navy in 1862. Had the Federal Navy supported the Army and placed the Confederate's pontoon bridge near the Bluff under fire as well as maintaining pressure against the river defenses, Butler might have achieved more success, but the torpedo defenses of the James River backed by the James River Squadron constituted a formidable barrier to the Federal ships.

The Confederate Navy maintained two Navy Yards at Richmond, Virginia, during the war, one on each bank of the James River. One of these was established at the end of Poplar Street in the section known as "Rocketts" (at the lower end of the city). The other was customarily known as the "Navy Yard opposite Rocketts" and was located in Manchester, across the James River from Richmond proper. The Marine Corps maintained a guard at each yard under the command of a commissioned officer.

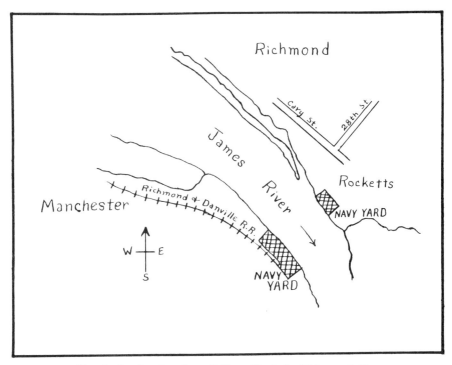

Sketch showing location of Navy Yards in Richmond, Va.

The Navy Yard at Rocketts had its origin early in the war when the *Yorktown*, a side-wheel steamer on the Richmond-New York run, was seized in the James River by the Virginia forces. The *Yorktown* was taken to the wharf at Rocketts where its conversion to a ship-of-war was undertaken by Naval Constructor Joseph Pierce with a group of mechanics from the Norfolk Navy Yard. The conversion was completed after several months, and the ship, under the command of Commander John R. Tucker, became known as the *Patrick Henry*.[26]

In early 1864, the ironclad *Fredericksburg* was fitted out at Rocketts, and the ironclad *Virginia, II*, constructed there. It was the need for seamen to man the *Fredericksburg* that compelled the Navy Department to withdraw those stationed at Drewry's Bluff and to transfer that post to the Marine Corps solely.[27]

The first Marines at the Yard at Rocketts were a Marine guard sent out from Camp Beall, Drewry's Bluff, for the protection of the public property on September 30, 1863. Second Lieutenant David Bradford, one sergeant, one corporal, and 12 privates reported to the Yard on the next day. Upon Bradford's transfer to the *Fredericksburg* on May 24, 1864, he was relieved by Second Lieutenant Lloyd B. Stephenson who commanded an enlarged guard of one sergeant, three or four corporals, and 23 privates until the close of the war.

Available records indicate that Marines were first assigned to the Navy Yard opposite Rocketts, which included duty on board the Schooner *Gallego*, probably in February 1863. Second Lieutenant Nathanieal E. Venable was in command until about May 26, 1863, when he was relieved by Second Lieutenant John S. Van de Graaff. He, in turn, was relieved on August 11, 1863, by Second Lieutenant Samuel M. Roberts. Upon Roberts' transfer to the *Richmond* on May 24, 1864, he was succeeded by Second Lieutenant Henry H. McCune who apparently remained on this assignment until the Yard was evacuated at the end of the war. The normal size of this guard was 21 or 22 men, including those serving on the Schooner *Gallego*, a storeship for the James River Squadron. After *Gallego* was sunk in late September 1864, its Marines were added to those assigned to the Yard. Although Marine recruits in the Richmond area were usually assigned to one of the companies at Drewry's Bluff, at least a handful were assigned directly to the Navy Yard opposite Rocketts according to the December 1864 muster rolls.

There must have been a certain degree of unified control exercised over the guards at the two Navy Yards beginning late in 1864 as Lieutenant Crenshaw remarked in his diary on October 19 that First Lieutenant R. H. Henderson had left the battalion at Drewry's Bluff "to take command of the two Marine Guards at the Navy Yards at Richmond."[28]

Enlistments were negligible in number in Richmond in both 1862 and 1863, current records indicating there were probably less than 20 in all. Instead, the depot company at Mobile transferred men to Richmond for assignment to the companies of the field battalion. Some 49 Alabama conscripts were listed on a descriptive roll dated May 8, 1863, and processed through Marine Head-quarters by Adjutant Israel Greene. These men were assigned almost immediately to their companies. This particular group was not run through the rolls of the Mobile depot company, but on September 19, 1863, a draft of one sergeant, one corporal, and 22 privates was transferred from the Mobile Barracks to Drewry's Bluff.

The picture was different in 1864 as enlisting was stepped up in Richmond to supplement the transfers from Mobile. Lieutenant Nathaniel E. Venable was the enlisting officer for all but one of the 73 men enrolled in Richmond in 1864. These men were almost all conscripts who chose service in the Marine Corps at the enrollment center, Camp Lee, Richmond. Another draft of 45 men was shipped out of the Mobile Barracks for Drewry's Bluff for the field battalion on June 8, 1864.

The aggregate present at Drewry's Bluff on June 10, 1864, was 76 with an aggregate battalion strength, present and absent, of 270. In connection with the planned expedition to free the prisoners at Point Lookout, the Marine bat-talion was away from Drewry's Bluff from 3 A.M. on July 3 until shortly after July 20 when it was ordered back from the Wilmington area.

The battalion at Drewry's Bluff had only 60 officers and men present for duty on August 31, 1864, with an additional 21 more on extra or daily duty or sick. These last were technically "present," making a total of 81. Of the remaining 232 members of the battalion, 214 were on detached service and 18 were absent and not available. (See Table on pp. 159-160.)

The last available strength report of the battalion dated January 2, 1865, showed just 81 available (27 in Company A, 30 in Company B, and 24 in Company C.)

With the transfer out of Navy personnel, the command of Drewry's Bluff had devolved upon Marine Major George H. Terrett in March 1864. To make his rank commensurate with the importance of the post and to prevent his be-ing ranked by less experienced and able officers who might occasionally be pres-ent at Drewry's Bluff, Terrett was given the temporary rank of colonel in the Provisional Army on June 17, 1864, ranking from May 23, 1864, and was assigned by General Robert E. Lee to the command of the Post of Drewry's Bluff on July 21, 1864.[29]

On May 23 and 24, 1864, the Confederate ironclads passed the obstructions in the James River at Drewry's Bluff and began to patrol the river for several miles below the Bluff. Flag-Officer John K. Mitchell took his ships downstream near Dutch Gap in June 1864 and engaged in a long range artillery duel with the Federal forces. He was reinforced in this effort by gunfire from a naval land battery [Battery Semmes] which had been established on the hill at Howlett's House and covered Trent's Reach by firing across a neck of land.

The Navy, having taught the Federals at Drewry's Bluff in 1862 the lesson of the need to control river banks of streams such as the James, landed the Marine guards of the squadron under the command of Lieutenant T. P. Gwynn and a division of small-arms men under Lieutenant Wilburn B. Hall, P.N.C.S., on June 21, at Cox's to picket the high ground close to Dutch Gap. But there was little activity other than some firing by the Marines into a Federal transport passing down the river.

Several nights later the Navy arranged to place a party on the river to examine the river channel for torpedoes and other obstructions. Again it was felt necessary to secure the bank of the river for protective covering, and all the Marines of the squadron under Lieutenant Gwynn were ordered landed on the night of June 25, 1864, at Cox's Landing to take care of the Federal pickets. A detachment of Army troops from Brigadier General George W. Custis Lee's command was to be on hand to cooperate at the same time.

Land picket duty on the right bank of the James River above Howlett's took place for some time in the summer of 1864. Finally, on July 9, Flag-Officer Mitchell wrote Major General George E. Pickett that for every night since June 13 he had stationed a picket guard of 20 men on the right bank from Osborne's to a mile upstream with instructions to fire on all boats passing in the vicinity. As this constant duty was beginning to interfere with more appropriate ship duties and heavy gun exercises, Mitchell requested General Pickett to substitute Army pickets.

Several days later Marine First Lieutenant T. P. Gwynn laid himself open to a severe reprimand from Flag-Officer Mitchell in connection with this picket duty. In his report of July 10 of picket service near Osborne's, Gwynn complained that several of the sailors on the detail had not more than one or two gun caps apiece. Mitchell promptly reminded him that this could not have happened if Gwynn, as the commanding officer of the party, had made the proper careful inspection of the men and their equipment before leaving the ship, and, furthermore, called him to task for failing to report the delinquents by name if they were to be blamed.

Mitchell pulled no punches in his letter, and Gwynn should have felt properly reprimanded.

Picket duty by the Navy on the James River seems to have continued for some time and probably right up to the close of the war. Lieutenant Edward Crenshaw, who succeeded Lieutenant Gwynn in command of the Marine Guard on the *Virginia*, leaves a record of picket duty. Under date of February 15, 1865, Crenshaw recorded:

> Went on picket duty last night with one midshipman, four seamen and two Marines, on the South bank of the river below "Signal Hill." Nothing unusual occured during my tour of duty. Returned to the ship at daylight.[30]

Such duty was not without its problems to the Navy. On March 10, 1865, an entire boat's crew on picket mutinied and deserted to the enemy taking along their arms and accoutrements. Crenshaw was particularly concerned as two of his Marines, Private [Richard] McGregor and Musician [John] Baines, were actively involved. Both of these men were old hands, having been enlisted originally in Mobile, in August 1861.

While the Marines of the James River Squadron were active, there is evidence that Marines from Camp Beall were also engaged in field activity. Captain T. S. Wilson, in accounting on June 30, 1864, for the loss of a camp kettle and three shovels, wrote:

> The camp-kettle was lifted out of the bow of a boat by a limb and unavoidably lost while my company was going down the Meherrin River in small boats.[31]

> [The Meherrin flows generally eastward from the vicinity of South Hill and Emporia, Virginia, to near Murfreesboro, North Carolina, and joins the Blackwater River near Winton, just before emptying into the Chowan River which in turn feeds into Albemarle Sound.]

The details of the participation of Confederate Marines in manning the naval battery on the James River at Bishop's (Battery Semmes) are sparse, and the Marines do not seem to have been assigned to the other naval batteries on the river, Brooke and Wood.

By an order dated September 21, 1864, a group of officers and men under Lieutenant Matthew P. Goodwyn, P.N.C.S., was assigned to duty with the battery at Bishop's. The group included 33 enlisted men from the *Virginia*, *Fredericksburg*, *Richmond*, and *Beaufort* of the James River Squadron. Ten of the 33 were Marines, including three from the *Virginia*, three from the *Fredericksburg*, and a sergeant and three privates from the *Richmond*.[32] Lieutenant Samuel M. Roberts, commanding these Marines, was taken ill and hospitalized on October 16, 1864. On November 13, 1864, the Marines were ordered to return to their ships, and Lieutenant Roberts was ordered back to the *Richmond* when discharged from the hospital. This he did on January 5, 1865.

Roberts made the mistake of getting separated briefly from his men when he took a small boat with two privates of the guard of his ship as a crew to go down river to Battery Semmes to get his baggage. On returning to the landing, he found his men had started off in the boat and were halfway across the river. They landed on the opposite or north side of the river and presumably deserted to the Federals. Flag-Officer Mitchell considered him guilty of neglect of duty and ordered him suspended for three weeks from January 14, 1865, with the usual restrictions. But just eight days later with the Squadron about ready to descend the river, Mitchell restored Roberts to duty.

One of the last adventures of Confederate Marines was the participation in an unsuccessful effort staged by the Navy to flank Grant's army in February 1865, capture a vessel on the James River, and break up the Federal base at City Point. A party of some 120 sailors, Marines, and soldiers under Lieutenant Charles W. ("Tacony") Read, P.N.C.S., started out from Drewry's Bluff on the morning of February 3, 1865, with four small boats mounted on the running gear of wagons. Unfortunately, the expedition was betrayed and narrowly escaped capture, finally getting back on February 13. The Marine contingent numbering 13 enlisted men under the command of First Lieutenant James Thurston, C.S.M.C., was assigned the job of serving as the rear-guard of the expedition. Here, again, was a dangerous mission in which the Marines participated actively and honorably, even though unsuccessfully.[33]

One of the last exploits of the Confederate Navy in Chesapeake Bay took place on March 31, 1865, when a yawl containing about twenty armed men captured first the schooner *St. Mary's* and then the schooner *J. B. Spafford* bound to New York. The Confederates were commanded by Master John C. Brain and Marine Lieutenant J. Campbell Murdoch.[34] But details of this exploit seem to be missing, and it is not known whether the crew included enlisted Confederate Marines or not.

With the evacuation of both Wilmington and Charleston, most of the Navy and Marine personnel from these stations were assembled in the Richmond area (at Drewry's Bluff) under the command of Captain (Flag-Officer) John R. Tucker. Here they were organized into Tucker's Naval Brigade and drilled in provisional companies as infantrymen.

The Marine field battalion at Drewry's Bluff marched off in the evening of April 2 on the retreat from the Richmond-Petersburg line to Appomattox

Court House as part of Tucker's Naval Brigade which in turn formed a part of General G. W. Custis Lee's scratch division of Local Defense Troops. On the retreat, the fifty-eight year old Major George H. Terrett fell into the hands of the Federal troops on April 5 near Amelia Court House.

One enlisted Marine, Private David Staples Woodson, has left us his story of the last year of the war as preserved by his oldest daughter, Emma Geneve Woodson Massie, and by a letter he wrote to the Virginia Pension Office in 1917.

> My business was growing nicely, serving a very large area for the big farm owners and their slaves 'till the War came in 1861. I served three of the four years, coming home only one time. I was stationed twelve miles below Richmond. I later got a furlough home for five weeks. I know the captain on the Packet Boat. I asked him if he could give me a ride to Galts Mill. He did, by putting me in his private closet. This put me within three miles of my father's home. After resting there several days I started for home (Lowesville), about forty miles. After about 35 miles I came to my sister Sue's home, about one mile of [from?] Mt. Moriah Church on Mill Creek. I went to a back room window to shave. My mother-in-law, Mrs. Sandidge, was there. She saw Yankies coming up to the house. When they came in she held their attention and talked with them as long as she could, to give me a chance to get away. I got out of the window and went down to the woods, got in a gully and covered up with leaves. They told her they saw a Southern devil go into the house. Their horses came within a few feet of me as they passed back. As soon as I could, I climbed a tree. I could see them with their spy glass on the next hill, looking for me. I stayed there until after night, then came down, and by going by paths and thickets, I reached home, about five miles [away], before day. The raid[ers] had been there also. Millie (my wife) didn't let me come in, but gave me a quilt, and sent me to a nearby ivy thicket. There I staid 'till the Yankies left the neighborhood, fed by the Negro servant.
>
> I spent 5 weeks providing for my family. I then returned to the army, 12 miles below Richmond, witnessing many sad scenes of wounded and dying soldiers in the battles around Richmond.

[In a statement in his pension file, Woodson commented, "Became dissatisfied. Promised a horse by a friend to enlist in Cavalry. Short furlough — went home — didn't get the Horse — overstayed leave — subject to punishment — remained at home unmolested — Gen Lee's amnesty proclamation led to return to original unit — served faithfully to surrender at Appomattox.]

> My last experience in the war was — We were marching from Richmond toward Appomattox. I looked some distance ahead of us and

noticed a big lot of pines. I said to the Irishman by me — "Do you
see that cluster of pines, the Yankies are coming out of them like
flies and wipe us all out." I am going to drop out of line right here.
I did. It came true . . .

[His statement in his pension file is quite similar. "All of my company including Capt Smiths Battallion of infantry were surrounded and taken Captive
in Amelia Co. The Federal Cavalry suddenly emerged from the thick growth
of Pines on Either side of the line of march, when I and 2 other Comrades,
Irishmen, were in the rear of the colum, and we managed to make an Escape
by dodging in the thick Pines. After which I never saw nor herd of a single
man of our Company and never knew what became of any [of] them."]

By hiding in the creek, brushes and sleeping on rails, with nothing
to eat, except what I could find along the way, I managed to get
to my father's house alive.

[From his pension file, "On arriving at Appomattox tired and hungry, and
suffering with my leg, I went out to my old home a short distance from the
Court House where I arrived *Sunday morning the 9th of Apl* when *the surrender took place*, where I remained for 3 weeks before I was sufficiently able
to go to my home in Amherst Co."

I stopped at a mill, got some meal, and got an old slave cook to
bake me a cake as quick as she could. I saw a man ahead of me
with a bag of corn on a horse. The bag fell and bursted. He left
some of the grain on the ground, which I got. I stopped under a
bridge and parched it. That was the sweetest meal I ever ate. I was
hungry. After sleeping out all night on a pile of rails. Early next
morning I saw a light up on a hill. I went up to the house and asked
if I could get something to eat. I had given some explanation as to
who the straggler was. After giving the names of many they knew
in that part of the country, I was invited to the breakfast table with
the family and found that I was in my own county. They directed
me through a near way to my old home.

When I came up in the yard, the old cook met me. She ran back
in the house to tell Miss Polly (my mother), "Mars Davy has come!"
Mother came out embracing and crying. After being there a while,
I heard quite a roar of big guns. I then remarked that "It was all
over, they (the guns) meant surrender." It was true. I had to rest
there several weeks due to sore feet and need of food. I then walked
home (Lowesville), a distance of forty miles, and found my wife and
baby well, and with something to eat.

I resumed my merchantile business. I did not find the country as I had left it. The slaves were free. The big farms were without labor. So many homes were with wounded sons. Others with one or more missing, never to return. Other weak and sick of starvation and fatigue. Food in the country was scarce, but it was April — yet time enough to plant corn . . .[35]

In the late afternoon of the next day, April 6, the pressure on Ewell's Corps by the pursuing Federal Sixth Corps (Wright's) forced the Confederates to form line of battle to their rear and make a stand. It had not been Lee's intention for Ewell's Corps to be the rear guard of the Army of Northern Virginia, but Gordon's Corps had turned to the right off the Jamestown Road and had followed the wagon train. (Gordon turned off on today's Route 417 at Hodnett's store at the intersection with Route 618, leaving Ewell's Corps the rear unit.)

Ewell's Corps consisted of Kershaw's Division of seasoned troops (DuBose's and Simms' Georgia brigades, Humphreys' Mississippi brigade, and Gary's dismounted cavalry brigade) and a rag, tag, and bobtail division under General G. W. Custis Lee consisting of Barton's Virginia brigade, Moore's brigade of local defense troops and Virginia Reserves, Crutchfield's brigade of heavy artillery from the Richmond defenses and Chaffin's Bluff serving as infantry, and Flag-Officer John R. Tucker's sailors and the Marine Battalion from Camp Beall at Drewry's Bluff.

Ewell reported his line on the high ground on the west bank of Sayler's Creek ran across a little ravine located at a right angle to the creek. Kershaw's Division was formed on the right and G. W. C. Lee's Division was on the left with Tucker's Naval Battalion behind his right.

Two days before, on the 4th, heavy rains had set in, and Sayler's Creek was up high on the 6th. The creek bottom land was muddy and marshy. In places the swamp was hip deep, and the ammunition of some of the Federal troops who were forced to wade through it became wet and useless.

The Confederate line braced to meet the Federal assault was exposed to a heavy artillery fire from Brinckle's Federal Battery E, 5th Regular Artillery, up until the time the Federal infantry pressed their attack. The initial Federal assault brought the 37th Massachusetts and the 121st New York regiments wading through the hip-deep marshland and up the western slope into contact with the Naval Brigade.

The 37th Massachusetts in particular was reported to have had "one of the fiercest, most hand-to-hand and literally savage encounters of the war, with the remnant of Stile's battalion and that of the Marines . . . . They clubbed their muskets, fired pistols into each other's faces, and used the bayonet savagely."[36] Brigadier General Truman Seymour, commanding the Federal 3rd Division, 6th

Army Corps, reported, "The Confederate Marine Battalion fought with peculiar obstinacy, and our lines, somewhat disordered by crossing the creek, were repulsed in the first onset."[37] Many years later a Confederate veteran recalled of the Marines,

> Their line of battle was just in front of Phillips' Georgia Legion of Infantry [DuBose's Brigade, Kershaw's Division] of which I was a member. Those marines fought like tigers and against odds of at least ten to one. The part they took in this fight with other commands ought to be written up.... This battle... has never been given the important place in history that it deserves.[38]

Major General Horatio G. Wright, the 6th Corps commander, reported a successful charge on the Confederate position "except at a point on our right of the road crossing the creek, where a column, said to be composed exclusively of the Marine Brigade and other troops which had held the lines of Richmond previous to the evacuation, made a countercharge upon that part of our lines in their front. I was never more astonished."[39] The ferocity of the fighting can be judged by the report of the commanding officer of the 37th Massachusetts who credited their Spencer (repeating) rifles as being the sole reason they were able to maintain their position and avoid the destruction or capture of the unit.[40]

After this initial contact, the Federal troops regrouped and swept over a confused field, aided considerably by the encircling movement of Custer's and Merritt's cavalry divisions, forcing unit after unit of Ewell's Corps to surrender until the entire command crumbled. All, that is, except Tucker's Naval Brigade which held out as an isolated command in a pocket. After the Naval Brigade's counter-charge, which had stopped the Federal advance in their sector, Tucker had withdrawn to a patch of dense woods in a depression in the bluffs. Here they remained unmolested as the Federal troops flowed fluidly around their flanks, leaving them isolated and pocketed.

The battle was essentially over, and dusk was beginning to set in when word reached Brigadier General J. Warren Keifer, commanding the 2d Brigade, 3d Division, 6th Army Corps, that a force of Confederates was still in that patch of woods. Two efforts on his part to get into communication with the commanding officer of these Confederates failed. Then Keifer began to have doubts of the unit's existence and rode alone into the woods to investigate.

Much to his surprise, he had only ridden into the woods a short distance when he came upon Tucker's troops in line of battle, partially concealed by the underbrush. Almost sure to be shot or captured, Keifer decided to bluff it out and shouted out the command, "Forward!" In instant readiness, the Confederate officers picked up the command and repeated it along the line. Keifer turned his horse to ride toward his own lines, but the dense thicket prevented any particular speed, and the Confederate Marines kept close behind him.

On reaching an open space, his true identity as a Union officer was discovered, and the cry, "Shoot him!", went up. He narrowly escaped losing his life in the confusion that ensued. It was only the prompt action of Captain Tucker and Marine Captain John D. Simms in knocking up the barrels of the nearest rifles with their swords that saved him. He then dashed off to safety lying close on his horse's neck.

After reaching his command, Keifer at once returned under a flag of truce to the wooded area where he met Tucker and explained to him his untenable situation. Tucker then surrendered his Naval Brigade to Keifer. Keifer estimated the Naval Brigade numbered about 2,000, including about 35 officers who had formerly served in the U.S. Navy before the war.[41] This seems too large a number as Ewell's entire corps numbered only about 6,000 at the time of the evacuation; a force of 300 or 400 was more likely the case. Incomplete records show that 45 enlisted Marines were captured this time in the general area as well as seven officers. The officers included Captains Holmes, Simms, and Wilson, First Lieutenants Gwynn and MacRee, and Second Lieutenants Albert S. Berry and Eugene R. Smith. But in spite of the growing debacle, the remnants of the Corps pushed on to oblivion.

When the final surrender was made at Appomattox three days later, Second Lieutenant H. H. McCune, the senior officer present with men, had 21 Marines with him, 4 from Company A, 4 from Company B, and 13 from Company C. In addition, four Marines not serving with their companies on the day of the surrender were paroled on a separate roll. Also surrendering at Appomattox on April 9 were three other Marine officers: First Lieutenants Richard H. Henderson (Co. C), Francis H. Cameron (Co. A), and Second Lieutenant Henry M. Doak. Taking his parole at Appomattox on April 10, 1865, was Major and Quartermaster Algernon S. Taylor. The Corps Adjutant, Major Israel Greene, was paroled at Farmville between April 11 and 21.

But the surrender at Appomattox did not account for all of the Marines in the Richmond area. Individual men were picked up in and around Richmond, and by April 10 a group of at least 29 Marines had been assembled in Libby Prison (all the Federal prisoners had been exchanged just before the evacuation of Richmond). Many of these men have been identified as having served at Camp Beall or at the Richmond Navy Yards prior to the evacuation.

Also to be accounted for are the Marines from the vessels of the James River Squadron commanded by Rear Admiral Raphael Semmes. On April 2, 1865, a letter from the Secretary of the Navy was sent to Semmes advising him that the Government was evacuating Richmond on the advice of General Lee, and that, unless otherwise directed by Lee, he should destroy his ships that night. His men were to be provided with rations, armed, and equipped for duty in the field, and the force was to join General Lee whose retreat was directed toward Danville.

The chapel and cemetery at Drewry's Bluff
By courtesy of VIRGINIA CAVALCADE and the Virginia State Library.

The James River Squadron was blown up at the obstructions in the river off Drewry's Bluff on the night of April 2. Lieutenant Crenshaw commented, "The blowing up of the *Virginia* was the most magnificent sight I ever saw."[42] The personnel of the Squadron was carried up the river in the wooden gunboats, reaching the city shortly after sunrise. After landing their passengers and crews on the Manchester side, the wooden gunboats were set on fire. The men were marched to the Danville Depot nearby where they assembled a scratch train composed of two old and worn-out engines and some old cars which had been abandoned.

Using palings and fence rails as fuel for the engines, the train got underway for Danville a few minutes after 8 A.M. On board were the men of Semmes' command as well as several hundred sick soldiers and stragglers. The struggling train reached Amelia Court House a few hours before sunset but kept on through the night and all the next day, reaching Danville the night of the 4th.

The men were kept on the cars all night, and all the officers were placed on duty around the cars in order to keep the men together.[43]

Semmes' command was organized on April 5 into a brigade of two regiments of five companies each and placed in the Army. Semmes was appointed a brigadier general in the Army and assigned to defend the city of Danville with a small force consisting of his Naval Brigade and two battalions of infantry. The Naval Brigade was placed in charge of the batteries on the north side of the River Dan.

The news of Lee's surrender reached Danville on the 9th in an atmosphere charged with depression and impending disaster. At 4 P.M. on April 12, Semmes was ordered to encamp within ten miles of Danville and to send 200 men to Pelham Station, North Carolina, [about 5 miles south of Danville] to guard stores. Lieutenant Crenshaw, temporarily hospitalized in Danville, looked from his hospital window and saw the troops moving out. Getting one of the attendants to carry his baggage for him, he walked down to the bridge where he "hitched" a ride on one of his brigade's ambulances.

Four days later, April 16 at one in the afternoon, Beauregard ordered the Naval Brigade to handle the trans-shipment of stores across a break in the railroad some twelve miles from Greensboro. Semmes' command was moved up close to Greensboro on the 19th and went into camp several miles from town. Semmes' men had begun to drift away by this time. In his "Memoirs" he says, ". . . before I reached Greensboro, North Carolina, . . . my command had dwindled to about 250 men [from 500]. Commissioned officers slunk away from me one by one, and became deserters."[44] Marine Lieutenant Crenshaw made a similar observation in his diary under date of April 19, "Several officers and many men deserted from the brigade on the march from Danville to this place [near Greensboro]. Two lieutenants from our ship [the *Virginia*] were among the number."[45]

About 10 A.M. on the 26th, Semmes brought his command into Greensboro, and, after marching nearly through the town, halted at a beautiful grove where orders were received to go into camp. Here they stayed while the surrender negotiations were conducted. Finally, on Monday, May 1, 1865, the surrender of the Naval Brigade was completed by the distribution of paroles to 245 officers and men of the Navy and Marines. The brigade rolls included three Marine second lieutenants: Edward Crenshaw, Samuel (?) Roberts, and Everard T. Eggleston, one sergeant, one corporal, and 15 privates.[46] This surrender was separate from that of Captain Tattnall's Company E of Marines which was surrendered and paroled at Greensboro as a separate unit and not as part of Semmes' Naval Brigade.

The surrender and parole of Semmes' Naval Brigade at Greensboro, North Carolina, concluded the history of the James River Squadron and of the Marines who were a part of that Squadron.

NOTES AND REFERENCES

Chapter III — Marines in Virginia

1. Memphis *Daily Appeal*, Fri., April 26, 1861, 1:1, quoting the correspondent "Medicus" of the Petersburg *Express*.

2. John W. H. Porter, *A Record of Events in Norfolk County, Virginia, from April 19th, 1861, to May 10th, 1862*, . . . (Portsmouth, Va., 1892), 70.

3. Order dated June 7, 1861, *Order Book, Gosport Navy Yard, F. Forrest Pp.*, Southern Historical Collection, University of North Carolina.

4. *O.R.* 2, 911.

5. MS. *Executive Journal, 1861, State of Virginia*, 281, in Virginia State Archives.

6. File of Otey Bradford, *"ZB" file*, Early Records Section, Operational Archives, Naval History Division, U.S.N. This source cited hereafter as *"ZB" file*.

7. J.R. Tucker to Hon. C. M. Conrad, Richmond, Aug. 22, 1861, papers of John R. Tucker, Microcopy 260, *C.S.N. Carded Records, R.G. 109*, U.S. National Archives, *Roll 7*.

8. *Letter Book, II, Gosport Dockyard*, 121, Dec. 6, 1861; and page 124, Dec. 7, 1861, *F. Forrest Pp., SHC, UNC*.

9. *N.O.R.* 6, 772.

10. Lt. Joseph N. Barney, C.S.N., to   , C.S.S. *Jamestown*, James River, Feb. 14, 1862, Letter #21, *Letters Sent by Comdr. Joseph Nicholson Barney, C.S.N., December, 1861-April, 1863, Entry 430, R.G. 45*, U. S. National Archives. Cited hereafter as *Barney's Letter Book, U.S.N.A.*

11. *N.O.R.* 7, 47: report of Flag-Officer Franklin Buchanan, C.S.N., March 27, 1862.

12. Lt. Joseph N. Barney, C.S.N., to 1st Lt. J. R. Y. Fendall, C.S.M.C., C.S.S. *Jamestown*, James River, April 29 (?), 1862, Letter #47, *Barney's Letter Book, U.S.N.A.*

13. Samuel A. Mann, *Recollections of service in the Army of Northern Virginia (Augustus Henry Drewry's battery of Virginia artillery) . . . at Drewry's Bluff, Chesterfield co., Va., 15 May 1862*, typescript MS., Virginia Historical Society. Also in *Southern Historical Society Papers*, vol. 34, 87.

14. *O.R.* 11, pt. 3, 505.

15. *N.O.R.* 7, 366.

16. *Ibid.*, 357.

17. Report of Capt. John D. Simms, Comdg. Marine Battalion, to Col. Lloyd J. Beall, Comdt., C.S.M.C., Drewry's Bluff Battery, May 16, 1862, *Van B. Pp.* Also see Richmond *Daily Examiner*, Mon., May 19, 1862, 1:3. The report is in the Richmond *Daily Examiner*, Sat., May 24, 1862, 1:2.

18. J. Thomas Scharf, *History of the Confederate States Navy* (New York, 1887), 716-717. Cited hereafter as "Scharf *Hist. C.S.N.*

19. Richmond *Daily Examiner*, Sat., May 3, 1862, 2:1 (also other issues).

20. Lt. Henry L. Graves, C.S.M.C., to "My Dear Sister," Camp Beall, Drewry's Bluff, Va., Nov. 23, 1862, in *Graves' Papers, Accession 2716, Southern Historical Collection, University of North Carolina.* Cited hereafter as *Graves' Pp., SHC, UNC.* Many of these letters are published in Richard Harwell (ed.), *A Confederate Marine:* . . . . (Tuscaloosa, Ala.: Confederate Publishing Company, 1963).

21. *N.O.R.* 8, 850.

22. Richmond *Sentinel*, July 29, 1863, 2:4; Sept. 5, 1863, 2:5; Sept. 28, 1863, 1:7; Oct. 15, 1863, 1:2; Oct. 22, 1863, 1:2; Oct. 23, 1863, 1:1; Aug. 31, 1864, 1:7. For a note on vegetables raised in a Marine garden, see letter of Ruffin Thomson to "Dear Pa," July 18, 1864, *Thomson Pp., SHC, UNC.*

23. Henry Kershaw DuBose, *The History of Company B, 21st Regiment, South Carolina Volunteers* (Columbia, S.C., 1909), 47.

24. Douglas S. Freeman (ed.), *A Calendar of Confederate Papers* . . . (Richmond, Va., 1908), 53.

25. Clement A. Evans (ed.), *Confederate Military History* (12 vols. & supp.; Atlanta, 1899), IV, 420. This source cited hereafter as *Evans' C.M.H.*

26. *N.O.R.* 7, 50.

27. *N.O.R.* 9, 806: Lt. R. D. Minor, C.S.N., to Comdr. Catesby ap R. Jones, C.S.N., March 23, 1864, and page 810: extract from Report of the Secretary of the Navy, April 30, 1864.

28. Entry dated Wed., Oct. 19, 1864, *Diary of Captain Edward Crenshaw.* This diary was made available for inspection in the original by Crenshaw's granddaughter, Mrs. Sarah Tatum Smith, through the intercession of a cousin, Mrs. Calvin Poole, both of Greenville, Ala. This diary has been published in the *Alabama Historical Quarterly.* His Marine Corps activities are to be found in issue #4 of Volume I and in all four numbers of Volume II. This source cited hereafter as *Crenshaw's Diary.*

29. For Terrett's temporary rank as a colonel, see *Confederate Archives, Chap. 1, Vol. 40, 402, R.G. 109,* U. S. National Archives. For his assignment to command at Drewry's Bluff, see S.O. 170, H.Q., Dept. No. Va. (Lee), July 21, 1864, in personal file of Col. Geo. H. Terrett, *Staff File, C.S.A. Carded Records, R.G. 109,* U. S. National Archives.

30. Entry dated Wed., Feb. 15, 1865, *Crenshaw's Diary.*

31. Requisition dated June 30, 1864, by Capt. T. S. Wilson, "OV" file, Box 37, *Miscellaneous Supplies, C.S.M.C., 2d Qr., 1864, R.G. 45,* U. S. National Archives.

32. S.O. 3, Sept. 21, 1864, Box 3, General Orders, *Comdr. John K. Mitchell Papers, Virginia Historical Society.* Cited hereafter as *J. K. Mitchell Pps., VHS.*

33. Freeman W. Jones, "A Daring Expedition," in George S. Bernard (comp. & ed.) *War Talks of Confederate Veterans* (Petersburg, 1892), 231-234. This article reprinted 1986 by Robert Hardy Publications, Suffolk, Va. One of the most quoted articles dealing with this expedition (by W. F. Shippey) names Lt. Crenshaw as the Marine officer on the expedition, but Crenshaw in his diary makes it clear that it was Lt. Thurston, C.S.M.C.; see entry dated Thurs., Feb. 2, 1865, *Crenshaw's Diary*. See also Ralph W. Donnelly, "A Confederate Forlorn Hope," *Military Affairs*, XXVIII, No. 2 (Summer 1964), 73-78. A chance encounter with this expedition by a Capt. Philip Dandridge, who believed these blue-coated men were a battalion of Marines, even though they carried cutlasses, is related in John Esten Cooke, *Wearing of the Gray* (New York: E. B. Trent & Co., 1867), 557-558.

34. *N.O.R.* 5, 540-542, and possibly 537-538.

35. David S. Woodson to Auditor of Public Accounts, Pension Office, Sept. 20, 1917, David S. Woodson Pension File, Box 8, "Amherst Co. V-W; Appomattox Co. A-O," Virginia State Archives. Also letter from Mrs. David B. Woodson to the author, Aug. 10, 1974.

36. Morris Schaff, *The Sunset of the Confederacy* (Boston, 1912), 107.

37. *O.R.* 46, pt. 1, 980: report of Brig. Gen. Truman Seymour, 3d Div., 6th Army Corps, U.S.A.

38. Letter by Daniel B. Sanford, *Confederate Veteran*, vol. 8, no. 4 (April 1900), 170. This fine tribute was called to my attention by Lee A. Wallace, Jr.

39. *O.R.* 46, pt. 1, 906: report of Maj. Gen. H. G. Wright, Comdg. 6th Army Corps, U.S.A.

40. *Ibid.*, 947: report of Capt. Archibald Hopkins, Comdg. 37th Mass., 3d Brig., 1st Div., 6th Army Corps, U.S.A.

41. Joseph Warren Keifer, *Slavery and Four Years of War*, ... (2 vols.; New York, 1900), II, 208-211, *passim*.

42. Entry dated Mon., April 3, 1865, *Crenshaw's Diary*.

43. *Loc. cit.,* entry dated Tues., April 4, 1865.

44. Raphael Semmes, *Memoirs of Service Afloat* (Baltimore, 1869), 819-820.

45. Entry dated Wed., April 19, 1865, *Crenshaw's Diary*.

46. *Greensboro Parolees, Roll 704, Semmes' Naval Brigade, R.G. 45*, U. S. National Archives.

Chapter IV

MARINES AT MOBILE, ALABAMA

Confederate Marine Corps recruiting in Mobile began in the summer of 1861. Captain Reuben Thom, seeking recruits for his Company C, began enlisting on July 24 and continued until mid-September, gaining some 46 men during the seven weeks. Thom then went on to Pensacola, Florida, to take command of his company of Marines, leaving Lieutenant George P. Turner as recruiting officer to forward recruits to Pensacola. Records show Turner in Mobile as late as November 5, 1861.

Marines on the Mobile Station were innocent pawns in an Army-Navy conflict when Lieutenant Thomas B. Mills, C.S.N., used them to back up his seizure of some coal stored at Hitchcock's Press. The Army protested, claiming their coal had been taken, but the matter smoothed out on the explanation furnished by Lieutenant James D. Johnston, C.S.N., then in charge of the Mobile Naval Station. The incident has little significance other than to show the presence of Marines on the Mobile Station in December 1861.[1]

But Marine Corps activity at Mobile was moderate as long as New Orleans remained a Confederate seaport. It was only with the surrender of New Orleans that the port of Mobile became of primary importance as a Confederate Navy and Marine Corps center.

As previously mentioned, Captain A. C. Van Benthuysen's company was ordered to Mobile from Pensacola on February 13, 1862, only to be shifted to Virginia in less than a month. Renewed activities of the Confederate States Marine Corps in Mobile apparently began in June 1862 by the assignment of Lieutenant Calvin L. Sayre to recruiting duty in an effort to obtain recruits for Flag-Officer Victor M. Randolph's infant naval squadron. Several weeks later word was received from Colonel Beall that Lieutenant James R. Y. Fendall would visit Mobile on recruiting service, and instructions were given Navy Paymaster Ware to advance the bounty to be paid for each recruit.

The Marine Corps unit at Mobile had a dual purpose. In part it was in the nature of a depot company, and in part it furnished the guard for the station and the ships of the squadron. The Marines enrolled at this station were given serial numbers in the order in which they were entered on Paymaster Ware's records. These numbers, similar in their utility to the service serial numbers of today, help identify individual Marines on various records. The numbers assigned Marines by Ware on the Mobile Station ranged from #1 in July 1862 through #375 on May 18, 1864. Occasionally the same man is found with two numbers on Ware's records. This resulted from men being returned to the barracks after serving on board one of the ships of the squadron and having been entered on the books of another paymaster in the interim. Of course, not all of these men actually served in the Marine Corps in the customary sense of "serving." Attrition was heavy in the group, some 101 not going beyond the recruit stage. Of these, 22 were returned to the Army, 5 died or were killed, 62 deserted and were not apprehended, 11 were discharged for various reasons, and 1 was exchanged for a soldier in the Army. On March 16, 1864, Captain Meiere reminded the Corps Quartermaster A. S. Taylor that he had "clothed & shod" some 412 men in a year and a half on the Mobile Station.[2]

Although #375 was enlisted on May 18, 1864, it may be assumed that recruiting continued until the battle of Mobile Bay on August 5, 1864. Recruiting was resumed shortly after the battle of Mobile Bay and is presumed to have continued until the surrender of Mobile on April 12, 1865.

Upon transfer to a permanent assignment with some field company, station guard, or vessel guard, the Marine's accounts were transferred to the Paymaster having charge of the accounts of that unit, and the Marine was then assigned a new serial number on the accounts of his new paymaster.

On September 17, 1862, about a month after his assignment to the Mobile Station, Admiral Franklin Buchanan wrote to Colonel Lloyd Beall, commanding the C.S. Marine Corps:

> Sir: There are now more than one hundred marines on this station, many of them fine looking men and would do credit to the Corps and service, if disciplined and uniformed. At present they are very badly off for clothing. You will oblige me by having them supplied as soon as possible as I require their services on board the various vessels of the squadron.[3]

The task of disciplining the recruited and assembled Marines was given by Colonel Beall in General Order 29, dated September 20, 1862, to Captain Julius Ernest Meiere, a career officer and son-in-law of Admiral Buchanan. Meiere reported on October 8, 1862, and assumed the command of the Marines on the Mobile Station.

Three days later Captain Meiere wrote the Corps Adjutant, Major Israel Greene, that the Admiral was negotiating for a cotton press to be fitted up as a barracks. When available, it was planned to bring all the Marines of the Squadron on shore to be disciplined and drilled. Meiere reported further that he had some 117 men and needed at least two officers to assist him as soon as possible. It was the increasing importance of Mobile as a naval station and the prospects of a permanent Marine center that contributed to the abandonment of the Receiving Ship for Marines and the substitution of a shore barracks by Admiral Buchanan.

The Naval Commandant ordered certain administrative changes made necessary by the establishment of the barracks. On October 24, 1862, he wrote Paymaster Ware of the Mobile Station:

A Marine Barracks has been established on shore and placed under command of Captain J. E. Meiere C.S.M.C. — You will please stop the rations of the Marines now on board the Dalman from breakfast time tomorrow morning as they will hereafter be furnished at the Barracks.[4]

Admiral Buchanan wrote Colonel Beall several days later of the establishment of these temporary Marine barracks needed in order to have the Marines of the squadron drilled and trained as soldiers. He described them as very comfortable and with a large yard suitable for a drill ground, the whole enclosed by high walls. The significance of this last is almost lost upon today's reader, but at that time the high walls around barracks served to make desertion difficult — yet note how many deserted in spite of this precaution. The Deserter's Roll Book of the U.S. Marine Corps for the same general period frequently carries the comment after the name of some deserter, "scaled the wall." Indeed, the brick wall around the Marine Barracks in Washington, D.C., today is a silent memento of that philosophy of control over the enlisted man.

Admiral Buchanan at the same time requested that two lieutenants be sent to Mobile to assist Captain Meiere since the men were new recruits and required strict attention.

The exact status of the Marines at Mobile was carefully delineated in a letter dated October 31, 1862, from the Corps Paymaster, Major Richard T. Allison, to Navy Paymaster Ware on duty at Mobile:

I received yesterday yours of the 25th inst. in reference to the Marines at Mobile.

You are correct in supposing that I have no desire to impose any portion of my duties upon you.

But in the instances you mention I do not think that such is the case, and am strengthened in my opinion in consultation with the Colonel commanding the Marine Corps.

The Marines under Captain Meiere are left at Mobile, not as in an ordinary Barracks, or Navy Yard, (which Mobile is not) but for the purpose of acting on board of the vessels there and forming part of their crews. They are placed in Barracks ashore merely for convenience, because the vessels are small. Were it otherwise the Marines would not be kept at Mobile at all, but ordered up here, to the Battalion at Drewry's Bluff. * * *[5]

Within a short time, Captain Meiere organized a company of Marines from the recruits who had been enlisted over the months by Lieutenant Fendall. The new company, designated Company "D", embraced those on board the ships of the squadron and consisted of four sergeants, four corporals, two musicians, and 78 privates, leaving four vacancies in the number of non-commissioned officers and six in the number of privates.

A detachment of one sergeant, one corporal, and 19 privates for Lieutenant Thurston of Company "E" at Savannah, Georgia, was reported ready for shipping out.

Meiere at the same time expressed his appreciation of "the many official acts of courtesy shown me by Lieutenant Fendall since my taking command, he having rendered me much aid and assistance." He then requested the Colonel to send two officers needed to assist him.[6]

The enlistment of Marines at Mobile was handled by a Recruiting Party separate from the Marine detachment commanded by Captain Meiere. As of December 20, 1862, First Lieutenant James R. Y. Fendall was on duty in the Marine Corps Recruiting Office in Mobile. He was assisted by three enlisted men, William Eihard, Albert Perkins, and George W. Jackson. In February 1863, Captain Reuben T. Thom, who replaced Lieutenant Fendall, was running a recruiting advertisement in the Mobile papers, giving his office location as the "Old Courthouse" on Conti Street, between Royal and Water. He dangled a bounty of $50, prize money, and commutation money before able-bodied men between the ages of 16 and 45 and offered higher pay for drummers, buglers, and fifers. The advertisement carried an explanation of the duties of Marines as "soldiers on board men-of-war or at Naval Stations, . . . not required to perform sailors' duty.'' Potential draftees were reminded of the provisions of the draft law by which they could ask for assignment to the Navy or Marine Corps. Similar advertisements continued almost daily into September. Captain Thom had moved his office to 33 Michael Street in June 1863. Thom and Meiere disagreed upon their respective authority over recruits once they had been placed with Meiere for instruction and training. The disagreement reached the point where communication between the two officers was conducted by letter and on a businesslike basis only.

The Marines at Mobile furnished guards for the various vessels of the Mobile Squadron as well as replacements for other guard units and for the field battalion, both as individuals and as groups.

Contingents of Marines were assigned to the vessels of the Mobile Squadron in August of 1862. Some 23 Marines were transferred from the Receiving Ship *Dalman* to the C.S. Ram *Baltic* on August 8. That group included one sergeant, one corporal, and 21 privates. Some 17 more Marines were transferred on August 20 from the *Dalman* to the C.S. Steamer *Gaines*. That group consisted of one sergeant, one corporal, and 15 privates. The next day, the 21st, 17 additional Marines (one sergeant, one corporal, and 15 privates) were transferred from the *Dalman* to the C.S. Steamer *Morgan*.

A group of eight Marines, exchanged prisoners of war who had been attached to the station as parolees, were transferred to Richmond, Virginia, to rejoin their companies on October 10, 1862, leaving Mobile by the Steamer *Mary Wilson* on the next day. Five of those men had been on the *McRae* at New Orleans.

A month later on November seven, 1862, a contingent of 24 Marines, consisting of one sergeant, one corporal, and 22 privates, was transferred from Mobile to the Naval Station at Savannah where most went on board the C.S.S. *Atlanta* as the nucleus of the Marine Guard of that ill-fated vessel. An additional 12 privates were transferred to the Savannah Station as a Marine Guard for that post on the last day of the year of 1862. During the two months a total of 36 men had been transferred from Mobile to Savannah.

From time to time additional assignments were made to the ships of the Mobile Squadron. On January 12, 1863, some seven additional privates were transferred to the C.S. Steamer *Morgan*. A week later more Marines were assigned to the ships of the squadron — eight privates were sent to the C.S.S. *Baltic*, one sergeant, one corporal, and three privates to the *Gaines*, and two privates as replacements for two of the *Morgan's* Guard detailed to special Government work.

These transfers conformed to Meiere's statement to Paymaster Allison that ". . . all the Marines of Company "D" will be distributed amongst the different vessels of the Squadron."[7]

On January 26, 1863, Admiral Buchanan made plans to capture a Federal ship lying at the outer edge of the Swash Channel off Mobile Harbor. Lieutenant John W. Bennett, commanding C.S.S. *Gaines*, commanded the expedition. Two small steamers which were active in the harbor were picked to carry the sailors and Marines of the expedition. The steamer *Crescent* was to be under the immediate command of Lieutenant J. R. Eggleston while the *Junior* would be under Lieutenants Hilary Cenas and Thomas L. Dornin.

The Marines of the expedition were to be under Captain J. E. Meiere in over-all command on board *Crescent* while part of the Marines were to be on the steamer *Junior* with Lieutenant David G. Raney in command.

In contemplation of the expected confusion attending the actual cutting-out of the Federal ship, the officers were ordered to wear white covers on their caps, and the men were to wear white shirts. All were to be armed with cutlasses and revolvers, if they could be obtained.

The Admiral enjoined silence in the operation to avoid attracting the attention of the Federal Blockading Squadron. It was his hope that the steamers could lay alongside of the Federal ship and capture her by boarding. Efforts were to be made to bring her back to Mobile. Failing this, she was to be burned.

But unforeseen circumstances frustrated the Admiral's plans. Buchanan, on board *Crescent* and accompanied by *Junior*, went down to Fort Morgan only to find the blockade runner *Alice* loaded with nearly 800 bales of cotton aground in the channel under the guns of the fort. This attracted the attention of the Federal Navy which sent another steamer into the channel. Then came a gale that lasted some thirty hours. The opportunity thus passed, and the expedition had to be called off.[8]

The usual pattern of a depot company, a constantly changing group of transients, continued unabated. Savannah again received a draft of men in March 1863, some 10 privates "shipping out" for that station on March 6. Only nine reached Savannah, however, as Private Eugene F. Moore deserted at Opelika, Alabama, taking four months' "French leave" until his voluntary return to duty on July 9, 1863. Some eight of this contingent were assigned to duty on board the C.S.S. *Savannah* upon their arrival at the station.

Captain Meiere received a letter in late March from Colonel Beall directing him to fill up the vacancies in his Company D from the recruits then in the barracks. Meiere then asked the commanders of the ships of the squadron for the number of Marines needed to fill their guard's complement. Any unassigned recruits were ordered shipped to Charleston. Few were left over and just two privates were transferred on March 31, 1863, to Captain John D. Simms, commanding the C.S. Marine Battalion temporarily stationed at Charleston. As of April 29 three more privates were sent on board the *Gaines*, three to the *Morgan*, and two to the *Baltic*.

Captain Meiere reported to the Corps Adjutant on March 20, 1863, that he had 63 recruits from the Conscript Camps in Barracks to be placed under instruction and drill and presumably to belong to Company "F". To assist in this work, he suggested that company officers be sent to serve with these recruits.[9]

Captain Meiere had begun the organization of Company "F" on the Mobile Station by April 1863, and on May 5 reported the detachment consisted of 23 men, three of whom were at the Recruiting Office. During this spring, some 27 recruits were received from the Conscript Camps of Alabama and enlisted in the Marine Corps at Mobile. These men were ineligible for bounty, accounting for the omission of account numbers for them from Ware's disbursement records. These conscripts accounted for practically the entire enlistment at Mobile during April and May of 1863.

Captain Meiere transferred more Marines from the Mobile Barracks to the *Morgan, Gaines,* and *Baltic* of the Mobile Squadron in July 1863. He made the mistake of transferring his men before giving Paymaster Thomas R. Ware advance notice so that their pay accounts could be prepared for transfer. Ware promptly and politely reprimanded Meiere. The administrative details had been placed in order by the next day, and the records then reflected the transfer of one corporal and two privates to the *Baltic*, one sergeant, one corporal, and three privates to the *Gaines*, and one corporal and six privates to the *Morgan*, making a group of 15 Marines in all.

Colonel Beall apparently wrote to Captain Meiere on July 31 on the subject of the transfer of the detachment of Company "F" from Mobile to Drewry's Bluff. Captain Meiere pointed out in his answer that frequent desertions from the ships of the squadron had reduced his Company "D" to about two-thirds of its original strength, and with guards required at the Naval Store House and Ordnance Department, the Naval Ship Yard, and at the Marine Barracks, all the men on the Station were needed. It was his suggestion that if the Commandant intended to break up the organization of Company "F", that the 54 men in the unit be consolidated into Company "D". He expressed the opinion that after the men really unfit for the service were weeded out, the consolidation would leave Company "D" at about the maximum strength authorized by law.

Captain Meiere explained that Company "F" would now number 76 men but for the large number of Army deserters returned and for the number of desertions. He volunteered the opinion that the ranks would soon be filled with conscripts, but they usually had proven to be physically unfit for service. Meiere further reminded Colonel Beall that upon the completion of the Ironclads *Tennessee* and *Nashville*, the Guards required for them would exhaust the strength of his command.[10]

A new demand now entered the life of the Marines at Mobile. For the first time a sizeable draft of men was sent to Richmond to fill up the ranks of the field battalion, Companies "A", "B", and "C" at Drewry's Bluff, Virginia. A contingent from Company "F" of 24 Marines including one sergeant, one corporal, and 22 privates, was transferred to Virginia on September 19, 1863.

The orders for the transfer so upset Admiral Buchanan that he wrote the Secretary of the Navy requesting the order be countermanded. He described the men as being "very important" in the scheme of things in Mobile and said they "Cannot well be dispensed with." In support of his plea, he stated that "The impression still prevails that Mobile will be attacked."[11]

Since the original order called for the transfer of 35 men to Drewry's Bluff and only 24 were actually transferred, it would seem that Meiere's letter and Admiral Buchanan's protest did bring some modification of the original order.

A return for Company "F" covering September and October 1863 is revealing as to the function and operation of a depot company:

Aggregate present & absent, August 31st/63	61
Recruits from August 31st/63 to October 31/63	23
Total	84
Transferred to Company "D" — Mobile, Ala.,	
September 19/63	37
October 19/63	3
Transferred to Drewry's Bluff, Va., Sept. 19/63	24
Deserted from Barracks	14
Discharged on Surgeon's Certificate	4
Recruits present for duty, joined since	
September 19/63	2
Total	84

In addition, some six deserters awaiting trial were on hand. The transfers to Company "D" were probably record transfers, the men being retained physically for drill and instruction as the cash requisition for pay purposes dated October 31, 1863, carries the names of one orderly sergeant, two sergeants, two musicians, and 54 privates, a total of 59 men.

A forerunner of the recruiting appeal of more modern days, "Join the Navy and See the World," headed an advertisement in January 1864 for recruits in the Mobile newspaper. The advertisement read, in part,

A Chance to See Something of the World

Wanted for Special Service
TWENTY RELIABLE MEN, between the ages of 18 and 35 years, for special service in the Marine Corps. None need apply who cannot bring recommendations as to character and evidence of their being out of the service.[12]

The advertisement was also run in February with the addition of a recruiting request for "Four thoroughly instructed DRUMMERS AND FIFERS for the Marine Barracks at Savannah, Geo."[13]

One wonders what this "Special Service" could have been. And so did a group of some 20 or 30 men who applied to Captain Meiere. Meiere reported to Colonel Beall that he had a chance of getting these men, whom he classified as "first rate men who have seen service," but they wanted to know the nature of the special service. He asked the Colonel to reply at once as the men were awaiting the details before re-enlisting elsewhere.[14] But there is no record of an answer, and the enlistment records do not show the enlistment of a group of 20 or 30 men about this time. Either the nature of the service was not revealed, it was not to the liking of the men, or the project was called off.

The commissioning of the C.S.S. *Tennessee* on February 16, 1864, soon brought about the transfer of the ship's Marine Guard from the Marine Barracks in Mobile. The first Marines to report, a party of nine, came on board and reported for duty just four days after the *Tennessee* was commissioned. On March 15, 1864, some 36 Marines were assigned to the *Tennessee*, consisting of First Lieutenant David G. Raney, two sergeants, two corporals, one musician, and 30 privates.

At the time this Guard was being sent on board the *Tennessee*, Captain Meiere wrote a letter of instructions to Lieutenant Raney. An important in-

1st Lt. David Greenway Raney, Jr.
The hand-written date of 1863 is on the back of the original photograph.
Photograph by the courtesy and permission of Mrs. Margaret Key and the Apalachicola (Fla.)
Historical Society.

struction was for Raney to have the Executive Officer of the ship assign him a suitable place on the ship for the keeping of the arms and accoutrements of the Guard. When the men had been issued sea bags, their knapsacks, canteens, and haversacks were to be turned in and stored in a convenient place. He further recommended that any harshness on the part of non-commissioned officers towards the men be reproved and that any punishment be used in preference to "tricing up" or "bucking" as there were other punishments more humane and quite as effective. Yet he advocated that prompt punishment follow all violations of military discipline or propriety.[15]

By March 1, 1864, Captain Meiere was reporting that the detachment of Company "F" had been gradually increased to thirty-odd men. Of these, six had been originally enlisted by Captain Thom, had deserted about the time the last draft had shipped out for Drewry's Bluff, and had been subsequently arrested, tried, and were serving out their sentences. Twelve of the new recruits had just completed three years as regulars [in the 1st Battalion Alabama Artillery] at Fort Morgan. It was the Captain's opinion that as a whole the detachment was very much superior to any yet enlisted.[16]

The return for Company "F" covering the five month period from November 1863 through March 1864 shows but a slow growth:[17]

Aggregate present and absent, November 1st/63	8
Recruits from November 1st/63 to March 31st/64	28
Total	36
Present for duty, March 31/64	29
Sick at Naval Hospital	2
Detached on Government work	2
In hands of Army, undergoing Sentence of General Court Martial	3
	36

During the next month (April 1864) some 16 recruits were added to the roll of Company "F".

A draft was made upon the Barracks on June 7, 1864, for the transfer of 45 Marines to the field battalion at Drewry's Bluff, Virginia. This draft took 42 of Captain Meiere's 57 available privates (one of whom was made a corporal and two were made sergeants), and three of those were under sentence of court-martial. The residue left to Captain Meiere to build on consisted of just 16 men (one orderly sergeant, one musician, and 13 available privates, plus one under sentence of a court-martial). On the same day Captain Meiere sent Adjutant Greene the enlistment papers on all Marines enlisted at the barracks since its establishment, retaining the duplicate records of the men attached to his company. This was apparently the elimination of Company "F" on the Mobile Station.

Efforts were made almost immediately to secure recruits for the Marine Corps in Mobile by advertising in the local newspaper:

To the Members
Composing the Local Military Organizations about
being placed in the Field.
A CHANCE to enter the military branch of the NAVAL SER-VICE. Good CLOTHING, PAY, RATIONS, and comfortable quarters furnished to persons who have or have not been conscripted, and who are desirous of remaining near their families, a chance is offered them of entering the Marine Corps. Before assignment, the Conscript has the privilege of selecting any branch of the service, and by expressing a preference will be assigned to the Marine Corps. None but healthy able-bodied men will be received. For particulars apply immediately at the Marine Barracks, Commerce Street, below Church.[18]

The Marine strength at Mobile ran about ten per cent of the total naval strength on the station. Only one record of the station strength and its distribution has been located. Fortunately, it is dated June 30, 1864, just five weeks prior to the battle of Mobile Bay.

Table 4

Officers and Crews of Vessels of the Mobile Squadron, 30th June 1864.[19]

	Officers	Crew	Marines	Total
Tennessee	22	125	35	179 [182]
Morgan	15	107	15	137
Gaines	18	117	17	152
Selma..................	13	89	—	102
Huntsville	14	63	—	77
Tuscaloosa	13	66	—	79
Receiving Ship	5	51*	—	56
Marine Barracks	3	—	20	23
Baltic..................	14	91	17	122
Officers on Shore Station ...	16	—	—	16
	113	709	104	927 [946]

* And recruits.

The services of the Marines afloat were unique and varied. On at least one occasion the Marine Guard of the *Tennessee* was instrumental in preventing the destruction of that vessel. The story is best told in the words of Dr. Daniel B. Conrad, Fleet Surgeon, C.S.N., who was serving on the *Tennessee*:

> During the four months that we were guarding the entrance to Mobile Bay we were not by any means safe from the danger of our con-trivances. One hot July morning we officers were up on the flat deck of the ram enjoying the sea breeze, when a floating black object was observed bobbing up and down, and supposed at first that it was a sort of a devilfish with its young, as we had killed one with its calf only a few weeks previously; but the motion was too slow, evidently. A telescope soon revealed the fact that it was a torpedo drifting in with the flood-tide. Here was literally the "devil to pay!" We could not send a boat's crew after it to tow it out of the way. You could not touch it; you could not guide it. There was no means in our power to divert it from its course. Finally at the suggestion of Captain David Rainey [Lieutenant David G. Raney] Jr. of the Marines, he brought up his whole guard with loaded muskets, who at once commenced to shoot at the floating keg and sunk it, but not a moment too soon, for it only disappeared under the water about twenty feet from the ram.[20]

The Marines at Mobile participated actively in the battle of Mobile Bay on August 5, 1864, both on board the vessels of the Mobile Squadron and in the defense of Fort Gaines. Marine guards were normally assigned to the *Tennessee*, the *Morgan*, and the *Gaines*. Although Confederate records do not show that Marines were assigned to the *Selma*, Federal reports of the battle of Mobile Bay name captured Marines from the *Selma* who had been assigned previously to the *Tennessee*.

After the capture of the *Tennessee* and the *Selma* in the battle of Mobile Bay, some 33 Marines from the *Tennessee* and one from the *Selma* were sent to the Federal prisons in New Orleans along with the captives from Fort Gaines. Some four of these men escaped from prison in New Orleans, three died before being exchanged, and two enlisted in the U.S. Navy. Many were transferred to Ship Island, Mississippi, until an exchange was effective on March 4, 1865, returning 17 (half the group) to Confederate service.

The crew of the C.S.S. *Gaines* escaped in six small boats on the night of August 5 from the sandy beach under the guns of Fort Morgan where they had beached their disabled and sinking craft. Some 129 officers and men, including the Marine Guard, reached Mobile at 7 A.M. on the 6th of August.[21] The C.S.S. *Morgan*, smoky, noisy, and slow, headed for the city of Mobile 25 miles away at 11 P.M. on a starlight night. Although hotly pursued and shelled by Federal cruisers, the *Morgan* reached the outer obstruction near Mobile at daylight only to find the opening through the obstructions closed. It was afternoon before the gate was pulled sufficiently aside to permit the *Morgan* to slip inside the barrier to safety, but she returned to port the sole survivor of the battle of Mobile Bay.[22]

With the approach of the Federal fleet, the town of Mobile was scraped clean of almost every available soldier. The Confederate Marines were no exception from this call for manpower. Captain J. Ernest Meiere and his two lieutenants, J. R. Y. Fendall and John L. Rapier, hastily organized a small company of Marines from the men on duty at the Barracks and men normally assigned to the C.S.S. *Baltic*, credited as numbering 40, but probably somewhat fewer in number. They were sent out to Fort Gaines to reinforce the garrison upon the appearance of a land force off Dauphin Island. These reinforcements were organized into a Provisional Battalion of 326 muskets under the command of Major W. R. Browne of General Dabney Maury's staff. The Major appointed Marine Lieutenant Rapier adjutant.

The battalion received its orders to go to Fort Gaines at midnight on August 3. After a night made miserable by a heavy rain, they reached the fort at sunrise the next morning, August 4. About 1 A.M. the night of August 4-5, the battalion took position on a picket line about 1100 yards from the fort in opposition to the advancing Federal Army troops of General Grainger. At daylight, the enemy's pickets were only 600 yards away, and a lively skirmish ensued. Unfortunately, the Federal forces had been allowed to occupy a pine forest on the island while the Confederate line, drawn too close to the fort, had to be content with bare sand hills, beach, and Palmetto trees.

The brisk skirmishing cost the battalion three killed and eight wounded. Major Browne was on the verge of advancing to the edge of the woods when an order was received to fall back into the fort. On the way back, the order was countermanded, and the battalion recovered almost all the ground voluntarily surrendered.

During the day there was a lull in the infantry combat. The Confederates on the line had a good, but discouraging, view of the naval battle in Mobile Bay.

On the morning of the 6th, Lieutenant Rapier recalled that the Federal sharpshooting continued, perhaps not so briskly, but with what seemed increasing accuracy. The battalion was relieved at daylight, and at 10 A.M. Major Browne and Lieutenant Rapier followed them back to the fort. They had hardly entered the fort when, to their surprise, they beheld their replacement troops on the picket line falling back in haste. Orders were sent to halt the retreat, but the damage had been done as the re-established line was only about 500 yards from the fort, a loss of about 600 yards.

Early on the morning of the 7th, Lieutenant Rapier was awakened by a friend with the news that Fort Gaines was to be surrendered. This thoroughly incensed him, as he preferred to go down fighting with honor to abject surrender. As far as his Marines were concerned, he had no doubt but that they were ready and willing to fight if so ordered.

The fort was surrendered at 8 o'clock on the morning of the 8th of August by Colonel Charles D. Anderson of the 21st Alabama Infantry, commanding, and shortly thereafter the prisoners were placed on board Federal ships, bound for New Orleans.[23] A document was later produced signed by many of the officers of the garrison purporting to show that the surrender was on their recommendation. This was a highly irregular procedure, which, when known, was condemned by Anderson's superior officers, and the Secretary of War recommended all officers for official reprimand who participated. Captain Meiere's signature appended to this document probably accounts for his absence from command after his return to duty. Neither Fendall nor Rapier signed the document.

Here, again, as so often during the war, the land side of seacoast fortifications proved to be the Achilles Heel. The only sure defense was to prevent the landing of troops, or, if landed, to keep them out of rifle shot distance of the fort.

As a result of the surrender of Fort Gaines, three Marine officers, one sergeant, one corporal, and 23 privates were sent to the Federal prisons at New Orleans and Ship Island. A group of four of these enlisted men escaped from prison on September 27, 1864, while a number were transferred to Ship Island, six finally being exchanged on March 4, 1865. There were nine who were released from prison to enlist in the U.S. Navy.[24]

Sergeant Ed W. Gardien, three privates, and a drummer boy were made prisoners of war about this same time, presumably at Fort Gaines. But they were back on the Paymaster's rolls by December 31, 1864, whether by parole or exchange is not known, being paid for time served as POW's.

Without designation of the vessel or fort at which they were captured, a Federal officer's letter states that four Marine officers (presumably Meiere, Raney, Fendall, and Rapier), four non-commissioned officers, and 52 privates captured in Mobile Bay, a total of 60 Marines, were proposed for exchange.

The number captured and enumerated above from the *Tennessee, Selma,* and Fort Gaines given above (63) is slightly in excess of the Federal report to Confederate authorities.

After the battle of Mobile Bay, we find no record of the operations of the Marine company in Mobile in the records of Paymaster Thomas R. Ware. The last cash requisition for the pay of Marines that he honored was dated June 30, 1864. The rapidly developing situation in the Mobile Bay area the last of July 1864 probably made it impossible to pay the depot Marines before they went on duty at Fort Gaines and were captured on August 8, 1864. The exchange of these men was not completed until March 4, 1865.

The capture of all the Marine officers stationed there must have constituted a virtual collapse of Marine Corps activities in Mobile. But by September 29, 1864, the Corps was again recruiting in Mobile with promises of good pay, rations, and clothing as inducements.[25] Captain Thomas S. Wilson, who had made a name for himself earlier in the year for his part in cutting out the U.S.S. *Underwriter* in the Neuse River, North Carolina, was ordered to Mobile from Camp Beall, Virginia, on August 18th. He reached there six days later to take command of the Marines on the station and to act as recruiting officer. Captain Meiere and Lieutenants Fendall and Rapier were not out of action long as they escaped from prison in New Orleans on October 13, 1864, and reported back at Mobile for duty. Fendall and Rapier arrived on November 10, 1864. Within a short time Fendall was assigned to command the Marine Guard of the C.S.S. *Nashville*, and on November 30 Rapier was ordered to assume command of the sixteen-man Marine Guard of the C.S.S. *Morgan*.

From March 27 through April 11, 1865, the partially armored C.S.S. *Nashville*, armed with three 7-in. Brooke rifles and one 24-pdr. howitzer, was stationed in support of the ground forces in Spanish Fort, Blakely, and batteries Tracy and Huger on the eastern shore of Mobile Bay. On the 31st, *Nashville* was struck eight times by a Federal land battery and was forced to withdraw to Mobile for two days of repairs.

Returning to her station, she resumed fire support of the Confederates on shore despite being plagued by faulty ammunition and fuses. *Nashville* assisted in the withdrawal of Confederate troops from the fortifications and finally helped rescue the crews and material from the ships *Huntsville* and *Tusccaloosa* which were scuttled and sunk in the channel of Spanish River.

In his report of the activity of *Nashville*, Lt. Bennett stated, ". . . to Lieutenant Fendall, commanding marines, I am under especial obligations for their [his] intelligent assistance and cordial cooperation."[26] Fendall commanded a Marine Guard of about 18 enlisted men, most of whom were finally surrendered and paroled at Nanna Hubba Bluff on May 5, 1865.

A companion ship of the Mobile Squadron the C.S.S. *Morgan* had managed to escape from the Federal fleet in Mobile Bay on August 5, 1864. Armed with two 6-inch rifled guns and one 6-inch and one 7-inch Brooke rifled guns, she had been repaired after the battle in Mobile Bay and was back in service. Partially armored and drawing only 7 '2 ", she was able to go places where *Nashville* with her deeper draft could not. Included in her crew on January 28, 1865, was a Marine Guard of 18 men under 2d Lt. John L. Rapier. Shortly before the Spanish Fort/Blakely campaign, Lt. Joseph Fry took over the command of *Morgan.*

On the afternoon of April 8th, a Federal battery of four 30-pounder Parrotts under Captain William P. Wimmer, 1st Indiana Heavy Artillery, opened up on the Confederate ships lying offshore. As Lieutenant Rapier later related,

> We were at anchor in the Tensas, just above Blakely Landing and just off the extreme right of the enemy. We had orders to shell their lines vigorously, and we did so up to dinner [lunch] time. Orders were then received by Captain Fry, instructing him immediately after dinner to move down stream, and attack the Federal left. All hands went to dinner and while we were quietly munching our corn bread and sour bacon, whiz! bang! and everybody jumped to their feet. We had been struck by a shell.

> ... In less time than it has taken to write this, the ship was ready for action, and the command to commence firing rang out fore and aft ... The Morgan was a wooden vessel with flush deck; every man was visible from his ankles up. Her position was about one thousand yards from the enemy's battery, which was mounted with Parrott guns, and countersunk under a hill.

> Pretty soon the Federal battery 'got range' on the ship, and then their *hits* were frequent. After one hour and a quarter's fight, the forward division was reported out of ammunition. Then in a few minutes more, a report that a plank had been ripped out of the ship's side just at the water line, and that it was impossible to plug the hole. Quick as thought, away went guns (rendered useless for want of ammunition) and chainboxes to the port side, to lift up the 'unpluggable' hole out of the water. Ten minutes more, and the after broadside guns reported out of munitions, and only two more shells for the seven-inch after gun left on hand.

> These reports came thick and fast, and this last one convinced Captain Fry that it was time to quit the fight, and try to save his ship, crippled as she was, and his men. He ordered the last two shots fired, and that we should then quit the action.

... The Morgan hauled off, and was so badly crippled that she could not be repaired and got ready to return to duty until the evening of the evacuation of Mobile, when she went over to the eastern shore to watch the movements of the enemy, and cover the retreat of our river transports. We then ascended the Tombigbee River to Demopolis, and there awaited in mournful inactivity the news of the sad sending of our long struggle.

A week passed, and we were ordered to return to Nana Hubba Bluff, to surrender our ship...[27]

A considerable number of the Marines captured at Mobile Bay on August 5, 1864, exchanged on March 4, 1865, and delivered back to Mobile were combined with new recruits to form a squad (or platoon?) of Company "D" which was utilized in the land defense of Fort Blakely. Within five weeks these men were again captured by Federal forces when Fort Blakely fell. Some 19 enlisted men (one sergeant and 18 privates) were shipped as prisoners of war to Ship Island. Exchange on parole was arranged swiftly in most cases and many of these men were shipped to Vicksburg, and re-entered the Confederate lines from there, only to be surrendered a few days later as a portion of Lieutenant General "Dick" Taylor's command at Citronelle, Alabama. Some 14 Marines (one sergeant and 13 privates) of Company "D", were paroled at Meridian, Mississippi, on May 9, 1865, one month to the day from the fall of Fort Blakely and just one day before the Nanna Hubba Bluff surrender.

The end was drawing near, and with the fall of Mobile, the *Nashville*, along with the *Morgan, Baltic*, and various auxiliary craft, retreated up the Mobile River to Nanna Hubba Bluff in the vicinity of the junction of the Tombigbee and Alabama Rivers, about 35 miles upstream from Mobile, where their surrender as the Confederate Naval Forces in the waters of the State of Alabama took place.

Included in the surrender on May 10, 1865, were Lieutenants J. R. Y. Fendall and John L. Rapier. Lieutenant David G. Raney, Jr., surrendered himself and gave parole as senior Marine officer for 24 Marines under his command (two sergeants, three corporals, one musician, and 18 privates).[28] Six of these Marines (one corporal and five privates) were from the guard of the *Morgan*, and, assuming the alphabetical listing to indicate that the remaining Marines were from the same vessel, the other 18 enlisted men (two sergeants, two corporals, one musician, and 13 privates) were probably the guard from the C.S.S. *Nashville*.

These two surrenders, at Citronelle and at Nanna Hubba Bluff, marked the end of the last remaining organized unit of the Confederate Marine Corps, Company D, accounting for a total of three officers and 38 enlisted men in all.

By coincidence, the first recruiting for the Confederate Marine Corps in 1861 and the last surrender of an organized unit of the Corps both took place within Alabama.

NOTES AND REFERENCES

Chapter IV — Marines at Mobile, Alabama

1. *O.R.* 6, 801-802.

2. *Mobile C.O. Day Book*, 243.

3. Admr. Franklin Buchanan, C.S.N., to Col. Lloyd Beall, C.S.M. Corps, Naval Commandant's Office, Mobile, Ala., Sept. 17, 1862, *Letter Book of Franklin Buchanan, 1862-'63* (typescript), 41, Southern Historical Collection, University of North Carolina. This source cited hereafter as *Buchanan's Letter Book, SHC, UNC.*

4. Admr. Franklin Buchanan, C.S.N., to Paymaster T.R. Ware, C.S.N., Naval Commandant's Office, Mobile, Ala., Oct. 24, 1862, *Misc. Records & Orders, Papers of Paymaster Thomas R. Ware*, R.G. 45, U.S. National Archives. Cited hereafter as *Ware Pp.*

5. Major and Paymaster Richard T. Allison, C.S.M.C., to Paymaster Thomas R. Ware, C.S.N., Richmond, Oct. 31, 1862, *Corres., '62-'64, Ware Pp.*

6. Capt. J. E. Meiere, C.S.M.C., to Col. Lloyd J. Beall, Commandant, C.S.M.C., Marine Barracks, Mobile, Nov. 2, 1862, *Mobile C.O. Day Book*, 4-5.

7. *Loc. cit.*, 26: Capt. J. E. Meiere, C.S.M.C., to Paymaster Richard T. Allison, C.S.M.C., Mobile, Dec. 15, 1862.

8. Admr. Franklin Buchanan to Lieut. John W. Bennett, Jan. 26, 1863, and Admr. Franklin Buchanan to Hon. S. R. Mallory, Secty. of the Navy, Feb. 1, 1863, *Buchanan's Letter Book, SHC, UNC.*

9. Capt. J. Ernest Meiere, C.S.M.C., to Major I. Greene, C.S.M.C., Marine Barracks, Mobile, March 20, 1863, *Mobile C.O. Day Book*, 54-55.

10. *Loc. cit.*, 129-130: Capt. J. Ernest Meiere, C.S.M.C., to Col. Lloyd J. Beall, Comdt., C.S.M.C., Marine Barracks, Mobile, Aug. 6, 1863.

11. Admr. Franklin Buchanan, C.S.N., to Hon. S. R. Mallory, Secretary of the Navy, Naval Commandant's Office, Mobile, Ala., undated, but letters on either side are dated August 31 and September 8, 1863, *Buchanan's Letter Book, SHC,UNC,* 216.

12. Mobile *Daily Advertiser and Register*, Fri., Jan. 22, 1864, 2:5, and subsequent issues.

13. *Loc. cit.*, Thurs., Feb. 4, 1864, 2:6, and subsequent issues.

14. Dispatch from Capt. J. Ernest Meiere, C.S.M.C., to Col. Lloyd J. Beall, C.S.M.C., C.S. Marine Barracks, Feb. 13, 1864, *Mobile C.O. Day Book*, 225.

15. *Loc. cit.*, 241-242: Capt. J. Ernest Meiere to Lt. David G. Raney, Mobile, March 12, 1864.

16. *Loc. cit.*, 234: Capt. J. Ernest Meiere to Major I. Greene, Mobile, March 1, 1864.

17. *Loc. cit.*, 247-248: statement of Comy F, C.S.M.C., from Nov. 1st 1863 to March 31st 1864.

18. Mobile *Register and Advertiser*, Sun., June 20, 1864, 3:6, and other editions. Punctuation edited.

19. Office Memo, *Letters for 3d Qr. '64, Ware Pp.*

20. Dr. Daniel B. Conrad, Fleet Surgeon, C.S.N., "Capture of the C.S. Ram Tennessee in Mobile Bay, August, 1864," *Southern Historical Society Papers* (Richmond, Va., 1876-1944), XIX (1891), 81-82. This same story is given in D. B. Conrad, M.D., "With Buchanan on the 'Tennessee'," in *Hero Tales of the American Soldier and Sailor* (A. Holloway, 1899), 414-415. Story reprinted 1986 by Robert Hardy Publications, Suffolk, Va.

21. *N.O.R.* 21, 590: report of Lt. J. W. Bennett, C.S.N., late commanding C.S.S. *Gaines*, to Hon. S. R. Mallory, Secretary of the Navy, Mobile, Ala., Aug. 8, 1864.

22. *Ibid.*, 584-585: report of Comdr. Geo. W. Harrison, C.S.N., commanding C.S.S. *Morgan*, to Admr. F. Buchanan, C.S.N., Mobile, Ala., Oct. 1, 1864.

23. Lt. John L. Rapier to "Dear Tom," U.S. Military Prison, Union Press, New Orleans, Sept. 5, 1864, in possession of Mrs. E. M. Trigg.

24. Marine Corps entries in *Auxiliary Register No. 4, New Orleans, La.*, August, 1864, captures, 19-20, *Entry 379, R.G. 109*, U.S. National Archives.

25. Mobile *Advertiser and Register*, Thurs., Sept. 29, 1864, 1:3.

26. *N.O.R.* 22, 102.

27. Jeanie Mort Walker, *Life of Capt. Joseph Fry . . . .* (Hartford: The J. B. Burr Publishing Co., 1875), 180-184. Her author for this segment was Lt. John L. Rapier.

28. Enclosure #8, Dispatch No. 109, *Letters of the West Gulf Squadron, Actg. R/Admr. H. K. Thatcher, Comdg., Volume for March-June, 1865*, 398-400, *R.G. 45*, U.S. National Archives. (Now in Microcopy 89, "Squadron Letters," Roll 196, Mar. 2 - July 7, 1865 (Thatcher), U.S. National Archives.)

Chapter V

MARINES AT SAVANNAH, GEORGIA

In 1861 on the Savannah Station, Commodore Josiah Tattnall was endeavoring to assemble some semblance of a naval squadron in the Savannah River to cover the coast of South Carolina and Georgia. In the fall of 1861 this "Mosquito Fleet" consisted of the paddle-wheel river steamer *Savannah* as flagship, the side-wheel steamers *Huntress*, *Sampson*, and *Resolute*, and the tug *Lady Davis*.

Tattnall's naval efforts were strengthened by the arrival of Marine Captain George Holmes' Company A, ordered north from Pensacola, Florida, on September 18, 1861. While the records of the services of these Marines are sparse, available information indicates that the company probably furnished contingents to the various ships of the squadron as well as officers. Second Lieutenant James Thurston is said to have been assigned to the C.S.S. *Sampson* at the time it was provisioning Fort Pulaski in late January 1862. Shortly before, Second Lieutenant Frances Hawkes Cameron reported for duty on board the C.S.S. *Huntress*. It seems reasonable to expect that a similar contingent was assigned to the flagship *Savannah*, probably including Captain Holmes and Lieutenant David G. Raney.

On a clothing receipt roll dated October 13, 1861, eleven Marines had their issues witnessed by Acting Lieutenant Wilburn B. Hall, C.S.N., who was serving on the *Savannah*. A 4th Quarter 1861 General Pay and Receipt Roll of Marines on the Georgia and South Carolina Stations carries the names of twelve Marines witnessed by Lieutenant Joel S. Kennard, C.S.N., who commanded the *Sampson* during the Port Royal fight. Just a few days before the Port Royal engagement, some sixteen Marines were transferred from the *Huntress* to the *Savannah*.

The approach of the Federal fleet to the bar of Port Royal, South Carolina, on November 4, 1861, was met by three of Tattnall's make-shift flotilla, the *Savannah*, the *Sampson*, and the *Resolute*. The *Huntress* and the *Lady Davis* were at Beaufort after having fired light ships three miles below Beaufort,[1] and joined Tattnall later. But Tattnall's cockle-shells had to content themselves with a few shots fired at long range, having neither the weight in armament nor the protective armor to challenge the Federal Navy.

Driven to the protection of the shallow waters of Skull Creek during the heavy bombardment on the 7th between the Forts Walker and Beauregard and the Federal ships, most of Tattnall's Marines under the command of Captain George Holmes landed shortly after 11 A.M. and marched to the support and relief of the garrison of Fort Walker. About an hour later, the available seamen from the *Savannah* and the *Sampson*, as well as a few Marines from the *Sampson*, under the temporary command of Lieutenant Phillip Porcher, C.S.N., were ordered to take naval ammunition to the heavily engaged battery. The Marines came within a quarter of a mile of Fort Walker, and the second group came within a half mile. The records of the *Savannah* show that every officer and man went ashore with the Marines at Hilton Head with the exception of the Engineer Department, all returning on board on the 8th.[2]

The battery was abandoned before this relief mission could be accomplished, and the two contingents returned to their ships. On the return march to the wharf at Skull Creek, Lieutenant David Raney, Holmes' second in command, commanded the main body of Marines. Holmes had separated himself from the company in order to make a personal reconnaissance and was feared captured.[3] The Confederate Marines covering the retreat from Fort Walker almost made contact with Federal Marines landed from the U.S.S. *Wabash* and sent out from Fort Walker as a protective picket line.

It is worth at least a passing comment that among the Army reinforcements reaching Fort Walker from Georgia on November 6 was Captain Jacob Read's battery of two 12-pounder howitzers and 50 men. The greater portion of this battery was brought into the fort on the 7th after 10:30 A.M. Both Read and his men were under the command of Colonel John A. Wagener who commanded Fort Walker. Captain Read, while commanding this Georgia Regular battery, was an old-time U.S. Marine officer and was holding a dual commission as a captain in the C.S. Marine Corps.

Company A was on the Savannah Station for the 4th quarter of 1861, and a payroll exists for the officers of the Company on the same station for the 1st quarter of 1862. The introduction of troops into a civilian situation is not without its problems, and the presence of Marines in Savannah was no exception. About half past eight on the evening of Thursday, January 9, 1862, City Patrolman Peter Smith reported a number of Marines on the corner of Fahm and Indian Street lane for using "abusive indecent language." Upon walking away, he was followed by one of the party who brought him down to the ground with a sling shot. In the altercation which followed, Smith received a two-inch deep stab wound. No arrests were made, but Smith felt he could identify his assailant.[4]

Orders sent to Marine Captain Holmes place him on the Savannah Station as late as April 22, 1862. Company A was moved early in July 1862 to Drewry's Bluff where it was reunited with Companies B and C.

On March 21, 1862, the 67-year old Captain Josiah Tattnall, C.S.N., was transferred from the command of the naval defense of Georgia and South Carolina to that of Virginia, in place of the wounded Franklin Buchanan, hoisting his flag on the C.S.S. *Virginia* (*Merrimack*). Tattnall was succeeded at Savannah by Captain Richard L. Page, C.S.N.

It was not until after the destruction of the *Virginia* and the Court Martial which on July 5, 1862, reversed the May 20 Board of Inquiry and cleared Tattnall of blame in the loss of the formidable ironclad that he was free to return to Savannah.

Upon his return to Savannah, he felt that much of his early work had been allowed to deteriorate. This feeling was expressed in family correspondence, one of the more pertinent letters reading . . .

> Cousin Josiah says, while he was away [in Virginia] they broke up his station here entirely. They transferred his vessels, guns and men to the army & he now had only one gun and scarcely any Marines, but of course they expect him to do *wonders*, & if he fails will abuse him.[5]

Tattnall's son, Captain John R. F. Tattnall, C.S.M.C., had reported to Savannah after being released from confinement at Fort Warren, Massachusetts, probably in late January 1862. It does not appear from the available records that he actually served on Marine Corps duty, but instead served as a volunteer aide-de-camp on the staff of General Robert E. Lee until he left Savannah on March 3, 1862. At the time Lee left Savannah, Captain Tattnall was left with an unexplained project of "getting up certain boats for operations on the water." But by mid-April Captain Tattnall had accepted temporary Army rank and was soon on his way to Alabama to command the 29th Alabama Infantry.

By the winter of 1862, Savannah was receiving Marines by transfer from Mobile. A draft of one sergeant, one corporal, and 22 privates was transferred from Mobile on November 8, 1862, and on December 31, 1862, an additional

1st Lt. Henry Lea Graves
The original picture is reported to carry the notation it was made in 1863 at Petersburg, Va.
*Photograph by courtesy of the late Richard Harwell and the permission of the Confederate
Publishing Co., Inc.*

12 privates were transferred from Mobile to Savannah, making 36 men within two months. These men formed the nucleus of the Guard for the C.S.S. *Atlanta*, Lieutenant James Thurston, commanding.

At about this time, Marine Captain John R. F. Tattnall became available for Marine Corps duty and was soon on the job in Savannah. His resignation as colonel of the 29th Alabama Volunteers was accepted on December 9, 1862, and his orders to report for assignment to Marine duty were issued the same day.[6] Existing muster rolls for Company E, the Marine company at Savannah, show enlistments in Savannah by Captain Tattnall as early as January 17, 1863.

Lieutenant Henry L. Graves reported in Savannah from Drewry's Bluff on February 2, 1863, for service on board the newly built ironclad *Savannah*. Upon reporting, he found that his first job would be to recruit a Marine Guard. He found only some 12 or 13 men available on the station with a requirement of 35 or 40 or more. Graves, armed with written authority from the Secretary of War, visited the various conscript camps and enlisted draftees for Marine Corps duty.[7] This was apparently the source of the numerous enlistments reported on the muster rolls of Company E as being made by Lieutenant Graves at Decatur, Georgia, site of a major conscript camp. But although enlistments were being made in Savannah and in the Georgia conscript camp at Decatur, another group of 10 privates was transferred from Mobile to Savannah on March 6, 1863.

For several months after arriving on the Savannah Station, Lieutenant Graves was apparently on board the tender *Sampson* along with his Marines pending the completion and commissioning of the new ironclad *Savannah* and/or the selection of a suitable barracks on shore. Finally, in May 1863, the men were placed in a new barracks described as "a beautiful place in the outskirts of the city. The house is surrounded by a large grove of old oaks and hickories, all covered with long moss. There is always a pleasant breeze and a plenty of green grass."[8] This estate, "Fair Lawn," survives today but has been converted into a school building and no longer fits Graves' description.

The designation of the Marines at Savannah as a "Marine Guard" was replaced by the designation of "Company E" in the spring of 1863. Captain Tattnall was making efforts in April to provide field music for his new company, and ran the following advertisement in the local paper:

C.S. Marine Barracks,)
)
April 18, 1863   )

MUSICIANS WANTED

For Company E, Confederate States Marines; four musicians — two Drummers and two Fifers.

Apply for further particulars at the naval offiec [sic.] on Liberty Street, between Bull and Whitaker.

J. R. F. Tattnall

Capt. C.S. Marines, Commanding.[9]

Company E apparently had difficulty in furnishing the required guards for the naval vessels of the Savannah Squadron. When Commander Webb, commanding the naval squadron, requested a Marine Guard for the C.S.S. *Georgia* in May 1863, he was advised that only 36 unassigned Marines were on the station and that 26 of these were in a course of drill preliminary to assignment to the C.S.S. *Savannah*, leaving only 10 raw recruits available. Flag-Officer Josiah Tattnall told him that since these raw conscripts had only received their muskets three days prior to the request that it would be advantageous to retain these men in the barracks until better drilled.[10] Efforts were made to increase the effectiveness of the various Marine Guards by requiring daily (except Sunday) drill under the direction of the Marine officers.

The *Atlanta*, the converted blockade runner *Fingal*, was commissioned on November 22, 1862. For some six months her activities were limited to patrolling the waters below Savannah and in maintaining contact with the river forts. Commander W. A. Webb, C.S.N., learned on June 14, 1863, of two ironclads inside Wassaw Sound and determined to attack them. He notified the Secretary of the Navy the next day of his intention to attack. The *Atlanta* left Savannah at 6 P.M. on June 15, anchored at 8 P.M., and coaled all night, then continued down river the 16th until about dark, being then 5 or 6 miles from the Federal ironclads.

Getting underway at 3:30 A.M. on the 17th, all went well until the *Atlanta* grounded about ¾ mile from the ironclads. Once off, attempts to regain the channel were ineffectual, and she was forced back upon the sand bank again by tidal action.

Aground, the *Atlanta* was at the mercy of the Federal *Weehawken*. Without maneuverability and with her gun deck tilted out of position for effective firing, the *Atlanta* rocked with the weight of the Federal firing. One shot from a 15-inch gun alone forced the armor plate back through the woodwork, tearing a gash inside three feet wide by the entire length of the protective shield. The shock of this blow caused

> . . . the solid shot in the racks and everything movable in the vicinity to be hurled across the deck with such force as to knock down, wound, and disable the entire gun's crew of the port broadside gun in charge of Lieutenant Thurston (Marine Corps) and also half of the crew at Lieutenant Barbot's bow gun, some thirty men being injured more or less.[11]

Primary sources are not clear as to who manned the guns of the *Atlanta*, but a biographical sketch of Lieutenant Thurston states that of the four guns on the *Atlanta* (two 7-inch Brooke rifles mounted on pivot carriages in the bow and stern, and two 6.4 inch Brooke rifles mounted on Marsilly carriages as broadside guns), two were manned by Marines, and one under Thurston's immediate command.[12] The presence of only two Marines on the list of wounded indicates Marines probably were not serving the port broadside gun, or else there was some exaggeration in Commander Webb's report.

Actually few shots were fired, seven by the *Atlanta*, and five by the *Weehawken*. But the five fired by the *Weehawken* were particularly effective. The *Atlanta* was in no position or condition to continue. With the tide not rising high enough to float the ship off the bar for another hour and a half, there was no alternative to surrendering the ship and its crew of 21 officers and 124 men, including 28 Marines.[13]

Two days later the captured Marines were received on board the U.S.S. *Vermont* in Port Royal Harbor, South Carolina. The unwounded prisoners were then transferred to the U.S.S. *James Adger* to be taken to Fort Monroe. Here they were paroled between June 29 and July 6, 1863. Some 74 of the *Atlanta's* crew left Richmond for Savannah on July 6. Many slipped off so that by the time Savannah was reached on July 8, only 33 men (including eight Marines) were delivered to the Steamer *Sampson*, the receiving ship. Three days later (July 11) the Marines from the *Atlanta* were sent on board the *Isondiga* at Savannah to replace temporarily the crew members who had been sent on loan to Charleston. News of the official exchange of the crew of the *Atlanta* reached Savannah on July 13.

In time, some 21 of the 27 enlisted Marines of the *Atlanta* returned to duty. Three of the remaining six were not exchanged until late in 1864, two deserted, and the fate of one has not been determined.

On December 21, 1863, Special Order No. 179 from the Colonel Commandant directed Captain Tattnall to make monthly inspections of the Marine guards on board vessels of the Savannah Squadron and to send the results to the Corps' Adjutant for the information of the Commandant. In conformity with the views of the Secretary of the Navy that all Marine guards afloat should be commanded by an officer, Captain Tattnall was ordered to place an officer of his company in command of the *Georgia's* guard or, if impractical, to have the officer of the *Savannah* make weekly reports to Captain Tattnall on the guard of the *Georgia*.[14]

Headquarters in Richmond issued orders in November 1863 to resume recruiting. Starting with December 29, 1863, the following advertisement for recruits appeared in the Savannah paper and ran for some time:

WANTED

C.S. Marine Barracks,)
Savannah, Ga., Dec. 28th, 1863)

For Company E, Corps of Marines, forty able bodied recruits. This Company will probably serve in the city of Savannah and on board the iron-clads, engaged in river defense, during the whole war. The platoon serving on shore is well quartered in excellent barracks, and for the sick the best hospital accommodation and medical attention is furnished by the regular medical department of the Navy. Privates receive fifteen dollars a month and abundant clothing of superior quality. At the end of each year the value of such articles of the clothing as have not been drawn is paid, in money, to each marine. Apply to the undersigned between the hours of 10 a.m. and 2 p.m., at the Marine Barracks (Fair Lawn) in this city.

John K. F. Tattnall, [sic.]
Capt. Co. E, C.S. Marines,
Comd'g.[15]

Among the various duties assigned to the Marines at Savannah was the guarding of Federal prisoners until their transfer to a prison camp. On September 10, 1864, Lieutenant T. St. George Pratt, C.S.M.C., with a detachment from the *Savannah*, was ordered to report to Lieutenant William E. Hudgins, P.N.C.S., for guarding prisoners. Upon inquiry from Secretary of the Navy, Flag-Officer William W. Hunter responded that Lieutenant Pratt was urgently needed to help guard some 4,000 prisoners suddenly sent to Savannah and that he would resume his duties afloat as soon as the urgency should cease.

These were prisoners transferred from the Andersonville prison to Savannah. One prisoner, John Ransom, 9th Michigan Cavalry, observed in his diary, "Rebel guards that I sometimes come in contact with are marines, who belong to rebel gunboats stationed in the mouth of Savannah River and are on duty here for a change from boat life. They seem a kindly set, and I don't believe they would shoot a prisoner if they saw him trying to get away."[16] The prisoners were moved out of the city after about five weeks. Colonel Edward C. Anderson, commanding in Savannah, released the sailors and Marines with thanks for their satisfactory services.

Another duty assignment for Marine officers at Savannah was to serve as Provost Marshal for the various Naval General Courts Martial which were convened from time to time. Flag-Officer Hunter asked the Navy Department in Richmond in January 1864 for a Marine Officer for Court Martial duty. Flag-Officer Tattnall, commanding the Savannah Station, received a letter on

January 9, 1864, from Commander John K. Mitchell, In Charge of the Office of Orders and Detail, directing him to order a Marine officer to this duty. This piqued Tattnall who wrote Mitchell that the letter from the Office of Orders and Detail was the first intimation that he had had that Flag-Officer Hunter required an officer for that duty and that any intimation on his part of his need would have made an application to the Department unnecessary. As a result, Lieutenant Edward F. Neufville, C.S.M.C., was detailed on January 13, 1864, as Provost Marshal and was ordered to report to Flag-Officer Hunter, the presiding officer, the next day. Following the courts-martial, Neufville reported for duty on board the *Savannah* on February 2, 1864.

The value of the Marines was apparently recognized by Flag-Officer Hunter who asked the Navy Department on December 29, 1863, to increase the number of Marines on both the *Savannah* and *Georgia* from 15 to 30. The request was approved, and on January 22, 1864, Hunter passed on the approval to Flag-Officer Josiah Tattnall for an additional 21 Marines for the *Georgia* and 15 for the *Savannah*, or such number as might be available.

In the meantime, Flag-Officer Josiah Tattnall, in his letter mentioned above of January 14, 1864, to Commander John K. Mitchell in Richmond, wrote that he considered the Marines on his Station as held chiefly for guards on board the ships of the Savannah Squadron. Those on shore he considered needed as replacements for the guards on board the ships of the Squadron, as a guard for the Navy store, and a few to take charge of the barracks and to serve as a nucleus for drilling recruits.[17]

After receiving Hunter's request, Tattnall wrote to Captain John R. F. Tattnall (his son), commanding the Marines on the Station, of the requisition approved by the Secretary of the Navy for sufficient Marines to increase the number on board the *Savannah* and the *Georgia* to thirty each. Captain Tattnall was therefore ordered to transfer all his Marines to the Squadron with the exception of a proper guard at the Navy store, a guard for the barracks and the prisoners confined there by sentence of a court martial, a cook for the barracks, and an orderly for the Naval Commandant. He was cautioned to retain the smallest number possible.[18]

The health of the Marines assigned to the *Savannah* became a matter of concern in the spring of 1864 to Fleet Surgeon Charles H. Williamson which he discussed with Flag-Officer Hunter, Commanding Afloat. Williamson observed that the greater portion of the Marine Guard of the *Savannah*, most of whom had been on the assignment since the vessel had been commissioned, were broken down by repeated attacks of intermittent fever and were unfit for duty most of the time. He then named some twelve Marines who he felt should be sent on shore to recover their health and be replaced.[19] Hunter transmitted a copy of this letter to Captain John R. F. Tattnall several weeks later, presumably for his information and action.

Later in the spring of 1864 at Savannah, the Navy made plans to attack one of the ships of the Federal squadron operating in the waters below Savannah similar to the cutting out of the U.S.S. *Underwriter* on the Neuse River, North Carolina, in February 1864.

On the afternoon of May 31, 1864, some 15 officers and 117 men from the Savannah Squadron (mainly from the *Savannah* and the floating battery or "Ladies Gunboat," the *Georgia*) left Savannah going downstream in seven boats under the command of Lieutenant Thomas P. Pelot, C.S.N., finally reaching Racoon Key on the night of June 3. Here the decision was made to make a night attack on a Federal vessel lying in Ossabaw Sound. After midnight of a dark and rainy night, the boats approached the ship, which turned out to be the U.S.S. *Water Witch*. Although challenged and fired upon, the Confederates managed to board her, and, after a sharp fight of some 10 minutes, captured her. The attack cost the life of Lieutenant Pelot and four men. Three officers and 10 men were wounded.

The part played by the Marines is not clear from the evidence located so far beyond the report that Private Thomas Veitch of the Marines was one of those who markedly distinguished themselves. The captured Federal sailors were met at Beaulieu Battery on the Vernon River by a Marine Guard under Lieutenant Edward F. Neufville, C.S.M.C., in turn under the over-all command of Lieutenant William W. Carnes, C.S.N. They took charge of the prisoners the next morning and escorted them to Savannah.

The final push of Sherman's army in December 1864 brought Federal troops to the outskirts of Savannah, and all available troops had to be placed in the defensive positions. The Marines available to Captain Tattnall consisting of a platoon of less than fifty men were assigned to a position near King's Bridge on the Ogeechee River. The platoon was in the trenches for twelve days, and Lieutenant Graves felt the position grossly undermanned. Graves was joined in the trenches by Lawrence, his body servant, who secured a rifle and participated in the defense.[20] He was much elated "with the idea at having shot at some Yankees" and the possibility of having hit one.[21] Finally, at dark on Tuesday, December 20, came the order to retreat and the position was abandoned. The Marines reached Savannah at midnight after a dreary march through water, mud, and darkness. Resting for an hour they then fell in with the long shuffling line of silent men leaving the city by the pontoon bridge joining the city with the South Carolina shore. They marched the remainder of the night and the whole of the next day until they reached Hardeeville where they took the "cars" to Charleston, South Carolina.[22]

The C.S.S. *Savannah* was fired by the Confederates on December 21, 1864, at 7:30 P.M. and the officers and members of the crew marched overland about eighteen miles to Hardeeville, reaching there on the morning of December 22.

Transportation was obtained that night to Charleston, South Carolina, and the crews of the Savannah Squadron (except those who had gone up river to Augusta) reached Charleston on the night of the 23rd.

With the commanding officer and at least a platoon of Marine Company E serving at Charleston, after having gone there on the evacuation of Savannah, a portion of the company serving as the Marine Guard on board the C.S.S. *Macon* had accompanied that ship on its trip up river from Savannah to Augusta, Georgia. Various Marines drifted in to Augusta and were assigned to duty with the *Macon's* contingent.

On January 16, 1865, the Marines of the *Macon* at Augusta, Ga., and enough crew members to make up a detail of 15 men were placed under the command of Master James W. McCarrick, P.N.C.S., and assigned to man the one-gun battery at Shell Bluff, about 45 miles below Augusta. The sole piece was a 68-pounder Columbiad (8-inch) and was to be used in defending the river against ascending Federal gunboats. Preliminary plans had been made almost three years before for obstructing the navigation of the river at this point.

This must have been essentially a Marine battery as there were about 10 Marines under Sergeant N. J. Harness on the *Macon* in mid-January 1865, and on January 26, 1865, Captain John R. F. Tattnall was informed by Flag-Officer William W. Hunter, P.N.C.S., that the detachment of Marines belonging to the *Macon* was stationed at this Battery and unavailable.[23] It is not clear whether these men ever rejoined the naval command at Augusta. The battery itself was not in the path of the Federal troops, and the situation may have simply deteriorated.

Details are almost totally lacking, but there is evidence that a Marine Guard was on duty at the Naval Ordnance Works in Charlotte, North Carolina. It is not clear where the detail came from, but the Savannah Station appears to be a likely source. The sole clue to the existence of this guard is the order of Colonel Lloyd J. Beall, Commandant, to Second Lieutenant Ruffin Thomson dated March 16, 1865, in which he said, in part, "You will make it your first duty to obtain provisions for Capt. Tattnall's command, and the *Marine Guard at Charlotte.*[24]

When Second Lieutenant Daniel G. Brent was ready in February 1865 to return to duty from his home in Greenville, Alabama, where he had been on sick leave, he sent a telegram to Augusta to Flag-Officer Hunter requesting assignment to duty as he had been cut off from his company at Charleston. Hunter answered that he had no authority to assign him to duty and suggested he communicate with Captain Tattnall.

Brent, with no knowledge of the actual location of his company, came on to Augusta where on March 1, 1865, he wrote Hunter requesting temporary assignment to the detachment of his company ("E") on board the C.S. Stmr. *Macon*. In view of the circumstances, Hunter assigned Brent to the *Macon* in command of the Marines of the *Macon* and *Sampson* until such time as he could rejoin his company. He was requested in the meantime to notify his captain by letter of his temporary duty and the causes therefor.

Finally, under date of March 29, 1865, Captain Tattnall wrote Flag-Officer Hunter that he was forwarding orders from Richmond for Lieutenant Brent and that Brent was being sent travel orders from Greenville, Alabama, to Augusta. Evidently the state of communications was such that as of March 29 Captain Tattnall was not aware that Brent had been in Augusta since March 1. Captain Tattnall telegraphed Hunter on April 9 that Brent had been ordered to report to Augusta where he was to collect and hold all Marine stragglers.

The number of Marines comprising Brent's command at Augusta these last weeks of the war is not known for certain. As of March 31, 1865, some 25 [28?] officers of all grades and 112 men, boys, and Marines were at Augusta under Flag-Officer Hunter. Of these, the *Macon* had 15 officers and 83 men, including Marines and boys, while the *Sampson* had 13 officers and 29 crew members with no mention of Marines.

The *Macon* had 11 Marines assigned in January 1865, but one had been left in the hospital in Savannah and one deserted on January 5 after the ship had arrived at Augusta. From time to time, additional Marines joined these nine, drifting in to the nearest naval installation, as well as being gathered up in the surrounding counties by Sergeant John Lewis, until some 20-25 were assembled.

By May 1, 1865, both Lee's and Johnston's armies had surrendered, and the war was over. Control was slipping in Augusta, and the Confederate commander, Brigadier General Birkett D. Fry, felt it expedient to parole his own men and to send them on their way home to minimize depredations. When the Federals arrived on May 3, they took up where Fry left off and completed paroling the Confederates. The Marine command at Augusta (and at Shell Bluff) may not have been surrendered formally as a unit. The assumption is that those in Augusta were paroled by Fry and discharged before the Federal troops appeared, as individual paroles turn up in scattered locations for these men. Yet, a letter from the family of one Marine states, "His group surrendered on May 7, 1865, at which time he [Jeptha Harbin] was, of course, Corporal of the Marine Guard of the C.S.S. *Macon*."[25]

NOTES AND REFERENCES

Chapter V — Marines at Savannah, Georgia

1. *O.R.* 6, 29: statement of Messrs. John Tuomey and Henry C. Robertson of occurrences at Beaufort, S.C., Nov. 7 & 8, 1861.

2. Entries for Nov. 7 & 8, 1861, *Account Book [of Ship's Steward] C.S.S. Savannah, Entry 418, R.G. 45,* U.S. National Archives.

3. *N.O.R.* 12, 295-298, quoting "Eyewitness" in the Savannah *Republican* for Nov. 12, 1861.

4. Savannah *Republican*, Sat., Jan. 11, 1862, 2:1.

5. Susan M. Kollock (ed.), "Letters of the Kollock and Allied Families, 1826-1884," *Georgia Historical Quarterly*, vol. 34, no. 3 (September 1950), 245: letter from Mrs. Edw. Neufville to Mrs. George J. (Susan) Kollock, Savannah, Ga., Oct. 1, 1862.

6. Col. John R. F. Tattnall, P.A.C.S. (Captain, C.S. Marines), to Gen. S. Cooper, A.& I.G., Pollard [Ala.], Nov. 24, 1862, in personal file of Col. J. R. F. Tattnall, 29th Alabama Infantry, *C.S.A. Carded Records, R.G. 109,* U.S. National Archives; also S.O. 288, para. 1 and 12, Dec. 9, 1862, A.& I.G.O.

7. Lt. Henry L. Graves, C.S.M.C., to "My Dear Mother," Savannah, Ga., Feb. 5, 1863, *Graves' Pp., SHC, UNC.*

8. *Loc. cit.,* Lt. Henry L. Graves, C.S.M.C., to "My Dear Mother," Savannah, Ga., May 27, 1863.

9. Savannah *Republican*, Fri., May 1, 1863, 3:2. (This ad began running on April 20 and was still being run on June 30.) These musicians were also advertised for in Mobile. See Mobile *Register and Advertiser*, Sun., Feb. 7, 1864, 2:6, and other issues.

10. *N.O.R.* 14, 699-700: Captain Josiah Tattnall, Comdg. Savannah Naval Station, to Comdr. W[illiam] A. Webb, Comdg, Naval Sqdn.

11. *Ibid.,* 291.

12. *Evans' C.M.H.,* 418.

13. *N.O.R.* 14, 266: report of Capt. John Rodgers, U.S.N.

14. *N.O.R.* 15, 698: S.O. 179, H.Q., C.S. Marine Corps, Richmond, Va., Dec. 21, 1863.

15. Savannah *Republican*, Tues., Jan. 19, 1864, 1:5, and other issues. Also in Augusta, Ga., *Daily Constitutionalist*, Jan. 26, 1864, through at least April 5, 1864.

16. John Ransom, *John Ransom's Diary* (New York: Dell Pub. Co., 1964), 125. Originally published in Auburn, N.Y., in 1881 under the title of *Andersonville*, it was reprinted in Philadelphia in 1883 under the title *Andersonville Diary*.

17. II *N.O.R.* 2, 573. The original document is MS. 274, *Savannah Sqdn. Pp., Emory U.*

18. *Loc. cit.*, MS. 287: unsigned [Flag-Officer Josiah Tattnall] to Capt. John R. F. Tattnall, C.S.M.C., Savannah, Jan. 27, 1864. Also see MS. 288 in the same collection.

19. Fleet Surgeon C. H. Williamson, C.S.N., to Flag-Officer W. W. Hunter, C.S.N., C.S. Stmr. *Savannah*, Savannah River, April 18, 1864, MS. 472 in *Letter Book (March-May, 1864* (unbound), Box 2, Papers of Comdr. William W. Hunter, C.S.N., Louisiana Historical Association Collection on deposit in the Howard-Tilton Memorial Library, Tulane University, New Orleans, La. Cited hereafter as *Hunter Pp., Tulane U.*

20. Richard Harwell (ed.), *A Confederate Marine: A Sketch of Henry Lea Graves with Excerpts from the Graves Family Correspondence, 1861-1865.* (Tuscaloosa: Confederate Publishing Company, Inc., 1963), 126-127: Lt. Henry L. Graves, C.S.M.C., to Sarah D. Graves ["My Dearest Mother"], Charleston, S.C., Dec. 28, 1864. The original is in the *Graves' Pp., SHC, UNC.*

21. *Ibid.*, 129: Iverson D. Graves to Mrs. Sarah D. Graves, James Island, S.C., Jan. 20, 1865.

22. *Ibid.*,126: Lt. Henry L. Graves, C.S.M.C., to Sarah D. Graves ["My Dearest Mother"], Charleston, S.C., Dec. 28, 1864.

23. Letter from Flag-Officer Wm. W. Hunter, Comdg., to Capt. J. R. F. Tattnall, Comy. E, C.S.M.C., Augusta, Ga., Jan. 26, 1865, *55 H-3, Letter Book, Savannah Squadron, October 18, 1864-April, 1865*, 77-78, *Hunter Pp., Tulane U.*

24. Col. Lloyd J. Beall, Commandant, C.S.M.C., to Lt. Ruffin Thomson, C.S.M.C., Richmond, March 16, 1865, *Thomson Pp., SHC, UNC.*

25. Letter to the author from James C. Stephens, of Fort Valley, Ga., Aug. 9, 1961. Mr. Stephens, a grandson of Corporal Jeptha Harbin, C.S.M.C., wrote for his mother, Mrs. L. D. Stephens.

Chapter VI

MARINES IN NORTH CAROLINA

There was a brief Marine Corps presence in Wilmington, North Carolina, in August 1861 when 1st Lieutenant George P. Turner set up a recruiting office. He advertised for able-bodied single men between the ages of 18 and 35 years. The promised pay was from $11 to $21 per month and a bounty of $10 was to be paid to each recruit for signing. But Turner's efforts seem to have been in vain as no records exist of recruits being obtained in Wilmington in 1861. Wasting no time, Turner was moved on to Mobile where he was recruiting Marines in September 1861.[1]

The activities of Confederate Marines in North Carolina came late in the war. The first was one of the most daring exploits of the Confederate Navy — the expedition against the Federal patrol boats operating in the vicinity of New Bern and Pamlico Sound which resulted in the "cutting out" of U.S.S. *Underwriter*.

Orders went out from the Navy Department in January 1864, to the naval commanders at Richmond, Wilmington, and Charleston or men to be detailed for special service under Commander John Taylor Wood at Wilmington. The force was planned originally to consist of about 250 seamen, 25 Marines, and 35 officers. Richmond, for instance, was asked to furnish 45 picked men under Lieutenant Francis L. Hoge. Additional officers named were Passed Midshipman Algernon S. Worth, and Midshipmen Richard Slaughter, Paul H. Gibbes, and J. De B. Northrop. The men were to be armed with rifles, cutlasses, and, as far as possible, revolvers, and be provided with 40 rounds of ammunition, cooked rations for three days, cooking utensils, and axes. They were to be well clothed and to have pea-jackets and blankets.

To make a long story short, the expedition left Wilmington by train and reached Kinston on Sunday, January 31, 1864. Here the expedition took to 14 small boats launched in the Neuse River and started downstream towards New Bern. About 2:30 in the morning of February 2, the expedition glided up to the *Underwriter* at anchor. In spite of being challenged, the Confederates closed in on the vessel before the Federals could fire their big guns.

Confederate Marines from Company C under the command of Captain Thomas S. Wilson were distributed among the small boats of the expedition. They stood upright in their unsteady craft and furnished covering fire for the initial wave of boarders, firing and re-loading under the small-arms fire of the Federal sailors.

One participant wrote that the Marines then joined the boarders, and as they were clambering up the sides and over the rail, he "... went forward to follow Mr. Loyall, when a Marine, shot through the heart, fell heavily upon me and crushed me down over the thwarts." Once on board the Marines obeyed their orders promptly. They were placed in formation on the hurricane deck, but not even the explosion among them of a large shell from a shore battery caused them to break ranks or turn a man from his post.[2]

The total losses of the expedition were five killed and eleven wounded. Of these, the Marine contingent had one man killed and four wounded. Marine Private William Bell, who lost his life in the attack, was singled out in Captain Wilson's report as "an excellent man, tried and faithful."[3] Private John Barrett received a slight head wound; Patrick Lambert a serious shoulder wound; Peter Marry a slight cheek wound, and William Shannon a serious thigh wound. Commander Wood acknowledged the help rendered by the Marines in his report, saying, "Captain Wilson, with 25 marines, rendered most valuable services."[4]

Wood commended his Marines to their Commandant, Colonel Lloyd J. Beall:

> Sir: It gives me pleasure to report to you the fine bearing and soldierly conduct of Captain Wilson and his men whilst absent on special duty. Though their duties were more arduous than those of the others, they were always prompt and ready for the performance of all they were called upon to do. As a body they would be a credit to any organization, and I will be glad to be associated with them on duty at any time.[5]

The Confederate Congress saw fit to extend its thanks to Commander Wood and his command for their various exploits, including the capture of the *Underwriter*. This was done by a Joint Resolution passed unanimously with a date of February 15, 1864.

The first Marines assigned to North Carolina were those sent out from Drewry's Bluff to Wilmington about January 20, 1864, primarily to supply Marine guards for the ironclads *North Carolina* and *Raleigh*, both nearing completion. First Lieutenant Richard H. Henderson probably accompanied the first contingent as records show him at Wilmington beginning January 21, 1864. A second draft was sent out from Drewry's Bluff on February 16 or 17, raising the number of enlisted men at Wilmington to about 45. This second draft was probably accompanied by First Lieutenant Fergus MacRee who served on the Wilmington Station from February 18 to March 18, 1864. He was relieved by Second Lieutenant J. Campbell Murdoch on or about March 12.

A guard was placed on board the *North Carolina* almost immediately, five reporting on January 22, 1864, and seven more the next day. In the absence of definite information, the guard of the *Raleigh* seems to have been composed of one sergeant, two corporals, and 15 privates. These men probably went on board the *Raleigh* during the spring. Second Lieutenant Henry M. Doak was ordered transferred from Savannah to Wilmington on February 27, 1864, to take command of the Marine Guard of *Raleigh* when completed. Arriving before his ship was ready for service, Flag-Officer Lynch temporarily assigned Doak to command the guard at the Navy cotton yard.

The cotton yard was located on the south side of the Cape Fear river on a marshy flat across from Wilmington. The steam cotton presses were located there, and it was there that the blockade runners took on their cargoes. The wharves were patrolled at all times to prevent deserters from stowing away on the ships being loaded.[6] Lieutenant Doak was placed in temporary charge of the Navy cotton yard on his arrival from Savannah but was soon transferred to the newly completed ironclad *Raleigh* in command of her Marine Guard.

On April 26, 1864, according to a Federal report, there was a fire at the cotton yards and some 15,000 to 20,000 bales were destroyed. A contemporary version, based on inaccurate research, credited boats' crews from U.S.S. *Niphon* with setting fire to the cotton yard. But the actual account reached *Niphon* from a contraband picked up from the beach.[7] The *Niphon's* boats could not have crossed the land behind Masonboro Inlet or negotiated the long trip up and back the Cape Fear river.

The Wilmington *Daily Journal* of April 29, 1864, carried a story of a tremendous fire and heavy loss during the night of April 28-29, 1864, at the cotton yards. The first early reports were that the Wilmington and Manchester Railroad offices were destroyed as were a number of freight cars belonging to a Georgia Road, all the sheds at the ferry, the Cotton Press, and B. W. Berry's Marine Railway. The preliminary estimate of loss was from 6 to 10 million dollars.[8]

The next day, the *Daily Journal* for April 30 gave more details including the loss by the Confederate Government of 800 bales of cotton (including 200 bales of Sea Island) with an estimated worth of $800,000. Berry's Ship Yard lost materials and work in progress with an estimated value of about $100,000. The losses of various other companies and individuals were also enumerated.[9]

The story of the fire reached Bermuda with the report that the destruction of cotton was upwards of 6,000 bales.

The fire was of suspicious origin, but whether done by a Federal agent or by carelessness of lurking deserters was not determined. In any event, the story of the boats' crews from U.S.S. *Niphon* was the product of unthinking reading and an over-active imagination. The mystery concerning the cause of the fire was finally publicly solved in 1900. D. R. McNary, one-time first lieutenant, 103d Pennsylvania Volunteers, disclosed that after his capture while recruiting Negro troops in North Carolina, the train taking him to prison went through Wilmington close enough to some immense piles of cotton for him to stick a lighted match into a bale of cotton. His little incendiary effort was highly successful and developed into the fire that virtually destroyed the Confederate Cotton Yard.[10]

The Marines had been at Wilmington but a short time when a tempest in a teapot was stirred up in March 1864 between Flag-Officer William F. Lynch, commanding the Naval Forces in North Carolina, and Major General W. H. C. Whiting, commanding the Department of Cape Fear, with headquarters at Wilmington, in which a Marine force was an innocent pawn.

Briefly, Lynch claimed that orders from the Secretary of the Navy had been received prohibiting either of the two State and privately-owned vessels, the *Hansa* and the *Alice*, from proceeding to sea unless the agents or owners consented to take the quantity of cotton which the Navy Department claimed the right to send. When the *Hansa*, a Collie steamer, left her wharf, Lynch detained her, ordered her to drop anchor alongside the *North Carolina*, and placed a half-company of Marines on board the *Hansa* on March 8, 1864.

Whiting became irate at what he claimed was a usurpation of authority by Lynch and a hindrance in the performance of his duty, and requested Lynch's replacement. The Marines were removed on March 10, and the problem was settled by Secretary of War James A. Seddon's refusal to interfere with the Navy's claim to a share of the cargo.

An official version says that Whiting ejected the Marines with a battalion of the 17th North Carolina Infantry under Lieutenant-Colonel John C. Lamb, and "...took possession of the steamer and hauled her upstream to her wharf."[11] Whiting himself reported to General Cooper, "I had turned the marine guard off from her, but without collision or difficulty."[12]

This little episode constituted the main war service of the *North Carolina* which never saw action against the enemy. Her engines were weak, and she was but little better than a floating battery. Her underside was apparently not sheathed with copper, and the sea worms performed their destructive work so well that she sank at anchor at Smithville, N. C., where she guarded the mouth of the Cape Fear River, in September 1864. Her Marines were detached and sent to the receiving ship *Arctic* on September 30, 1864.

When the *Raleigh* was ready for service, Doak joined his ship. The newly completed ironclad steamed down the Cape Fear River, crossed the bar, and engaged the Federal blockading fleet off New Inlet on May 6-7, 1864. Doak wrote later that during the engagement a fifteen-inch shell exploded on or just over his post between the two guns "inciting a momentary fear that Atlas had carelessly dropped this planet." [13] At one time in the dark and confusion, Doak, ordered to fire his starboard gun at the next light, threw a shell into Fort Fisher. Flag-Officer Lynch sent him below under arrest, but he was promptly restored to duty on the intervention of his captain, Pembroke Jones, who recognized that the firing was in obedience to a faulty order.

The next day the Federal blockaders, all wooden ships, closed in on the *Raleigh*, but a few shots from her long-range rifled guns convinced them of their error.

Unfortunately, the *Raleigh* ran hard aground crossing a bar on her way back up the Cape Fear River and broke her back, ending her naval service. As Lieutenant Doak expressed it, "We had done all we purposed — all we could do — and prow was turned shoreward — Ft. Fisher giving us a hearty salute as we ran by. Owing to careless sounding or a reckless pilot, we ran aground going over the bar — the "Raleigh" and months of labor and thousands of dollars all gone for nothing." [14] The Navy Court of Inquiry gave its opinion that the loss was not due to any negligence or inattention on the part of any one on board but was due primarily to her heavy draft.

After the loss of the *Raleigh* her Marines were then assigned to the C.S.S. *Arctic* serving as a receiving ship. On board the *Arctic* as of July 1, 1864, were 38 Marines (two sergeants, three corporals, and 33 privates), all on detail from Companies A, B, and C, the field battalion, stationed at Drewry's Bluff, Va. Four of these privates were detailed on July 31 to the C.S.S. *North Carolina* while the others were still on the *Arctic* through September 30.

Captain Alfred C. Van Benthuysen, lately returned to duty after suspension from duty in lieu of the recommendation of a Court Martial that he be dismissed from the service, was in Mobile when contacted by Colonel Beall on June 15. He was asked whether he wished to be returned to the command of his company at Drewry's Bluff or assigned to the separate command of superintending the guard of Wilmington. Van Benthuysen chose the latter, and on the next day he received orders to proceed immediately to Wilmington where he would find further orders. He reported at Wilmington on June 29, 1864. Van Benthuysen's own Company B remained at Drewry's Bluff under the command of Captain John D. Simms. Van Benthuysen's choice of the Wilmington assignment was not surprising in view of the fact that he was definitely on bad terms with Captain Simms who had been instrumental in bringing about his courts-martial.

An intelligence report received by Major William Norris in Richmond from Southern Maryland may have been instrumental in sparking what almost became the most daring exploit of the Confederate Marines. An agent identified only as "DARST" wrote Norris on June 9, 1864:

> We think it all important that a diversion should be made, either to capture or release our prisoners at Point Lookout or a raid upon Washington with a view to the destruction of the military supplies and public property, or both at the same time would certainly be better, if the necessary troops can be spared at this time. There is not a troop stationed in our county [probably Charles County, but possibly St. Mary's] or Prince George at this time. We therefore infer that the garrison at Point Lookout must be weak.[15]

The degree of influence of this report is not known for certain, but on June 26, 1864, General Robert E. Lee wrote a letter to President Davis speculating on the possibility of freeing the Confederate prisoners at Point Lookout, Maryland, located at the confluence of the Potomac River with Chesapeake Bay. The plan contemplated crossing the lower Potomac with the Marylanders of the Army of Northern Virginia and overwhelming the garrison at Point Lookout, thought to be largely Negro troops who were not expected to offer a stubborn resistence. Lee suggested Colonel John Taylor Wood as an able Navy officer for conducting the operations on the river. (Wood held dual commissions, being an Army colonel as well as a Navy captain.) The released prisoners would be marched overland around Washington, crossing the upper Potomac into Virginia where fordable.[16]

Three days later (on June 29) Lee again raised this proposition in connection with Early's successes in the Valley of Virginia.

Davis apparently made up his mind on July 2 and sent a letter to General Lee at Petersburg by Colonel John Taylor Wood. Lee, in reply, wrote Davis on the 3rd some of the details as he envisaged them.[17] First, it was Lee's belief that close security precluded any attempt to communicate with the prisoners at Point Lookout themselves. Second, he discarded his original thought of crossing the Potomac River into Southern Maryland with supporting troops as too dangerous. Part of the plan evidently involved the boarding and capture of the Federal gunboats since Lee commented that "the first indications of relief must be borne to them [the prisoners] by the guns of the *captured gunboats.*" [Italics added by author.] Boarding parties of sailors and Marines in the style of John Taylor Wood offered a hope for success in capturing the gunboats.

Events moved along swiftly once Davis approved of the project. That same day (July 2) Captain John D. Simms, commanding the Marine Battalion at Drewry's Bluff, received an order for all his available officers and men under Captain Holmes to be sent to Wilmington, to report to Flag-Officer Lynch. About 3 A.M. on Sunday, July 3, Captains Holmes and Wilson and Second Lieutenants Eggleston, J. De B. Roberts, and Crenshaw with about 90 men took the steamer at Drewry's Bluff for Richmond. Reaching Richmond at 6 A.M., the contingent was joined by Second Lieutenant McCune with 40 men from the Marine Guards of the two Navy Yards in Richmond. This made over 130 Marines who were joined by about 150 seamen under their naval officers, and the entire party left on the Danville Railroad at 7 A.M. At the Junction [Burkeville?], they were forced to detrain as the Federal raiders had torn up the road beyond this point. At 10 P.M. after marching 13 miles more, they bivouacked for the night.

This naval contingent continued its march on July 4 to Roanoke Station where the cars were boarded for Danville. (Roanoke Station, or Staunton River Bridge, was the scene of a gallant defense conducted by Captain Benjamin L. Farinholt, 53rd Virginia, on June 25 which saved the bridge and turned back Wilson's raiders.) This made a stretch of almost 30 miles that had to be marched because of the destroyed railroad. They reached Danville before sunset, passed through Greensboro during the night, and continued on their way to Goldsboro. On the forenoon of the 5th they reached Goldsboro and left for Wilmington that night, reaching there on Wednesday, July 6, 1864. Here at Wilmington the Marines went into camp pending the organization of the expedition.

Part of the mechanics of the operation called for a party to go to Cherry-stone and cut the telegraph wire to Old Point Comfort, i.e., the Naval Forces in Hampton Roads and the wire to Washington before the attack. Officers known to the prisoners who were capable to organizing, inspiring confidence, and putting the men into motion quickly were to accompany Wood. The men were to be separated into the various arms of the service and officered accordingly. The practice of separating officers from their men while prisoners broke units into individuals.

On July 5th Colonel Wood and three officers were on the road from Lee's headquarters to the Stony Creek depot, 28 miles away where they would take the cars [train] for Weldon. Lee reported to President Davis that General Whiting had been directed to provide two 20-pounder Parrots, if possible, and all possible assistance so that the expedition could sail on Saturday, July 9th.

With the arrival of the top officers, Wood, General Custis Lee, of President Davis' staff, Lieutenant Colonel Andrew J. Hays (who held a permanent commission as a captain of the Marines), a member of General Braxton Bragg's staff, and Lieutenant John Wilkinson of the Navy, the expedition began to shape up quickly. The rumors were flying fast, and Lieutenant Crenshaw confided to his diary as early as July 7 that Lieutenant Wilkinson was to superintend the fitting out of some fast blockade runners for a secret expedition. It was also whispered that Colonel Wood would command, assisted by General Custis Lee and Lieutenant Colonel Hays, and that the expedition had as its objective the release of Confederate prisoners confined at Point Lookout.

General Early, on whom so much depended if the scheme was to be successful, had to be notified of the part he was to play since the freeing of the Point Lookout prisoners had become an objective after his campaign had begun. Lee promised (July 3) to send an officer with the message to Early that an effort would be made to release the prisoners about July 12. Early could expect to hear of the operation's success through Northern sources. His part would involve sending a brigade of cavalry with Generals [John B.] Gordon and [William Gaston] Lewis to command the prisoners and lead them around Washington.

The chosen messenger was General Lee's son, Captain Robert E. Lee, who recalled that his order to report "at once to the commanding general" aroused wild guesses among his companions. After an evening of rest at headquarters, Captain Lee was given a letter to carry to General Early. In view of the real possibility of capture, he was told of its contents and instructed to destroy the letter should the possibility of capture develop. Captain Lee traveled by rail from Richmond to Staunton where he had a relay of horses to the Potomac. By riding day and night he caught up with Early and his troops in Maryland some miles beyond the old battlefield of Sharpsburg (Antietam) and delivered his letter on July 7 or 8.

Meanwhile, back in Richmond, news of the expedition was leaking out. Of necessity, Josiah Gorgas, the Chief of Army Ordnance in Richmond, became associated with this expedition by being directed to send 2000 stand of arms to Wilmington. But, he wrote in his diary under date of July 7, "I know nothing of it, except what I hear, ... It seems, however, impossible to keep State Secrets, and the expedition is talked of in the streets . . . ."[18]

Two fast blockade runners at Wilmington, the *Let-Her-B* and the *Florie*, were seized by the Government and fitted out for the expedition. On July 8 Custis Lee telegraphed President Davis that the promised arms had not arrived and should be received before the next evening (the 9th). These were the guns which were to be used to arm the former prisoners upon their release from Point Lookout by the expedition. Davis, in turn, reported the non-arrival of arms, and the discussion of the expedition on the streets of Richmond, to General Robert E. Lee and authorized him to call off the expedition if he deemed it best. During the evening Lee was forced to report to President Davis that the expedition was a topic of discussion all through the army, information having been brought from Richmond.

News travels fast. In fact, Union General Ben Butler had received a report from a Confederate deserter on the previous day (July 7) that it was a part of Early's plan to attack Point Lookout and release the prisoners, meanwhile "amusing" the Federals at Martinsburg. This was apparently the basis for an order from Secretary of the Navy Gideon Welles to Commander Foxhall A. Parker, Commanding Potomac Flotilla, at St. Mary's, Maryland, to "take additional precautions relative to covering the camp of prisoners at Point Lookout and its approaches by your gunboats." This order was followed by the sending of another gunboat to the Point Lookout area, making three in all.

But preparations continued at Wilmington. On Saturday, July 9, the Marine Battalion was divided into two equal detachments and sent on board the blockade runners. Captain Holmes and Lieutenants Henderson, Stephenson, Eggleston, and Crenshaw were with one detachment on the *Florie* while Captain Wilson and Lieutenants McCune and J. De B. Roberts were with the other detachment on the *Let-Her-B*. Colonel Wood, commanding the two vessels, in company with General G. W. C. Lee and Colonels Hays and Cox of General Bragg's staff, were on the *Let-Her-B*. Lieutenant Roberts fell down a hatchway on the *Let-Her-B* and hurt himself too badly to remain on duty so Lieutenant Crenshaw was shifted from the *Florie* to the *Let-Her-B* to fill his place. That night the vessels dropped down the river and anchored off Smithville for the night.

On this day (July 9th) War Office clerk J. B. Jones in Richmond recorded in his diary the rumor of the success of the expedition to Point Lookout from Wilmington to liberate 20,000 prisoners of war who would march on Washington and cooperate with General Early.

The expedition was still having trouble getting the necessary rifles. Custis Lee telegraphed Davis that of the 2000 rifles shipped from Columbia on the 8th, some 1400 had been ordered back by Gorgas. Lee protested that even with the 2000 and those which General Whiting in Wilmington could furnish they had little enough and requested that the full 2000 be furnished.

Later the same day Lee again telegraphed Davis that the arms hadn't been received but that General Whiting was making every effort to get them. He explained that Whiting was releasing 1600 Austrian rifles, but they were an undesirable caliber, they lacked accoutrements, and were too few in number.

J. Taylor Wood telegraphed the President (also on the 9th), "Will try and get out tonight. Am badly off for officers, but hope for the best. I request that you will not act on Wilkinson's case until I see you." The reference to "Wilkinson's Case" is enigmatic, but a chatty letter from Lieutenant Van R. Morgan to [Catesby ap R.] Jones on July 28, 1864, seems to be explanatory,

> Wood is ordered to take command of a vessel at Wilmington, blockade runner, fitted up as a war vessel to go to sea. Wilkinson (John) was ordered to report to him and resigned. This is a far worse blow to the Navy than that it received from the immortal fifteen; it destroys the Navy.[19]

President Davis apparently declined to accept a resignation from Lieutenant Wilkinson, assuming it was tendered, and the effect upon the Officer Corps feared by Lieutenant Morgan was avoided.

Also on the 9th, John Tyler at Petersburg, Virginia, wrote a distorted version of the expedition to Major General Sterling Price in Arkansas. He credited Wood with using five gunboats and with carrying 20,000 stand of arms, but was fairly accurate as to the plan. Of the general plan he commented, "This I regard as decidedly the most brilliant idea of the war."[20]

On the same day Early's Confederate troops won the battle of Monocacy, brushing aside the Federal forces which barred his way to Washington. The Confederate strategy called for Bradley Johnson's cavalry brigade (formerly "Grumble" Jones') to take position north of Frederick, early on the morning of July 9th and watch Early's left during the battle to be fought on the Monocacy River. Once assured the battle was a Confederate success, Johnson was to strike across country, destroying railroads and telegraph lines north of Baltimore, cut the railroad between Baltimore and Washington, and then push on for Point Lookout to rendezvous with John Taylor Wood's amphibious prisoners liberation expedition.

On the morning of Sunday, July 10, President Davis telegraphed Colonel Wood that the object and destination of the expedition were so generally known that he feared they would meet "unexpected obstacles." He recommended "calm consideration and full comparison of views before proceeding." That afternoon, at Cockeysville, Lieutenant Colonel Harry Gilmor with only 135 men from the 1st and 2d Maryland Cavalry made his start on a diversionary strike against the Philadelphia, Wilmington, and Baltimore Railroad. On the evening of July 10 the two former blockade runners, the *Florie* and the *Let-Her-B*, started down the Cape Fear River and had just passed Fort Fisher when they were signalled to stop to receive a communication from the President to Colonel Wood. The vessels hove to and in a short time the deciphered dispatch was in Wood's hands. This must have been Davis' 6:15 P.M. telegram (or a similar one to Wood) to Custis Lee which read, "Sent telegram this morning to Colonel John T. Wood to indicate my belief that the attempt would now be fruitless. If you have not other information I advise abandonment of project."[21]

Crenshaw recorded in his diary under date of July 11 that the expedition had been called back by the President since the Federals had learned all about the intended expedition, removed the prisoners to Elmira, and were prepared to give the expedition "a warm reception and no quarter."[22] On the same day, back in Richmond, Robert G. H. Kean, Head of the Bureau of War, wrote in his diary that the news of the supposedly secret expedition from Wilmington to free the prisoners at Point Lookout had leaked out from Navy sources, and that the latest Northern news was that the prisoners had been removed to the interior of New York. He further remarked that the expedition had been in everybody's mouth for more than a week past.[23]

With action not developing in the Point Lookout area, the attention of both the Federal Army and Navy high commands was quickly and forcefully turned to the threats against Washington and Baltimore generated by the Confederates under Generals Jubal E. Early and Bradley T. Johnson. On July 12, the day set for the release of the prisoners, Colonel Gilmor cut his railroad line, destroyed the railroad bridge over the Gunpowder River, captured two trains, and Major General William D. Franklin, U. S. A. (who escaped), and withdrew successfully, frustrating the Navy's efforts to save the bridge by the presence of a gunboat.[24] Early's troops had appeared before Washington on the 11th. On the 12th the Confederates skirmished with the Federals manning the ring of forts around Washington. Johnson, with his brigade, less Gilmor's detachment, had been coming across Maryland from Cockeysville since the 10th. On the 12th he had cut the railroad between Washington and Baltimore near Beltsville in Prince Georges County. From this point he directed his march toward Upper Marlboro on his way through Southern Maryland to Point Lookout over 80 miles away. But the news of gathering Federal forces had been received. These forces included the 19th and part of the 6th Corps from Grant's Army before Petersburg. Back on the Cape Fear River the two vessels had returned to Wilmington and anchored off the city, and Colonel Wood had gone to Richmond to report.

On July 13, faced with gathering Federal hosts and with no news of an attack on Point Lookout, Early was forced to take up the retreat back to Virginia, having recalled Johnson. On the same day Josiah Gorgas was confiding in his diary that the removal of prisoners from Point Lookout to Elmira, N. Y., rendered abortive the proposed prisoner liberation expedition. Finally, oñ the 15th, orders were received to unload all the Government stores and to return the vessels to their owners. The vessels were returned to them on Monday, July 18.[25]

So the effort failed, and over the years the full significance of Early's Raid has been lost. Not lost, however, is the picture of the instant readiness for dangerous service of the Confederate Marine battalion.

Anticlimactically, four refugees from the South gave the story of the expedition to the commanding general at Point Lookout, on July 18, the same day the vessels had been returned to their owners at Wilmington. They reported that some 800 sailors and Marines under John T. Wood left Richmond on the 7th or 8th of July to man two armed blockade runners at Wilmington. The object was to release the Point Lookout prisoners. Not recognizing this story as being the same as the one reported previously by General Butler, it created a sensation at Point Lookout, and telegrams were sent that afternoon to the Secretary of the Navy and to the senior officer at Fort Monroe. The Navy immediately sent orders to the blockading vessels off Wilmington to exercise "great vigilance."

But by this time the expedition had been abandoned. The Charleston, S. C., *Mercury* freely admitted that the expedition had never got to sea and ascribed the leakage of information as the cause of its frustration. The paper conceded it was probably just as well since if the [New York] *Herald* of the 27th [17th] was correct then most of the prisoners had been removed from Point Lookout to Elmira.

Actually there had not been a complete removal of Confederate prisoners from Point Lookout. Before the expedition had gone beyond the planning stage, the Federal Commissary General of Prisoners, Colonel William Hoffman, had ordered 2,000 enlisted prisoners transferred to Elmira on June 30. This camp was just being opened for the first time. Then, again, on July 15, several days before news of the Confederate expedition had filtered North, some 3,000 more prisoners were ordered to Elmira. By July 27, 1864, some 3,059 prisoners had been transferred, leaving 11,430 still at Point Lookout with more scheduled to be moved out. Actually a low point of 7,088 prisoners was reached on August 31, 1864, at Point Lookout, but this figure tended to increase as the close of the war drew nigh.

At 1 P.M. on Monday afternoon, July 18, 1864, the Marine Battalion received orders to march to Smithville at the mouth of the Cape Fear River. Reaching there at sundown, they pitched their tents and established a camp on the sandhills a mile from the village. At least there was a fair chance of enjoying a delightful sea breeze at this spot, a real pleasure in mid-July, as well as meals of oysters and fish. Several days later (the 20th) the Marine Battalion, less Lieutenant Crenshaw and 25 enlisted men, was ordered back to Richmond and Drewry's Bluff. These exceptions were intended for assignment to a regular Confederate cruiser.

Camp life was boring and monotonous to Lieutenant Crenshaw, and he began to find fault with his Marine Corps life and yearn for his former Army life. A state election coming up in North Carolina was the occasion for Captain Van Benthuysen commanding the Marines on the Wilmington Station to suggest to Lieutenants Doak and Crenshaw that they have their men vote for Governor Vance. They were assured their votes would not be challenged, and a packet of Vance tickets was enclosed. Lieutenant Crenshaw, without commenting on the morality of the situation, simply wrote in his diary, "None of my guard being entitled to vote, I, of course, did not do as he requested."[26]

Several days later, Crenshaw and his 25 men went to Wilmington and went on board the *Atalanta*. The next day (July 30) five privates were transferred to Captain Van Benthuysen's Wilmington company, and the remainder were mustered as part of the crew of the *Atalanta*, now known as the *Tallahassee*. After returning from its first cruise of August 6-26, 1864, the command of the guard of the *Tallahassee* was transferred to Lieutenant H. M. Doak on October 3, Crenshaw being ill. A Marine Guard of one sergeant and 10 "efficient" privates for the *Chickamauga* (late the *Edith*) was sent out from Drewry's Bluff under the command of First Lieutenant David Bradford and reported on board on September 3, 1864.[27]

Lieutenant Henderson left Wilmington on June 10, 1864, on a 30-day furlough to marry Sarah (Sally) Power Williams, of Society Hill, South Carolina. His orders called for him to report to Drewry's Bluff for duty with his company upon the expiration of his leave of absence. By the end of August 1864, the Wilmington Guard consisted of some 14 men from Company A (one corporal and 13 privates), 17 men from Company B (one sergeant, two corporals, and 14 privates), and 15 men from Company C (one sergeant, two corporals, and 12 privates), a total enlisted strength of 56 Marines. Most of these men had been sent to Wilmington during January and February 1864. Second Lieutenant J. De B. Roberts reported on September 30, 1864, for duty in command of one of the Marine Guards of the Cape Fear River Squadron. Unfortunately, earlier that month the C.S.S. *North Carolina* had sunk and this left

2d Lt. Henry Melville Doak

Pictured in an artist's conception of a Confederate Marine officer's uniform.
Picture from the Tennessee State Library by the courtesy of Mrs. Frank L. Owsley.

little afloat at Wilmington for the Marines except the floating battery *Arctic* and the cruisers. Among the Marines at Wilmington were at least seven recruits whose names were not carried at this time on the muster rolls of Companies A, B, or C, indicating they may have been North Carolina recruits or draftees. There is a brief mention dated July 28, 1864, of Lt. H. M. Doak commanding the Marine Guard at Smithville (now Southport), but no details have been located which explain the number of men composing this unit or what its assignment might have been.

General Whiting urged the Secretary of the Navy Mallory in October 1864 that both the *Chickamauga* and the *Tallahassee* (*Olustee*) be retained in port at Wilmington. He commented,

> ... I should never think of employing such vessels to fight. It is the men and guns that are wanted as well as the ships, not only to man the naval batteries now being substituted for the *North Carolina* and the *Raleigh*, which were to defend the inner bars, but to guard or picket the entrance and river, a duty devolving upon the Navy, and for which there are neither forts nor vessels here.[28]

Both these vessels were in port in time to meet the Federal assaults of December 24-25, 1864, and of January 15, 1865, and the enlisted men supplemented the strength of the Marine Guard Company at Wilmington under the command of Captain Alfred C. Van Benthuysen.

Colonel Lamb, commanding at Fort Fisher, recorded in his diary, October 27, 1864, that the battery commanding the rip would be a Navy battery commanded by a naval officer and manned with a naval garrison under the name of "Battery Buchanan."[29] Captain Van Benthuysen detailed 23 enlisted Marines of his detachment under Second Lieutenant J. De B. Roberts on November 3, 1864, to Confederate (or Federal) Point to serve as a guard for this battery.

Shortly thereafter, seven more Marines were sent from the Wilmington Station to supplement the Guard at Battery Buchanan. In December, Lt. Roberts was replaced by Lt. J. Campbell Murdoch, and the return of the Battery for the month showed 19 officers and warrant officers, 136 Navy enlisted men, and 25 Marines assigned there. The Marine Guard consisted of Murdoch, two sergeants, three corporals, and 20 privates. The ratings of the Navy personnel show that the complement of the Battery was similar to that of a regular Navy ship-of-war.[30]

The Marine Guard of nine men from the floating battery, C.S.S. *Georgia* at Savannah, was entrained on the Charleston & Savannah Railroad on December 20, 1864, to reinforce Ft. Fisher below Wilmington. There may have been desertions from this party as only five were captured at the fall of Ft. Fisher. The last record of the other four was that of their transfer to Wilmington on December 20.

The casualty records indicate that the Marine Guard of C.S.S. *Savannah* under Lt. Thomas St. G. Pratt was also transferred to the defense of Ft. Fisher. Pratt and 11 of his guard were captured (the normal complement was 20). Pvt. James P. Thompson was paroled at Greensboro, N. C., on April 28, 1865, while Pvt. William H. Cook was paroled at Lynchburg, Va., April 15, 1865. Whether these last two were members of the Guard transferred to Wilmington is not clear.

Additional naval personnel under Lieutenant Francis M. Roby and Marines under Captain Van Benthuysen reinforced Battery Buchanan on Christmas Eve, and Lieutenant R. T. Chapman, commanding, requested that rations be issued to them and charged off as to supernumeraries.

On Christmas Day, 1864, Union troops made a landing and advanced upon Fort Fisher. A message which was received about 5:20 P.M. was sent to Battery Buchanan requesting reinforcements. About two-thirds of the Battery's complement were double-quicked to Fort Fisher under Lieutenant Arledge and the officers of the companies, reaching there in time to assist in repelling the assault.

One detachment of officers, sailors, and Marines under Lieutenant Francis M. Roby was serving two 7-inch Brooke rifled guns in Fort Fisher during the heavy Federal bombardment. On Sunday afternoon (the 25th) both guns burst, wounding a number of the men, but they requested to be assigned to other guns, and continued their skillful firing. The detachment of Marines under Captain Van Benthuysen reinforced the garrison and was praised to Flag-Officer Pinkney by Major General Whiting for their "welcome and efficient aid."[31]

On December 31, 1864, a number of the Marines at Battery Buchanan were detached, presumably returned to Captain Van Benthuysen's Wilmington Guard Company. The detachment numbered 12 and was followed on January 4, 1865, by five more. Between these two detachments a party of five Marines made their own provision for their future by deserting to the enemy on New Year's Day. Of these, Corporal Thomas Lawler furnished information to the commander of the U.S.S. *Pontoosuc* of the bombardment of Battery Buchanan.

At 12:50 P.M. on January 13, Lieutenant Arledge reported to Colonel Lamb at Fort Fisher with 50 Marines from Battery Buchanan. The fighting continued for three days, and on Sunday, January 15, Colonel Lamb noted in his book at 1:25 P.M., ". . . mention should be made of the gallantry and determined bravery of Sergeant Philip Smith and [Private] Arthur Muldoon of Captain Van Bothielus' [Van Benthuysen's] Marines, ..."[32]

When the Federal fleet and troops began the January attack, Lt. Doak, C.S.M.C., was assigned to a battery of three 9-in. Dahlgren guns, known as "porter bottles" from their shape. By the 15th, all three guns had been dismounted and put out of action. Doak was then assigned to operate a mortar battery used for shelling the rifle pits. He had just found the range with his mortars and scored a direct hit when a large shell from the fleet exploded and wounded him. Eight of his guns' crews were either killed or wounded by the same shell.[33]

In the final defense of Fort Fisher we have left to us a picture of desperately fighting, weary men defending the Fort to the last position, falling back slowly from one gun chamber to the next as the Federal forces gradually squeezed their way into the mighty fortress. This fighting from traverse to traverse took from 3 o'clock in the afternoon of January 15th until 10 o'clock at night. Captain Van Benthuysen, though badly wounded himself, took a squad of Marines and picked up the wounded General Whiting and Colonel Lamb, and forced their way from Fort Fisher to Battery Buchanan, hoping to find refuge there.

But it was not to be. On reaching Battery Buchanan it was found to be evacuated, and there were no boats or means by which the brave retreating garrison could escape; they had been abandoned to their fate. The only alternative was to await capture which took place about 10 P.M.[34]

The statement made in a Confederate Midshipman's diary seems to express the consensus, official and public, "The company of Marines fought splendidly."[35]

An additional group of Marines had been sent from Savannah to assist in the defense of Wilmington. Some 18 enlisted Marines of Company E under the command of Second Lieutenant Thomas St. George Pratt were captured at the fall of Fort Fisher, and the assumption is that perhaps a few from Company E may have escaped this fate.

The Marines serving at Wilmington were largely, if not wholly, serving in Fort Fisher and Battery Buchanan when those key fortifications fell into Northern hands after the determined defense of January 13-15, 1865. Some six Marine officers were captured here on that fateful day, four of them wounded. The six were Captain Alfred C. Van Benthuysen (Co. B), First Lieutenant David Bradford (Co. B), and Second Lieutenants Henry M. Doak (no company assignment known), J. Campbell Murdoch (Co. C), Thomas St. George Pratt (Co. E), and J. De Berniere Roberts (Co. C).

Some 66 non-commissioned officers and privates, a large company as companies went those days, were captured at Fort Fisher and Battery Buchanan and shipped to Point Lookout, Elmira, Fort Monroe, and Fort Hamilton. There were 13 from Company A, 19 from Company B, 14 from Company C, 18 from Company E, one from Company F, and one without a company designation.

Even so, the war was not over for all of these men as Lieutenant Doak, for one, returned South on exchange, was rehospitalized for his wound, and was discharged from the Naval Hospital on the day Richmond was evacuated. He left Richmond in the company of Lieutenant David Bradford, and the two followed Lee's retreating Army. Doak surrendered and took his parole at Appomattox on April 10, 1865. Bradford, a nephew of President Davis, went on to join the President's party. At Abbeville, Ga., he was paid $300 in gold from the specie train to cover travel expenses to the Trans-Mississippi Department in accordance with his orders. Lieutenant Murdoch was also exchanged in February 1865 and returned to duty, taking his parole at Society Hill., S. C., on May 27, 1865.

Captain Van Benthuysen was severely wounded at Fort Fisher and was hospitalized in a New York hospital until exchanged on February 25, 1865. He returned to Richmond where, along with his two brothers, he was part of President Davis' party on his attempt to escape. The three brothers were separated from the main party and took Davis' papers with them. Alfred Van Benthuysen was paroled at Baldwin, Florida, the end of May or early in June 1865, making him probably the last Marine officer to surrender.[36]

NOTES AND REFERENCES

Chapter VI — Marines in North Carolina

1. Wilmington *Journal*, Mon., Aug. 19, 1861, 2:5, and 2:2.

2. Correspondent to the Richmond *Dispatch* quoted in the Charleston *Mercury*, Fri., Feb. 19, 1864, 1:4-5. This story has been used with slight variation in Scharf, *History of the C.S.N.*, 399.

3. *N.O.R.* 9, 452: report of Comdr. J. Taylor Wood, C.S.N., to Secretary of the Navy S. R. Mallory, Richmond, Feb. 11, 1864.

4. *Ibid.*, 452: report of Comdr. J. Taylor Wood, C.S.N.

5. *Ibid.*, 453-454: Comdr. J. Taylor Wood, C.S.N., to Colonel L. Beall, Comdg. Marine Corps, Richmond, Feb. 16, 1864.

6. Harriet Gift Castlen, *Hope Bids Me Onward* (Savannah, Ga.: Georgie Collier Comer, 1945), 189.

7. *N.O.R.* 9, 714: report of Actg. Vol. Lt. J. B. Breck, comdg. U.S.S. *Niphon*, to Comdr. W. A. Parker, U.S.S. *Niphon*, Off New Inlet, N.C., May 1, 1864.

8. Wilmington *Daily Journal*, Fri., April 29, 1864, 3:1.

9. *Loc. cit.*, Sat., April 30, 1864, 2:1.

10. D.R. McNary, 1st Lt., 103d Pa. Vols., "What I Saw and Did Inside and Outside of Rebel Prisons," *Kansas M.O.L.L.U.S. Series* (Dec. 3, 1900). Reprinted by Robert Hardy Publications, Suffolk, Va., 1987.

11. This incident is given *O.R.* 33, 1217-1229, *passim*, and in John Johns, "Wilmington During the Blockade," *Harper's New Monthly Magazine*, vol. 33 (June-November 1866), whole no. CXCVI (196), September 1866, 500. This last was reprinted in *Civil War Times Illustrated*, vol. 13, no. 3 (June 1974), 34-44.

12. *O.R.* 51, pt. 2, 830.

13. *MS. Memoirs, H. M. Doak Papers*, MS. Section, Archives Division, Tennessee State Library and Archives, 36. This source cited hereafter as *Doak MS. Memoirs*.

14. *Loc. cit.*, 37.

15. *O.R.* 51, pt. 2, 1000-1001.

16. *O.R.* 37, pt. 1, 767.

17. Douglas S. Freeman (ed.), *Lee's Dispatches: Unpublished Letters of General Robert E. Lee, C.S.A., to Jefferson Davis and the War Department of the Confederate States of America. 1862-65* (New York, 1915), 269-271: #149, Lee to Davis, Camp Petersburg, July 3, 1864.

18. Frank E. Vandiver (ed.), *The Civil War Diary of General Josiah Gorgas* (University, Ala., 1947), 124. This source cited hereafter as *Gorgas' Diary*.

19. Van R. Morgan to [Catesby ap R.] Jones, Naval Station, Marion Court House, S.C., July 28, 1864, *"NA" file, Box 22, Subject File of the C.S. Navy - 1861-1865, R.G. 45*, U.S. National Archives.

20. *O.R.* 40, pt. 3, 758-759: Hon John Tyler to Maj. Gen. Sterling Price, Comdg. Dist. Ark., Petersburg, Va., July 9, 1864. Also found in *N.O.R.* 10, 721.

21. *Ibid.*, 761: telegram from President Jefferson Davis to Gen. G. W. C. Lee (c/o Gen. Whiting), Richmond, July 10, 1864, 6:15 P.M. Also found in *N.O.R.* 10, 722.

22. Entry dated July 11, 1864, *Crenshaw's Diary*; also see II *O.R.* 7, 458.

23. Edward Younger (ed.), *Inside the Confederate Government: The Diary of Robert Garlick Hill Kean* (New York, 1957), 164, entry for July 11, 1864.

24. Geoffrey W. Fielding (ed.), "Gilmor's Field Report of His Raid in Baltimore County," *Maryland Historical Magazine*, vol. 47, no. 3 (September 1952), 234-240; W. W. Goldsborough, *The Maryland Line in the Confederate Army. 1861-1865* (Baltimore, 1900), 204-206; *O.R.* 37, pt. 1, 349: report of Lt. Gen. J. A. Early; and Bradley T. Johnson, "Maryland," *Evans C.M.H.*, II, 126-129.

25. Entries dated July 15 and 18, 1864, *Crenshaw's Diary*.

26. *Loc. cit.*, entry dated July 28, 1864.

27. S.O. 69, para 2, H.Q., C.S.M.C., Aug. 29, 1864, and endorsement showing he reported Sept. 3, 1864, file of David Bradford, "ZB" file, Early Records Section, Operational Archives, Naval History Division, U.S.N. This source cited hereafter as *"ZB" file*.

28. *N.O.R.* 10, 774-775: Maj. Gen. W. H. C. Whiting, C.S.A., to Secretary of the Navy S. R. Mallory, Wilmington, N.C., Oct. 6, 1864.

29. *Ibid.*, 800: entry dated Oct. 27, 1864, Col. Lamb's Official Diary.

30. List of Officers & Crew of the C.S.N. Battery *Buchanan* for the month of December, 1864, Item B, Folder 17, Pkg. 3-E, C.S. Navy Papers, Georgia Historical Society, Savannah, Ga.

31. *N.O.R.* 11, 365: report of Maj. Gen. W. H. C. Whiting, C.S.A., transmitting Col. Lamb's report, to Lt. Col. A. Anderson, A.A.&I.G., H.Q., Dept. of No. Car., Dec. 31, 1864.

32. Entry for Sun., Jan. 15, 1865, 1:25 P.M. from Record of Events book kept by Col. Wm. Lamb, C.S.A., Comdg. Ft. Fisher, as published in the New York *Herald*, Thurs., Jan. 26, 1865, 8:2.

33. *Doak MS. Memoirs*, 41-42.

34. *O.R.* 46, pt. 1, 440: report of Maj. Gen. W. H. C. Whiting, C.S.A. (P.W.), to Gen. R. E. Lee, Comdg. Armies Confederate States, Hospital, Ft. Columbus, Governor's Island, New York Harbor, Feb. 19, 1865.

35. *N.O.R.* 11, 377-378: extract from Diary of Mdsn. Clarence Cary, C.S.N.

36. Alfred J. Hanna, *Flight Into Oblivion* (Richmond, Va., 1938), 123.

Chapter VII

CONFEDERATE MARINES AT CHARLESTON, SOUTH CAROLINA

The part played by Confederate Marines at Charleston has remained obscure in spite of numerous efforts to locate details of their activities. From time to time various Marine contingents appear to have been sent to Charleston, but the force on permanent assignment was probably no more than the Marines assigned to the ships of the Charleston Squadron.

Following the engagement at Port Royal Sound on November 7, 1861, the small steamer *Huntress* carrying Marine Lieutenant Francis H. Cameron and, presumably, a small detachment of Marines escaped to Charleston. Cameron was detached from the *Huntress* and ordered back to Savannah on January 15, 1862, reporting three days later.

One of the more interesting projects for the Marines was a special expedition to destroy the Federal monitors in Charleston harbor. On February 19, 1863, the Navy Department ordered Lieutenant William A. Webb, C.S.N., to prepare several boarding parties for attacking the enemy fleet. The somewhat fantastic plan called for boarders to drive iron wedges between the turret and the deck, jamming the revolving turret. A second man was to cover the pilothouse with wet blankets, while a third was to either cover the smoke stack or throw powder down it. Other men were to be provided with turpentine or camphine in glass vessels which were to be smashed over the turret, followed by an inextinguishable liquid fire while still others, watching every turret or deck opening, were provided with sulphuretted cartridges and other equipment for smoking out the enemy.

One section of the special boarding group was composed of fifteen men (one captain, one sergeant, and 13 privates) from Marine Company C. Listed as Stackmen were Captain Thomas S. Wilson and Sergeant James A. Mercer. Bottle and Sulphur men were Hugh Aird, Patrick Hart, William Bell, and Stephen Caul. Blankets and Powder were assigned to Henry Curran, James

Grogan, Thomas Crilley, and Theodore Davis. Richard McGregor and John Barrett were assigned to the Bottles and Sulphur; Abraham W. Bessant and Anthony Cannon were the Axemen while S. C. Curtis was Plateman.[1] However, in April 1863, the Navy Department ordered the officers and men of this expedition back to Richmond.[2]

It does appear that a Marine battalion of 200 men under the command of Captain John D. Simms was sent to oppose the expected attempt by the Federal Navy to force Charleston harbor in the spring of 1863. They are reported to have remained at Charleston about a month and then returned to their Drewry's Bluff camp. As of March 26, 1863, orders had been received in Mobile for the available recruits to be sent to Charleston, and on April 12, 1863, just two privates were reported transferring to Captain Simms commanding the Marine battalion at Charleston.

Correspondence concerning the pay accounts of these men reveals that the Marines had returned to Drewry's Bluff by April 29, 1863.[3]

The battalion's presence in Charleston was not without incident. A Private Welsh, who had deserted from the Marines, was arrested on the street by Lieutenant Bradford. Welsh made an attempt to escape by running away, but Bradford brought him down with three shots from his revolver, two taking effect, one wounding him in the right side and the other in the leg. Neither wound was considered dangerous, and Welsh was soon lodged in the Guard House.[4]

Second Lieutenant Henry M. Doak was ordered to Charleston in the spring of 1863 to locate and recover deserters, presumably those who had succumbed to the siren song of the port city. One approach was to place an advertisement in the newspaper starting May 2 promising amnesty to those who returned voluntarily.

> I am authorized by Col. Beall, Commandant of Marines, to give notice to the Marines of Companies B and C, who are absent from their Commands without leave, that if they will return to duty they will not be punished. They will report to me at the Pavilion Hotel, or to Sergeant ALLIE [ALLICE] on board the Stono, by the 5th of May, and receive transportation to Drewry's Bluff.[5]

Doak recalled many years later that his search for deserters led him to visit Fort Sumter, then commanded by Colonel Alfred Rhett, commanding the 1st South Carolina Regular Artillery. Colonel Rhett "very properly" refused to let Doak inspect his garrison, only permitting a review of his muster roll. Of course, the Marine deserters, several of whom he actually saw, could not be identified by name. Later, when Doak was stationed in Charleston, he secured the muster roll names of the deserters and again approached Colonel Rhett. Rhett explained that these were the best men he had. Doak realized the men were quite useful in a fort from which there was no escape and agreed with Rhett that it would be best to leave the men where they were. An appeal to Richmond secured the requisite approval for Colonel Rhett to retain them.[6]

During the summer of 1863, Lieutenant Doak was ordered to Charleston for duty on board the new ironclad *Charleston* in command of her broadside guns. Years later he recalled that he had participated in three naval engagements and one land attack at Charleston. One engagement he mentions was the firing into a number of small boats carrying three Federal regiments up the channel between Battery Wagner and James Island in an attempt to land and attack Battery Wagner. Doak recalls *Charleston* laying alongside the northern end of the channel where it opens into Charleston Harbor with her guns double-shotted with grape and her decks crowded with riflemen. Within a few minutes the combined fire of the ship's big guns, the riflemen on deck, and the Confederate forces on shore had cleared the channel, and the enemy boats were sunk and the men drowned, killed, or surrendered. But this action is difficult to identify among the many actions in the Charleston area, particularly when neither Army or Navy published records mention any such participation by *Charleston*.

Doak mentions as his second engagement participation in repelling the night assault on Fort Sumter, crediting *Charleston* with the firing of grape, canister, and rifles into the Federals.[7] This must be a reference to the night attack on September 8-9, 1863, made by Union sailors and Marines. Reports credit an ironclad with assisting the fort in repelling this assault, but the credit is given to the *Chicora*.[8]

Doak failed to mention the third naval action, nor did he give any details concerning the land action. Since his writings seem to have been made at an advanced age (he was 80 when the questionnaire was completed), the accuracy of detail is subject to question.

This third naval action could have been the boat expedition under the command of Lieutenant Commanding A. F. Warley, C.S.N., of the C.S.S. *Chicora*, which captured and broke up the enemy's picket stationed at the unfinished battery at the mouth of Vincent's Creek (between Morris' and James Islands) on the night of August 4, 1863. Lieutenant Warley took four small boats with a Navy party and joined with about 30 men from the 25th South Carolina (the Eutaw Regiment), under Captain Sellers. They were guided to the northern entrance of Light-House Creek where the soldiers were landed. Lieutenant Warley, with two boats, went around to the mouth of Vincent's Creek to cut off the enemy's barges. One of the barges was cornered and captured with a captain and 10 men of the 100th New York being captured. A few soldiers escaped under heavy fire in the other barge. One Confederate was killed.[9]

The Richmond newspaper carried a report from Charleston that the affair was staged by "some Marines and a detachment of the Eutaw regiment."[10] It is quite likely that Warley took a combined party of sailors and Marines with him.

The need for trained troops to meet emergencies in the defense of Charleston led to a Navy General Order (dated June 29, 1864) organizing a landing force to be known as the "Naval Battalion." Although not specifically mentioning the Marines of the Squadron as comprising a portion of the battalion, it seems they must have been included as they were among those who could be spared most easily without disrupting the minimum ships' organization.[11] Lieutenant Berry of the Marine Corps, who had gone on board the *Charleston* on November 5, 1863, was named adjutant of the battalion.

On July 10, 1864, a company of Marines of undetermined strength was able to assist the garrisons at Battery Simkins and Fort Johnson in repulsing a Federal barge attack. Although no details are given about this company, it was probably composed of the Marines of the Squadron organized as part of the Naval Battalion.

The Marine Guard on board the C.S. Steamer *Charleston* as of August 31, 1864, consisted of one sergeant, one corporal, and 14 privates under Lieutenant Berry. These men were from the Marine battalion at Drewry's Bluff and represented Companies A, B, and C. It appears that no Marine Guard was stationed on board the C.S.S. *Palmetto State* about this time as Lieutenant Commanding James H. Rochelle, C.S.N., was notified by Flag-Officer Tucker that the standard complement of his ship was a total of 155 (26 officers, 35 petty officers, and 94 enlisted men), but that "If a Marine Guard is allowed to your command, an equal number of Landsmen will be deducted from the allowance."[12] Back in late July and early August 1863, some of the Marines just released after being captured on board the *Atlanta* were assigned temporarily to both the C.S.S. *Chicora* and the *Palmetto State*, but they were transferred to Savannah, their home station, on August 11, 1863.

The approaching completion of the strong new ironclad ram, the *Columbia*, brought about the organization of a Marine Guard for that vessel. On October 6, 1864, a contingent of 21 men (one sergeant, one corporal, and 19 privates) was assigned to the *Columbia*, followed by four more privates on November 4, making a guard of 25 enlisted men. This guard, composed largely of new conscripts from North Carolina, was commanded by Second Lieutenant Eugene R. Smith, formerly a Tennessee infantry officer, who reported on board January 1, 1865. These men were probably most of a group of 32 North Carolina conscripts who had been assigned to the Corps by October 30, 1864, according to the Colonel Commandant's report of that date.[13] Shortly after going aground in Charleston Harbor at the time of her launching on January 12, the Guard of the *Columbia* (reduced to 22 men) was transferred to the C.S. Guardship *Indian Chief* on February 7, 1865.[14]

On the evening of December 23, 1864, a contingent of sailors and Marines from the Savannah Squadron under Commander Thomas W. Brent arrived at Charleston. On Christmas Day some 100 men under Lieutenant Dalton, C.S.N., from the crews of the *Isondiga* and the *Georgia*, and including the Marines from the *Savannah* under Lieutenant Pratt, briefly were sent to reinforce Fort Johnson in the Charleston defenses.

Seaman Robert Watson recorded in his diary that he was "turned out" at 6 A.M. on a very cold Christmas day. Some 20 men were sent to the Ram *Charleston* while all the remainder, except the crew of the *Savannah*, were sent to James Island. Watson noted he went in a miserable old slow and leaky boat which bucked a head wind and tide to carry a party of officers and Marines, presumably to James Island. The next day (the 26th) after breakfast, he was again in a boat to carry some Marines to James Island, remained there a short time, returning to his ship (the *Indian Chief*) at 1 P.M.[15]

Almost immediately after the Savannah Marines arrived in Charleston, Lieutenant Thomas St. Geo. Pratt and many, if not all, of the *Savannah's* Marines were shifted north to Wilmington where they arrived just in time to join with Captain Van Benthuysen's provisional company in the final and unsuccessful defense of Fort Fisher on January 15, 1865. Here Lieutenant Pratt and at least eighteen of his Company E men were captured by the North.[16]

The remainder of Company E officered by Captain John R. F. Tattnall and Lieutenant Henry L. Graves were quartered in the vacant Middleton house on the Battery in Charleston. With every expectation of being stationed there for some time, Captain Tattnall went ahead with plans to build the strength of his company. Having no accoutrements for recruits, and wishing to avoid two kinds of accoutrements in the same detachment, Tattnall decided to secure the equipment in the hands of the Marine Guard of the *Macon* which was at this time at Augusta. He wrote Flag-Officer William W. Hunter there on January 23, 1865, asking if he would arrange to have the accoutrements in the possession of the *Macon's* Guard boxed and expressed to Tattnall. It was his suggestion that this equipment could be replaced by the military authorities in Augusta. Hunter, in his reply, simply pointed out that he was unable to meet the request at this time as the detachment of Marines referred to were stationed at a Battery [Shell Bluff, Georgia] many miles from Augusta.[17]

Captain Tattnall was the senior Marine officer on the Charleston Station and as such was ordered to report to Brigadier General W. B. Taliaferro, commanding the 2d and 3d Sub-Districts of South Carolina at Charleston. Lieutenant Albert S. Berry, commanding the Marine Guard of the Charleston Squadron, was ordered on February 10, 1865, to report to Tattnall with his Marines, or to march to James Island in the event Captain Tattnall had left the city with his command. The Marine Guard detailed for this shore duty were those whose transfer would be the least injurious to the organization of the ships.

Charleston was evacuated on the night of February 17 and the morning of the 18th. The defending troops marched out to form a junction with General Beauregard, reaching Monck's Corner on the 19th.[18] Flag-Officer J. R. Tucker with some 400 men and officers reached Florence, South Carolina, on the same day and reported by telegram to General Braxton Bragg. Major General Hoke acknowledged by sending the cryptic order, "Go on with your force."[19] On the 20th of February, General Hoke reported he had telegraphed Commodore Robert F. Pinkney to organize all the Naval forces in his department (Wilmington) into one command for duty at the batteries at the obstructions, the surplus to be used as infantry support.[20]

Flag-Officer Tucker halted at Whiteville, North Carolina, on the trip north and telegraphed General Hoke on the 21st for clearance as to whether it was safe to continue his trip. It seems that the railroad superintendent, a Captain Henry M. Dram, had stated that events had occurred since the 19th which precluded the safe arrival of Tucker's train. General Bragg answered this telegram from Wilmington and suggested that Tucker should remain at Whiteville to check any enemy advance, if possible, and fall back for the protection of the Fayetteville Arsenal.

Tucker answered that with his force of only 350 sailors unused to marching, no artillery, and no transportation for stores or baggage, that he doubted his ability to check the enemy. He proposed moving by train to Cheraw, South Carolina, and thence to Charlotte, North Carolina [where a Naval Ordnance Works was located], but would await instructions to move in any direction Bragg would think best and requested an immediate answer. But Bragg had problems of his own for on the next morning (February 22) Wilmington was evacuated.

In any event, Tucker proceeded to Fayetteville, but on February 27 he telegraphed either General Bragg or General Hoke that he had received orders to report to Richmond with his entire command and proposed to leave at once with such of his command as was present. He requested that Lieutenant William E. Evans' detachment [from the C.S.S. *Columbia*] be ordered to report to Richmond also.[21] Tucker then went to Virginia with his force, effected an organization at Drewry's Bluff known as "Tucker's Naval Brigade," and later participated in Lee's retreat to Appomattox.

Two post-war letters from a Marine who belonged to the guard of C.S.S. *Columbia* give a story of the group,

> Since I received your letter my mind has been wondering a great deal over about Charleston Harbor; Indian Chief; Gun Boat Charleston; Dry Dock; the Sinking & Sunk Gun Boat Columbia; Palmetto States; "Chicora;" the unfinished Gun Boat Ashley; the Marsh Hen &c &c, Even James Island; the breast works there; the Yankee lookout; our wormy crackers; the Soldiers graves; our ragged old clothes; our black shirts, and Oh! me, I hate to name it now — the Lice the Lice! or as some politely called them the "Confederates." Your letter brings all these things to my mind. Besides it makes me think of old Commodore Tucker Capt Brown, Capt Ray, Capt. Evans and that old *devil catcher* Capt. Hunter. I think of all the mean Marine Officers and often wonder why an all wise Providence permitted them to live.[22]

Another letter written over three years later elaborates on the same theme,

> . . . Capt. Brown, Lt. Evans, Capt Hunter, Commodore Tucker, &c. Capt. Brown was a gentleman and so was Tucker but Tucker was not smart. I think of our filthy clothes, the lice, the salt and fresh water, the crackers, the "duff" and of the sure enough Coffee and rice, and also the Nassau pony or beef, and how good it was [to?] we poor soldiers; and how we had to submit to anything to gratify the whims and notions of our Superiors on the water. I think of how we could see the infernal Yankee fleet out at sea, and of how the "darned critters," shot at us, as if they meant to kill us.

It is in this letter of August 30, 1874, that the route taken by the *Columbia's* Marines (and others in Charleston — possibly on board *Indian Chief*) from Charleston to Drewry's Bluff is given.

> I think of the night we left Charleston, with all the devilment that was done — the fire, smoke and blowing up and sinking of our noble Boats, Torpedoes, &c. How we came to Florence — thence to Whiteville, then the route step to Fayetteville, thence to the arsenal; then the Western RR, Jonesboro [now Sanford] — where Waddill, Cameron Morrison Kanedy & others left us then the route Step again across the Cape Fear River to Pages station [now Cary] on the NCRR; then to Hillsboro, then to Greensboro, then to Danville, then to Richmond beyond the James — looked at Castle Thunder and other scanes [scenes], thence down the James to Drewry's Bluff we

went down on the "Patric[k] Henry" — then up the Bluff to grave yard; then to the Marine Barracks, and even to the branch of fresh water beyond. Well do I remember How we all enjoyed Washing in the fresh water there at the Branch. Little Rowe enjoyed it much . . . Boggs was a good Cook, he could get a good dinner out of nothing & [have] a big pot of soup besides . . . .[23]

Captain Tattnall's Company E of the Marines made the trip from Whiteville on the Wilmington and Manchester Railroad to Fayetteville and Raleigh, and from the latter place, to Greensboro.

Finally, on April 28, 1865, at Greensboro, Captain John R. F. Tattnall, First Lieutenant Henry L. Graves, Second Lieutenant Ruffin Thomson, and 14 enlisted men of Company E were paroled in accordance with the Johnston-Sherman agreement. Major and Corps Paymaster Richard T. Allison, who had left Richmond on April 2, 1865, was paroled at the same time on the same roll.[24]

NOTES AND REFERENCES

Chapter VII — Confederate Marines at Charleston, South Carolina

1. Scharf, *History of the C.S.N.*, 687-689. Various misspellings of personal names have been corrected.

2. *Ibid.*, 690-691, and *O.R.* 14, 908: Gen. G. T. Beauregard, C.S.A., to Gen. S. Cooper, C.S.A., A.&I.G., Charleston, S.C., April 23, 1863.

3. Paymaster Henry Myers, C.S.N., to Paymaster Thos. R. Ware, C.S.N., Naval Station, Charleston, S.C., April 29, 1863, *Letters for April-May-June, '63, Ware Pp.*

4. Charleston *Mercury*, Tues., March 24, 1863, 2:1.

5. Charleston *Daily Courier*, Tues., May 5, 1863, 1:3.

6. *Doak MS. Memoirs*, 31½ and 32.

7. *Loc. cit.*, 33.

8. *N.O.R.* 14, 636-637, 639.

9. *Ibid.*, 738-739, 747-748.

10. Richmond *Daily Examiner*, Fri., Aug. 7, 1863, 2:7.

11. General Order dated June 29, 1864, Flag Ship *Charleston*, Charleston, S.C., *January-June, 1864, folder, Box 9, Papers of Lt. James H. Rochelle, C.S.N.*, Duke University, Durham, N.C. This source cited hereafter as *Rochelle Pp., Duke U.*

12. *Loc. cit.*, Box 9: Flag-Officer J. R. Tucker, Comdg. Afloat, to Lt. J. H. Rochelle, C.S.N., Comdg. C.S.S. *Palmetto State*, Sept. 29, 1864, *July-September, 1864, folder.*

13. II *N.O.R.* 2, 749.

14. Transfer Roll of Men Transferred to C.S. Guardship *Indian Chief* from C.S.S. *Columbia*, Roll 1, undated, *Entry 419, R.G. 45*, U.S. National Archives.

15. William N. Still, Jr. (ed.), " 'The Yankees Were Landing Below Us': The Journal of Robert Watson, C.S.N.," *Civil War Times Illustrated*, vol. XV, no. 1 (April 1976), 12.

16. Point Lookout P. W. Register #2, parts 1 and 2; Elmira P. W. Register #3; also Rolls of Prisoners of War Received from Ft. Fisher, N.C., Jan. 22, 1865 (14 rolls, 537 names), Records of the Office of the Commissary General of Prisoners, U.S. National Archives. The Registers are also in Microcopy 598, Rolls 114, 115, and 221, U.S. National Archives.

17. Flag-Officer Wm. W. Hunter, C.S.N., Comdg., to Capt. J. R. F. Tattnall, Co. E, C.S.M.C., Augusta, Ga., Jan. 26, 1865, *55-H-3*, 77-78, *Hunter Pp., Tulane U.*

18. *O.R.* 47, pt. 2, 1223: Maj. Gen. L. McLaws, C.S.A., to Gen. S. Cooper, A.&I.G., Monk's [sic.] Corner, Feb. 19, 1865.

19. *Ibid.*, 1227: telegram from Flag-Officer J. R. Tucker, C.S.N., to Gen. [Braxton] Bragg, Florence, [S.C.], Feb. 19, 1865, and answer from Maj. Gen. R. F. Hoke. Also in *N.O.R.* 12, 188.

20. *Ibid.*, 1234: telegram from Maj. Gen. R. F. Hoke to Major [Francis S.] Parker, Forks Road, Feb. 20, 1865. Also in *N.O.R.* 12, 188.

21. *Ibid.*, 1289: telegram from Flag-Officer J. R. Tucker, C.S.N., to Gen. Bragg or Gen. Hoke, Fayetteville [N.C.], Feb. 27, 1864. Also in *N.O.R.* 12, 190.

22. Wm. McLeod to Aaron Wollard, April 24, 1871, extracts from xerox copy of letter in author's possession.

23. Wm. McLeod to Aaron Wollard, Aug. 30, 1874, extracts from xerox copy of letter in author's possession.

24. *Greensboro Parolees, List of Commissioned and Non-Commissioned Officers and Privates, C.S. Marine Corps, Roll 705, R.G. 45*, U.S. National Archives.

Chapter VIII

MARINES ON THE HIGH SEAS

The first Confederate cruiser to go to sea was C.S.S. *Sumter* out of New Orleans under the command of (then) Commander Raphael Semmes. The Marine Guard commanded by First Lieutenant Becket K. Howell consisted of 20 enlisted men. Their services were utilized for regular shipboard duty, guarding prisoners from the captured vessels, and serving as members of prize crews placed on captured ships. For instance, when the *Sumter* captured the brigs *Machias* and *Cuba* off Cienfuegos on July 4, 1861, only a midshipman, Albert G. Hudgins, and four men could be spared for a prize crew: two sailors (Henry Spencer and John Davison), and two Marines, probably Privates John Dunlee (Donnelly?) and John Bryan.

Semmes, who didn't have a high opinion of his Marines, lost many of them as his crew was reduced by desertions. Semmes landed one unnamed Marine on shore on January 11 in accordance with the order of a Court Martial. Five of the crew deserted at Cadiz on January 14 and nine more on the next day. Some of these could have been Marines. One Marine private, William Ryan, gave the story to the press later that he made a try that day but was recaptured and punished with 30 days in double irons, three months police duty "polishing brasses," and no shore liberty for six months.

The *Sumter* left Cadiz on January 17, 1862, and reached Gibraltar the next evening. Here she stayed in commission until April 9 when Semmes discharged and sent off nearly all the remaining men. At muster on March 30 the crew was down to 46. Private Ryan's story was that when he jumped ship at Gibraltar, there were 40 of the crew, including officers, still on board. He left with Bernard Conway, another Marine, by swimming ashore and going to the U.S. Consul who gave them clothing and money for the passage home. Another Marine deserter was Corporal William Hudson who jumped at Cadiz. All three of these men were reported to have their homes in the North.[1]

These stories account for only five of the Marine Guard of the *Sumter* by name, and it is not clear just what happened to the remainder of the Guard,

Officers of C.S.S. *Sumter*. **Sitting, left to right, Lt. Evans, Cdr. Raphael Semmes, Chief Engineer Freeman; standing, left to right, Surgeon Galt, Lt. Stribling, 1st Lt. Kell, Lt. Chapman, and Lt. of Marines Howell.**
U.S. Navy Dept. Photo. NR&L (Old) #36, by courtesy of the Naval Historical Center.

Officers of C.S.S. *Sumter*. **Sitting, Cdr. Raphael Semmes; standing, left to right, 4th Lt. W. E. Evans, Marine 1st Lt. B. K. Howell, 3d Lt. J. M. Stribling. 1st Lt. J. M. Kell, 2d Lt. R. T. Chapman, Engineer M. J. Freeman, Clerk W. B. Smith. (Identifications as published in Wiley & Milholland,** *Embattled Confederates* **(N.Y., 1964), 152. Lt. of Marines Howell was improperly identified in this same picture in** *Civil War Times Illustrated***, Nov. 1978, 33.**
Photograph courtesy of Eleanor S. Brockenbrough Library,
The Museum of the Confederacy, Richmond, Virginia.

whether they were discharged and paid off, or whether they were among the deserters. Just two more can be accounted for in the surviving records.

Semmes did recommend to Captain James D. Bulloch, C.S.N., on April 28, 1862, that "The Marine, Thompson, I would recommend to be sent to the Confederate States."[2] He was probably referring to Sergeant H. I. Thomason, the senior enlisted Marine of the *Sumter's* Guard.

The next ranking Marine enlisted man was Corporal (later Sergeant) George Stephenson. He remained with the few men left on board *Sumter* at Gibraltar when that ship was laid up from active service. While here a most unusual happening took place. The second-in-command, Acting Master's Mate Joseph T. Hester, killed the commanding officer, Midshipman William Andrews, in an altercation on October 15, 1862. Sergeant Stephenson reported this tragedy to the Confederate naval authorities in London and received orders to assume command of *Sumter* until such time as a Navy officer could be sent to take over.[3] This he did, and we have here the unique situation of a Marine sergeant in formal command of a Confederate ship-of-war. Sgt. Stephenson was apparently kept in service and seems to have been on board C.S.S. *Georgia* during its brief life between April 9, 1863, when commissioned, and late January 1864 when she was under repairs at Cherbourg. Commander James D. Bulloch wrote on May 31, 1864, from Liverpool:

> Sergeant Stephenson has just handed me your note of the 18th Inst. and I have directed him to remain on board the Georgia for the present. I suppose his pay ought to go on and think Paymaster Senac will take his account up.[4]

Stephenson was later returned to the Confederate States and served until surrendered and paroled at Greensboro, as a member of Semmes' Naval Brigade. Semmes does not seem to have recruited for his guard from among the crews of his captured vessels.

After laying up the *Sumter*, Semmes went to England and took the *Alabama* to sea for its famous commerce destroying cruise. For some unexplained reason the Colonel Commandant of the Marine Corps stated in a report to the Secretary of the Navy dated April 28, 1864, "There is also a marine guard at sea on board of the C.S.S. Alabama."[5] On this question we call upon the *Alabama's* commanding officer as a witness. Semmes states in his book, without equivocation, "We had no marine guard on board the *Alabama*, and there was, consequently, no sentinel at the gangway in the daytime. We were necessarily obliged to rely upon the master-at-arms, and the quartermaster, for examining all boats that came alongside, to see that no liquor was smuggled into the ship."[6] The only Marine on board *Alabama* was Lieutenant Becket K. Howell who had been Semmes' Marine officer on *Sumter*.

Apparently one effort was made during the *Alabama's* cruise to recruit for a Marine guard from those on board a captured vessel. On December 7, 1862, the *Alabama* captured the mail steamer *Ariel* bound from New York for Aspinwall. The passengers included five officers and 105 enlisted U.S. Marines commanded by Major Addison Garland. They were on their way to the Marine Barracks at Mare Island, Calif. They were permitted to continue their voyage, but were disarmed and paroled.[7] Major Garland reported that Lieutenant Richard F. Armstrong of the *Alabama* gave the Federal Marines an impromptu recruiting spiel, offering kind treatment and good pay, but failed to gain a single recruit.[8]

Among the cruisers which neither started from nor returned to a Confederate port was C.S.S. *Shenandoah*. While a Marine guard was not sent out from the Confederacy for service on this vessel, the commanding officer, James I. Waddell, arranged to recruit, arm, and clothe his own guard. On February 8, 1865, after leaving Hobson's Bay at Melbourne, Australia, a group of 34 young American seamen and eight of other nationalities were found to have smuggled themselves on board *Shenandoah*.

Now, for the first time, Waddell had enough men to organize a small Marine Guard. Available records show Sgt. George P. Canning, Corpl. David Alexander, and Privates John Moss, Robert Brown, Henry Riley, and William Kenyon were enlisted on February 18, 1865. One Marine, probably J. A. Exshaw (later a sergeant) was enlisted on April 1, 1865. On April 17, 1865, Henry Canning, an Englishman who had shipped at Melbourne, Australia, was transferred from the fire department to the Marine Guard. On June 12, 1865, Maurice Murray and Emmanuel Sylvia [Silver?], both from the captured bark *Abigail*, a new Bedford whaler, were added to the *Shenandoah's* Marines, and finally, on June 16, 1865, William Burnett was enlisted in the Guard. Waddell says in his memoirs that the crews of some 11 whalers last captured, 336 men in all, produced nine men, all intelligent soldiers, men who had been taught to respect military authority and knew how to use the Enfield rifle. He implies they became part of his Marine Guard, but he doesn't actually say so.

Waddell remarked that the uniforms for his Marines had to be made from head to foot,[9] but their trousers were probably those from a captured shipment of two dozen infantry pants and coats originally destined for trade with the Ascension Island natives.[10]

Little information has been located concerning the presence of a Marine Guard on C.S.S. *Stonewall* beyond a brief mention of the presence of a sergeant of Marines in the ship's complement. A roster of its officers was obtained when *Stonewall* put in at Ferrol, Spain, in March 1865, and was published in a New

York paper. The list included a J. M. Prior, of Virginia, as the ship's sergeant of Marines, but no mention is made of the size of his guard.[11] John M. Prior had been a sergeant of Marines on board C.S.S. *Rappahannock* at Calais, France, on May 16, 1864, when she was decommissioned, and he was kept in service until assigned to C.S.S. *Stonewall* circa January 24, 1865.

When the Marine battalion stationed temporarily at Smithville, (now Southport) North Carolina, was ordered on July 20, 1864, to return to Richmond and Drewry's Bluff, Lieutenant Edward Crenshaw, one sergeant, two corporals, and 22 privates remained behind for assignment as Marine Guard for a naval vessel. They were transferred to Wilmington nine days later where they went on board *Atalanta* (also known as *Atlanta*).[12] The next day, July 30, the crew as mustered included 20 Marine enlisted men, five of the group having been sent to Captain Van Benthuysen's company at Wilmington.

The *Atalanta*, rechristened *Tallahassee*, put to sea on August 6, 1864, and soon succeeded in upsetting the people of the Northeast coast of the United States with her captures and destruction of shipping. On August 12, 1864, *Tallahassee* spoke with *Adriatic* from London to New York with 163 passengers, nearly all foreigners. When the passengers learned their ship was to be burned, there was considerable consternation until they were finally persuaded they were not to be burned with it. To enforce order and quiet, Lieutenant Crenshaw and a guard of Marines were sent on board until she was fired.[13] *Tallahassee* arrived at Halifax, Nova Scotia, on the 18th where she took on enough coal to enable her to return to Wilmington, and was forced to leave port the next day.

Many of the men on shore leave during this brief stay in port proceeded to vsit the local grog shops with disastrous results on their mobility. British officials, prodded by Federal consular agents, were obliged to order *Tallahassee* to leave promptly, and Lieutenant Crenshaw left a word picture of the departure in his diary:

> We took on coal until after dark, when all the shore boats and people on board were sent off, and I was sent on shore with other officers [and] a guard to gather up and bring off our missing liberty men, 60 or 70 of whom had not yet come off — being drunk and scattered all over town as is the custom with sailors. With the aid of the Town police and their officers, we succeeded in gathering together and carrying to our boats all but 27 of our men. Some of them were so drunk that they had to be carried on the shoulders of the guard to our boats. The police were very polite and kind to us, and very good-naturedly took some hard knocks from our drunken sailors and marines without using their clubs.[14]

Among the 27 of the crew left on shore at Halifax were three Marines: Private John Berry, a Canadian by birth; Private Stephen J. Saunders, English-born, and Private John O'Brien, born in Ireland. Was there a story in the fact that none of the three Marine "deserters" was a native-born American?

Upon entering the harbor of Halifax on the morning of August 18, the ship's officers and crew were paid off in gold. Wardroom officers received $100, steerage officers, $50, and all others $10. Lieutenant Crenshaw took the occasion to go ashore and buy a valise full of clothing. Crenshaw must have extended himself financially as he borrowed some gold from members of his Guard.

Soon after returning to Wilmington, he paid off his debt to Private J. S. Jones who thanked him for it in his letter of October 19. Jones wrote, "I am truly thankful for the interest you took to pay me. I must also acknowledge that you overpaid me by 15cts. which is indeed not much except in times like these."[15] On December 18, 1864, Crenshaw paid off another of his debts when he sent $10 in gold to Sergeant Montgomery Smith, also of his old Guard, by Lieutenant Bradford.

After returning to safety under the protective guns of Fort Fisher on August 25, Lieutenant Crenshaw, who had become ill, was detached and was succeeded by Lieutenant H. Melville Doak on October 1, 1864, in the command of the Marine Guard of 17 men. Navy Lieutenant George Gift wrote on October 4 that he was in no hurry to go óut in *Tallahassee* as the yellow fever was still prevalent in Bermuda and not expected to abate for several weeks.[16] *Tallahassee*, under her new name of *Olustee*, sailed from Wilmington the night of October 29 for a short cruise.

Although the cruise of *Olustee* from October 29 through November 7, 1864, is not covered by any Confederate reports in the Navy *Official Records*, a brief version is given by Lt. Doak in his post-war memoirs:

> I was next ordered to the double-screw propeller *"Tallahassee"* — also sailing under an alias as the "Olustee," to confuse the enemy — originally the blockade runner "Atalanta" — sent out to destroy trading ships. As international law then was this was lawful, although we were known as pirates. After a very successful cruise — . . . we encountered dreadful weather somewhere off Ft. Delaware — cyclones that swept our boats from their davits. We were pursued by two sidewheel cruisers — luckily as night was drawing on. They had the *"Tallahassee"* greatly at a disadvantage. As we rode a wave the engineer — hand on throttle-valve — had to shut off steam to

prevent racing. As we thus lost time our pursuers had their sidewheels always in the water at work. We were unable to unlimber [!] our heavy stern gun to reply to their fire. With that in use we could have kept them out of range. They threw a few shells close astern and some through our rigging. As soon as night fell, all holes [holds] were battened down and we ran with "doused glim," showing no ray of light — turning squarely southward on our course at right angles. At daylight no sail was seen. . . .

As we neared Cape Hatteras — weather now calm — furnace fires drawn to clean flues — day dawned on five steamers all around us, beginning to fire although at long range. Capt. [Wm. H.] Ward . . . did some very skilful maneuvering. First with long-range bow and stern guns he showed it was best to keep at a respectful distance. Next he drew them this way and that until we were inshore of them — could risk running ashore and getting through the surf — all the while running up steam. When we had full steam on we easily distanced them — being the fastest ship afloat.

According to our reckoning we were due to reach the mouth of Cape Fear River before night. Our reckoning was luckily wrong. We passed our Half-Moon Battery after dark — giving no signal and risking shots fired. Ft. Fisher was also passed without signalling — without their sighting our dim, grey-painted form. The tide was not yet full and we grounded while trying to run over the bar. We had shipped most of our prisoners on Federal ships not worth destroying which we bonded — my name yet on bonds to fall due six months after a treaty of peace, etc. — given when I was boarding officer — some prisoners shipped on slow foreign vessels not likely to get in soon enough to announce our presence. We had about twenty prisoners left over. These, with the crew, were put to shifting coal forward. One Federal cruiser was dimly seen in the offing all unconscious of our presence. With shifting of coal and rising of the tide we soon ran in and dropped anchor, safely at home.

[William] May, our English boatswain, piped all hands aft in his deep bass — "All hands lay aft for a pull o' the Gospel halyards." Capt. Ward read the English service suited to escape perils of sea — closely following "Amen" with, "Purser, open a basket of champaign in the wardroom and give the men grog aft." Next morning was Sunday — all hands again piped aft for a pull o' the Gospel halyards — Lieut. [Mortimer M.] Benton reading the morning service — A man never suspected of over-piety and yet "took orders" — last I heard of him was preaching in Ohio.[17]

The Confederate Government purchased the blockade runner *Edith* at Wilmington in the summer of 1864 and converted her into a cruiser or commerce raider. On August 11, 1864, Marine Sergeant William L. Purvis and nine privates were assigned to duty on board *Edith* or *Chicakamauga* as she was re-named.[18] First Lieutenant David Bradford was assigned to the command of this unit. Two enlisted men were transferred before sailing.

Chickamauga put to sea on the night of October 29, 1864, and proceeded immediately to harass Federal shipping. Less than two weeks later the ship put in at St. George's, Bermuda, where the Guard was practically eliminated by desertions, some six of the seven privates deserting on November 11, 1864. Thus, on the return of the ship to Wilmington, virtually no Marines were on board.

When consideration was first being given to the acquisition of ships in Europe for use as Confederate warships and cruisers, Commander James D. Bulloch suggested to Secretary of the Navy Mallory in November 1862 that there should be selected "officers for each ship, also a few leading men and marines — noncommissioned officers who are natives of the South, or bona-fide citizens of the Confederacy — to give nationality to the crew and to insure the actual possession of the ship until the men shipped at large are got into a good state of discipline."[19]

Commander James H. North wrote to the Confederate Navy Department on April 3, 1863, about the ship being constructed under his supervision that "trusty men should be sent to form a marine guard, as the Federal Government will resort to any and every means to capture our vessels."[20] He followed this letter with a coded dispatch on April 11, 1863, "Spies employed by the Federals are to be found everywhere, and nothing will be left undone to frustrate our plans and if possible to capture our ships. For the safety of our ships a marine guard formed of good and trusty men from our own country . . . . should be sent immediately."[21] On several occasions, North asked that Lieutenant James Thurston (his nephew?) be sent to him, but Thurston was assigned to duty on board *Atlanta*, was captured on June 17, 1863, and was not exchanged until October 18, 1864.

There is evidence of the presence of Confederate Marine sergeants in France in late summer of 1864. Captain Samuel Barron's *Diary* carried the notation that on August 8, 1864, he wrote Lieutenant Commanding Charles M. Fauntleroy, C.S.N., about the sergeants of Marines.[22] Then, three days later, he wrote that he had issued orders to Fauntleroy to send home his master's mates and sergeants of Marines. Orders went to the "paymasters to advance 100 frs. to Lt. [George A.] Borchert for the expenses to the Confederacy of each one of them."[23] The cruiser *Rappahannock*, which was forced by French authorities to be little more than a receiving ship at Calais, France, picked up two Marines, Orderly Sergeant W. P. Montague and Sergeant John M. Prior.[24] Flag-Officer Samuel Barron probably intended to retain them in service.

A Marine Guard for a naval vessel was apparently considered a necessary and integral part of a ship's complement, and the old-line naval officers in command of the ships originating in European ports attempted to recruit their own. The cruisers sailing from Confederate ports carried a regular Marine guard.

NOTES AND REFERENCES

Chapter VIII — Marines on the High Seas

1. *Augusta, Ga., Daily Chronicle and Sentinel*, Thurs., June 12, 1864, 3:2, quoting the Boston *Journal* of May 24, 1862.

2. *N.O.R.* 1, 684.

3. *Ibid.*, 688.

4. Correspondence, May-June 1864, *Wm. C. Whittle Pp.*, Norfolk [Va.] Public Library.

5. *N.O.R.* 9, 808, also II *N.O.R.* 2, 648.

6. Raphael Semmes, *Memoirs of Service Afloat* (Baltimore, 1869), 511.

7. *N.O.R.* 1, 595 and 811. Also "California, Mare Island Marine Barracks," in *Posts and Stations File*, Reference Section, Division of History and Museums, H.Q., U.S.M.C.

8. Maj. A[ddison] Garland, U.S.M.C., to Col. Comdt. John Harris, U.S.M.C., California Steamer *Ariel*, near Aspinwall, Dec. 12, 1862, *Entry 42*, "Letters Received: 1818-1915," *R.G. 127, Records of the United States Marine Corps*, U.S. National Archives.

9. *N.O.R.* 3, 814.

10. *Ibid.*, 819.

11. New York *Herald*, Mon., April 10, 1865, 4:1.

12. Entry dated July 29, 1864, *Crenshaw's Diary*.

13. *Loc. cit.*, entry dated Aug. 12, 1864.

14. *Loc. cit.*, entry dated Aug. 19, 1864.

15. J. S. Jones to Lt. Crenshaw, C.S. Stmr. *Tallahassee*, Oct. 19, 1864, copy of letter in author's possession.

16. Castlen, *Hope Bids Me Onward*, 187.

17. *Doak MS. Memoirs*, 37-38.

18. Muster Rolls for Companies A and C, C.S.M.C., for November-December 1864, Wrappers #9 and #3, *Entry 426, R.G. 45*, U.S. National Archives.

19. James D. Bulloch, *The Secret Service of the Confederate States in Europe* (2 vols.; New York, 1959), I, 392: Comdr. James D. Bulloch, C.S.N., to Secretary of the Navy S. R. Mallory, Liverpool, England, Nov. 7, 1862.

20. II *N.O.R.* 2, 398.

21. *Ibid.*, 401.

22. *Ibid.*, 817.

23. *Ibid.*, 818.

24. Correspondence, May-July 1864, *Wm. C. Whittle Pp.*, Norfolk [Va.] Public Library.

Chapter IX

LIFE AS AN ENLISTED MAN

The Corps was distinctive in the Confederate service in that it was organized on a permanent regular status, with officers appointed on a career basis. As such, life in the organization was different from the Army (with the exception of a very few units) and even from the Navy itself which developed two separate officer organizations, the Regular Navy and the Provisional Navy.

Naturally, life in the Marines was not the same for all the men, yet there were sufficient similarities to warrant certain generalizations. Of necessity, some aspects have to be touched lightly, or even ignored, simply because there are not sufficient facts now available to warrant generalizations.

Let us look at this time at such topics as bounty, pay, conscription, age, barracks and housing, the role of Marines, discipline, desertions, punishment, medical care and funerals, and Marine music. Our generalizations may not give a complete picture of the life of an enlisted Rebel Marine, yet perhaps the web-footed Johnny Reb will be somewhat more "real" from this sampling of his life.

BOUNTY

Under the original laws, the term of enlistment was for four years. There was not a specific legislative provision in 1861 for a bounty to be paid Marine recruits although the pay estimate for the year ending February 4, 1862, provided $6000 for "Transportation and expenses for recruiting." The New Orleans *Daily Delta* called attention in its news column to "a liberal bounty" being offered the Marine recruits and further commented on the fine advantages offered by the Corps, "little work, and excellent food, clothing and pay." The bounty was $10 with an additional $2 paid those who produced good men for the service, payable as soon as the recruits were accepted.[1] Advertising for recruits at Wilmington, N. C., in August 1861 continued to offer a $10 bounty to Marine recruits.[2]

In view of the 4-year long enlistment period as compared to the one year term in the volunteer Army units and the growth of the bounty system, Secretary of the Navy Mallory recommended on February 27, 1862, that the term of enlistment be cut to three years. He further recommended that the same $50 bounty provided for Army and Navy enlistments be extended to recruits for the Marine Corps. On April 10, 1862, a new Act of Congress established the term of enlistment as for the war or for three years as elected at enlistment.

The Confederate Congress passed a bounty act on April 10, 1862, which provided a $50 bounty to be paid Marines on enlisting and a bonus equivalent of $40 for those already in service who had enlisted for three years. The Act appropriated $40,000 to finance its provisions.[3] In addition to the $50 bounty, by 1862 prospective recruits were being promised prize money whenever engaged in the capture or sinking of enemy vessels, or even when witnessing such an action.

On June 27, 1862, Flag-Officer V. M. Randolph at Mobile requested Paymaster Ware to pay the bounty to all the Marines that Lieutenant Fendall enlisted, and that reimbursement would be made by Marine Paymaster Richard T. Allison. A few days later, on July 8, Secretary of the Navy Mallory requested Paymaster Ware to pay the Marines recruited by Lt. Fendall the bounty to which they were entitled at the same rate as that paid Navy personnel. Colonel Lloyd J. Beall, the Marine Corps Commandant, wrote Lieutenant Fendall in December 1862 that the Comptroller had decided that conscripts entering the Marine Corps were not entitled to bounty. Paymaster Ware, upon reading this letter, wrote the 1st Auditor of the Treasury, Bolling Baker, asking if this letter applied to persons enlisting in the naval service.

This bounty question finally reached Attorney General Thomas H. Watts who decided that persons enrolled under the Acts of April 16 and September 27, 1862, who enlisted voluntarily in the Marine Corps would be entitled to the $50 bounty provided by the Act of April 10, 1862. But, enrollees who later transferred to the Marine Corps were not entitled to the bounty.[4] Then followed a clarification from Bolling Baker of the Treasury Department, based on the Attorney General's opinion, advising Paymaster Ware that "All persons between 18 & 35 are liable to conscription [and are] not entitled to bounty unless they enlist in [the] Marine corps prior to enrollment in [the] army."[5] Little was done other than pay the bounty until the passage of the Act of June 7, 1864.

On February 17, 1864, the Confederate Congress passed an Act to Organize Forces to Serve During the War, which contained a special bounty section providing that at the expiration of a six-month period beginning April 1, a 6% $100 Government bond would be paid to men in service or to the beneficiary entitled to "arrearages of his pay," provided that no one would be eligible who had been absent without leave during this period. As so frequently done by the Confederate Congress, the wording of this Act did not specifically refer to Navy and Marine Corps personnel. Congress corrected this omission by the Act of June 7, 1864,[6] which specifically extended the provisions of the Act "to the warrant officers, pilots, seamen, ordinary seamen, landsmen and boys of the navy, and to the non-commissioned officers, musicians and privates of the marine corps."

PAY

Once the operation of the Conscription Act of 1862 began, it became increasingly difficult to obtain recruits for the Corps. The Act placed all eligible men in the Army with the provision that seamen could be transferred from the land forces on the application of the Secretary of the Navy. Colonel Commandant Beall asked for an amendment that would permit those subject to the draft to volunteer for existing Army units or the Navy or Marine Corps, enabling them to exercise their choice of assignment. This suggestion was incorporated into the new Navy and Marine Enlistment Act of October 2, 1862, along with a base pay increase of $4 a month for privates,[7] raising them to $15 per month. But the transfer system was far from successful and was characterized as availing but little by Captain S. S. Lee, C.S.N., in charge of the Office of Orders and Detail, in his report of October 31, 1864.[8]

Recruiting advertisements in 1863 called attention to the higher pay of drummers, buglers, and fifers. Ordinary privates were paid less than these musicians. To promote enlistments in the Marine Corps, persons presenting recruits to the Recruiting Officers were paid $2 for each recruit they brought, the same as in the United States service.[9]

The initial pay scale for the Marine Corps seems to have been basically the same as that authorized for infantry of the proposed Regular Army and was still in effect as of October 27, 1863, for officers, the enlisted rates having been raised on October 2, 1862.

Table 5

Confederate Regular Army and Marine Corps Pay Scales

Regular Army Scale (3/6/61)		Marine Corps Scale (10/27/63)	
Colonel	$ 195	Colonel Comdt	$ 195
Lt. Colonel	170	Lt. Colonel	170

	P.M., Adjt., Q.M. 162
Major..................... 150	Major..................... 150
Captain 130	Captain 130
1st Lieutenant.............. 90	1st Lieutenant.............. 90
2nd Lieutenant............. 80	2nd Lieutenant............. 80
Sgt. Major 21	Sgt. Maj. & Q.M. Sgt........ 25*
1st Sergeant 20	1st Sergeant 24
Sergeant................... 17	Sergeant................... 21
Corporal 13	Corporal 17
Musician 12	Drummer and Fifer.......... 16
Private.................... 11	Private.................... 15

* While the budget carries pay for these ratings at $21 a month, disbursement records show their actual pay was $25 a month.

Officers were paid an additional $9 a month for each 5 years service, and field officers (major or higher) received a monthly forage allowance for three horses at the rate of $8 each, the same as for Army officers of like rank. Extra pay for enlisted men was limited to that authorized for detailed or detached men for "uncommon skill or industry" in the performance of their assigned duties.

Available records show that a battalion teamster was paid $24.75 for 99 days, or 25¢ a day. Two hospital stewards were paid at different rates. One, a Marine, was paid at the rate of 25¢ extra per day, while another, a naval enlisted man, was paid $40.00 a month. Four Marines doing extra duty as carpenters at Camp Beall worked a total of 241 days at 40¢ extra pay per day. A Marine doing extra duty as a mechanic worked 152 days at 40¢ per day extra. Shoemakers, in great demand, received $3 a day extra pay.

By the Act of October 2, 1862, the pay for enlisted Marines was increased a flat $4 per month over the original pay scale which would have been the same as that for the Regular Army. On June 9, 1864, the enlisted man's pay in the Army was increased a flat $7 per month, leaving the Marine pay $3 less than the Army scale.[10] Secretary of the Navy Mallory promptly asked Attorney General George Davis as to whether the enlisted men of the Marine Corps were entitled to the pay increase authorized for the Army, but he received a negative opinion.

On October 30, 1864, Colonel Beall, in making his report to the Secretary of the Navy, reminded him that the pay of the Marine enlisted man was still $3 a month less than that of the Army infantryman. The Secretary incorporated this objection in his report to the President, remarking that:

The organization of the Corps is that of a regiment of infantry, to which in pay and allowances it should be assimilated, and, as the monthly pay of its noncommissioned officers, musicians, and privates is now $3 less than that of the same grades in the infantry, an increase to this extent is recommended.[11]

His plea was recognized, and by the Act of January 19, 1865, Congress set the pay of the enlisted men of the Marine Corps at that authorized for the same grades in the infantry of the Army.[12] The Army pay increase was for one year only. But, on March 4, 1865, it was extended until June 30, 1866, automatically extending the pay increase for the Marine Corps enlisted man.

In December 1862, the Marine noncommissioned officers on the Mobile Station were scheduled to receive $50 and the privates 50% of the pay due them. From then on, until through the June 30, 1864, pay day, Marines on the Mobile Station were paid all or part of their pay regularly. The Commandant reported in November 1863 that up to that date the Corps had been paid promptly at the regular fixed periods. Except detachments afloat had been paid in the usual manner, presumably by the cruise, by the Navy paymaster on board ship with the privilege of drawing against their accounts. It was not until payment was due for September-October 1864 that a major unit missed getting paid on time. This was Company E at Savannah, and the failure to pay on time was caused by the interruption of communications between Richmond and Savannah, not to a lack of funds. Then in December 1864, Company E missed a pay day because of the lack of funds. A pay record of this calibre in the Confederacy was no mean achievement.

Nothing illustrated the plight of the military man in inflation times so much as the Paymaster's record for November 1864 which showed the Colonel Commandant receiving pay of $248.80 for the month while the Headquarters' Clerk, a civilian, was drawing $333.33.[13]

Pay could be allotted. Before sailing on the C.S.S. *Sumter* from New Orleans in 1861, Lieutenant Becket K. Howell made an allotment for $30 a month for 24 months beginning September 30, 1861, to W. B. Howell, the Naval Agent at New Orleans.

Pay deductions were allowed in certain situations. For example, on the Mobile Station the Navy Paymaster was not infrequently directed to deduct sums due the laundresses on the Station before transferring the men's accounts to another paymaster.

Marines on board ship drew various small stores items from time to time which were charged against their pay. The two items most commonly drawn were soap and tobacco. An interesting and varied list of items drawn by the

Marines of the floating battery C.S.S. *Georgia* at Savannah in August and September 1863 along with the charges made for them follows:[14]

Pocket handkerchiefs	10¢
Papers of needles	86¢
Thimbles	10¢
Jackknives	20¢
Razors	$2.75
Razor strops	$2.21
Shaving boxes	$1.37
Shaving brushes	44¢
Cakes of shaving soap	86¢
Fine combs	$1.01
Coarse combs	$1.72
Tin pots	72¢
Tin pans	$1.03
Box of blacking	$1.26
Blacking brush	Not given
Pair scissors	Not given
Blue Thread	Not given

The surprise is not that the Marines needed so many items, but that the articles were apparently available. Certainly life on board ship must have been considerably more luxurious than Army life!

Other charges against men's pay were the cost of lost articles of clothing or equipment, deductions to pay fines imposed by courts-martial, and the standard flat monthly deduction of 20¢ a month per man for the hospital fund. In one instance, a private's pay was stopped until stolen pistols had been paid for; another private was charged $2 for a lost haversack, and still another was charged $75 for a lost overcoat.

CONSCRIPTION

With the operation of the conscript law, the Corps began to draw its recruits from the various camps of instruction. On March 10, 1863, some 13 conscripts were transferred from the Army to the Marine Corps, followed by 36 more on March 13. These men were enrolled between August 2, 1862, and March 16, 1863, mostly from the counties of Central Alabama. During May and June 1863, some 27 more conscripts from Central Alabama were transferred from the conscript camp to the Marine Corps depot company at Mobile. Lieutenant Henry L. Graves from Savannah secured conscripts from the Decatur, Georgia, camp, mostly during 1863. Between January 1 and July 1, 1864, the Marine units in the Richmond area received more than 70 conscripts from Camp Lee in Richmond recruited by Lieutenant Nathaniel E. Venable. These were men who had enrolled between July 20, 1863, and June 1, 1864. On October 30,

1864, the Colonel Commandant reported that 32 recruits from the conscript camp near Raleigh, were at the Naval Station at Charleston.[15]

The time spent in the various conscript camps before assignment to the Marine Corps varied widely with little pattern. Many spent less than a week in camp while others were in camp from one to two months. Then there were the occasional men who were in camp six or seven months before assignment. One suspects these were either too ill to be assigned or had been used to supplement the administrative staff at their particular camp. From 1863 until the end of the war practically all the Marine recruits were conscripted into service. An occasional youth or foreigner enlisted outside the operation of the draft.

Some insight into the lives of conscripts going into the Marine Corps from rural North Carolina can be obtained from two letters which have surfaced recently.[16] Henry Hunter Bowen was a 41-year old married conscript who lived in Washington County, close to the Beaufort County line. Sent first to the Camp of Instruction near Raleigh, Camp Holmes, he was soon transferred to Charleston, where he went on board the Receiving Ship *Indian Chief* as a Marine recruit for the ironclad C.S.S. *Columbia* when completed. His newsy letter was written to his wife the day after his going on board *Indian Chief*.

The letter, which follows, was edited by dividing it into paragraphs and sentences. Sentences are started with added capital letters and ended with periods to aid the clarity of understanding. The original spelling and structure are retained.

[Monday] Oct 10th 1864
charleston south carolina

My dear wife [Ann Latham Bowen]
    I take the opertunity to inform you that I left camp homes [Holmes] on friday [Oct. 7] morning and we got to charleston on Sunday morning [Oct. 9] a bout 8 oclock and went out to the ship and we are here on the receaveing ship and we shal remain thare until the iron clad [C.S.S. *Columbia*] is done and then we shal go a bord of her as mariens which duty is they all say is the lightist of all of the services and drest the finest.

    I am well at present and hope these few lines may find you all the same and I want you to rite to me as often as you can. We are a fairing first rate here. We have a pound of beef or bacon a day and a plenty of sugar and coffey twice a day and a plenty of hard tack and potatoes and we are not exposed to the weather at all. I like my position just as well as I can to be from home in the service. Men say that has tried both say they had rather be a private here than to be a lutenant in the in fantry. Two lutenants left camp homes with us and threw up there comishions to come with us to this place. We can see the yankeys fleet, out so we can just hear the report of ther guns and see the smoke rise. We can see fort Sumpter from heare and a good maney other forts in site and we have two and three iron clad done here now that is all ready for service.

I dont think we shal have any fight here soon and I believe it is the common oppinion that the war will soon be over and I prey to god it may be so. I have seen more sights [?] since I left home than I ever saw before in all of my life before and when you rite to me direct your letters to Mr. H. H. Bowen receaving ship Indian Chief charleston S.C., at present for it will be some time before our iron clad is finished some month or two and I will rite you as soon as I get on it. This flag ship is to receive all troops that comes to the navy as camp homes, reserve all of the troop, for the unfantry. Thare is about one hundred on bord of this ship at this time. She lies still all the time out in the stream about a quarter of a mile from charleston but not to wards the yankey fleet.

I love to ride in the steam cars first rate. We have come over rivers and under bridges, and traveld day and nite.

You direct your letters at present to Mr H. H. Bowen receiving ship indian chief charleston S.C., and you must carry on the best you can untel I can get home again. I want to get a furlow to come home a bout christmas if I can and I think I can if nothing turns up more than common. We had frost heare on sunday morning. It is cooler down hear than any where I have bin but I ges it is cool at home now. As to the news we have heard nothing of urgent importance. You must send me the [news?], if you have any. It is said that there is some cases of the yallow fever in the town but they think this cool weather will stop it now and I dont think there is much danger of getting it on the ship.

I will come to a close by saying I remain your dear husband until death &c.

H.H. Bowen
[Henry Hunter Bowen.]

Shortly after Henry Hunter Bowen left home for the service, a brother, W. J. Bowen, wrote a letter to Henry H. and George Washington Bowen giving news of their home area and families.

Goldsboro [Thursday] Oct 27 1864
Dear Brothers H. H. & G. W. Bowen

I take this oppertunity to Drop you a few Lines as we have to Lay over here till nine ock [o'clock] to Knight. Conscripted and on our way to camp Homes [Holmes], and very sorry to say It. tho I am in tolerable Good health at this time and Left my family and yours all in reasonable health Last sunday [Oct. 23] when we Left home and I hope when I hear from you that you may be Enjoying the same Great blessing.

I have no news of importance more than they have taken Every man out of our county Except militia officers & magistrates. Every detail[ed] man, Every blacksmith, and miller is now on there way to camp homes [Holmes]. No one Left at all between 17 & 50 years of age. The senior reserves are yet at plymouth.

The Enemy on friday before we left home [Oct. 21] Burned all the Bridges from Bath to Leachville and I understand they have Been through Hyde [County] and done Likewise.

You must [write?] me as soon as you hear from me again. I can not tell you now where to Direct to me.

Yours Rspy
W. J. Bowen.

AGE

Early in the war, recruits were expected to be at least 21 years of age. Persons under that age were required to have the approval signature of a parent before being enlisted. The Conscription Act of 1862 changed the age limit declaring all white males, not exempt and between the ages of 18 and 35, members of the Army.

The youngest Marines were those recruited as musicians (drummers or fifers). For example, William Edward Howard enlisted in Richmond on March 1, 1864, at the age of 15 years. Dudley Marvin Stone enlisted in Richmond on February 23, 1864, at the age of 13 years, 6 months. Still younger was James Leonard Stevenson who enlisted in Richmond February 17, 1864, at the age of 12 years, 10 months. He deserted November 14, 1864. Because of his youthfulness, his leaving was officially recorded as a discharge. Possibly the youngest was Henry Klocke, enlisted at Mobile, May 18, 1864, at the age of 12 years (no months mentioned). Presumably captured, he was paid on February 9, 1865, in Mobile for time as a prisoner of war.

Among the youngest enlisted for regular Marine service was Joseph Camp, of Campbell County, Georgia, who enlisted in Richmond on May 30, 1864, giving his age as 17 years. At Savannah, the youngest was Macarton Campbell Kollock who was only 16 years, 1 month, and 27 days old when he enlisted on December 1, 1863. He was a cousin of the Tattnalls and was assigned to duty as orderly to the Naval Commandant, Flag-Officer Josiah Tattnall.

At the other end of the age scale, while most enlisted Confederate Marines were in their 20s and 30s, there were some who were in their 40s, and even a few who were in their 50s.

Perhaps the oldest was John W. Willey who enlisted in Mobile on November 10, 1862. A record in 1863 gave his age at that time as 59 years. He remained in the Marines until the end of the war, finally surrendering at Mobile on July 21, 1865. At this time he should have been 61 years old. Two other Marines were probably in their 50s when they served. First Sergeant Jacob Scholls, who was reported to be 51 when he died in the spring of 1862, and Vincent Jordan, who was conscripted at Talledega, Alabama, on March 6, 1863. Jordan's service came to an end on October 27, 1864, when he was discharged on a Surgeon's Certificate of Disability at age 52. A third older Marine was Thomas J. Dunphy, enlisted at Mobile on November 22, 1862, who gave his age as 49 in 1864, making him 50, or close to it, at the end of the war.

On May 5, 1864, an 18-year-old grocer from Sussex County, Virginia, Samuel B. Grant, a conscript at Camp Lee, Richmond, was assigned to the Marine Corps on June 7. He served first at Drewry's Bluff, and then on board C.S.S. *Fredericksburg* of the James River Squadron. He was hospitalized in Richmond when captured at the close of the war. After the war, he returned to Sussex County where he died on August 23, 1944, at the age of 98 years, 8 months, and 15 days.

Even at this age, Grant was not the oldest survivor of the Corps. That honor seems to have been earned by David Staples Woodson, a merchant and postmaster at Lowesville, Amherst County, Va., who was also conscripted at Camp Lee on February 20, 1864, and assigned to the Corps on March 3, 1864. His Marine service was also performed at Drewry's Bluff. He was captured and paroled on April 9, 1865. He died March 27, 1938, at the age of 99 years, 1 month, and 5 days.

BARRACKS AND HOUSING

The Marines sent to the Pensacola area in the spring of 1861 were to be housed in tents. Secretary of the Navy Mallory instructed that an appropriate place for an encampment be selected, having due regard to health, shade, and water. It was not long, however, before they moved into the Warrington Navy Yard, presumably occupying the Marine barracks there.

The Marines at Mobile were originally housed on board the Receiving Ship *Dalman*. But, on October 24, 1862, orders were issued to stop the rations of the men on the next day as a Marine barracks had been established on shore. The Mathews Press and wharves located on Commerce Street, below Church, were rented from M. Waring Goodman for use as a Marine barracks at a rental of $4,000 per year.

A similar barracks was established at Savannah for the Marines belonging to Company E which furnished the guards for the vessels of the Savannah Squadron. In May 1863 the Marines on shore moved to a house on the outskirts of the city known as "Fairlawn." It had been the manor house of a pre-Revolutionary plantation and General Robert Howe's headquarters in December 1779, before the British occupied Savannah. In 1959 it was St. Benedict's, a Catholic School. Recruiting advertisements referred to the Savannah Marines on shore as being "well quartered in excellent barracks."[17]

When the Savannah Marines reached Charleston, in late 1864, the Marines there were housed in the Middleton House on the Battery. Investigation in Charleston has produced the opinion that the house referred to is now known as the Ross House, #1 Meeting Street, right on the Battery, which was occupied by William Middleton in 1861.

In September 1862, Colonel Beall requested an appropriation of $15,000, mainly for lumber, for the construction of temporary barracks at Drewry's Bluff before the arrival of winter. He based his appeal upon the preservation of the efficiency of his men by looking after their health, comfort, and morale. These barracks were built in November and December 1862 at a cost of $13,971.92 to get the men out of tents[18] and were used for the rest of the war. Captain Charles M. Blackford, P.A.C.S., wrote home in August 1864 that the soldier [Marines?] at Drewry's Bluff lived in small whitewashed cabins with beautiful walkways in the area beautified by grass and flowers.[19] These could have been the Marines' quarters since Private Routt of Company C was on daily duty during the summer as a gardener at Drewry's Bluff. Besides flowers and grass, he raised fresh vegetables which graced the mess-tables of the garrison. The field battalion from Drewry's Bluff and Richmond was under canvass for a brief time in July 1864 in the Wilmington-Smithville, North Carolina, area.

Marines assigned to the ships of the Navy had varied fortunes. In Mobile, for instance, the Marines were usually housed on shore for convenience because of the small size and limited space on the ships of the Mobile Squadron. This was preferable to service on the ironclads which frequently required the presence of the guard at all times. The ironclads did not have enough air, ventilation, or light. A Confederate Naval Medical Survey recognized the extreme heat on and in the ironclads in summer and recommended remedial measures be taken. They included anchoring where there was a free circulation of air, keeping all air apparatus open unless absolutely necessary to close them, that wind sails or ventilators of canvass, metal, or wood be fitted to them, and that awnings be used constantly. The heat from the galleys alone was sufficient to render that portion of the berth decks assigned to the crew virtually uninhabitable.[20] The Engine Room of the C.S.S. *Richmond*, reputed to be one of the hottest in the Confederate Navy, sometimes reached 150° Fahrenheit, and the rest of the ship was probably hot in proportion. Lieutenant Thomson wrote home that, "To be aboard an Iron Clad or on a Southern Station during the summer months is not at all desirable."[21] On another occasion, when officers were being sent to Charleston, to serve on the ironclads, he expressed the hope that his position at Drewry's Bluff would save him from assignment to "that disagreeable berth."[22]

Life on board the cruisers *Sumter*, *Chickamauga*, and *Tallahassee* was undoubtedly more comfortable if only because of being out of the hot, humid, stagnant air of the coastal rivers, and because basically these ships were better designed for general living conditions, light, and ventilation, being converted merchantmen. Cruising on the open sea removed the men from exposure to the malaria-bearing mosquitos of the swampy regions around the Southern port cities.

ROLE OF MARINES, THEIR DRILL AND INSTRUCTION

Marine Corps instruction then, as now, was varied and covered many phases of military and naval life. As early as April 1861, the first contingents sent to the Pensacola area were actively drilled in the use of great guns and small arms. Captain Van Benthuysen received orders from the Secretary of the Navy in May 1861 to see that his Marines were instructed and drilled in the use of their arms so as to make efficient soldiers of them in the shortest time. He was advised to hold early morning and late evening drills during the hot weather. In addition to their infantry drill at Pensacola, one company actively manned a 10-inch Columbiad erected in battery in the Navy Yard. While in barracks, Marines drilled until sufficiently proficient to be assigned to the vessels of the several squadrons or the cruisers.

General Orders issued to the Savannah Squadron in April 1863 directed that the Marine guards be drilled every day except Sunday, under the direction of the Marine officers.[23] This order was in line with the regulation which provided:

ARTICLE 12. They are to be frequently exercised by their own officers. A suitable place on deck will be assigned for that purpose, upon the application of the senior marine officer, when the other duties of the ship and weather will, in the opinion of the commanding officer, permit.

Lieutenant Edward Crenshaw, C.S.M.C., of the Ironclad *Virginia, II*, wrote in his diary in March, 1865 that he was training sailors and Marines of the ship in infantry drill and the manual of arms. The infantry exercises were conducted on shore while practice in the manual of arms was held on the fantail of the ironclad.[24]

The participation of Marines on shore in parades, reviews, inspections, and related ceremonies was governed by the Army rules and regulations for the same purposes. Little has been found of the participation of Marines in ceremonial affairs. One exception was the participation of the Marines from the *Savannah* and the *Isondiga* in the funeral procession of Commander William McBlair in Savannah on February 17, 1863.

Marine regulations prescribed that Marines could be employed on board ship as gun's crews at the great guns under their own officers, or even as individuals assigned to regular gun crews. But such assignments were to be made only in case of necessity. It was pretty well understood that many Marines had been trained as heavy artillerists. In October 1863, Major General William H. C. Whiting at Wilmington, North Carolina, found that the increased fortifications defending Wilmington required more artillerists. In discussing his problem with President Davis, the thought was expressed that perhaps some Marines and artillerists could be spared from the forts on the James River. This thought, expressed as a request, was sent to Adjutant General Cooper. Again, in August 1864, when General Dabney Maury at Mobile requested some "tried artillery troops from Charleston," President Davis suggested as an alternative making an inquiry whether any Marines instructed as artillery could be sent.[25]

Lieutenant Ruffin Thomson attempted to explain to his father the functions of Marines, "The Marines are drilled in Artillery as well as Infantry tactics & in truth in their proper sphere they are simply *Naval Artillerists* . . . . Still they retain their rifles, which are useful in enforcing subordination among a crew, in boarding, & repelling boarders &c, &c . . . . ." He then went on to point out that the Corps furnished guards of from 15 to 30 men for the different navy yards and ironclads under the command of lieutenants. Here, in a brief form, he presented his interpretation of the role of Marines in the Sixties.[26]

Another function of the Corps developed during the war. It provided a mobile striking force for special assignments and to meet emergencies. This was an important function which had its beginnings in the U.S. Marine Corps before the war, particularly the Marine participation in the Seminole War, in the Mexican War, and at the capture of John Brown. The function was recognized, yet its significance was scarcely comprehended; it remained for the function to be elaborated upon in the next century.

The amphibious nature of the Corps was explained in its advertising literature which stated, ". . . service in the Marine Corps is particularly attractive to persons who would like to combine a military with a naval life."[27] or, "Marines are SOLDIERS on board men-of-war or at naval stations, and are not required to perform sailors' duty."[28]

It was common practice to call upon the ships of the squadron in the area to furnish the required Marines from their guards whenever a special force was needed. For large groups or in the Richmond area, the field battalion at Drewry's Bluff was called upon to furnish the men. Flag-Officer John K. Mitchell, commanding the James River Squadron, on June 15, 1864, requisitioned manpower for "Expedition Parties" to be held in readiness for immediate service. Under this order, the *Virginia*, the *Richmond*, and the *Fredericksburg* were to furnish ten Marines each, and two Marine officers were to be furnished, one each, by the *Virginia* and by the *Fredericksburg*.[29]

The designation in advance of need made prior training possible and eliminated much confusion in the event of a sudden call for a special force. The danger in that advance designation of specific personnel was that care had to be taken in their regular assignments not to give them key positions.

In November 1863, Colonel Commandant Beall reported that while the Corps had not been recruited up to its authorized strength, it had met all requisitions for guards of vessels and navy yards and had still been able to keep up a camp of instruction which had been beneficial to officers and men alike. Beall ascribed the failure to reach authorized strength to the difficulty of obtaining recruits "suitable for Marines." At this time practically all of the recruits for the Corps were products of the Conscription Law. But Beall repeated the opinion of Captain Meiere at Mobile (at this time the source of most of the new men for the Corps) that the conscripts "have in almost every instance proven physically unfitted for the service."[30]

Although Colonel Beall did not name or locate the Marine camp of instruction in his report, all the available evidence points to it having been Camp Beall located at Drewry's Bluff. Captain Van Benthuysen said the Marine camp was merely quarters assigned to the Marines within the Post of Drewry's Bluff.

Supporting this belief is the fact that except at the beginning of the war, Camp Beall was the only permanent camp where Marines were stationed; the largest concentration of the Corps (three companies) was at Camp Beall, and most, if not all, of the new officers in 1863 and 1864 were first assigned to duty at Camp Beall immediately after being commissioned, presumably for a training and indoctrination period, before being given a duty assignment on a ship or a station.

The enlisted men of the Corps were usually on one of three basic assignments; (1) with the field battalion at Drewry's Bluff, Va., (2) serving on the Marine guard at a navy yard or naval station, or (3) on board ship as a member of a ship's guard, either on river or harbor duty, or on a cruiser on the high seas.

Although Marines companies were maintained close to authorized strength, the various detachments kept the number available for field service at a very modest figure. The following table gives the distribution of the men of the battalion stationed at Drewry's Bluff as of August 31, 1864:

Table 6

Distribution of Marine Companies A, B, and C: August 31, 1864.[31]

	Co. A	Co. B	Co. C	Total
Detached Service:				
On C.S. Str. *Charleston*	4	10	3	17
(Charleston Squadron)				
On C.S. Str. *Fredericksburg*	12	2	4	18
(James River Squadron)				
On C.S. Str. *Richmond*	4	7	11	22
(James River Squadron)				
On C.S. Str. *Drewry*	2	0	0	2
(James River Squadron)				
On C.S. Str. *Virginia, II*	0	12	7	19
(James River Squadron)				
At Navy Yard Rocketts'	8	12	9	29
(Richmond, Va.)				
At Navy Yard opposite Rocketts'	6	10	6	22
and on C.S. Schr. *Gallego*				
(Manchester, Richmond, Va.)				
Provisional Company	15	17	16	48
(Wilmington, N. C.)				
ON C.S. Str. *Tallahassee*	6	9	6	21
(Wilmington, N. C.)				
For C.S.S. *Edith* (*Chickamauga*)	6	0	3	9
(Smithville, N. C.)				

	Co. A	Co. B	Co. C	Total
Detached Service:				
Miscellaneous assignments	3	3	1	7
Absent: On Leave	0	3	1	4
Without leave	1	0	3	4
Sick	1	2	2	5
In arrest or confined	2	0	3	5
Present:				
At Drewry's Bluff	28	25	28	81
(including sick and on daily duty)				
Totals:	98	112	103	313

The same situation prevailed with Company E based at Savannah with many members of the company assigned to the vessels of the Savannah Squadron. The Marine establishment at Mobile, Company D, had been considerably disrupted by the heavy losses by capture in the battle of Mobile Bay and the surrender of Fort Gaines earlier in August 1864, but was recruiting a new company.

Individual men were assigned to special duty from time to time, detailed as shoemakers, gardeners, carpenters, teamsters, guard over "Navy flour" at the flour mill, hospital steward, and as orderlies to various commanding officers. Others served at times as post office runners and as company baker.

The Marines performed guard duty on board ship and at Navy shore installations. A Marine guard protected naval property at the Farnsworth depot on the railroad near Pensacola for months in 1861. At Savannah a small guard watched the Navy store, and helped guard Federal prisoners in September and October 1864. In Mobile, Marines were used to guard the Naval Store House and Ordnance Department, the Naval Ship Yard, and the Marine Barracks as well as furnish the guards on board the ships of the Mobile Squadron.

While much of this duty was bound to be routine, it had its moments. One such episode took place on board the C.S.S. *Savannah* on Christmas Eve 1863. Lieutenant Henry L. Graves, the senior Marine officer on board, was engaging in concocting eggnog with several other officers when he was called up on deck. As he tells the story:

> I went up and found about 20 sailors drunk and like so many wild beasts. I called out my Guard immediately, had them load and fix bayonets & form around them, and one after another were dragged out and ironed. It was near two o'clock before we got them all secured. The wind was biting cold and I like to have frozen. Fortunately the moon shone very brightly. I suppose two or three of the men will be court martialed and shot. The men had broken into the spirit room and stolen several gallons of whiskey from the Surgeon's supply.[32]

DISCIPLINE, DESERTION, AND PUNISHMENT

Punishment played an important part in enforcing discipline in the Confederate Marine Corps. The forms of punishment were not unusual to Regular units for that day although some of them have no standing today. The emphasis was on the negative approach of punishment rather than on the currently prevailing positive approach of reward and the development of morale. Basically the punishments could be grouped into physical punishment, deprivation of money or leave, incarceration, humiliation, and the attempt to secure public disapproval.

The Marine officer commanding on board ship, with the approval of the commander of the ship, could both reduce noncommissioned officers, and promote to fill vacancies. He also had the power to regulate, under the over-all control of the ship's captain, the permission for Marines to go on shore — to have "liberty."

When on duty in a navy yard or a garrison, the Marine officer commanding could reduce noncommissioned officers, provided he reported the particulars to the Corps Commandant, and he could promote to fill noncommissioned officer vacancies with the sanction of the Commandant. He also controlled the customary "liberty" for the enlisted men.

Commander (later Rear Admiral) Raphael Semmes, while in command of the C.S.S. *Sumter* in late 1861, reported in his journal under date of December 16 that "A Marine having been found asleep last night at his post over the prisoners, I have ordered a general court-martial for his trial."[33] This Marine was kept in irons until the ship reached Cadiz, Spain, where he was discharged from the service and, with the consent of the Spanish Civil Governor, was put on shore, stranded, in a foreign country. Yet he did escape being executed by a firing squad as his punishment could have been. Two days before Christmas a Marine on the *Sumter* made the mistake of cursing the corporal while on post and wound up in the ship's brig for the offense.

At Mobile in early 1863, Captain J. E. Meiere first bought an iron ball and chain (at a cost of $18.00) and later followed up with two iron chains and shackles. A brig was constructed at the Mobile Marine Barracks in October 1863, indicating that confinement as a punishment was there to stay. Some punishments were not without an element of humor, such as the reduction of Corporal Nugent to the ranks for killing hogs at Smithville, North Carolina, in July 1864.

The generic term "desertion" covered a major difficulty with the men enlisted or drafted into the Mobile Station. Between July 1862 and May 1864, some 375 men passed through the paymaster's books on the Mobile Station. Of these, 16 were returned to the Army units to which they properly belonged, four died, eight were discharged, one was exchanged for an Army man, and 53 deserted and were not apprehended. There were some 13 more who deserted and were arrested while one deserter returned voluntarily.[34]

A 5'3" Irish-born Marine by the name of Patrick Geelan deserted from the Mobile Barracks in November 1862 and achieved the dubious distinction of being advertised for in the Mobile *Daily Tribune* at a $30 reward. He was soon picked up, court-martialed, and sentenced on January 15, 1863, to six months with a ball and chain at hard labor on public works, to have his head shaved in the presence of the Marines of his command, to forfeit all pay due or which might become due, and to have his sentence read aloud at all naval stations and on board all vessels in commission. It developed that there were no public works on which he could be employed, so his captain ordered him to clean arms. But he refused to do this and then deserted again. Admiral Franklin Buchanan described him as "an old offender and a mutinous bad character" and requested an example be made of him and that he be again tried by court-martial in order to secure the efficiency and discipline of the Marines. Finally the Marine Corps washed its hands of Geelan by transferring him to the Army as a deserter on October 10, 1863.

Another source of irritation (and, one suspects, desperation) in the Mobile Marines was Private Thomas Farley. Buchanan reported to the Navy Department that he had inquired of the Provost Marshal whether Farley might not be sent to Richmond as a Yankee prisoner. The Admiral considered this as the surest mode of punishment but had been told that it could not be done. He stated firmly that Farley was not to be trusted in the Confederate service. But Buchanan lost again when one of President Davis' proclamations required the release of Farley from confinement. His last move in the Farley case was to transfer him to Drewry's Bluff on September 19, 1863. One is lead to suspect that he deserted on his trip to this station as none of the available records of the companies stationed at Drewry's Bluff carry his name.

Private J. W. Oats was sentenced at Savannah to wear a barrel shirt marked "Deserter" two hours daily for 30 days and to forfeit liberty for three months. Private James T. Barber was sentenced to be confined at hard labor in any penitentiary in the State of Georgia, or any other prison designated by the Secretary of the Navy, for not less than three years, or as long thereafter as the war might continue. Private John Carson at Mobile was sentenced for desertion to three months solitary in double irons, three days each week on bread and water, deprivation of liberty for six additional months, and to forfeit all due pay, and two-thirds of his pay for the next nine months.

Desertion was a continuing problem, and the Corps was not free from it from the very beginning. The best available records for 1861 are for Captain Alfred C. Van Benthuysen's company and show that for the two months period ending June 30, 1861, his company had 11 deserters; for the period ending August 31, 1861, three deserters; for the period ending October 31, eight more, and for the period ending December 31, an additional six deserters, making 28 in all in eight months. A good number of these, however, were Northern men or sympathizers who were practically forced into the Confederate service and took their first opportunity to leave.[35]

In the closing months of the war it seems fair to ascribe the desertions to discouragement and to the feeling that the war was lost.

MEDICAL CARE AND FUNERALS

The Confederate Marine Corps had no medical service of its own but relied upon the services of the Confederate Navy Medical Corps in much the same manner as the United States Marine Corps today. Each Marine from the Commandant down had assessed 20¢ a month for the hospital fund deducted from his pay. Any actual hospitalization took place in a Confederate naval hospital, if available. Recruiting notices mentioned that "for the sick the best hospital accomodacion and medical attendance is furnished by the regular medical department of the Navy."[36] Recruits were medically examined by Navy surgeons, if one was available, otherwise by civilian doctors who were allowed $2 for each recruit they examined, whether accepted or rejected.

So far only one medical report exclusively concerning the Corps has been located. This is an abstract record for October 1861 for the "1st Regt. Marines" stationed at the Pensacola Navy Yard prepared by Doctor Joseph D. Grafton. At this time the so-called "1st Regt." consisted of only 208 officers and men.

An analysis of this report shows 29 sick men carried over from the last report while 22 remained sick at the end of the month. During the month some 72 went on sick report for an assortment of reasons. Some 77 were returned to duty, one was furloughed, and one died. The major causes for going on sick report were acute diarrhoea, 17 cases; acute dysentary, seven cases; acute rheumatism, six cases; and catarrah, five cases. Signs of fights showed up in the two hospitalized for contusions, four fractures, and two cuttings. V.D. only appeared in two hospitalizations for gonorrhoea.[37]

Records are available for admissions and discharges for the sickbay of the C.S. Steamer *Gaines* at Mobile between August 22, 1862, and August 30, 1863. With a guard consisting usually of 17 Marines, there were 52 hospitalizations during this period of about a year. Some 42 admissions were for intermittent fever, defined today as malarial fever in which the proxysms occur at intervals, generally regular. Many made return visits, and the usual period of hospitalization was from three to ten days.

Rarely a man was discharged on a surgeons's certificate as unsuited physically for the service. Company B had a cleaning out before leaving Pensacola in the spring of 1862, and some nine men were discharged for disability. Outside of this one episode (which may have taken place in the other companies at the same time as well), such discharges were individual occurrences.

There were men who died in the hospitals. In Mobile funerals were handled by Noah Higgins, Undertaker, who furnished a stained top pine coffin for $30 (raised in 1864 to $50) and a hearse for $10 (raised in 1864 to $15). There was a additional charge of $10 if a cab was furnished. These funeral costs were charged to the deceased's account by the Paymaster, and the proceeds from the sale of his effects, which sometimes brought more than his funeral expenses, were credited to his account.

Available records say very little about the operation of the medical service for Marines and only in a few instances do we know the names of the doctors assigned to this duty. One, Dr. Joseph D. Grafton, already mentioned, was apparently the medical officer for the Marines at Pensacola in 1861. Surgeon Lewis W. Minor, C.S.N., was assigned to the Marine Barracks at Mobile on August 16, 1864, and presumably remained on this assignment until the end of the war. A third identified doctor was Assistant Surgeon Marcellus Ford, P.N.C.S., who was transferred in late 1864 from the *Water Witch* to the Marine Detachment serving in the Savannah trenches. Upon the evacuation of Savannah, Ford accompanied the Marines to Charleston, and remained on duty with them on that station.

Among the Navy doctors serving with the Marines at Drewry's Bluff were Assistant Surgeon Edwin G. Booth (May 16, 1862 - September 10, 1862); Passed Assistant Surgeon Charles E. Lining (January 3, 1863 - March 10, 1863); Assistant Surgeon Henry B. Melvin (May 20, 1863 - September 3, 1863); and Assistant Surgeon Pike Brown (September 14, 1863 - September 8, 1864).

Enlisted men were assigned to work as hospital stewards at the Marine Barracks, Mobile. One was Emile Atsinger (January - June 1864). He was a true "Corpsman," however, as he had enlisted as an Ordinary Seaman in August 1862 at the Jackson, Mississippi, Naval Station. Another hospital steward was Prescott C. Caldwell (September 1863 - February 14, 1864) who enlisted as a Marine and detailed to this duty. Marine Private Henry Forbes received extra duty pay of 25¢ a day as a hospital steward at Drewry's Bluff for the period

November 1, 1863 - March 15, 1864. Orville T. Shaffer was serving as a hospital steward when captured in Richmond on April 3, 1865. John H. Slack, a private in Company B, surrendered as a "Hospital Steward, Navy Battalion" on April 5, 1865.

MARINE MUSIC

The Marine Band has long been a source of pride to the citizens of the United States and has occupied a preeminent position among the military bands of the world for years. It is only natural that the question should be asked, "Did the Confederate Marine Corps have a band?"

One author has made a reference to a Marine band. In discussing Richmond in the closing days of the war, Clifford Dowdey referred to a Confederate Marine band of twenty-two musicians[38] as though all the Corps' musicians were gathered into a single unit, but this was not the case.

In general, provision was made by legislation for strictly field music by drummers and fifers in the Confederate Marine Corps rather than for the assembly of a small regimental band. The rather wide distribution of the units of the Corps and the apparent scarcity of musicians made it difficult to consider the organization of a band if the units were to have any music at all.

The original Act of March 16, 1861, prescribed 12 musicians for the six-company battalion. The Reorganization Act of May 20, 1861, increased the number of authorized musicians to ten drummers, ten fifers, and two [principal] musicians. On September 24, 1862, the number of authorized musicians was increased by an additional twenty drummers and twenty fifers, making thirty of each as well as the two principal musicians. But there is no record that the authorized strength was ever reached. Since there were three main Marine stations: Drewry's Bluff, Savannah, and Mobile, records of musicians normally would be expected to be found on the rolls of Marine units at these stations.

The Richmond papers in May 1862 carried recruiting advertisements for a few boys to be enlisted as learners of music, provided they had the consent of their parents or guardians.[39] Recruiting advertisements were run for months in the Mobile paper for recruits for the Corps between the ages of 16 and 45 years of age which promised higher pay for drummers, buglers, and fifers.[40] During part of April, May, and June 1863, Captain John R. F. Tattnall, organizing Company E at Savannah, advertised for two drummers and two fifers for his company.[41]

The presence of three companies at Drewry's Bluff usually guaranteed some musicians on the post. One officer, in writing his family, mentioned with some acerbity, "The drum & shrill fife, the first sound in the morning & the last thing at night, also at breakfast dinner & supper, strikes harshly on the ear . . . ."[42]

Efforts were made to include one or more musicians in the Marine guards placed on board the larger ships of the Confederate Navy. The C.S.S. *McRae* carried a drummer in 1862 while a musician (type unknown) was on board the *Virginia* (*Merrimack*) during its famous fight as well as one on the *Jamestown.*

In November 1864, the C.S.S. *Georgia* (floating battery) was reported as having a deficiency in Marines that included two musicians. One of the privates on the *Georgia*, John Broderick, did qualify as a fifer. One musician was on board the C.S. Ironclad *Fredericksburg* according to the July-August 1864 muster roll for Company C. One musician was ordered to the C.S.S. *Virginia, II,* on October 31, 1864, and another to the same ship on December 31, 1864, from Company C.

The records indicate there were at least five musicians on duty at Mobile at one time or another with the depot companies. Francis Farley was assigned to the C.S.S. *Tennessee* on March 15, 1864, and served until captured. A twelve-year old youth, Henry Klocke, was enlisted on May 18, 1864, at Mobile as a Marine musician.

The specialty of the musicians is not always mentioned, but those that are mentioned were either fifers or drummers. Their main utilization was not for music but for the transmission of orders.

The authorization of two principal musicians could have been for the purpose of appointing skilled musicians to train others, or for the purpose of heading up a regimental fife and drum corps should the regiment ever be assembled as a single unit. No record has been found of the appointment of either of the two authorized principal musicians, nor is there any record of the assembly of more than a few musicians at any single time or place.

As to the equipment and uniform of Marine musicians, it will be remembered that in September 1861 the Secretary of the Navy requested, among other things, the purchase of twenty bugles with extra mouth pieces. But there is no record of their receipt. On March 17, 1864, equipment was drawn from the Corps Quartermaster for a drummer on duty at Drewry's Bluff. Specifically, the equipment consisted of one drum, one pair of drum sticks, and one canteen strap for use as a drum sling.

NOTES AND REFERENCES

Chapter IX — Life as an Enlisted Man

1. New Orleans *Daily Delta*, Fri., April 12, 1861, 6:4, and advertisement in issues for April 9, 10, 11, and 12, 1861, 7:1.

2. Wilmington *Journal*, Mon., Aug. 19, 1861, 2:5, also 2:2.

3. Matthews, *Public Laws . . . .*, *op. cit.*, Chap. XXIII, Sections 2 and 3, April 10, 1862.

4. Attorney General Thos. H. Watts to Secretary of the Navy S. R. Mallory, Dept. of Justice, Richmond, Dec. 27, 1862, MS. #4, *Savannah Sqdn. Pp., Emory U.*

5. B[olling] Baker to Paymaster Thomas R. Ware, C.S.N., Richmond, Dec. 30, 1862, *Letters for November-December, '62, Ware Pp.*

6. Matthews, *Public Laws . . . . 1st Sess., 2d Cong., 1864, op. cit.*, Chap. XX, 259.

7. IV *O.R.* 2, 191-192: G.O. 89, Nov. 18, 1862, which quotes Act No. 29, "An Act to permit enlistments in the Navy and Marine Corps."

8. II *N.O.R.* 2, 754: report of Capt. S. S. Lee, In Charge, Office of Orders and Detail, to Secretary of the Navy S. R. Mallory, Richmond, Oct. 31, 1864.

9. Secretary of the Navy S. R. Mallory to Lewis Cruger, Comptroller, Navy Dept., Richmond, Feb. 20, 1862, *Area File #7, p. 458, Microcopy 625, Roll 412*, U.S. National Archives.

10. IV *O.R.* 3, 492: Act of June 9, 1864.

11. II *N.O.R.* 2, 750: Col. Lloyd J. Beall, Comdg. C.S.M.C., to Secretary of the Navy S. R. Mallory, Richmond, Va., Oct. 30, 1864. The Secretary's Report to the President, II *N.O.R.* 2, 636, is incorrectly dated April 30, 1864; internal evidence indicates the correct date to be *circa* November 7, 1864, the date of the opening of the session of Congress.

12. Ramsdell, *op. cit.*, 19: Act No. 26 of Jan. 19, 1865.

13. Vouchers #11 and 20, Abstract of Payments, November-December 1864, Wrapper #6, *Entry 426, R.G. 45*, U.S. National Archives.

14. Various listings of small stores issued to crew of C.S.S. Georgia, *Entry 419, R.G. 45*, U.S. National Archives.

15. II *N.O.R.* 2, 749: report of Col. Lloyd J. Beall, Comdg., C.S.M.C., Oct. 30, 1864.

16. Xerox copies of originals of these letters in the possession of the author by the courtesy of a family member.

17. Savannah *Republican*, Tues., Jan 19, 1864, 1:5, and other issues.

18. Lt. Henry L. Graves, C.S.M.C., to "Dear Aunt Hat," Camp Beall, Nov. 17, 1862, and to "My Dear Sister," Camp Beall, Drewry's Bluff, Va., Nov. 23, 1862, *Graves' Pp., SHC, UNC.*

19. Susan Leigh Blackford, compiler (Charles Minor Blackford, III, ed.), *Letters from Lee's Army* (New York, 1947), 269.

20. *N.O.R.* 10, 735-736: report of Board of Surgeons (W. B. Sinclair, James F. Harrison, and W. F. Carrington) to Surgeon W. A. W. Spotswood, C.S.N., In Charge, Office of Medicine and Surgery, Richmond, Aug. 26, 1864.

21. Lt. Ruffin Thomson, C.S.M.C., to "Dear Pa," Drewry's Bluff, Va., June 2, 1864, *Thomson Pp., SHC, UNC.*

22. *Loc. cit.,* Lt. Ruffin Thomson, C.S.M.C., to "Dear Pa," Drewry's Bluff, Va., Nov. 3, 1864.

23. *N.O.R.* 14, 691: G.O. 1, para. 16, April 17, 1863, Comdr. R. L. Page, Comdg. Naval Forces Afloat, Savannah River.

24. Entries dated Tues., March 14; Wed., March 15; Mon., March 20; and Wed., March 29, 1865, *Crenshaw's Diary.*

25. *O.R.* 52, pt. 2, 724.

26. Lt. Ruffin Thomson, C.S.M.C., to "Dear Pa," Camp Beall, Drewry's Bluff, Va., March 14, 1864, *Thomson Pp., SHC, UNC.*

27. Richmond *Daily Examiner*, Sat., May 3, 1862, 2:1.

28. Mobile *Register and Advertiser*, Tues., Feb. 3, 1863, 1:3, and numerous other issues.

29. G.O. 7, June 15, 1864, James River Sqdn., Box 3, General Orders, *J. K. Mitchell Pp., VHS.*

30. II *N.O.R.* 2, 535: Report of Secretary of the Navy S. R. Mallory to President Jefferson Davis, Nov. 30, 1863, and *ibid.*, 563, report of Col. Lloyd J. Beall, Comdg., C.S.M.C., to Secretary of the Navy S. R. Mallory, H.Q., C.S.M.C., Richmond, Va., Nov. 7, 1863. Also *Mobile C. O. Day Book*, 130: Capt. J. E. Meiere, C.S.M.C., to Col. Lloyd J. Beall, Mobile, Aug. 6, 1863.

31. Muster and Pay Roll, Co. A, C.S.M.C., for July-August, 1864, dated Aug. 31, 1864, at Camp Beall, Va., Wrapper #9; and Muster and Pay Roll, Co. B, C.S.M.C., for July-August, 1864, dated Aug. 31, 1864, at Camp Beall, Va., Wrapper #2; and Muster and Pay Roll, Co. C, C.S.M.C., for July-August, 1864, dated Aug. 31, 1864, at Camp Beall, Va., Wrapper #3, all of *Entry 426, R.G. 45*, U.S. National Archives.

32. Lt. Henry L. Graves, C.S.M.C., to "My Dear Sister," Stmr. *Savannah*, Dec. 26, 1863, *Graves' Pp., SHC, UNC.*

33. *N.O.R.* 1, 730: Semmes' *Journal*, entry dated Mon., Dec. 16, [1861].

34. *Ware Pp., passim.*

35. II *O.R.* 2, 96-97, and II *O.R.* 3, 205.

36. Savannah, Ga., *Republican*, Tues., Jan. 19, 1864, 4:5, and other issues.

37. Medical Director's Consolidated Report of the Sick and Wounded serving in the Army near Pensacola, Fla., commanded by Maj. Gen. B. Bragg for the month of October 1861, *C.S. Miscellaneous Papers, Portfolio #10*, Manuscripts Division, Library of Congress.

38. Clifford Dowdy, *Experiment in Rebellion* (New York, 1946), 402.

39. Richmond *Daily Examiner*, May 6, 1862, 1:5.

40. Mobile *Register and Advertiser*, Sat., Feb. 21, 1863, 1:4. This advertisement continued to run until the fall of 1863.

41. Savannah *Republican*, Fri., May 1, 1863, 3:2. This advertisement ran from April 20 until at least June 30.

42. Lt. Henry L. Graves, C.S.M.C., to "My dear Aunt," Camp Beall, near Drewry's Bluff, Va., Nov. 19, 1862, *Graves' Pp., SHC, UNC*.

Chapter X

THE MARINE OFFICER

The Confederate States Marine Corps was intended to virtually duplicate the U.S. Marine Corps. The Confederate Congress made all United States laws for Marines not inconsistent with Southern law applicable to the Confederate Marine Corps.[1]

The creation of a Confederate Marine Corps was heavily promoted by the large number of officers who left the U.S. Marine Corps to join their fortunes with the South. Another contributory factor was the large number of Navy officers who did likewise and who knew the value of a Marine Corps. Various historians today are of the opinion that the rather modest record of the U.S. Marines during the Civil War was due to the fact that many of the better trained and more experienced officers still of an age for active service did "go South." No less than 19 former U.S. Marine officers were on the rolls of the Confederate Marine Corps at some time during the war. A twentieth officer, First Lieutenant Alexander W. Stark, who was not dismissed from the U.S. service until January 9, 1862, became a Confederate Army artillery battalion commander and the author of one of the few military texts produced in the Confederacy. He was an Army colonel at the end of the war. Those former U.S. officers who went into active Confederate Marine service gave a tone to the new Corps which from the beginning was a "regular" unit, not a "volunteer" unit.

Table 7

U.S. Marine Corps Separations

"List of all officers of the United States Navy and Marine Corps who left the service between December 1, 1860, and December 1, 1863, by resignation, dismissal, or desertion, to engage in the rebellion against the government, or otherwise." An excerpt from Executive Document No. 3, 38th Congress, 1st Session, Marines only.

NAMES	RANK	HOW LEFT THE SERVICE	REMARKS
Henry B. Tyler	Major	Dismissed	At the South
George H. Terrett	do.	do.	do.
Jabez C. Rich	Captain	do.	do.
Algernon S. Taylor	do.	do.	do.
Robert Tansill	do.	do.	do.
John D. Simms	do.	do.	do.
Israel Green	1st Lieutenant	do.	do.
J. R. H. Tattnall	do.	do.	do.
Adam N. Baker	do.	do.	do.
Chas. A. Henderson	do.	do.	do.
Henry B. Tyler, Jr.	do.	do.	do.
Julius E. Meiere	do.	do.	do.
George P. Turner	do.	do.	do.
Thos. S. Wilson	do.	do.	do.
Alex'r W. Stark	do.	do.	do.
Jacob Read	do.	Resigned	do.
And'w J. Hays	do.	do.	do.
George Holmes	do.	do.	do.
S. H. Matthews	do.	Dismissed	Whereabouts Unknown
Robert Kidd	do.	do.	do.
Geo. W. Cummins	2d Lieutenant	do.	do.
Calvin L. Sayers	do.	Resigned	At the South
Henry L. Ingraham	do.	do.	do.
Becket K. Howell	do.	do.	do.
J. H. Rathbone	do.	do.	Not at the South
Oscar B. Grant	do.	do.	do.
J. M. Reber	do.	Dismissed	do.
D. M. Sells	do.	Resigned	do.

[Errors in spelling names have not been corrected.]

It is a mistake to assume that all the U.S. Marine officers who were dismissed or resigned during the Civil War entered the Confederate service although this is the impression conveyed by a report of the U.S. Secretary of the Navy Gideon Welles.[2] For instance, Second Lieutenant George W. Cummins, dismissed, served as a lieutenant and captain in the 15th Ohio Infantry; Second Lieutenant Joel Howard Rathbone, resigned January 16, 1862, served as a captain in the 12th U.S. Infantry from February 1862 until December 1864, and Second Lieutenant David Miles Sells, resigned July 17, 1863, became lieutenant colonel and brevet colonel, 107th U. S. Colored Infantry.

The officers of the Confederate States Marine Corps were appointed on a company level first. Most of the field and staff officers were appointed later by original appointment rather than by promotion. For example, the Corps adjutant, Israel Greene, was originally appointed a captain, and, having qualified under the law, was appointed the next day as major and adjutant. Likewise, the second quartermaster, Algernon S. Taylor, received an original appointment as a line captain followed by an almost immediate transfer to the staff as major and quartermaster. In effect, at least, both were original appointments rather than promotions.

The first staff officer appointed was Major and Quartermaster Samuel Z. Gonzalez in April 1861. The remaining officers above company rank were appointed after the secession of Virginia and the enlargement of the Corps to regimental size. These top positions were allocated to Maryland and Virginia, either intentionally or otherwise. The post of colonel commandant and that of paymaster went to Marylanders while the lieutenant colonelcy, the field majority, and the post of adjutant went to Virginians. The second (and last) permanent major and quartermaster was also a Virginian. The Lower South had no Marine officers above the rank of company officers.

When the Corps was originally organized, all former U.S. Marine officers were commissioned as first lieutenants or higher. Of the five who had been second lieutenants in the U.S. Marine Corps (Turner, Wilson, Sayre, Ingraham, and Howell), all were originally commissioned as first lieutenants in the C.S. Marine Corps. Of those who had been first lieutenants in the U.S. Marine Corps (Simms, Greene, Read, Tattnall, Hays, Holmes, Baker, Tyler, Jr., and Meiere), six were originally commissioned captains in the C.S. Marine Corps (Simms, Greene, Read, Tattnall, Hays, and Holmes), while the other three (Baker, Tyler, Jr., and Meiere), new in their grades in the U.S. Service, were originally commissioned at their same grade of first lieutenant. Of the four captains from the U.S. Marine Corps (Terrett, Rich, Taylor, and Tansill), the senior captain (and brevet major), Terrett, was originally commissioned as a major and the other three in their same grade as captains. The Adjutant and Inspector of the U.S. Marine Corps with the rank of major (Tyler, Sr.) was originally commissioned in the C.S. Marine Corps as the lieutenant colonel of the Corps. By the end of the war, all the former U.S. Marine officers remaining in the C.S. Marine Corps had reached the rank of captain or higher.

A few of the top officers of the Corps were not products of the U.S. Marine Corps. These included the Colonel and Commandant, Lloyd J. Beall, the first Major and Quartermaster, Samuel Z. Gonzalez, the Major and Paymaster, Richard T. Allison, and two of the foremost company commanders, Reuben T. Thom and Alfred C. Van Benthuysen.

Table 8

Seniority List of Confederate Marine Officers
from U.S. Marine Corps

	Original entry into U.S.M.C.
General Staff	
Tyler, Henry B. (Major, A & I)	3 March 1823
Captains	
Terrett, George H. (Bvt. Major, 13 Sept. 1847)	1 April 1830
Rich, Jabez C.	12 June 1834
Taylor, Algernon S. (Bvt. Captain, 10 Mar. 1847)	21 February 1839
Tansill, Robert (Bvt. Captain, 17 Nov. 1847)	3 November 1840
First Lieutenants	
*Simms, John D. (Bvt. Captain, 13 Sept. 1847)	7 October 1841
Greene, Israel	3 March 1847
Read, Jacob	3 March 1847
Tattnall, John R. F.	3 November 1847
Hays, Andrew J.	4 December 1847
Holmes, George	3 March 1849
Baker, Adam N.	12 September 1853
Tyler, Henry B., Jr.	2 January 1855
Meiere, Julius Ernest	16 April 1855
Second Lieutenants	
Turner, George P.	27 September 1856
Wilson, Thomas S.	13 December 1857
Sayre, Calvin L.	3 June 1858
Ingraham, Henry L.	1 July 1858
Howell, Becket K.	1 August 1860

*Simms was promoted to captain, U.S.M.C., just before going South, but did not accept the promotion.

There can be little doubt that it was the intention of the former U.S. Marine officers to create a regular establishment for the Confederacy on the pattern of the prewar U.S. Marine Corps, and this philosophy was impressed upon the newly appointed junior officers. One newly appointed second lieutenant observed:

> Everything is so different from the Vol. Army to which I have been accustomed. Here all the formalities & etiquette of the Regular Service are rigidly enforced. I have been so used to treating men as my equals that I find it rather novel to treat them otherwise. However that will all wear off in course of time & the Government of men will come natural. All the officers here [at Camp Beall, Drewry's Bluff, Va.] are very obliging in giving any instructions we juniors may wish. There are only five here at present (besides the new appointments) and they are old U.S. Marine officers & each has served from 15 yrs to 30 years. They are old [hands?] though with one exception still young men — and wedded to their manner of life.[3]

It was precisely the opposite situation (that is, the virtual *absence* of experienced officers) in the U.S. Marine Corps during the war which apparently kept that organization from making the excellent record to which Americans have grown accustomed.

The Confederate Marine Corps at the outbreak of the war found itself supplied with officers for the rank of first lieutenant and above who were well equipped to act in a much higher capacity on the war-time standards which were thrust upon the new country. In fact, the inability to recruit the Corps to full strength combined with the pressing need of a mushrooming Army for trained officers led to the assignment of various experienced officers to Army duty.

With the over-supply of experienced officers available for the posts of first lieutenant and higher ranks, filling these posts was no problem. But the supply of junior officers (and by arbitrary definition, let us mean second lieutenants when we speak of "junior officers") was a problem. The original bill establishing the Corps called for the appointment of only six second lieutenants, but by April 26, 1861, Secretary of the Navy Mallory was urging the appointment of an additional second lieutenant for each company on the grounds that the frequent requirement for Marines to serve in small groups justified more junior officers than would be needed in any other arm of the military service. The Act of May 20, 1861, in effect, increased the number of companies from six to ten and at the same time provided two second lieutenants for each company. This increased the authorized number of second lieutenants from six to twenty.

The pattern of the source of junior officers was discernable by the close of 1861. It was the procurement of men from the Army with experience, usually as a commissioned or a noncommissioned officer.

Several facts stand out in an analysis of the officer personnel of the Confederate Marine Corps. First, those who had been on active duty in the U.S. service and had resigned were given the majority of the top positions in the Corps in preference to civilians. Second, all field and staff positions were filled by original appointments (as qualified above); no promotions being made to a rank above captain. Third, the main source of junior officers soon became the ranks of the Army with apparently no appointments being made from civilian life after 1861. Finally, and significantly, there was not one officer in the Confederate Marine Corps who was appointed by promotion from the ranks of the enlisted men of the Corps.

The assimilation of civilian appointees with a group of professional officers is always a difficult matter, and the Confederate Marine Corps was no exception. The problem was complicated further by the introduction of additional professional officers from time to time as they resigned from the Federal service or as they were released from Northern prisons where they had been confined since the outbreak of hostilities and sent South.

The determination of seniority was no easy task and caused some difficulty within the Corps. In the tables of seniority presented herein, the dates given for the date of appointment, date of acceptance, or date to rank from do not necessarily indicate the true date on which the officer first acted in the rank to which he had been appointed or promoted.

For instance, Becket K. Howell was appointed a captain to rank from February 1, 1863, vice Jacob Read who had been dismissed from the Corps as of that date, yet his promotion to that rank actually took place some time later. When the 1864 Navy Register was published, carrying the status of Marine officers as of October 31, 1863, Howell was still ranked as a first lieutenant. His nomination as a captain was received in the Senate on December 23, 1863, and confirmed on December 29, 1863. Yet he does not seem to have used the rank of captain during the war. During his service on the *Alabama*, up through her sinking on June 19, 1864, all references to him were as first lieutenant. Even on November 23, 1864, he was referred to as "Lieutenant Howell,"[4] indicating that as of that late date he had not been informed of his promotion.

The same seems to have been true about Calvin L. Sayre whose nomination and confirmation dates were the same as Howell's, but his rank dated back to December 11, 1862, the date of Turner's dismissal. Sayre's services after

Table 9
Seniority List of Captains, C.S.M.C.

Name	Born	App'd from	Relative rank in U.S.M.C.	App'd, accepted, or date of rank	Nominated in Congress or Senate	Confirmed	March '61	May 21 '61	June '61	July 15 '61	Aug. 14 '61	Oct. 26 '61	Dec. 3 '61	Dec. 4 '61	Dec. 5 '61	Jan. 22 '62	Feb. 15 '62	Oct. 10 '62	Dec. 11 '62	Feb. 1 '63	Notes
Rich, Jabez #	Me.	Va.	1	10/26/61	12/7/61							1	1	1	1	1	1	-	-	-	Dropped 10/10/62.
Taylor, Algernon S.	Va.	Va.	2	12/3/61	12/7/61								2	-	-	-	-	-	-	-	Prom. Q.M. 12/4/61.
Tansill, Robert	Va.	Va.	3	1/22/62	1/27/62										2	-	-	-	-	-	Resigned 2/15/62.
Simms, John D.	Va.	Va.	4	7/15/61	7/30/61 10/4/62	8/13/61 4/18/63				1	1	2	3	2	2	3	2	1	1	1	
Greene, Israel	N.Y.	Va.	5	6/19/61	7/30/61	8/13/61			1	2	-	-	-	-	-	-	-	-	-	-	Prom. Adjt. 6/19/61.
Read, Jacob @	Ga.	Ga.	6	5/21/61	5/21/61 10/4/62	5/21/61 *		1	2	3	2	3	4	3	3	4	3	2	2	-	Dismissed 2/1/63.
Tattnall, John R. F.	Conn.	Ga.	7	1/22/62	5/21/61 10/4/62	5/21/61 4/18/63									5	4	3	3	2	
Hays, Andrew J.	Ala.	Ala.	8	3/29/61	5/21/61 10/4/62	5/21/61 4/18/63	1	2	3	4	3	4	5	4	4	6	5	4	4	3	
Holmes, George	Me.	Fla.	9	3/29/61	7/30/61 10/4/62	8/13/61 4/18/63	2	3	4	5	4	5	6	5	5	7	6	5	5	4	
Thom, Reuben T.	Va.	Ala.		3/25/61	5/21/61 10/4/62	5/21/61 4/18/63	3	4	5	6	5	6	7	6	6	8	7	6	6	5	
Van Benthuysen, Alfred C.	N.Y.	La.		3/30/61	5/21/61 10/4/62	5/21/61 4/18/63	4	5	6	7	6	7	8	7	7	9	8	7	7	6	
Meiere, Julius E.	Conn.	D.C.	10	12/5/61 4/19/62	4/21/62 10/4/62	4/21/62 4/18/63									8	10	9	8	8	7	Vice Taylor.
Turner, George P.	Va.	Va.	11	12/5/61 4/19/62	4/21/62 10/4/62	4/21/62 4/18/63									9	11	10	9	-	-	Vice Tansill. Dismissed 12/11/62.
Wilson, Thomas S.	Tenn.	Mo.	12	10/10/62	10/10/62	4/18/63												10	9	8	Vice Rich.
Sayre, Calvin L.	Ala.	Ala.	13	12/11/62	12/23/63	12/29/63													10	9	Vice Turner.
Howell, Becket K.	Miss.	La.	14	2/1/63	12/23/63	12/29/63														10	Vice Read.

Officers ranking 1-9 in the U.S.M.C. originally appointed as captains; those ranking 10-14 were promoted to captains.

Jabez Rich left the U.S.M.C. at Gosport Navy Yard, 4/20/61, and went on duty immediately with the Virginia State Marine Corps. His dismissal from the U.S.M.C. was dated 5/22/61. The Virginia forces were transferred to Confederate service on 6/8/61.

* Although the Senate Journal does not show these nominations were recalled, these officers had been dismissed from the Corps before the nominations submitted 10/4/62 were confirmed.

@ Jacob Read accepted appointment as a captain, Co. D, 1st Regiment Georgia Regulars, 3/5/61.

Number authorized by Act of March 16, 1861 — 6.
Number authorized by Act of May 20, 1861 — 10.

Table 10

Seniority List of First Lieutenants, C.S.M.C.

Name	Born	Appd. from	Relative rank in U.S.M.C.	Appd., accepted, or date of rank	Nominated in Congress or Senate	Confirmed	March '61	April '61	May '61	June '61	July '61	August '61	Nov. 22, '61	Dec. 10, '61	Dec. 10, '61	Jan. 24, '62	Feb. 15, '62	July 4, '62	Oct. 10, '62	Dec. 11, '62	Jan. 11, '63	Feb. 1, '63	
Baker, Adam N.	Pa.	Fla.	1	6/6/61	7/30/61	8/13/61				1	1	1	1	1	1	1	1	1	-				Deserted 11/13/61. Dropped 10/10/62.
Tyler, Henry B., Jr.	D.C.	Va.	2	8/20/61	8/23/61	8/24/61						2	2	2	-								Dismd. 12/10/61.
Meiere, Julius E.	Conn.	D.C.	3	5/8/61	5/21/61	5/21/61			1	2	2	3	3	-									Prom. 12/5/61.
Turner, George P.	Va.	Va.	4	7/2/61	7/30/61	8/13/61					3	4	4	-									Prom. 12/5/61.
Wilson, Thomas S.	Tenn.	Mo.	5	1/24/62	1/27/62	2/13/62?										2	2	2	-				Prom. 10/10/62.
Sayre, Calvin L.	Ala.	Ala.	6	3/29/61	5/21/61, 10/4/62	5/21/61, 10/10/62	1	1	2	3	4	5	5	3	2	3	3	3	1	-			Prom. 12/11/62.
Ingraham, H. Laurens	S.C.	S.C.	7	3/29/61	5/21/61	5/21/61	2	2	3	4	5	6	-										Resgd. 11/22/61.
Howell, Becket K.	Miss.	La.	8	3/29/61	5/21/61, 10/4/62	5/21/61, 10/10/62	3	3	4	5	6	7	6	4	3	4	4	4	2	1	1	-	Prom. 2/1/63.
Henderson, Richard H.	D.C.	D.C.		4/16/61	5/21/61, 10/4/62	5/21/61, 10/10/62		4	5	6	7	8	7	5	4	5	5	5	3	2	2	1	
Raney, David G., Jr.	Fla.	Fla.		11/22/61	2/13/62, 10/4/62	2/15/62, 10/10/62							8	6	5	6	6	6	4	3	3	2	Vice Ingraham, 11/22/61.
Fendall, James R. Y.	D.C.	D.C.		12/10/61	2/13/62, 10/4/62	2/15/62, 10/10/62									6	7	7	7	5	4	4	3	Vice Tyler, Jr., 12/10/61.
Johnson, Wilbur F.	Ga.	Ga.		2/15/62?													8	-					Vice Meiere, 12/5/61. Resgd. 7/4/62.
Gwynn, Thomas P.	Wisc.	Va.		2/15/62	10/4/62	10/10/62											9	8	6	5	5	4	Vice Turner, 12/5/61.
Thurston, James J.	S.C.	S.C.		7/4/62	10/4/62	10/10/62												9	7	6	6	5	Vice Johnson, 7/4/62.
Cameron, Francis H.	N.C.	N.C.		10/10/62	10/4/62	10/10/62													8	7	7	6	Vice Baker, 10/10/62.
Claiborne, James F.		La.		10/10/62	10/4/62	10/10/62													9	8	-		Vice Wilson, 10/10/62. Dismd. 1/14/63.
Fergus, MacRee	Fla.	Mo.		10/10/62	10/4/62	10/10/62													10	9	8	7	Vice vacancy?
Bradford, David	La.	Miss.		12/11/62	12/23/63	12/29/63														10	9	8	Vice Sayre, 12/11/62.
Venable, Nathaniel E.	Va.	Texas		1/11/63	12/23/63	12/29/63															10	9	Vice Claiborne, 1/14/63.
Graves, Henry L.	Ga.	Ga.		2/1/63	12/23/63	12/29/63																10	Vice Howell, 2/1/63.

Number authorized by Act of March 16, 1861 - 6.
Number authorized by Act of May 20, 1861 - 10.

Table 11
Seniority List of Second Lieutenants, C.S.M.C.

Name	Born	Appd. from	Apptd., accepted, or date of rank	Nominated in Senate	Confirmed	APRIL '61	JULY '61	AUG. '61	OCT. '61	NOV. '61	DEC. '61	FEB. '62	JULY '62	AUG. 31 '62	OCT. 10 '62	OCT. 24 '62	NOV. 12 '62	DEC. 11 '62	JAN. 14 '63	FEB. '63	MAR. '63	APR. '63	JULY 11 '63	SEPT. 11 '63	FEB. '64	MAR.-APR. '64	MAY '64	JUNE '64	SEPT.-OCT. '64	
Raney, David G.	Fla.	Fla.	4/22/61	5/21/61	5/21/61	1	1	1	1	-	-	-	-	-	-	-	-	-	-	-	-	-	-	-	-	-	-	-	-	Prom. 1 Lt. 11/22/61, vice Ingraham.
Stockton, E. Canty	Fla.	S.C.	June '61?	7/30/61			2	-	-	-	-	-	-	-	-	-	-	-	-	-	-	-	-	-	-	-	-	-	-	Nomination rejected 8/16/61. Congress adjourned 8/31/61.
Fendall, James R. Y.	D.C.	Miss.	7/3/61	7/30/61	8/13/61		3	2	2	1	-	-	-	-	-	-	-	-	-	-	-	-	-	-	-	-	-	-	-	Prom. 1 Lt. 12/10/61, vice Tyler.
Johnson, Wilbur F.	Ga.	Ga.	6/29/61	7/30/61	7/30/61		4	3	3	2	1	-	-	-	-	-	-	-	-	-	-	-	-	-	-	-	-	-	-	Prom. 1 Lt. 2/15/62?, vice Meiere.
Lloyd, Edmund J.	Va.	Va.	Did not accept.	7/30/61	8/13/61		5	4	4	3	-	-	-	-	-	-	-	-	-	-	-	-	-	-	-	-	-	-	-	Nominated captain, C.S.A., 12/5/61.
Gwynn, Thomas P.	Wisc.	Va.	9/20/61	12/7/61	12/13/61				5	4	2	-	-	-	-	-	-	-	-	-	-	-	-	-	-	-	-	-	-	Prom. 1 Lt. 2/15/62, vice Turner.
Thurston, James J.	S.C.	S.C.	9/20/61	12/7/61	12/13/61				6	5	3	1	-	-	-	-	-	-	-	-	-	-	-	-	-	-	-	-	Prom. 1 Lt. 7/4/62, vice Johnson.
Cameron, Francis H.	N.C.	N.C.	9/20/61	12/7/61	12/13/61				7	6	4	2	1	1	-	-	-	-	-	-	-	-	-	-	-	-	-	-	Prom. 1 Lt. 10/10/62, vice Baker.
Claiborne, James F.		La.	10/28/61	1/27/62					8	7	5	3	2	2	-	-	-	-	-	-	-	-	-	-	-	-	-	-	Prom. 1 Lt. 10/10/62, vice Wilson.
Fergus, MacRee	Fla.	Mo.	10/9/61	12/7/61	12/13/61				9	8	6	4	3	3	-	-	-	-	-	-	-	-	-	-	-	-	-	-	Prom. 1 Lt. 10/10/62, vice vacancy?
Ramsey, Robert M.		Tenn.	10/28/61	12/7/61	12/13/61				10	9	7	5	-	-	-	-	-	-	-	-	-	-	-	-	-	-	-	-	Dismissed 7/9/62.
Fowler, John D.	Va.	Ala.	10/26/61	12/7/61	12/13/61				11	10	8	6	4	-	-	-	-	-	-	-	-	-	-	-	-	-	-	-	Died 8/31/62.
Bradford, David	La.	Miss.	11/22/61	12/7/61	12/13/61					11	9	7	5	4	1	1	1	-	-	-	-	-	-	-	-	-	-	-	Prom. 1 Lt. 12/11/62, vice Sayre.
Venable, Nathaniel E.	Va.	Texas	10/24/62	1/20/63	1/23/63											2	2	1	-	-	-	-	-	-	-	-	-	-	Prom. 1 Lt. 1/14/63, vice Claiborne.
Graves, Henry L.	Ga.	Ga.	10/24/62	1/20/63	1/23/63											3	3	2	1	-	-	-	-	-	-	-	-	-	Prom. 1 Lt. 2/1/63, vice Howell.
Doak, Henry M.	Tenn.	Tenn.	11/12/62	1/20/63	1/23/63												4	3	2	1	1	1	1	1	1	1	1	
Berry, Albert S.	Ky.	Ky.	2/15/63	2/27/63	3/6/63															2	2	2	2	2	2	2	2	2	

Continued on page 179.

Table 11 contd. Seniority List of Second Lieutenants, C.S.M.C.

Name	Born	Appd. from	Appd. accepted, date of rank	Nominated in Senate	Confirmed	APRIL '61	JULY '61	AUG. '61	OCT. '61	NOV. '61	DEC. '61	FEB. '62	JULY '62	AUG. 31 '62	OCT. 10 '62	OCT. 24 '62	NOV. 12 '62	DEC. 11 '62	JAN. 14 '63	FEB. '63	MAR. '63	APR. '63	JULY 11 '63	SEPT. 11 '63	FEB. '64	MAR.-APR. '64	MAY '64	JUNE '64	SEPT.-OCT. '64	Remarks
Neufville, Edward F.	Ga.	Ga.	2/23/63	3/3/63	3/6/63															3	3	3	3	3	3	3	3	3	3	
Van de Graaff, John S.	Ky.	Texas	3/17/63	3/10/63	3/17/63																4	4	4	-	-	-	-	-	-	Resigned 9/11/63.
Brent, Daniel G.	D.C.	Fla.	3/30/63	3/30/63	3/30/63																5	5	5	4	4	4	4	4	4	
Murdoch, J. Campbell	Md.	Md.	4/8/63	4/1/63	4/8/63																	6	6	5	5	5	5	5	5	
Roberts, Samuel M.	Pa.	La.	4/8/63	4/1/63	4/8/63																	7	7	6	6	6	6	6	6	Vice Johnson.
Rapier, John L.	Ala.	La.	7/11/63	12/23/63	12/29/63																		8	7	7	7	7	7	7	Vice Raney.
Stephenson, Lloyd B.	Va.	Va.	2/11/64	2/9/64	2/11/64																				8	8	8	8	8	Vice Fendall.
Thomson, Ruffin	Miss.	Miss.	2/11/64	2/9/64	2/11/64																				9	9	9	9	9	Vice Gwynn.
Pratt, Thos. St. Geo.	Md.	Md.	2/11/64	2/9/64	2/11/64																				10	10	10	10	10	Vice Thurston.
McCune, Henry H.	Mo.	Mo.	3/14/64	5/5/64	5/20/64																					11	11	11	11	Vice Cameron.
Crenshaw, Edward	Ala.	Ala.	4/11/64	5/5/64	5/20/64																					12	12	12	12	Vice MacRee.
Eggleston, Everard T.	Va.	Texas	5/20/64	5/30/64	5/31/64																						13	13	13	Vice Claiborne.
Roberts, J. De Berniere	N.C.	S.C.	6/16/64	6/7/64	6/9/64																							14	14	
Smith, Eugene R.	Tenn.	Tenn.	9/13/64	11/10/64	11/23/64																								15	Vice Fowler.
Pearson, John A.	Ark.	Ark.	10/8/64	11/10/64	11/23/64																								16	Vice Bradford.

Number authorized by Act of March 16, 1861 - 6.
Number authorized by Act of May 20, 1861 - 20.

August 28, 1862, were in the Provisional Army with the rank of major. It is not possible to tell from the existing records when he first used the Marine rank of captain. There is a record of his requesting permission to purchase uniform cloth from the Naval Storekeeper at Mobile Bay on May 17, 1864, signing his request as a captain, C. S. Marine Corps.[5]

Upon the renomination of the officers of the Marine Corps on October 4, 1862, necessitated by the transition from a provisional to a permanent form of government, the list was referred to the Committee on Naval Affairs. Upon the report of the Committee, the nominations were first ordered on October 7 to lie on the table, and then on October 10, 1862, all nominations except those for captain were approved. The President was requested at that time to furnish the Senate with the rank and grade of the resigned U.S.M.C. officers and to verify whether John R. F. Tattnall was commanding the 29th Alabama Infantry Regiment.

President Davis replied the next day that John R. F. Tattnall had been given the provisional rank of colonel and assigned to the command of the 29th Alabama Infantry by authority of Act No. 383 of the Provisional Congress. He submitted at the same time a letter from Secretary of the Navy Mallory dealing with the resigned U.S. Marine Corps officers. Mallory explained that John D. Simms was at the head of the grade of first lieutenant in the U.S. Marines, and had been commissioned captain in the Federal service but had refused the commission and resigned. Following him in the grade of first lieutenant were Jacob Read, John R. F. Tattnall, Andrew J. Hays, and George Holmes, in that order. All of these had been advanced a grade and appointed captains in the Marine Corps of the Confederate States. They had been nominated and confirmed in this order by the Provisional Congress at its second session. Mallory then stated that Captain Tattnall had been ordered to report to the Secretary of War for duty on the application of the War Department. The Navy Department had not been informed of his duty assignment.

The confirmation of these officers finally reached the debate stage in the Senate on April 10, 1863, to no decision. Debate was resumed on the 17th, only to be postponed again "until tomorrow." Finally, on April 18, the Senators reached a decision. Mr. Clay, of Alabama, introduced a resolution supporting his contention that Captain Reuben Thom was entitled to be the senior captain of the Corps. Clay argued that Thom had been the first Marine captain to be appointed and since Captains Simms, Read, Tattnall, Hays, and Holmes had only been first lieutenants in the U.S. Marine Corps, their automatic seniority in the Confederate service applied only to appointments as Marine first lieutenants. The resolution called upon the President to renominate the Marine captains upon consideration of the facts and law "in such order of rank as he may seem just and proper." But after a close vote, the resolution was defeated and the nominations confirmed.[6]

Had the resolution been approved and the nominations submitted as Senator Clay desired, Thom would have been the senior captain in the Corps. Captain Alfred C. Van Benthuysen would have been the fourth ranking captain after Thom, Andrew J. Hays, and George Holmes until outranked by the appointments of Jabez Rich, Algernon S. Taylor, and Robert Tansill, all formerly captains in the U.S. Marine Corps. The appointments of these last three were all of a fairly temporary nature. Most significant, both Thom and Van Benthuysen would have ranked the officer who actually served as senior captain of the Corps from October 10, 1862, until the end of the war, John D. Simms.

In view of another happening in the Corps at this time, it is an open question whether Senator Clay's fight over the captains' nominations might not have been designed to help Captain Van Benthuysen out of a predicament. He was being court-martialed during October 1862 as a result of a report submitted to Captain Simms and passed on to higher authority after the original complainant requested to withdraw the report. In a draft of a statement prepared for the officers of the Court Martial (which may or may not have been submitted), Van Benthuysen stated, "I would here remark . . . that there is a question of rank between myself and the said Capt Simms . . . ."[7] After April 18, 1863, this question of rank was moot.

Van Benthuysen apparently was not aware of the decision of Attorney General Thomas H. Watts on February 13, 1863, concerning the relative rank of former U.S. officers in the Confederate service. Watts ruled that the Relative Rank Law *authorized* the President to date commissions for officers resigning before the date of the Act, March 16, 1861, so as "to secure to them the same relative position that they held in the former service," but it was not *imperative* nor *required* that he do so. The Act of May 20, 1861, applying to those resigning before or after the Act also *authorized* the President, but it was not *imperative*.

The Attorney General's basic conclusion was that "the rank and position such Officers hold in the Confederate Navy, depend on the will of the President. Such Officers, when they receive appointments, will be entitled to hold such rank and relative position in our Navy as the President chooses to assign them."[8]

OFFICER SELECTION

Once the Corps had been organized, a set procedure was established for the selection and qualification of new second lieutenants.

Marine regulations provided that any citizen receiving an appointment in the Corps should appear before a Board of Officers constituted by the Secretary of the Navy. The Board was to examine the candidate as to his physical ability, moral character, attainments, and general fitness for the service, and his commission depended upon the favorable report of the Board. The candidate from civil life for second lieutenant could not be over twenty-five years of age.

The first step toward obtaining a commission was to make application in writing, usually supported by letters of recommendation, preferably by individuals of political importance. It was expected that a man already in the military service would also present the endorsements of his superior officers.

The general procedure is covered in the following excerpt from a letter to the father of a potential Marine officer:

> I enclose your authority for your son to appear before the Examining Board in this city for examination for the position of 2nd Lieut. in the Marine Corps. I could not get an appointment as 2nd Lieut. in the Navy, but this position will probably suit your son better.
>
> He had best get a furlough of 30 days or longer — come here and undergo his examination, and if he pass, then resign to take the command in the Marine Corps. He will thus have his command in the Army to fall back upon, if he fail to pass examinations.
>
> He will be examined upon English grammar, arithmetic, and geography mainly. His bearing and deportment will have much to do in deciding his success. Gentlemanly bearing has great influence upon the board. . . .
>
> NB. The applicant is required a short letter or essay to test his knowledge of English grammar.[9]

Assuming that the written application was acceptable, a letter (such as referred to above) would then be sent from the Secretary of the Navy to the candidate authorizing him to appear before the Examining Board. One such letter reads as follows:

> Sir:
>
> If between twenty one and twenty five years of age, you are authorized to appear before a Board of officers of the Marine Corps for examination for admission into the Corps as a Second Lieutenant, and will present this letter to Col. Lloyd J. Beall Commandant of the Corps in this City.[10]

This was not a fast procedure. Ruffin Thomson submitted his letter of application in April 1863, and it was not until December that he received his letter authorizing him to appear before the Board.

Thomson wrote about both his written examination and his personal appearance before the Board. His written exam in 1864 was based on

> a good English education, grammar, arithmetic, algebra, geometry, mathematical and physical geography, a knowledge of the governments of England, France and Russia, a question or two as to the Crimean War, and wound up by requesting a statement of my services in the field.[11]

The Board apparently examined the various testimonials on file with the application while the personal appearance apparently covered such intangibles as to whether the candidate was a "gentleman" and whether he would make a proper representation of the Corps in society. In order to make as favorable an impression as possible, Ruffin Thomson records how he felt obliged to borrow clothes from some of his acquaintances so that he could appear before the Board as well dressed as possible.

The examination does not seem to have been superficial, but, on the contrary, a wearing experience. Henry Graves wrote after his examination was over, "I am too tired to add more tonight than that the examination is over and I passed."[12]

Thomson was examined on January 14, 1864, and on February 11, 1864, he was officially notified of his appointment by the following letter:

> Sir: You are hereby informed that the President has appointed you by and with the advice and consent of the Senate a Second Lieutenant, in the Marine Corps of the Confederate States. You are requested to signify your acceptance or non-acceptance of this appointment; and should you accept you will sign before a magistrate, the oath of office herewith, and forward the same with your letter of acceptance to this Department.[13]

Where the new second lieutenant was already holding an Army commission, it became necessary for him to resign it before his Marine commission could be effective. Here is a sample of the type of letter sent in such a case:

> Sir — The Board by which you were last examined for the position of 2d Lieut of Marines have made a favorable report in your case, and upon producing the acceptance of your resignation as an officer in the Army you will receive the appointment of Second Lieutenant in the Marine Corps.[14]

Once the newly appointed second lieutenant had taken the oath and forwarded it to the Navy Department along with his letter of acceptance, he received his first orders and duty assignment. They were sent to Camp Beall at Drewry's Bluff for Marine training and indoctrination. Here they came under the observing eyes of senior officers who were "old timers" from the U.S. Marine Corps, bent upon molding these new officers into Marines.

The demands upon the new officers were far from excessive. Thomson commented that he had a daily lesson in tactics, guard duty once a week, and the duty to attend Company Roll Call each alternate week.

After orientation for several months at Camp Beall, the new officer was transferred to either the Marine Company D stationed at Mobile, Company E at Savannah, to a naval station or yard, or to the command of the Marine guard on a naval vessel. Those Marine guards usually numbered from 12 to 30 men. A definite attempt was made to have all newly appointed officers have duty on board ship by rotating their assignments. For instance, in November 1863, Colonel Lloyd J. Beall wrote Flag-Officer William W. Hunter, Commanding Forces Afloat, at Savannah, that the various commanders of the guards on board ship should be relieved every six months and replaced with an officer serving on shore duty with Captain John R. F. Tattnall. This was an order from the Secretary of the Navy.

The education of the new Marine officer was not considered complete at the end of his initial training and indoctrination period. At Savannah, at least, orders were issued by Captain Tattnall for his officers to report for bi-weekly examinations to test their progress in certain elementary military works. At 3 P.M. on Thursdays the junior officers were to be tested on Hardee's *Light Infantry Tactics*, and Volumes I and II of *General Army Regulations*. At the same hour on Saturdays the examinations were to be on Mahan's *Field Fortifications* and *Outpost Duties*. The Officer of the Day was to be excused from attending these examinations unless they should be adjourned to the Barracks.[15] Flag-Officer Hunter was approached on the propriety of having the Marine officers of Company E serving afloat report to Captain Tattnall for these sessions.

Edward Crenshaw made various notations in his diary relative to his studies at Drewry's Bluff in late 1864. He mentioned studying English grammar, arithmetic, Army regulations, artillery and infantry tactics, Todd's *Manual*, history, *Outpost Duty*, etc. His cultural readings included the Bible, a chapter on the philology of the English language, and chapters from *Thadeus of Warsaw*.[16] Crenshaw's assignment to ship duty apparently curtailed his studies as they were rarely mentioned in his diary from then on.

We can obtain a good picture of the life of a Marine officer assigned to ship duty in one of the Confederate defensive squadrons from the letters of Lieutenant Henry L. Graves.

After serving an indoctrination period at Camp Beall, Graves was ordered to Savannah to serve on the ironclad being completed in that city. The *Savannah*, as this new ironclad was named, was launched on Wednesday, February 4, 1863, but she was not ready for occupancy by her crew. Two months later he wrote home that he was currently rooming on board the *Sampson*, a converted river steamer used as a tender. He went ashore for his meals and ate at a boarding house. Fortunately, he carefully recorded a daily schedule in a letter to home:

> My daily programme is as follows: rise at 7½ — receive my Sergeants morning report. attend to various little company morning duties — have the boat manned, go ashore & walk a half mile up town to breakfast at Eight. After breakfast I returned immediately to the Ship and remain till 1½ when I walk up to dinner. The morning hours have been spent mostly in writing and putting the company accounts to rights. After dinner I come back and stay till suppertime — Some times going ashore a half hour sooner in order to take a walk up "Bull Street" and meet the pretty girls. After supper I return aboard ship and go to sleep by 8½ or 9.[17]

It was not until July 21, 1863, that he wrote that he was finally going on board the *Savannah*. Then for some six months he would be serving on board ship, to be replaced by another officer at the expiration of that time in order to rotate the duty and experience.

Graves made a point of writing home that his mother need not worry about him because of the *Savannah's* trips down the river as he was never called upon for guard duty, only midshipmen and master's mates going on that duty. But Marine officers of the James River Squadron did draw assignments of this nature. Lieutenant Edward Crenshaw had hardly reported for duty on board the C.S.S. *Virginia* in February 1865 than he was sent down river on night picket duty with a party of seven others (one midshipman, four seamen, and two Marines). This type of picket duty, involving all-night duty, recurred every few days.

DISCIPLINE AND PUNISHMENT

During the winter of 1861 occurred one of those unpleasant episodes that mar the smooth functioning of a military organization.[18] On November 10 First Lieutenant Henry B. Tyler, Jr., obviously under the influence of liquor, confronted Second Lieutenant James R. Y. Fendall in the Warrington Navy Yard and commenced an insulting and abusive verbal attack. Fendall, who was on duty as Officer of the Guard that day, avoided taking up the argument and left for dinner. Tyler followed into the Mess Room and continued the verbal attack, and, becoming more incensed, shook his fist close to Fendall's face, calling him "a damn scoundrel, damn son of a b____, and damned aboli-tionist!" Lieutenant Isaac S. Hyams, C.S.A., assigned to Marine duty, who was in the room, then ordered Private Conner to restrain Tyler from making a personal assault upon Fendall. Fendall then left for the Guard House.

About half an hour later, Tyler again met up with Fendall at the Central Wharf Guard House and renewed his verbal attack upon the harassed officer. In front of Captain Douglas West, Louisiana Infantry and Captain of the Guard, Tyler proclaimed he distrusted the loyalty of Fendall, citing a brother or brothers in the Federal service as proof of his contention. (This must have been a reference to Lieutenant Philip R. Fendall, Jr., of the U.S. Marine Corps, who was James' brother.) Tyler finally desisted under pressure from Captain West, and Fendall promised settlement on the morrow when he was off duty.

Tyler managed to make quite a day of it by getting caught attempting to pinch a bottle of whiskey from the Officers' Mess. He claimed the whiskey had been given him by Lieutenant Richard Henderson. Still not satisfied, he wandered over to the camp of the Louisiana Infantry where his intoxication was so evident that the officers avoided him.

This was too much, and on November 29, 1861, Tyler was court-martialed, found guilty, and recommended for dismissal from the Corps. The sentence was approved by General Bragg and the dismissal published on December 10, 1861, as a part of General Orders No. 17 of that date.

This must have been a real blow to his father, the lieutenant colonel of the Corps, who started 30 days leave that same day. Young Tyler had been ar-rested in New York City less than six months previously for being drunk and disorderly and for using seditious language. At that time he had only been in port a few days off the slaver *Nightingale* which had been captured off the coast of Africa and brought to port by a prize crew from the sloop-of-war *Saratoga*.

Tyler had injudiciously chosen the vicinity of Police Headquarters to in-stitute a noisy street-corner tirade of cursing the Stars and Stripes, calling General Scott a "hoary-headed old villain," and proclaiming him to be a traitor who would be shot if they could once get him to Virginia. Finally the heavy hand of the law took him to Police Headquarters where he was detained for the night and sent to the Navy Yard the next morning.[19] Tyler apparently tendered his resignation as an officer in the U.S. Marine Corps, but it was not accepted, and he was dismissed as of June 21, 1861, just six days after reaching port. Here was the unenviable record of a man who had been dismissed from both the United States and Confederate Marine Corps within less than six months.

Another officer who encountered disciplinary problems and almost lost his commission as a direct result was Captain Alfred C. Van Benthuysen. Captain Van Benthuysen became involved in two courts-martial, one right after the other, based on incidents in late 1862. The first incident took place on October 2, 1862, at a picnic given by Major Drewry at Drewry's Bluff. The first charge was conduct unbecoming an officer and a gentleman, and the second charge was using reproachful words in violation of the 15th Article for the better government of the Navy. Specifically, Van Benthuysen was accused of assaulting and striking Surgeon Algernon S. Garnett, C.S.N., with his hand, of calling on Second Lieutenant James F. Claiborne, C.S.M.C., to shoot Surgeon Garnett, and with charging Surgeon Garnett with ungentlemanly conduct.[20]

The detailed information on his court-martial is derived largely from an address to the Officer of the Court written by Captain Van Benthuysen which may or may not have been delivered.[21] Available evidence indicates that when a somewhat intoxicated Dr. Garnett threatened to smack the Captain's face, Van Benthuysen responded by striking him. Whether or not ladies were present is not clear. It seems that in the midst of the altercation Van Benthuysen called on Lieutenant Claiborne to shoot the doctor who was holding the captain on the ground. On the other hand, Dr. Garnett was accused of being armed while searching for Lieutenant Claiborne. Captain Van Benthuysen, conscious of Dr. Garnett's some two hundred and thirty pounds in opposition to a much slighter built Claiborne, felt amply justified in calling the doctor "a damned coward."

Dr. Garnett apparently reported the incident that evening to Captain John D. Simms, the senior Marine officer, only to minimize the incident and attempt to withdraw his charges the next morning. But the charges were submitted by Captain Simms and led to the court-martial which was conducted October 20-28, 1862, with Lieutenant Colonel Henry B. Tyler, C.S.M.C., as presiding officer.

In any event, the Court found Van Benthuysen guilty as charged and recommended his dismissal from the Marine service. However, the Secretary of the Navy deemed the sentence "unwarranted by the testimony and uncalled for by the interests of the service and recommended a mitigation of the sentence." President Davis confirmed the sentence but reduced the punishment to suspension from rank and command for four months from October 28, 1862.[22] Van Benthuysen was released from arrest for these offenses on January 21, 1863.

But in the meantime, Van Benthuysen had managed to get into trouble again on December 5, 1862, while still awaiting sentence from his first court-martial. According to the new charges and specifications, he was drunk or sufficiently under the influence on that day to attract attention, violate his arrest, disobey the orders of his superior officer, treat his superior officer with contempt, utter seditious or mutinous words, and use provoking or reproachful words.

The story of the incidents leading to these charges can be reconstructed to a degree from the specifications. It seems that Captain Van Benthuysen, who had been doing some drinking, was ordered by Captain Simms to go to his quarters in camp. Van Benthuysen apparently responded that he didn't acknowledge Simms as his superior officer and refused to accept orders from him. He further retorted that if he was taken back to camp he would have to be carried. In the words that were passed, Van Benthuysen threatened Simms, "I can take those men (referring to the guard) and arrest you," and, exploding with wrath from the circumstances surrounding the first court-martial, angrily charged Simms, "Either you, Doctor Garnett, or Captain Thom, told a G_____ D_____d lie!"

Also involved was an order issued January 2, 1863, by Captain Simms from Headquarters, C. S. M. Battalion, Camp Beall, requiring that officers in arrest leaving camp by permission must report their return to Captain S. S. Lee, C.S.N., commanding the Post through their immediate commanding officer. This order was presented to Van Benthuysen by Second Lieutenant N. E. Venable in his capacity as Acting Adjutant at the Camp. Van Benthuysen's immediate response to Venable was to say he would pay no attention to the order unless it came from Flag-Officer Forrest or Captain Lee.

The incident of December 5, 1862, plus the other incident of January 2, 1863, apparently attracted considerable attention as six witnesses appeared before the court, namely, Captain John D. Simms, First Lieutenants R. H. Henderson and T. P. Gwynn, Second Lieutenants David Bradford and N. E. Venable, and Sergeant Grogan.[23] Details of this second court-martial are sparse, but apparently Van Benthuysen was again found guilty as charged, sentenced to dismissal, and had his sentence commuted by the President to suspension from rank and command.

This last suspension lasted for more than a year, and it was not until May 26, 1864, that Van Benthuysen was restored to duty and ordered to report to then-Brigadier General George W. C. Lee, commanding the local forces in Richmond. Just a few days later, June 3, Van Benthuysen was ordered to Mobile to report to Admiral Buchanan for duty. He reported on June 13, but just two days later was offered his choice of the command of his company at Drewry's Bluff or the command of the guard at Wilmington, North Carolina. With Simms still at Drewry's Bluff, it is no surprise that he chose to go to Wilmington, arriving on June 29, 1864, to enter upon the duties of his new assignment. Probably an outgrowth of these courts-martial was the dismissal of Lieutenant Claiborne from the service on January 14, 1863, but details have not been located.

Among the Marine officers who were severely disciplined was Second Lieutenant Robert M. Ramsey, of Tennessee. Ramsey was not in the Corps very long and very little about him is to be found in the records beyond his appointment on October 28, 1861, and his dismissal as of July 9, 1862. According to his father, several Marine officers got one day's leave to participate in the battle of Malvern Hill, which took place on July 1, 1862. They overstayed their leave until the close of the battle and were arrested for being absent without leave when they returned. Their excuses were not accepted, and they resigned their commissions.[24]

Ramsey did not resign; he was dismissed as of July 9, 1862. One trouble with this story is that there was only nine days between the battle of Malvern Hill and Ramsey's dismissal date. The dismissal date could have been back-dated to the date when the offense was committed. A second problem with the story is that no other Marine Corps officer was dismissed or resigned around the same general time frame.

The case of Captain George P. Turner develops a certain amount of admiration for a man who literally fought his way back. Turner was dismissed on June 25, 1861, from the U.S. Marine Corps after almost five years service. Starting as a first lieutenant, he was soon promoted to captain in the Confederate Marine Corps. Then something went wrong and what was described only as an "unfortunate occurance" took place. Turner's sister, Henrietta, later wrote that her brother had said that she must not grieve for his dismissal might prove a blessing to him. She was active in his behalf and succeeded in securing the promise of the Secretary of War to give her brother a commission on his pledge to "abstain during the War from all intoxicating drinks."

Turner went to Chattanooga immediately after his dismissal and enlisted as a private in the 1st Kentucky Cavalry. Attending strictly to his business, he soon proved his worth, and in less than six months was commissioned in the Army as an assistant adjutant general with the rank of captain. By June 1864, he was being recommended for a Regular Army commission or the restoration of his Marine Corps commission. Discussions were under way to restore his Marine Corps commission, and an appointment between the Secretaries of the Navy and War was virtually arranged when the war ended. There seems little doubt but that Turner would have had his commission restored.

Simple justice requires the recitation of the facts above to eliminate the black mark of dismissal that stands unqualified in the Navy Register. Turner settled in North Alabama after the war, and older residents remember him today with respect and affection even though many years have passed since his death in 1905.

PRISONERS OF WAR AND ESCAPE

On two separate occasions Confederate Marine officers were involved in daring prison escapes. One was the temporarily successful escape of Lieutenant James Thurston from Fort Warren, Massachusetts, in August 1863, and the second was the escape of Captain J. Ernest Meiere and Lieutenants James R. Y. Fendall and John L. Rapier from a Federal prison in New Orleans in October 1864. While neither of these experiences played any particular part in the development of the Corps, they were at least illustrative of the aggressiveness, daring, and personal courage of those representatives of the officer personnel.

Lieutenant James Thurston, C.S.M.C., was captured when the C.S.S. *Atlanta* was captured by the U.S.S. *Weehawken* in Wassaw Sound, below Savannah, on June 17, 1863. First sent to Fort LaFayette, he was transferred to Fort Warren, on July 4, 1863.

The prisoners at Fort Warren were confined in the casemates of the old fort. Each casemate had a musketry slit through the thick masonry wall perhaps six or eight feet high and about seven inches wide at the outside edge of the wall, the opening flaring inward to permit the movement of muskets within the casemate. Lieutenant Joseph W. Alexander, C.S.N., also of the *Atlanta*, experimented and found that he could slip through this musketry slit by stripping down to his shirt. Alexander confided this information to Major Reid Sanders, an Army quartermaster by rank, but better known as the son of the mysterious Confederate Agent George N. Sanders. As the word was passed around, each prisoner cautiously tested his body against the narrow opening, but only four officers were found who had the requisite narrow frames — Alexander, Sanders, Navy First Lieutenant Charles W. Read, the commander of the notorious *Tacony*, and Marine First Lieutenant James Thurston.

The occasional walks allowed the prisoners were now eagerly utilized to familiarize themselves with the number of guards, their posts, the position of the loopholes or musketry slits in relation to the outer works of the fort, and the neighboring islands. There were a formidable set of obstacles to overcome once out of the casemate. Once out, the moat had to be crossed, the coverface or demilune to be scaled, all sentries to be eluded, and, once the water's edge of George's Island was reached, a half mile of water to be traversed to the nearest of the adjacent islands, Lovel's Island. And none of the four slender men who could squeeze through the casemate openings could swim!

A try was made on the dark and drizzly night of Sunday, August 16, 1863, by Sanders, Read, Alexander, and Thurston. The men let themselves out of the casemate by means of a knotted rope, collected their clothing and various articles to make floating easier, crawled cautiously over the bank of the moat and slid down its outer slope. They passed through a thicket of weeds and reached the water's edge a few hundred feet farther away. They then assembled the materials for a crude raft and shoved out into the cold and rough water. Buffeted by an adverse wind and rough waves, shivering with cold, and unable to steer their fragile float, they were forced to abandon the struggle and allow the wind to blow them back to the shore of George's Island where the prison was located.

They were then forced to retrace their steps back to the casemate and return themselves to custody. By doing this without alerting the Federal guards, they kept the stage set for another try under more favorable circumstances.

The four then invited Thomas Sherman, a Federal seaman who had been imprisoned for voicing treasonable sentiments, and N. B. [J. N.?] Prydé, quarter gunner of Read's ship, the *Tacony*, to join them in the next bid for freedom. Both of these men were small enough to squeeze through the casemate loophole, and both of them were good swimmers.

The group made the second escape attempt two nights after the first try. The new plan called for Sherman and Prydé to swim to Lovel's Island, steal a boat, and return for the other four, two at a time. Sherman and Prydé swam off as agreed, but they never returned, and were never heard of again. After hours of waiting for Sherman and Prydé to return with a boat, the remaining four drew lots for two to cling to a crude raft composed of an old target, a plank, and an assortment of empty tin cans and try to get to Lovel's Island for the boat. It fell by lot for Sanders and Read to remain and upon Thurston and Alexander to make the try.

Sanders and Read lay hidden in the weeds with their coats wrapped around them. A Federal sentry, observing the absence of the target, called the neighboring sentry to help him search for it. They searched the area for the missing target, threw rocks around in vain hope of hearing them land on the missing target, and even prodded into the weeds with their bayonets. During this process both Sanders and Read received blows from rocks and were even prodded with a bayonet without their presence being suspected.

With the approach of dawn and the failure of Alexander and Thurston to return, the two fugitives decided to return to confinement in the casemate. They were unsuccessful in their efforts to slip back into prison and were discovered by the astonished guards and recaptured.

Thurston and Alexander pushed off from the prison island on their frail raft and finally made Lovel's Island, exhausted, wet, and weary. After a short rest, they paddled a dory to a sailboat lying at anchor a short distance off shore, boarded her, and took possession of the vacant craft. They sailed over to the rendezvous point to pick up Read and Sanders, satisfied themselves that the contact could not be made, then pushed out to sea. Their trip took them past Nahant, Swampscot, Marblehead, Beverly, Manchester, and finally to Gloucester. At Cape Ann Light, they landed in an attempt to get additional clothing and food, but were forced to settle for bread and water.

Resuming their escape attempt, they reached Rye Beach at night where they purchased hats and pantaloons with some of the $15 Thurston had with him. They again put out to sea, but were hailed by a boat from the U.S. Revenue Cutter *Dobbin* and boarded at about 11 A.M. on August 20, 1863. They almost succeeded in passing themselves off as Eastport fishermen, but a roll of $300 of Confederate money in Thurston's shirt pocket was their undoing. That evidence against them was too strong, and they finally confessed to being escaped prisoners. The two fugitives were taken to Portland, Maine, and placed in jail, being returned to Fort Warren on September 7, 1863.[25]

A year after the prison attempt, Mrs. Anna J. Sanders, of Abingdon, Virginia, wrote President Davis on August 25, 1864, requesting that the name of her son, Reid, be placed on the list of the first prisoners to be exchanged. At the same time, she requested that the "gallant Lieutenant Read of the *Tacony*" be included. She referred to him as "my dear son's companion in this escape through the loop-hole of the fort."[26]

Secretary James A. Seddon notified Mrs. Sanders on September 8, 1864, that attempts had been made to exchange her son, but they had failed. He reported the Commissioner of Exchange had gone as far as the policy of the Government would permit to bring about an exchange. But this correspondence was to no avail. Major Reid Sanders, the 27-year old son of the mysterious Confederate Agent, George N. Sanders, had died at Fort Warren, Boston, on September 3, 1864.[27]

Among those captured at Fort Gaines, Alabama, on August 5, 1864, was Second Lieutenant John L. Rapier, C.S.M.C., who managed to escape from a Federal prison in New Orleans shortly thereafter. Fortunately for our history of the Confederate Marine Corps, he later told his story for publication, and it is given here in condensed form.[28]

The prisoners were first confined in the Picayune Press, but a few days later were transferred up town to the Union Press building. [These references to "press" buildings refer to cotton presses, not newspaper presses.] Here Rapier almost succeeded in walking out of prison and was only prevented by the corporal of the guard insisting that he get the permission of the sergeant before going off for a cup of coffee. Unfortunately, the sergeant became suspicious and, throwing the beam from his lantern upon Rapier, discovered his true identity and returned him to the prison proper.

After about three weeks, some eighteen prisoners (including Rapier) were selected as special "trading material" by the Federals to bring about the exchange of an Admiral's son and several of his brother officers. [I have not been able to verify this.]

The group was transferred to the former offices of Hewitt, Norton & Co. on Common Street, between Carondalet and Baronne, under the special guard of U.S. Regulars.

The men resolved to escape, if possible, and began planning to cut through the brick wall. The work on the escape was handicapped by eight or ten roll calls a day. To provide a noisy cover for their work, they obtained permission to scrub the prison daily and worked noisily every day for several hours on this job while several of the group worked on the wall. But it seemed to be in vain since time after time, just when progress was being made, a Federal officer would appear with a stone mason and calmly order him to repair all the prisoners had managed to accomplish.

The Federal officer was positively uncanny in timing his appearance and in locating where they had been working, and the prisoners were confused and frustrated. Finally came a tip-off from one of the sentinels. Several times the sentinel muttered some unintelligible words to Rapier in passing. After several tries, Rapier finally caught the words, "Ye have a spy amongst ye's."

There it was. After some time and careful investigation this traitor's identity was discovered. The younger and rasher of the prisoners were all for putting him to death by strangulation, but calmer counsel prevailed, and it was decided to confront him with evidence of his treachery, force a signed confession, and request his removal from the group.

Paymaster Richardson, C.S.N., the oldest of the group and respected by all as a most excellent Christian gentleman made the accusation for the group. Richardson accused the Judas of being a spy and showed him a copy of a letter which the spy had written to Federal authorities, asking to be taken out of the prison as he was suspected by his comrades. Richardson reminded him that he was really a Confederate deserter who had taken the oath and not a true prisoner.

The wretch attempted to protest his innocence when one of the young hotheads sprang upon him and was ready to hurl him off the window balcony when stopped by the leveled muskets of the guard. Second Lieutenant William E. Dougherty of the 1st Infantry[29] had been attracted by the commotion and had brought up the guard saving the traitor's life. The traitor, no longer living a·life of pretense, sent out for a mint julep and drank it leisurely within view of the loyal Confederates, signifying his defiance. [This traitor has been identified by others as Acting Master's Mate Robert B. Holly.]

This event led to one of those civilities of warfare which seem so strange today. An appeal was made to the Federal commander protesting the unfairness of having a known spy in their midst and requesting his removal. The Confederates claimed their right as prisoners to attempt to escape, and acknowledged the right of the sentinels to shoot them should they be caught in the attempt. It is not clear whether this novel request moved the prison commander. But it was only a short time until the offensive traitor was removed and the group could again enjoy the right to scheme and plot.

An opening in a small closet under the stairs resulting from an earlier attempt to dig out had not been bricked up again. The Federal guards contenting themselves with closing the door and nailing it tightly. This promised an opportunity, and the imprisoned Confederates pried open the door and broke the points off the nails so that when it was closed it gave the outward appearance of being securely nailed. They then arranged that one man should be working constantly on the brickwork and mortar behind the closet door during the daylight hours.

Having only a chisel and an ear syringe, work was necessarily slow. The procedure was to furnish the worker with tin cups of water which were used to moisten and soften the mortar by means of the syringe. Then the man on the next shift would use the chisel. Finally all but the last row of bricks had been removed and on the evening of October 13, 1864, all was ready for the escape attempt.

Paymaster Richardson, whose thigh wound was too severe to make an escape try advisable, aided his companions by stationing himself near the sentinel and playing his flute. He was considered an able musician, and that night he concentrated on playing "Home, Sweet Home" and lulled the sentinel practically to a state of unconsciousness with this nostalgic melody.

Led by Lieutenant Rapier, the escaping prisoners broke through the final barrier to find themselves in the medical purveyor's office next door. They then walked to the front of the building, undid the fastenings of the front windows and emerged on a balcony on Common Street.

By a process of balcony-hopping, they progressed to Baronne Street, rounded the corner, and continued until they ran out of balconies. At this point they discovered a staircase leading to a street entrance. Fortunately, although locked, the key was on the inside. By unlocking the door, they stepped upon the sidewalk of Baronne Street as free men.

Shooting began almost immediately, and it was only due to the crowds and confusion that Rapier managed to escape. After walking around town for several hours, he determined to locate the family of his boyhood friend, John T. Gibbons. He was unable to locate the family where he expected to find them so he resolved to hazard questioning a neighbor lady who, fortunately, was able to give him the Gibbons' new address.

Going to the address furnished him, Rapier quietly entered the yard through the back gate. He was unable to distinguish anything by sight as it was now pitch black, but to his welcome relief he heard the sound of the rattle of the beads of a rosary being said. This sound spoke volumes to him and signified safety as it was undoubtedly Mrs. Gibbons saying her rosary in retirement on the back porch as was her evening wont. Speaking quietly, he made himself known and was promptly welcomed by all the family.

His brother officer, Lieutenant Fendall, was probably lost in trying to locate the Gibbons' home and in danger of capture, so it was arranged for Mr. Gibbons to go to look for him. Sure enough, Fendall was in the vicinity of the first address and, as luck would have it, approached Gibbons himself for the new location of the Gibbons family. Following the simple command of "Follow me," Fendall was guided to the Gibbons' home where he rejoined Rapier.

Then Mrs. Rapier was sent for, and she hastened to the Gibbons' home for a reunion with her son even though it was then past midnight. The two officers stayed at the Gibbons' home for ten days before making their move to leave New Orleans for the Confederate lines. First, there was a meeting with the local Prisoners' Relief Committee to discuss and discard various plans of escape. It was finally decided for the two officers to make the try on their own aided by a contribution of Federal greenbacks.

They were taken out of town on the evening of October 23, 1864, to a point where they could plunge into the swamp to start their bid for escape. Shortly, they rendezvoused with an Alabamian named Scott, a Confederate spy, who accompanied them on the perilous trip.

Most of the traveling was done at night to avoid being seen by the numerous pickets and roving bands of Federal soldiers. An added hazard was the shortage of good water, and the fugitives had to exercise rigid self-discipline to resist drinking the unsafe water of the swampy regions.

After making the river about 2 A.M., they hiked up the levee to Bonnet Carre, then headed due North through the swamp toward Lake Maurepas. One stop was made at the cabin of an old German who was known to Scott as a Union sympathizer. Pretending likewise to be Union sympathizers, the party received good treatment, a supper and breakfast, and lodging. The old man became suspicious of their need for a boat the next morning, and the party was obliged to reveal its true status. They were forced to threaten him with death to secure a boat.

The trio continued their try for escape in a small overloaded pirogue. About two miles from the mouth of the Blind River, they sighted the Federal gunboat *Commodore*, but their very insignificance was their salvation as they escaped discovery. Reaching Bear Island, they continued onward uneventfully, crossing the Amite River, and finally reaching Ponchatoula, seven days and nights after leaving New Orleans. This was comparative safety, and the party then followed the railroad (now the Illinois Central) to Jackson, Mississippi, then by railway to Meridian, and from Meridian to Mobile.

Their expense account called for $272 for board and transportation as follows:

Board at Lake Maurepas.........................	$ 16.00
” ” Bear Island............................	12.00
” ” Springfield	32.00
” ” Tickfaw................................	8.00
” ” Amite City	16.00
Transportation from Amite to	
Summit	78.00
Board at Summit	18.00
” ” Brookhaven	92.00
	$272.00

The voucher reports the expenses were incurred in coming from New Orleans to Mobile, after escaping from prison at New Orleans and were incurred between October 25 and November 10, 1864.[30] Arrival at Mobile was apparently on November 10 as the voucher gives that date as the last day of travel and since orders were issued that day from Naval Commandant's Office in Mobile for Rapier to report to Captain Thomas S. Wilson, C.S.M.C., who had been sent from Richmond to reorganize the Mobile Marines.

On November 30, Lieutenant Rapier was ordered to duty on board the C.S.S. *Morgan*, and Lieutenant Fendall probably received his orders on or about this same day to report to the C.S.S. *Nashville*. Their odyssey was over, and it was back to routine duty.

NOTES AND REFERENCES

Chapter X — The Marine Officer

1. Section 9 of the Act to Provide for the Organization of the Navy approved March 16, 1861, to be found in the *Register of the Commissioned and Warrant Officers of the Navy of the Confederate States to January 1, 1863* (Richmond: Macfarlane & Fergusson, 1862), 35.

2. Executive Document No. 3, January 5, 1864, 38th Congress, 1st Session.

3. Lt. Ruffin Thomson to "Dear Pa," Camp Beall, Drewry's Bluff, Va., March 14, 1864, *Thomson Pp., SHC, UNC.*

4. II *N.O.R.* 2, 819: quoting from Diary of Capt. S. Barron, C.S.N., Nov. 23, 1864.

5. Major C. L. Sayre, P.A.C.S., and endorsement by Capt. C. L. Sayre, C.S.M. Corps, to Admr. Franklin Buchanan, Mobile, May 17, 1864, *Misc. Correspondence, '61-'64, Ware Pp.*

6. C.S. Congress *Journal, op. cit.*, III, 314.

7. Statement of Capt. A. C. Van Benthuysen prepared for presentation to the Officers of the Court Martial, Oct. 28, 1862, p. 4, *Van B. Pp.*

8. Rembert W. Patrick (ed.), *The Opinions of the Confederate Attorneys General, 1861-1865* (Buffalo, 1950), 213-215.

9. C. C. Clay, Jr., to W. H. Crenshaw, Richmond, Va., Feb. 22, 1864, a transcript of a letter in the collection of Crenshaw Letters owned by R. E. Townsend of Annapolis, Md., in 1963.

10. Secretary of the Navy S. R. Mallory to Ruffin Thompson [Thomson], Richmond, Dec. 26, 1863, *Thomson Pp., SHC, UNC.*

11. *Loc. cit.*, Ruffin Thomson to "Dear Pa," Richmond, Jan. 18, 1864.

12. Henry L. Graves to "My Dear Mother," Richmond, Oct. 20, 1862, *Graves' Pp., SHC, UNC.*

13. Secretary of the Navy S. R. Mallory to Second Lieutenant Ruffin Thomson, C.S.M.C., Richmond, Feb. 11, 1864, *Thomson Pp., SHC, UNC.*

14. Secretary of the Navy S. R. Mallory to Capt. E. R. Smith, C.S.A., Navy Dept., Richmond, Aug. 20, 1864, in personal file of Capt. Eugene R. Smith, Co. B, 25th Tennessee Infantry, *C.S.A. Carded Records, R.G. 109*, U.S. National Archives.

15. Copy of Orders No. 25, C.S. Marine Barracks, Savannah, Ga., Dec. 26, 1863, MS. 261, Box 2, *Hunter Pp., Tulane U.*

16. Entries dated Tues., Nov. 22, 1864, and Wed., Nov. 23, 1864, *Crenshaw's Diary. Todd's Manual* apparently refers to Rev. John Todd, *The Students' Manual: designed, by specific directions, to aid in forming and strengthening the intellectual and moral character and habits of the student.* This manual had numerous editions; the 18th edition, for example, was published in Philadelphia in 1854. *Thaddeus of Warsaw* was a novel written by Jane Porter, authoress of *Scottish Chiefs*, and dealt with John Sobieski and his attempts to free Poland, and a suitable theme for a Confederate's reading.

17. Henry L. Graves, C.S.M.C., to "My Dear Mother," Savannah, Ga., April 22, [1863], *Graves' Pp., SHC, UNC.*

18. G.O. 17, H.Q., Dept. Ala. & W. Fla., near Pensacola, Fla., Dec. 10, 1861, *Van B. Pp.* These orders contain the charges, specifications, findings, and sentence of Tyler's Court Martial.

19. Washington *Evening Star*, Wed., June 19, 1861, 3:2, quoting the New York *Commercial* "of yesterday."

20. Flag-Officer F. Forrest, Chief of Bureau, to Capt. A. C. Van Benthuysen, C.S.M.C., undated, but containing charges and specifications arising from the October 2, 1862, incident, *Van B. Pp.*

21. *Loc. cit.*, MS. statement of Capt. A. C. Van Benthuysen to the Officers of the Court Martial, Drewry's Bluff, Oct. 28, 1862.

22. *Loc. cit.*, Secretary of the Navy S. R. Mallory to Capt. A. C. Van Benthuysen, C.S.M.C., Richmond, Jan. 16, 1863.

23. *Loc. cit.*, Flag-Officer F. Forrest, C.S.N., Chief of Bureau, to Capt. A. C. Van Benthuysen, C.S.M.C., charges and specifications dated Richmond, Dec. 15, 1862.

24. William B. Hesseltine (ed.), *Dr., J. G. M. Ramsey: Autobiography and Letters* (Nashville: Tennessee Historical Commission, 1954), 130.

25. The story of this prison escape is given in several different articles. See Anon., "Escape from Fort Warren," *Harper's New Monthly Magazine*, vol. 28 (Dec. '63 - May '64), Single No. 167 (April 1864), 697-701; also J[oseph] W. Alexander, "An Escape from Fort Warren," in Walter Clark (ed.) *Histories of the Several Regiments and Battalions from North Carolina in the Great War 1861-65*, ... (Raleigh and Goldsboro, N.C., 1901), IV, 733-743. Also see a brief version in *The Photographic History of the Civil War*, VII, 139.

26. II *O.R.* 7, 679.

27. W. J. Tenney, *Military and Naval History of the Rebellion* (New York, 1865), 789, under date of Sept. 3, 1864.

28. John L. Rapier, "A War Incident," New Orleans *The Times Democrat*, Wed., Jan. 31, 1894, 9:5-7, and 10:1-2. This article was later reprinted under the title, "Thrilling Experiences of Col. J. L. Rapier: An Account of His Escape from Prison in New Orleans," *Confederate Veteran*, vol. 8, no. 2 (February 1900), 77-81.

29. 2d Lt. William Edgworth Dougherty, pvt, general service, and corporal, sergeant, and 1st sergeant, Companies K and G, 1st Infantry, April 10 '60 to March 18, '63; 2d Lt., 1st Infantry, Feb. 19, '63; 1st Lt., April 9, '65; captain, March 1 '78; brevet 1st Lt, July 4 '63 for gallantry and meritorious service during the siege of Vicksburg, Miss. Dougherty was from Washington, D.C., and son-in-law of William Hickey, Chief Clerk of the U.S. Senate. Hickey's two sons served in the Confederate Army. Dougherty was a graduate of the Class of 1858 at Georgetown University.

30. Voucher #1054, *Ware Pp.*

Chapter XI

BIOGRAPHICAL SKETCHES OF MARINE OFFICERS

The biographical sketches of the officers are arranged into five general classes. The first group consists of four senior officers who, while not having been Marines, nevertheless contributed to the creation of the Confederate Marine Corps. They have been termed "The Converts" as they were converted to the Marine Corps way of life.

The second group of eleven officers from the "Old Corps," who were instrumental in training the enlisted men as Marines and who trained and indoctrinated the new officers have been termed the "Torch Bearers."

Termed the "Short Timers" is a group of ten officers whose service as Marine officers averaged slightly over seven months. Their service was satisfactory, but their time of service was so short as to minimize their effect and influence upon the development of the Corps.

The largest group consists of 25 officers commissioned in the Marine Corps 1861 through 1864. These officers, none of whom had previous Marine Corps service, have been termed "The New Breed" and are subdivided into four sub-groups based upon the year of entering the Corps.

The last group of eight officers consists of those who didn't measure up for one reason or another and were dropped from the Corps. The term of "Bilgers" has been applied to this group.

THE "CONVERTS"

Considered as converts to the Marine Corps way of life are four officers who were particularly instrumental in the organization and development of the C.S. Marine Corps although never having served in the U.S. Marine Corps. These officers were the Colonel-Commandant Lloyd J. Beall, who brought 35 years Army service to his new position; Major and Paymaster Richard T. Allison, who had been a U.S. Navy Paymaster for 11½ years; and two captains and original company commanders, Reuben T. Thom and Alfred C. Van Benthuysen. Both of these were combat veterans, Thom in Mexico, and Van Benthuysen in Italy.

BEALL, LLOYD JAMES. Beall was born October 19, 1808, at Fort Adams, Rhode Island, the son of Lloyd Beall, of Maryland, who had been a captain in the American Revolution. He had two brothers in the U.S. Army, Thomas Jones Beall, and Benjamin Lloyd Beall. His family home was in Georgetown, D.C.

He was appointed to West Point from Maryland in 1826 and graduated in 1830, two years after Jefferson Davis. He was commissioned a second lieutenant, 1st Infantry, on July 1, 1830, and served as regimental adjutant from March 1, 1833, to June 11, 1836. Beall and Jefferson Davis were second lieutenants in the same regiment from July 1, 1830, until March 4, 1833. Beall transferred to the 2nd Dragoons as a first lieutenant on June 11, 1836, and was then promoted to captain October 19, 1836. From 1840 to 1842 he attended the French Army's Cavalry School at Saumur. He was promoted to major and paymaster on September 13, 1844, and was serving on this duty when the outbreak of the war was imminent.

Beall was stationed in St. Louis, Missouri, when he resigned, effective April 22, 1861, and headed South. Arriving in Charleston, South Carolina, on April 22, he then went to Montgomery to offer his services. Two days after the Act of May 21, 1861, increased the new Confederate Marine Corps to regimental size, Beall was appointed colonel-commandant of the Corps and served in this capacity until the end of the war.

On May 25, 1862, General Joseph E. Johnston wrote General Robert Lee suggesting that Colonel Beall was eminently qualified for the grade of brigadier-general. But nothing came of the suggestion.

Colonel Beall was pardoned on November 30, 1866, on the recommendation of General U. S. Grant and Mayor Addison, of Georgetown, D.C. General Grant endorsed his application, "I am satisfied thet he never dreamed of taking arms against this government, but like many others, supposed secession would be peaceable, and it was left to him to select what government he would live under. I recommend that amnesty be granted in this case."

Beall died in Richmond, on November 10, 1887, in his 80th year, and was buried in Hollywood Cemetery, Richmond (lot no. 101, Section K). His grave marker erroneously gives his year of death as 1888.

Beall had married Fannie [Frances Alston] Hayne, the only daughter of U.S. Senator Arthur P. Hayne, at Maryetta, near Georgetown, South Carolina, on December 7, 1843. She was also niece of the one-time Governor of South Carolina and U.S. Senator Robert Y. Hayne. He was survived by Mrs. Beall, his son, Arthur Hayne Beall, and a daughter, Mrs. William T. Mitchell [Elizabeth Alston Beall].

He should not be confused with former Captain Lloyd Beall, 2nd Infantry, U.S.A., also of Washington, D.C., who served in the Confederate Army as a private of artillery.

ALLISON, RICHARD TAYLOR. Allison was born in Jefferson County, Kentucky, near Louisville, on June 6, 1823, the son of Capt. John S. Allison. He moved to Baltimore in 1845 where he practiced law. He was appointed a Paymaster in the U.S. Navy on October 30, 1849, by his uncle, President Zachary Taylor.

Allison first served in the Pacific Squadron and on the coast of California. He then accompanied Commodore Perry's expedition to Japan, followed by duty with the China Squadron. He returned to the United States in 1856 and was assigned to duty as Inspector of Provisions at Washington, followed by an appointment as Paymaster of the Washington Navy Yard.

He tendered his resignation from the U.S. Navy on April 20, 1861, but remained on duty until May 1 at the request of Secretary of the Navy Welles. He then left for Richmond where he telegraphed President Davis at Montgomery, Alabama. Summoned to Montgomery, he accepted an appointment as Paymaster of the C.S. Marine Corps dating from May 10, 1861. He moved to Richmond upon the establishment of the seat of government and the headquarters of the Marine Corps at that city and remained on that assignment until the evacuation in 1865.

Although out of town from time to time during the war, Allison was in Richmond in April 1865, leaving there on the second and making his way to North Carolina. He surrendered as a part of General Joseph E. Johnston's command and was paroled at Greensboro, North Carolina, as of April 28, 1865. On May 6, 1865, at Richmond, he applied to Major General E. O. C. Ord for the benefit of the "Amnesty Proclamation," and took the Oath of Allegiance five days later on the 11th. It was after the war that he discovered that his resignation from the U.S. Navy had not been accepted, and the records showed that he had been dismissed.

He returned to Baltimore after the war where he became, in time, clerk of the Superior Court of Baltimore, serving for many years.

Allison was first married to Maria Key Taney, daughter of Chief Justice Roger B. Taney of the U.S. Supreme Court. She died April 15, 1887. His second wife, who also predeceased him in 1904, was Elizabeth Buchanan, daughter of John Philpot of Baltimore County.

Allison lived the last years of his life near Phoenix, Baltimore County, Maryland, dying at Rockford, near Phoenix, on April 10, 1909. He was buried in the churchyard of St. James' P. E. Church, My Ladies Manor, or Monkton, Maryland.

THOM, REUBEN TRIPLETT. Thom was a member of a prominent Fredericksburg, Virginia, family where his father was a postmaster for many years. His father, Reuben Triplett Thom (c. 1782-5/7/1868) and his mother, Eleanor Reat (c. July 1786-11/20/1865) are both buried in the churchyard of St. George's Episcopal Church in Fredericksburg, where his father had been Senior Warden.

During the Mexican War, Thom served first as a first lieutenant in the Alabama Regiment of Infantry and then as captain of Company G, same regiment, June 1846-May 1847. When the 13th U.S. Infantry was raised, he was commissioned and served as a second lieutenant, August 3, 1847-July 15, 1848.

Serving as Quartermaster General of Alabama prior to the war, he was sent North by Governor Moore to purchase arms. On February 5, 1861, Thom, as a captain of artillery, began recruiting for Alabama service at Montgomery. Appointed a captain, C.S. Marines, on March 25, 1861, he continued recruiting for his Marine company in Montgomery until April 29, 1861. Between May 23 and July 12, he recruited in New Orleans, and from July 24 to September 14 in Mobile.

Captain Thom and 55 Marines were among the troops landed on July 6, 1861, on Ship Island, Mississippi, which fought off the Federal ships on July 9. Returning to the mainland, he recruited at Mobile between August 7 and September 14. He and his company were then sent to Pensacola to help organize the Marine battalion.

Thom and his company were transferred on the request of the Secretary of the Navy from Pensacola to Norfolk, Virginia, leaving on November 29 and arriving December 7, 1861. Here he was assigned to the C.S. Steamer *Virginia* (*Merrimack*). On February 20, 1862, while on board C.S.S. *Virginia*, Thom asked to be transferred to the Army, remarking, "I only accepted this [Marine Corps commission] to get into active service." He received favorable mention for his services in the engagements in Hampton Roads, March 8-9, 1862.

Shortly after the Hampton Roads engagements, Thom was detached from his company and sent South. He was in Montgomery, as of May 6, 1862. Thom was on detached duty at Mobile during 1863, and records show he witnessed bounty payments to recruits from February through September of that year.

On September 28, 1863, the Marine Corps authorized Thom to seek service with the Army for reasons of health. As of October 31, 1863, Thom was on duty with the Army at Mobile, and in 1864 was an assistant inspector-general on the staff of Brigadier General Richard L. Page, surrendering with Page at the fall of Fort Morgan on August 23, 1864. Imprisoned at Fort Lafayette, New York, until transferred on March 13, 1865, to Fort Delaware. While in prison, he assisted with the distribution of supplies obtained by the Confederate Agent, Brigadier General W. N. R. Beall.

Thom was released on oath on June 10, 1865. His prison life was apparently severe on him, and in July 1865 a relative who saw him remarked he was "in a low state of health brought on by long confinement and bad treatment." It was feared that his lungs were diseased, and recovery was considered doubtful.

He made a partial recovery, living in Montgomery, until his death on December 25, 1873. He was buried in the City Cemetery the next day. His widow, Basilisa Valdes Thom, filed for a Mexican War pension in August 1895 while living at Cerulean Springs, Trigg County, Kentucky, and received $8 a month (Certificate #12336) until March 1906 when she died, presumably in Mexico. Thom married his wife while in Mexico on June 10, 1848, at Orizaba, Mexico. She had been born in Spain and was just past 15 years of age.

A first cousin, also named Reuben Thom, served as a private, 3rd lieutenant, and 2nd lieutenant in Co. H, 11th Alabama, October 25, 1861, until he resigned March 28, 1864. Born in Virginia, he was 45 years old during the war. He made his home in Livingston, Alabama, where he became Clerk of the Court. He married Margaret, a daughter of Judge Samuel Chapman, of Sumter County, in 1843.

VAN BENTHUYSEN, ALFRED CRIPPEN. Alfred C. Van Benthuysen was born in 1836[?] in Brooklyn, N. Y., but he was taken to New Orleans in the 1850's by his father. His aunt, Eliza, was the wife of Joseph Davis, brother of Jefferson Davis.

He is reported to have fought in China with the Chinese 1857-8 and then sailed for Italy in 1859 after his return to the United States. In 1860 he was with Guiseppe Garibaldi in his Italian campaign, serving on the staff of General Avezzana, was present at the battle of Caseria, and participated in Garibaldi's triumphant entry into Rome.

He returned to the United States and was appointed a captain in the C.S. Marine Corps from Louisiana on March 30, 1861, at the age of 24. During April and May 1861, he enlisted men at New Orleans for Marine Company B. Van Benthuysen's company formed a part of Braxton Bragg's Army of Pensacola and manned a battery in the Warrington Navy Yard (Pensacola) at the time of the Federal bombardment on November 22-23, 1861.

Van Benthuysen and his company were ordered to Mobile on February 13, 1862, but their stay was brief as they were soon ordered North to the Gosport Navy Yard at Norfolk, Virginia. They reached the Yard on March 11, 1862, just two days after the famous *Monitor-Virginia* engagement, and were ordered to duty as the Marine Guard for the Yard.

Van Benthuysen and his company were transferred to Drewry's Bluff upon the evacuation of the Norfolk area and participated actively in the turning back of the Federal gunboats at Drewry's Bluff on May 15, 1862.

It was while stationed at Drewry's Bluff that Van Benthuysen came into conflict with Navy Dr. Algernon S. Garnett and was court-martialed in October 1862 as a result of the altercation and related problems. The Court sentenced him to be dismissed from the service, but the sentence was commuted by President Davis to suspension from rank and pay for four months from October 28, 1862.

This suspension was still in effect on December 5, 1862, when, while under the influence of liquor, he violated his arrest and refused to acknowledge Captain John D. Simms as his superior officer. This brought about a second court-martial, and he was apparently again suspended from rank and command until about May 26, 1864.

He was first restored to duty and ordered to report to Brigadier General George W. C. Lee, commanding the local forces at Richmond, but on June 3, he was ordered to Mobile. He reported to Mobile on June 13, but two days later Colonel Beall sent a telegram to Van Benthuysen at Mobile offering him the choice of commanding his own company at Drewry's Bluff or of the separate command of the guard at Wilmington. He received orders by telegram on the 16th to proceed to Wilmington.

Van Benthuysen and his provisional company of Marines were commended by Major General William H. C. Whiting for their services in the defense of Fort Fisher on December 24-25, 1864. He was wounded in the fighting at Fort Fisher on January 15, 1865, but received special commendation for carrying the wounded Colonel Lamb and General Whiting out of danger.

Van Benthuysen was then forced to surrender and was shipped North as a wounded prisoner. He was hospitalized in the U.S. General Hospital, Fort Columbus, New York Harbor, for a gunshot wound to the head. He was paroled for exchange at Fort Columbus on February 25, 1865, and transferred to City Point, Virginia, that same day. By March 7 he was back in the Richmond-Drewry's Bluff area.

Van Benthuysen, along with his brothers, Watson, a quartermaster captain, and Jefferson Davis, also an Army captain, apparently accompanied President Davis on his flight South from Richmond. They left Charlotte, N.C., with Davis' baggage wagon train on April 26, 1865. Van Benthuysen shared in the disposition of the Confederate Treasury funds on May 23, receiving 400 gold sovereigns valued at $1,940, plus $55 for travel expenses. He is reported to have been paroled at' Baldwin, Florida, about the end of May 1865.

The family recollection is that Alfred Van Benthuysen returned to New Orleans and later became active in the Ku-Klux-Klan. He was a deputy sheriff in New Orleans in 1867.

He married Rosario [Rose] Trezevant, of New Orleans, but died shortly afterwards on November 15, 1871, at the home of his brother, Watson Van Benthuysen, also in New Orleans. There were no children of this marriage. His wife was a daughter of Dr. Octavius Undecimus Trezevant, of Scotland (March 1, 1810-1866) and Maria Dorothea J. S. D. E. D'Argaine y Belgrano, of Montevideo. She married a second time to George Mongomery, a planter from Monroe, Louisiana.

THE "TORCH BEARERS"

The term "Torch Bearers" is applied to officers from the "Old Corps" who entered the Confederate States Marine Corps and constituted the extension and continuation of the U.S. Marine Corps into the Confederacy. These officers were Israel Greene, George Holmes, Becket K. Howell, J. E. Meiere, John D. Simms, John R. F. Tattnall, Algernon S. Taylor, George H. Terrett, Henry B. Tyler, Sr., and Thomas S. Wilson. They had combined experience of about 157 years, or an average of over 15 years each. Arbitrarily, Richard H. Henderson, who was exposed to Marine attitudes, philosophy, and traditions all his life as the son of the Commandant Archibald Henderson, is included as one of the "Torch Bearers." It was up to those men to not only train their enlisted men but to teach and indoctrinate the new officers.

GREENE, ISRAEL C. Israel Greene was born at Plattsburg, N.Y., in 1824 and moved with his family to Wisconsin when he was ten years old. He entered the U.S. Marine Corps on March 3, 1847, as a second lieutenant. He married Edmonia Taylor of Virginia in 1851. In the summer of 1857, Greene was sent by the Corps Commandant to the U.S. Military Academy at West Point to secure knowledge of artillery preparatory to introducing artillery into the Marine Corps. His most conspicuous service in the Marine Corps took place at Harpers Ferry on October 18, 1859, when he led the Marines who stormed the Fire Engine House and personally captured John Brown. He was listed in the 1860 Navy Register as Instructor of Artillery at the Marine Barracks, Washington, D.C.

On May 2, 1860, he was ordered to command the Marine Guard of U.S.S. *Niagara* which was to take the Japanese Embassy home. *Niagara* sailed from New York on June 30, rounded the Cape of Good Hope, and arrived at Yedo (Tokyo) November 8, 1860. It was April before he returned to the United States.

Upon attempting to resign from the U.S. Marine Corps on May 2, 1861, he was dismissed instead, effective May 18, 1861. Entering the Provisional Army of Virginia, he accepted appointment as a captain on May 25, 1861, but he declined an appointment as a lieutenant-colonel of infantry on June 19, 1861. Whether he accepted a commission as a major in the Virginia service is not clear. He was assigned to recruiting duty in Richmond.

Greene was commissioned in the Confederate States Marine Corps from Virginia as a captain on June 19, 1861. This rank was confirmed August 13, 1861, and on the next day he was nominated as adjutant of the Corps with the rank of major. This appointment was confirmed on August 24, 1861.

He served at Marine Headquarters at Richmond for the remainder of the war and apparently left only upon the evacuation of that city. He seems to have joined the retreat of the Army of Northern Virginia and took his parole at Farmville, Virginia, between April 11 and 21, 1865.

There is a record of Greene visiting Washington, D.C., on August 2, 1865, for the purpose of obtaining a pardon. At that time he was residing near Berryville in Clarke County, Virginia.

He moved to South Dakota in 1873 and farmed on his government claim located about two miles east of Mitchell until his death on May 25, 1909, in his 86th year. He is buried in Mitchell, South Dakota.

HENDERSON, RICHARD HENRY. Richard H. Henderson, born August 27, 1831, in the District of Columbia, was a son of the long-time Commandant of the U.S. Marine Corps, Brevet Brigadier-General Archibald Henderson (1783-1859) and Anne Maria Cazenove (1803-1859).

When William A. Graham of North Carolina was Secretary of the Navy (1850-1852), Henderson was offered commission in the U.S. Marine Corps but declined it. One brother, Charles A. Henderson, did serve as an officer in the U.S. Marine Corps but was retired on December 4, 1861, as "unfit for duty - sick" and then was dismissed on July 22, 1863. He died soon afterwards on July 25, 1865. Another brother, Octavius Cazenove Henderson was on the faculty at Virginia Military Institute and served as a captain, 1st Virginia Battalion, C.S.A.

At the beginning of 1861, Henderson seems to have been a lawyer in Washington, D.C., as well as the captain of a militia or drill company known as the "Henderson Guards." He resigned this post under pressure in late February 1861 and stated his intention of joining the Confederacy. After having offered his services to Virginia, he was appointed a first lieutenant in the C.S. Marine Corps from Virginia, dating from April 16, 1861.

He was ordered to command the Marine Guard of the C.S. Steamer *McRae* on June 27, 1861, but by August he was serving with Capt. Van Benthuysen's Company B at Pensacola. As of December 27, 1861, he was on board the C.S.S. *Patrick Henry* operating on the James River and participated in the battles in Hampton Roads on March 8-9, 1862. Shortly thereafter he was succeeded on the *Patrick Henry* by Second Lieutenant James F. Claiborne.

Henderson then joined his company at Drewry's Bluff. One source says he was on the Charleston Station during part of 1862-'63. He was on the Wilmington Station in 1864, serving first on *Raleigh* and then on the Receiving Ship *Arctic*. Going on a leave of absence on June 11, Henderson married Sarah Power Williams, of Society Hill, South Carolina, on June 15, 1864. She was the youngest daughter of Colonel John Nicholas Williams and his second wife, Sarah Cantey Witherspoon. Her paternal grandfather was Governor David Rogerson Williams, of South Carolina. Henderson was detached from *Arctic* on July 21, 1864, with orders to report to Drewry's Bluff on the expiration of his leave. Shortly after his arrival in Richmond, Henderson was transferred from Company B to Company C on August 18, 1864, at Drewry's Bluff due to a shortage of officers. He was assigned to the command of the Marine Guards at the two Richmond Navy Yards in October 1864. He surrendered and was paroled at Appomattox Court House on April 9, 1865.

Immediately after the war, he is reported to have purchased a little farm near Richmond. He later returned to Washington, D.C.

Henderson died at the age of 49 years in Washington, D.C., of heart disease on May 3, 1880, shortly after having been appointed to a clerkship in the Pension Bureau. He was buried in grave 175, range 54, in Congressional Cemetery, Washington, D.C. A large obelisk marks his family plot. The obituaries fail to mention his wife, who secured a divorce from him in South Carolina on May 17, 1876, on grounds of alcoholism, or his two children, Archibald (1/16/1867 - 12/2/1914), or Alice (2/24/1871 - ?).

HOLMES, GEORGE. Holmes, born in Portland, Maine, around 1825, served as a second lieutenant and captain in Captain R. C. Livingston's Company of Florida Volunteers in the Mexican War, August 1847 until disbanded in July 1848. He was appointed a second lieutenant, U.S. Marine Corps, from Florida on March 3, 1849. He served until he resigned on February 28, 1861.

About a month later, on March 29, 1861, he was appointed a captain in the Confederate Marine Corps and immediately entered upon recruiting duty. During most of April and early May 1861, he recruited men at New Orleans. Holmes then went on duty at Pensacola, being transferred with his company to Savannah, on September 18, 1861. While in this area, he participated in the battle of Port Royal, South Carolina, on November 7, 1861. In the spring of 1862, Holmes and his Company A reported to the Marine Camp at Drewry's Bluff, where he was stationed until the closing days of the war.

Captain Holmes served in Commodore Tucker's Naval Brigade on the evacuation of Richmond and was captured at Sayler's Creek, Virginia, on April 6, 1865. After a short confinement at Johnson's Island, Ohio, he was released on taking the oath of allegiance to the United States on July 25, 1865. He was described as 40 years old with a light complexion, dark hair, hazel eyes, and 5′6″ tall. He gave his residence as Jacksonville, Florida, where he died before July 1888.

HOWELL, BECKET KEMPE. Becket K. Howell, the eighth child of William Burr and Margaret K. Howell, and a grandson of Governor Richard Howell, of New Jersey, was born at Natchez, Mississippi, December 24, 1840. He was a brother-in-law of President Jefferson Davis, being a younger brother of the second Mrs. Davis, Varina Howell. He spent much of his youth with the Davises and was placed in a Quaker school in Alexandria, Virginia, at Davis' expense.

Howell was commissioned a second lieutenant in the U.S. Marine Corps on August 1, 1860, but resigned effective March 1, 1861. He was then commissioned a first lieutenant in the C.S. Marine Corps on March 29, 1861. One of his first assignments was to accompany a party of recruits from New Orleans to Pensacola in May 1861.

He was assigned shortly thereafter to the command of the Marine Guard on the C.S.S. *Sumter* and was carried on the payroll from April 2, 1861. He was on the *Sumter's* famous cruise under Semmes until *Sumter* was laid up at Gibraltar on April 9, 1862. In June Howell was at Nassau with Semmes.

When Semmes assembled his officers for the C.S.S. *Alabama*, Howell was included although there was no Marine Guard on the ship. He participated in the engagement with the U.S.S. *Kearsarge* off Cherbourg, France, on June 19, 1864. Howell was picked up from the water by the English yacht *Deerhound* after the sinking of the *Alabama* and returned safely to England.

As of November 23, 1864, he was planning to leave on the 25th for the Confederacy on the steamer *Emily*. The end of the war found him at St. Georges, Bermuda, unable to complete his journey back to the Confederacy.

Howell was nominated as a captain in the Marine Corps, vice Captain Jacob Read, on December 23, 1863. He was confirmed on December 29, 1863, his commission dating back to February 1, 1863. Strangely enough, he was never referred to as "Captain Howell."

There is a report that in 1867 he and his brother, Jefferson Davis Howell, were jobless in Montreal. Becket came to the Davis plantation, "Brierfield," as overseer in May 1882, but was taken ill with fever and died on September 12, 1882. He never married.

MEIERE, JULIUS ERNEST. Julius Ernest Meiere was born November 25, 1833, at New Haven, Connecticut, where his French-born father, Julius Meiere, was an instructor in French and German at Yale College. The elder Meiere was Receiving and Copying Clerk for the Navy Department from October 8, 1839, until November 9, 1840, when he was appointed a Professor of Mathematics in the Navy. Most of his service was performed at Philadelphia. He was dropped from the service by a legislative cut-back on September 4, 1848.

Julius Ernest Meiere is reported to have been Private Secretary to Lewis Cass, U.S. Senator from Michigan, in the late 1840s.

Meiere was appointed a second lieutenant, U.S. Marine Corps, on April 16, 1855. Two years and four months of his sea duty was spent cruising for slavers off the coast of Africa. He was at sea for over two years in the Gulf of Mexico, taking part in the fight which resulted in the capture of Admiral Marin's Mexican Squadron. Meiere was serving as Acting Consul of Vera Cruz at the time of the bombardment of that city by General Miramon. In June 1860 he was on duty at the Marine Barracks, Washington, D. C.

Meiere was promoted to first lieutenant in January 1861. On April 3, 1861, he married Nannie Buchanan, daughter of Captain Franklin Buchanan, U.S.N. (later Admiral, C.S.N.), at the Washington Navy Yard, and both President Abraham Lincoln and Senator Stephen A. Douglas attended the wedding. The President is reported to have cut the wedding cake. On April 20, 1861, Meiere commanded a Marine detachment of 20 men sent on board the U.S.S. *Anacostia* at Washington. Colonel John Harris, Commandant of the Marine Corps, reported on May 18, 1861, to Secretary of the Navy Welles that all of the Marine detachment of the *Anacostia* were still on board with the exception of Lieutenant Meiere who had resigned. His resignation was refused, and he was dismissed from the service as of May 6, 1861.

Going to Montgomery, Meiere was appointed a first lieutenant in the Marine Corps from the District of Columbia, ranking from May 8, 1861. He was soon sent to Pensacola to serve with the Marine battalion forming a part of General Braxton Bragg's command. He was ordered on September 19, 1861, to join Captain Holmes' company at Savannah, reporting on September 21. Promoted to Captain on December 5, 1861, he served on the Savannah Station in the winter of 1861-'62. He was transferred to the Richmond area in the spring of 1862. He was serving on board the C.S.S. *Virginia* (*Merrimack*) when she was abandoned and destroyed on May 11, 1862. On May 15, 1862, he commanded Captain Thom's Marine Company C at the battle of Drewry's Bluff. He was then in Richmond during June-July 1862 on recruiting service.

Captain Meiere was ordered to Mobile, on September 20, 1862, to command the Marines on that station and reported on October 8, 1862. He enlisted, trained, and organized Marines at this station for the vessels of the Mobile Squadron and for transfer to Savannah and Richmond (Drewry's Bluff). He was captured at the surrender of Fort Gaines, Alabama, on August 8, 1864, and imprisoned at New Orleans but managed to escape on October 13, 1864. On February 17, 1865, he visited the Marine Camp at Drewry's Bluff. He is reported to have surrendered at Mobile on May 4, 1865, and to have taken the oath of allegiance at Key West, on May 20, 1865. In 1865, a Marine lieutenant reported Meiere was considered "one of the best officers in our Corps, . . ."

Meiere went North after the war and graduated from the Medical College of the University of New York in 1869. He went to Colorado in 1873 but returned to the East the next year. He applied for an apointment as an Army Contract Surgeon on March 28, 1874. (During one of these periods in the East, he is reported to have practiced medicine in the Pennsylvania coal fields.) He again went to Colorado in 1878, settling in Leadville where he was appointed City Physician in 1879.

The story is told that while living in Leadville in 1888, Dr. Meiere was appointed consul to Amoy, China, by President Cleveland. Going to Washington a few days later, Meiere had a chance encounter with a former friend and shipmate, an officer in the Navy. Meiere enthusiastically thrust out his hand in greeting only to have his one-time friend draw back, fold his arms, and declare he would not shake hands with a traitor. The doctor then slapped the officer on the face with his gloves.

Soon after this incident, Meiere was called to the President's office where he was reminded of his assault on the naval officer and was asked to apologize. He declined to do so. "Then," said Mr. Cleveland, "I will revoke your commission as consul." In reply, Dr. Meiere is reported as having replied, "Revoke and be d____d." With that he turned on his heel and left the executive presence.

A one-time president of the Lake County and of the Cripple Creek Medical Societies, he died of pneumonia at the Sisters' Hospital (St. Nicholas's Hospital run by the Sisters of Mercy) in Cripple Creek on December 3, 1905, aged 72 years. Funeral services were scheduled to be under Masonic auspices.

Captain Meiere and Mrs. Meiere were divorced, and he was estranged from many members of his family.

SIMMS, JOHN DOUGLAS, JR., was born circa 1822 in Virginia. His father, John D. Simms, Sr., served as Chief Clerk to the Secretary of the Navy from April 5, 1827, until his death on March 2, 1843. The family name was in the process of being changed from "Semmes" at this time. Simms' half-sister, Emily Douglas Simms (6/3/1810 - 4/9/1880) married Flag-Officer French Forrest, U.S.N., and C.S.N.

Simms entered the U.S. Marine Corps from the District of Columbia on October 7, 1841, and was promoted to first lieutenant on September 14, 1847. He was brevetted captain as of September 13, 1847, "For gallant and meritorious conduct at the storming of the castle of Chapultepec, and in the capture of the San Cosme gate, 13th September, 1847." While serving on the U.S.S. *San Jacinto*, he participated in the storming and destruction of the Canton Barrier Forts in China in November 1856. From April to December 1857, Simms was on detached duty from the U.S.S. *San Jacinto* to visit Formosa, ostensibly to locate any missing American or European seamen but also reporting on the island's fortifications and the availability of coal. In 1860 he was stationed at Marine Barracks, Pensacola. Simms was nominated for promotion to captain by President Lincoln according to the Washington *Evening Star* of June 4, 1861, but he did not take the oath signifying his acceptance.

Simms submitted his resignation from the U.S. Marine Corps, but it was refused, and he was dismissed as of July 8, 1861. He entered the C.S. Marine Corps from Virginia as a captain on July 15, 1861.

Simms is reported to have served on the Savannah Station in 1861. He was at the Gosort (Norfolk) Navy Yard on November 25, 1861, where he was detailed to command the various companies of armed workmen in the Yard. On March 19, 1862, he was assigned to duty as "Commandant of the Post of Marines" at the Gosport Navy Yard. With the evacuation of Norfolk, Simms went to Drewry's Bluff where, as senior captain, he commanded the provisional battalion of two companies which acted as sharpshooters against the Federal fleet before Drewry's Bluff on May 15, 1862.

Simms commanded the battalion of Confederate Marines sent to Charleston in the spring of 1863 as reinforcements against the expected monitor attack. Other than this expedition, Simms seems to have served at Drewry's Bluff until the close of the war. During most of this time he was in command of Company B and served as Inspector and Mustering Officer at Camp Beall, Drewry's Bluff. He was also second-in-command to Colonel George H. Terrett, commanding the battalion and post.

Simms was captured at Sayler's Creek on April 6, 1865, and released on oath from Johnson's Island prison on July 25, 1865. At the time of his release his age was given as 43 years, height as 5 '8 ", light complexion, blue eyes, and light hair. His residence was given as Norfolk, Virginia. Extensive efforts to locate information on his postwar activities have been unsuccessful.

He was pardoned July 6, 1867, still at Norfolk.

TATTNALL, JOHN ROGERS FENWICK. John R. F. Tattnall, the son of Flag-Officer Josiah Tattnall and Harriet Fenwick Jackson, was born at "Arawana," near Middletown, Connecticut, in 1829 and was sent abroad for his education. After six years in France, he returned to Georgia at the age of 17. He was unable to obtain his father's assistance in securing a commission as the older Tattnall was on naval service in Mexico. Securing his own recommendations, young Tattnall secured a commission as a second lieutenant, U.S. Marine Corps, on November 3, 1847, much to his father's astonishment. He was promoted to first lieutenant on February 22, 1857.

On February 28, 1861, while on board the U.S.S. *Constellation* off the West Coast of Africa, Tattnall wrote a letter to Governor Brown of Georgia offering his services should Georgia leave the Union. This was finally forwarded to the Governor with a covering letter from his father at Savannah on June 6, 1861.

Tattnall was serving on board the steam sloop *San Jacinto* of the African Squadron at the outbreak of the Civil War. While still at sea, he threw his sword overboard to avoid handing it over to his commanding officer. He was placed under arrest on October 7, 1861, put in irons, and then imprisoned in Fort Warren, Boston Harbor, on November 27, 1861, after his ship reached port.

Tattnall was exchanged after considerable negotiation on January 10, 1862, and released from Fort Warren on January 13, 1862. He then made his way South via Baltimore. Although published as a captain (#10 out of 20) in one of Georgia's two Regular regiments, he accepted a commission as a captain in the C.S. Marine Corps as of January 22, 1862.

He was ordered from Savannah to Norfolk on February 11, 1862, returning on March 4, 1862. During March he was mentioned as a Marine captain serving as a volunteer aide-de-camp on the staff of General Robert E. Lee, then on duty in Savannah in charge of the coastal defenses of South Carolina, Georgia, and Florida.

Tattnall was reported on April 9 as desiring an Army commission, and on April 19, 1862, he was appointed a colonel in the Provisional Army ranking from April 17, 1862. Nine days later he was assigned to the command of the 29th Alabama Infantry stationed at Pensacola. By June 30, 1862, Colonel Tattnall was commanding a Detachment of Observation of brigade strength stationed near Pollard, Alabama, and as such was an acting brigadier general.

Without explanation, he resigned as colonel of the 29th Alabama on November 24, 1862, and requested duty with the Marine Corps. General John H. Forney endorsed him as "an efficient and faithful officer" and expressed regret at his resignation. Colonel Lloyd J. Beall of the Marine Corps endorsed the resignation on December 8, 1862, with the remark, "The services of Col. Tattnall are required with his Corps proper." The next day his resignation was accepted in orders, and he was ordered to report to Colonel Beall.

He was soon sent to Savannah, to organize Company E of the Marine Corps and served there until the evacuation of that city in December 1864. Tattnall then transferred his activities to Charleston. Upon the evacuation of Charleston, the remnants of Company E under Captain Tattnall withdrew to Greensboro, North Carolina, where they were surrendered as part of General Joseph E. Johnston's command on April 28, 1865.

Tattnall resided at Halifax, Nova Scotia, for a time after the war, eventually returning to Savannah. He became connected with the Cotton Press Association in Savannah, but retired on account of ill health. He was treasurer of the Chatham County Board of Education during the closing years of his life.

Tattnall left Savannah in June 1907 to visit friends in Middletown, Connecticut, and died there at "Walnut Grove" on August 17, 1907. That was within a half mile of his birthplace.

His body was returned to Savannah for burial. The funeral was conducted by the Georgia Naval Militia and the Confederate Veterans' Association. Burial was on August 21, 1907, in Bonaventure Cemetery, Savannah, the site of the former ancestral home of the Tattnalls.

Tattnall never married, and his nearest relatives in Savannah were a niece, Mrs. W. J. B. Adams (née Mary Fenwick Neufville), and two cousins, John F. and Macarton Campbell Kollock.

Tattnall's attitude toward being a Marine Corps officer was best expressed by his remark on resigning his commission as a Confederate Army colonel and acting brigade commander that he would rather command a company of Marines than a brigade of volunteers!

TAYLOR, ALGERNON SIDNEY. Taylor was born in Alexandria, on February 17, 1817, when Alexandria was still a part of the District of Columbia. He married Susan M. Meehan, daughter of the Librarian of Congress, in Washington, on July 5, 1837. He was appointed a second lieutenant in the 5th U.S. Infantry on August 1, 1838. By Army General Order No. 50 of November 23, 1838, he was authorized to transfer to the U.S. Marine Corps by exchange with Lieutenant A. W. Allen. The exchange was probably effective February 21, 1839, as this is the date in the Marine Corps records for entry into the Corps. He was promoted to first lieutenant on March 3, 1847, and to captain on July 17, 1857. Taylor received a brevet rank as a captain dated March 27, 1847, for gallant and meritorious conduct at the bombardment and capture of Vera Cruz and the capture of Tuspan, Mexico. In February 1852, he commanded the Marine Guard landed at Buenos Aires, Argentina, from the U.S.S. *Congress*.

Taylor acted as the chief aide and representative of the President of the United States to the Japanese Ambassadors and their party on board the U.S.S. *Powhatan* in 1860. The party left Japan February 13, was escorted across the Isthmus to the Atlantic side where it boarded the U.S.S. *Roanoke*, and arrived at Washington, D. C., May 14, 1860 on board the steamer *Philadelphia*.

Taylor commanded a contingent of 40 Marines stationed for 15 days beginning January 5, 1861, to defend Fort Washington, Maryland, below Washington, D. C., on the Potomac.

Taylor submitted his resignation from the U.S. Marine Corps on April 25, 1861, but it was not accepted, and he was dismissed as of May 6, 1861. Returning home he offered his services on April 27 to the State of Virginia, and two days later was appointed a lieutenant-colonel of Light Infantry in the Provisional Army of Virginia, his commission carrying the date of May 8. Taylor was assigned to duty with the volunteers from Washington, D. C., on April 30, and on May 2 was assigned to the command of all troops in Alexandria. He was commanding in Alexandria on May 5 when he evacuated the town prematurely. He was superseded by Colonel George H. Terrett on May 10. In June 1861, he was a lieutenant-colonel on duty at Camp Henry, Culpeper Court House, Virginia. He was mentioned on October 4, 1861, as in command of the Post at the county seat, Redwood, (Culpeper County ?).

He entered the C.S. Marine Corps on December 3, 1861, as a captain and was appointed Quartermaster the next day. His resignation as lieutenant-colonel in the Provisional Army of Virginia was announced in orders dated December 6, 1861. On the 7th, he was officially nominated to the Senate as a captain, C.S.M.C., and as captain and quartermaster on December 24, 1861. His nomination as captain was postponed on February 8, 1862.

Finally confirmed as major and quartermaster of the Corps, he seems to have served uneventfully in the Richmond area until late in the war. On February 15, 1865, the Secretary of the Navy ordered the court martial of Major Taylor and a Sergeant Smith [Samuel B. Smyth?]. Taylor was accused of being cognizant without taking action on Sergeant Smith's use of Government transportation to bring goods from Augusta to Richmond to be sold on private account. No record has been found of the court martial or of any outcome of the incident.

Taylor was paroled at Appomattox on April 10, 1865, according to one record, or on April 26, 1865, at Richmond, according to another. He took the oath of allegiance at Richmond on June 20, 1865. Records show he was visiting his family in Washington on August 1, 1865.

Mrs. Taylor died in Detroit, January 11, 1885. Taylor applied for a Mexican War pension which was finally allowed on April 17, 1889, for $8 per month (Application #12839, Certificate #18061). This supplemented a monthly stipend from his brother, Admiral Alfred Taylor, U.S.N., who died April 19, 1891. His pension was finally increased to $12 a month on May 4, 1895. Major Taylor died May 26, 1899, at the age of 82 years at the Maryland Confederate Home at Pikesville, Maryland (then outside Baltimore), and was buried in Loudoun Park Cemetery, Baltimore, Confederate Section, row D, grave #81 (next to the last grave in row). He was survived by a daughter.

TERRETT, GEORGE HUNTER. George H. Terrett, the son of Captain George Hunter Terrett and Hannah Butler Ashton, was born in Fairfax County, Virginia, in 1807. He received a commission as a second lieutenant in the U.S. Marine Corps on May 18, 1830, dating from April 1, 1830.

Terrett served on the punitive expedition to Quallah Battoo, Sumatra, in 1832. He also served with the Marines fighting the Indians in the Seminole War, 1836-1838. On September 14, 1839, he participated in a duel at Harper's Ferry. He escaped unhurt, but shot his opponent, a Mr. West of the Treasury Department, through both legs. In 1840 he returned to Florida to fight in the Everglades.

He entered on duty on August 9, 1843, at Mahon in the Mediterranean, in charge of the Marine Stores kept there.

During the Mexican War, he served as a captain with the Marines of General Winfield Scott's command and was brevetted major for his conduct at Chapultepec on September 13, 1847. Marines led by him were largely instrumental in capturing the San Cosme gate to Mexico City. He left Mexico City to return to the United States on March 20, 1848.

Terrett submitted his resignation from the U.S. Marine Corps on April 22, 1861, upon the secession of Virginia, but his separation was recorded as a dismissal under the date of May 6, 1861. He was promptly commissioned a colonel in the Provisional Army of Virginia, and preliminary plans were made for him to be the colonel of a regiment of Washington City volunteers if it could be organized. On May 10, 1861, he was placed in charge of the troops and defense of Alexandria, Fairfax, Loudoun, Prince William, and Fauquier Counties. He was in direct command of the city of Alexandria from May 10 until the city was evacuated and the troops withdrawn to Manassas on May 25, 1861.

Colonel Terrett was placed in command of a newly formed Fourth Brigade composed of Moore's , Garland's, and Corse's regiments of Virginia volunteers (the 1st, 11th, and 17th Regiments) on June 20, 1861, but the arrival of a newly commissioned Confederate brigadier, James Longstreet, brought about Terrett's replacement. He then commanded Camp Pickens at Manassas from about July 10 to August 22, 1861, when he resigned his Virginia commission.

In the meantime, he was commissioned the line major of the recently enlarged Confederate States Marine Corps, accepting the commission on June 20, 1861.

Terrett was assigned to duty at Drewry's Bluff, commanding the Marine battalion in the summer of 1862 upon the establishment of the Marine Camp at that site. During February-June 1863, he served as Recruiting Officer in Richmond.

Secretary of the Navy Mallory wrote President Davis on May 21, 1864, of the ''justice and expediency'' of conferring such provisional rank on Major Terrett, commanding at Drewry's Bluff, as would keep him from being out-ranked on the occasional presence of a less experienced and able officer of superior rank. The suggestion was accepted by President Davis who suggested his appointment to the temporary rank of colonel. This appointment was effective May 23, 1864, and Terrett was assigned to command the Post at Drewry's Bluff on July 21, 1864. Terrett commanded the Marine forces which assisted in repelling the Federal attacks of the May 1864 on Drewry's Bluff.

There was a rumor among the Marine officers in the spring of 1865 that Colonel Terrett was to be promoted to brigadier-general, but this failed to materialize before the close of the war.

He participated in the retreat to Appomattox but was captured near Amelia Court House on April 5, 1865, and was sent to Johnson's Island via Old Capitol Prison. He was released on oath and parole on July 25, 1865. He returned to Washington, D. C., and took up a temporary residence there.

Colonel Terrett later returned to and rebuilt his family home, "Oakland," about four miles west of Alexandria, near the Episcopal Seminary. He died November 27, 1875, and was buried originally in the family plot at Oakland. His body was later placed in the Abbey Mausoleum, located adjacent to Henderson Hall (a U.S. Marine Corps post), just outside the Hobson Gate to the Arlington Cemetery.

TYLER, HENRY BALL. Henry Ball Tyler, son of William and Priscilla Tyler, was born in Virginia September 13, 1800, and admitted to the U.S. Military Academy on September 28, 1818. He was found deficient in his studies at the end of the second year and dropped. On March 3, 1823, he was appointed a second lieutenant in the U.S. Marine Corps and promoted to first lieutenant in May 1830. In May 1836, Tyler served as regimental adjutant for the Marines serving in the Creek Indian War. He was promoted to captain in 1853. Tyler commanded two companies of Marines called to disperse a mob of "Plug-Uglies" on election day (June 1, 1857) in Washington, D. C. He received much credit for dispersing the mob and for capturing the cannon in their possession.

While in the U.S. Marine Corps, he served on the Frigate *Constitution* in 1824 and later on the *Erie, Macedonian, Pennsylvania, Columbus*, and at many navy yards, including Brooklyn, Boston, Norfolk, and Washington. He resigned the post of Adjutant and Inspector with the rank of major on May 2, 1861, to go South after 37 years' service.

Tyler was commissioned lieutenant-colonel of the Confederate Marine Corps on June 18, 1861. On or about July 26, 1861, he reported to General Bragg at Pensacola where he served as the senior Marine officer for the Marine battalion assembled there. He served briefly as a brigade commander in the Army of Pensacola in September 1861. He was relieved from duty with the Army of Pensacola on January 21, 1862, and ordered to report to the Colonel of his Corps upon the expiration of his leave. Records of his further service are sketchy, consisting of court martial duty, examining boards, and other headquarter's duty. He was paroled at Lynchburg in April 1865.

Tyler married a cousin, Elizabeth Browne Tyler, on June 26, 1828, at "Mill Park." After the war he made his home at Fairfax Court House, where he died on December 17, 1879, survived by his wife, three daughters, and six sons. He was buried in the Fairfax Cemetery, Fairfax Court House.

WILSON, THOMAS SMITH. Thomas S. Wilson was born on June 21, 1837, near Murfreesboro, Tennessee. After attending Union University at Murfreesboro, he was appointed a second lieutenant in the U.S. Marine Corps on

December 13, 1857. He was serving on board the Frigate *Congress* of the Brazil Squadron at the outbreak of the war. When his ship returned to the United States in August 1861, he refused to take the oath of allegiance and attempted to resign from the Corps. He was dismissed instead on August 24, 1861, and was held as a prisoner of war at Fort Lafayette along with his shipmates, Captain Robert Tansill, U.S.M.C., and Midshipmen Henry B. Claiborne and Hilary Cenas. He was transferred to Fort Warren on October 30, 1861.

After considerable correspondence between Confederate and Federal authorities, Wilson was sent on January 19, 1862, to Norfolk, Virginia, paroled for 45 days, and released in anticipation of his proper exchange.

His commission as a first lieutenant, C.S. Marine Corps, was dated January 24, 1862. He was ordered to Pocohontas, Arkansas, on March 6, 1862, to report for duty to Major General Earl Van Dorn, commanding. This must have been his first duty assignment as he stated at the close of the war that he entered the C.S. Marine Corps on March 7, 1862. He was on ordnance duty at Abbeville [Miss. ?] as of November 28, 1862. His commission as a captain came through about this time (dating from October 10, 1862) and on December 1, 1862, he was ordered from the Army at Holly Springs, Mississippi, to report to the Colonel Commandant of the Marine Corps in Richmond for assignment to duty.

Wilson was regularly assigned at Drewry's Bluff, to Company C of the C.S. Marine Corps from January 1863 until August 18, 1864. During this time he was on several special assignments. He commanded a contingent of 14 enlisted men from Company C sent to Charleston in the spring of 1863 to be organized and trained as monitor boarders. He commanded a Marine detachment in January 1864 that composed a part of the expedition which boarded and captured the U.S.S. *Underwriter*. This expedition received the thanks of the Confederate Congress. Captain Wilson accompanied the Marine battalion to Wilmington in July 1864 on the planned amphibious expedition to release the prisoners of war at Point Lookout, Maryland.

When the news of the battle of Mobile Bay and the capture of Fort Gaines reached Marine headquarters, Wilson was ordered on August 16, 1864, to transfer the command of Company "C" to Lieutenant Richard H. Henderson and go to Mobile as commander of the Marines there. He reported in Mobile on August 25, 1864. Here he took steps to re-organize and recruit the Marines of the Mobile Station. After the escape of the Mobile officers from Federal prisons and their return to duty, Wilson returned to Drewry's Bluff.

He was captured at Saylor's Creek on April 6, 1865, and was sent to Johnson's Island, where he took the oath and was released on July 25, 1865. He gave his age as 28 years and his residence as Springfield, Missouri, upon his release.

Wilson returned to Greene County, Missouri, where he taught school, became a farmer, and served later as a county official. He married Mary A. White in 1872 and had nine children. He died November 7, 1900, and was buried in the Brick Church Cemetery, Springfield.

THE "SHORT TIMERS"

Grouped together are ten officers whose service with the Confederate Marine Corps, while adequate, was of such a short duration as to have only a moderate effect upon the development of the Corps. Four of these officers were former U.S. Marine Corps officers: Captains Andrew Jackson Hays, Robert Tansill, Calvin L. Sayre, and First Lieutenant Henry L. Ingraham. Six of the ten officers had varied backgrounds. These were Samuel Z. Gonzalez, Wilbur F. Johnson, John D. Fowler, and John S. Van de Graaff. Lt. Isaac S. Hyams was an Army officer assigned to duty with the Marines for a little over 10 months. Edmund J. Lloyd never accepted his Marine Commission. The average active duty time of the eight officers who accepted Marine commissions was slightly over seven months.

HAYS, ANDREW JACKSON. Andrew J. Hays was born in Alabama and appointed from that state to the U.S. Marine Corps on December 4, 1847. With the approach of the war, Hays commanded a detachment of 30 U.S. Marines at Fort McHenry in Baltimore, January 9-12, 1861, then returned to Washington, D. C.

Hays resigned his commission as a U.S. Marine first lieutenant on March 1, 1861, and was appointed a captain in the Confederate Marines on March 29. On or about May 17, 1861, he was assigned to recruiting duty, and during much of August-October he recruited in Memphis, Tenn. He then reported to Pensacola for duty with the Marine battalion, but on December 3, 1861, he was placed in command of nine companies of Mississippi volunteers at Camp Quitman, Florida. Characterized by General Bragg as "an excellent disciplinarian, a very good drill officer, and has no superior, if an equal, of his grade, in this Army." Hays was recommended as lieutenant-colonel of the 27th Mississippi, but President Davis nominated James L. Autrey.

Reverting to his permanent rank of captain of Marines, Hays seems to have served on Bragg's staff until May 6, 1862, when he was promoted to lieutenant-colonel and assigned to the 27th Mississippi. This assignment was made permanent on August 11, 1862, dating from July 17, 1862. He took over the command of the regiment on August 20, but was ordered to report to Bragg's headquarters on November 30, 1862. Several days later, on December 4, 1862, he was assigned to duty in the Inspector-General's Department of Bragg's command.

While serving in this capacity, Hays was commended for his services in the Stone River Campaign (December 26, 1862-January 5, 1863) by General Bragg. He continued on staff duty as a lieutenant-colonel and Assistant Inspector General, Army of Tennessee. Under General Joseph E. Johnston's assuming command, Hays continued on his staff for a short while until ordered to report to the President in Richmond for assignment to inspection duty on April 28, 1864. In July 1864, he was in Wilmington helping to organize the sea-going expedition designed to free the Confederate prisoners of war at Point Lookout.

He was ordered to North Alabama on August 24, 1864, to inspect Roddey's command. There is another mention of Hays as a lieutenant-colonel on inspection duty as of October 26, 1864.

The last mention of Hays was an order for him to report to General Bragg commanding at Wilmington for assignment to duty on February 17, 1865.

Andrew J. Hays married Miss Laura M. Kirtland of Memphis, Tennessee, in that city on June 20, 1861; his son, Jack, married Adabelle Slaughter. Hays' brother, Charles, was a first lieutenant in the Confederate Navy and another brother, Archer, was an Assistant Surgeon in the same Navy. His grandson, William Slaughter Hays, was graduate #7575, Class of 1924, at the U.S. Naval Academy.

Hays died on December 25, 1896, and was buried in what is known as "the Old Hays' Cemetery" at Finchburg, Alabama, about 15 miles from Monroeville. His Confederate Marine Corps duty time was just over 8 months.

GONZALEZ, SAMUEL ZACHARIAS. Samuel Z. Gonzalez, the son of Don Manuel Gonzalez who came to Pensacola in 1763, was born in Florida and was appointed a U.S. Navy Storekeeper from that State on June 6, 1854. Stationed at Pensacola in 1860, he resigned from the U.S. Navy on January 12, 1861.

Gonzalez was appointed major and quartermaster of the C.S. Marine Corps on April 3, 1861, and served with the Marines at Pensacola. Ordered to Richmond on August 19, 1861, he met with Secretary of the Navy Mallory and resigned his Marine commission on September 13, 1861, and reported to Commander Thomas W. Brent at Pensacola for duty as Navy Storekeeper the same day. He later served at Montgomery and at Mobile. He was paroled on May 7, 1865, at Albany, Georgia. His Marine Corps duty time was 5 months, 10 days. Gonzalez was an uncle of Lt. Daniel G. Brent, C.S.M.C.

TANSILL, ROBERT. Robert Tansill was born June 12, 1812, at Occoquan, Prince William County, Virginia. He served as an enlisted man in the U.S. Marine Corps from March 16, 1833, until November 3, 1840, when he accepted a commission as a second lieutenant of Marines.

Tansill saw service in the Florida Indian War in 1841-42, and in January 1847, while assigned to U.S.S. *Dale*, was in battle near the mission of Santa Clara, California. He was promoted to first lieutenant effective March 16, 1847. He served as Military Governor of San Francisco (Yerba Buena) for a brief time in 1847. On November 17, 1847, he commanded the Marines of U.S.S. *Dale* in a landing operation near Guaymas, Mexico. He was brevetted captain for gallantry and meritorious conduct during this operation on October 24, 1848, his rank dating from November 17, 1847.

While serving on board U.S.S. *Powhatan* in Asiatic waters, Tansill was one of the Marines Commodore Matthew C. Perry landed in Japan on March 8, 1854. He also accompanied a punitive landing at Tumai on July 6, 1854.

Tansill was promoted to captain on November 29, 1858. His resignation, an exposition of his political beliefs, was written on board U.S.S. *Congress* in South American waters under date of May 17, 1861.

Tansill was arrested upon his arrival in New York on August 23, 1861, his resignation was not accepted, and he was dismissed from the Marine Corps as of August 24, 1861. He was confined in prison at Ft. Lafayette and later at Ft. Warren without charges, a hearing, or a trial until finally exchanged as a prisoner of war on January 10, 1862.

Reaching Richmond on January 20, 1862, he accepted a captaincy in the C.S. Marine Corps on January 22, 1862. On February 13, 1862, as a captain of infantry, C.S.A., he was ordered to report to the Governor of Virginia, and the next day he was appointed colonel, 2nd Regiment of Virginia Artillery. He was nominated to the Congress as a captain of infantry on February 15, 1862, and his resignation as a Marine officer dates from this day.

His regiment was disbanded on May 22, 1862, and he reported to General Whiting to serve on his staff as a captain. He was promoted to colonel, P.A.C.S., on May 27, 1863, and served at this rank until the close of the war. He was paroled as colonel and Inspector-General at Jamestown, N. C., April 28, 1865, and took the oath at Richmond on May 22, 1865, giving his age as 52.

Tansill first married Frances ("Fannie") Weems, the daughter of the Rev. Jessee Ewell Weems, and granddaughter of Parson Weems, the biographer of

George Washington. She was born 1825 and died in 1846. Both are buried in the graveyard at the family home, "Vaughnland," located about five miles northwest of Dumfries, Virginia, off County Road 643. Tansill's second mar-. riage was to Anna Lucinda Bender on October 18, 1849, in Washington, D. C.

SAYRE, CALVIN LAWRENCE. Sayre, the son of Philemon Dickerson Sayre and Caroline Virginia Clayton, was born on January 9, 1832. He matriculated at Franklin College (now the University of Georgia) at Athens in the Class of 1852, but apparently did not graduate. He was appointed a second lieutenant, U.S. Marine Corps, on June 3, 1858. During his first cruise, he commanded a landing party at Panama City, Columbia (now Panama) on September 28, 1860.

On February 14, 1861, Sayre resigned his Marine commission and tendered his services to the Confederacy at Montgomery, on February 22, 1861. While doing duty under the War Department, he was appointed a first lieutenant, C.S. Marine Corps, from Alabama on March 29, 1861. His Army duty terminating on May 27, 1861, he soon reported for duty with the Marine battalion before Pensacola.

Sayre participated in the engagement on Santa Rosa Island, Florida, on October 9, 1861, and lost his right leg from a musket ball wound. Captured, he was paroled and returned to the Confederate lines.

Made a first lieutenant of artillery, and later a major, P.A.C.S., Sayre went on Army duty and remained with the Army until the end of the war, finally taking the Oath of Allegiance at Montgomery on July 23, 1865, and was pardoned September 12, 1865. Since Sayre retained his Marine commission while serving in the Army, the seniority system brought his promotion to a Marine captain dating from December 11, 1862.

Sayre married Ella Lansdale in April 1879. They had two children, Clayton and Ella Hargrove. After residing in Washington, D. C., he returned to Montgomery, where he died on November 4, 1894, and was buried in Oakwood Cemetery in Montgomery. His active duty as a Marine officer from commissioning until receiving his wound was 4 months, 12 days.

INGRAHAM, HENRY LAURENS. Ingraham, the son of Duncan Nathaniel Ingraham and Harriett Horry Laurens, was born in South Carolina about 1837. He entered the U.S. Naval Academy on May 29, 1852, but resigned after two years on June 22, 1854. Ingraham was appointed a second lieutenant, U.S. Marine Corps, from South Carolina on July 1, 1858, tendered his resignation December 31, 1860, and it was accepted March 8, 1861.

Ingraham was commissioned a first lieutenant, C.S. Marine Corps, on March 29, 1861, and reported for duty at Pensacola, on April 3, 1861. He resigned his Marine commission on November 22, 1861.

Ingraham was appointed a first lieutenant, Corps of Artillery, C.S.A., as of November 16, 1861, accepting this commission on November 22. He served on Army duty until the end of the war, being paroled as captain and Ordnance Officer of Kirkland's Brigade at Greensboro, North Carolina, on May 1, 1865. He took the oath of allegiance to the U.S. on August 5, 1865, at Charleston and applied for a pardon August 23, 1865.

Ingraham married Sarah Moultrie (12/11/1838 - 5/1/1910), daughter of Dr. William L. Moultrie and his first wife, Hannah C. Harleston. Ingraham died in Charleston on July 9, 1878, aged 41 years. He and his wife were buried in the churchyard at Strawberry Chapel on the Eastern side of the Western Branch of the Cooper River, near Charlestown. His active duty with the C.S. Marine Corps was for 7 months, 23 days.

JOHNSON, WILBUR F. Johnson, a native of Georgia, served in the U.S. Coast Survey before the war. He enlisted as a private in Company D (the "Macon Volunteers"), 2nd Georgia Infantry Battalion, at Macon, on or about April 20, 1861, but was transferred to the C.S. Navy [Marine Corps] June 27, 1861, receiving his Army discharge July 11, 1861.

Johnson accepted a commission as a second lieutenant of Marines on June 29, 1861, and reported for duty at Pensacola on August 1, 1861. He received favorable mention for his services as volunteer aide-de-camp to General Richard H. Anderson on October 8-9, 1861, on the Santa Rosa expedition. After brief Marine Corps duty, General Bragg used him on ordnance duty. He was promoted to first lieutenant approximately February 15, 1862.

Johnson was called to Richmond on May 3, 1862, to report to the Commandant of the Marine Corps for assignment to duty. A request by General Richard H. Anderson for his services was denied by the Secretary of the Navy, and shortly afterwards Johnson resigned his Marine commission on July 4, 1862.

The next day, July 5, 1862, Johnson was appointed a first lieutenant of artillery. He served on ordnance duty for the remainder of the war. No post war record has been found.

His Marine Corps commission was effective for 1 year, 5 days, although his actual Marine Corps duty assignments were limited to about 7 months.

LLOYD, EDMUND JENNINGS. Edmund Jennings Lloyd, the son of Anne Harriotte Lee and John Lloyd, was born in Alexandria, Virginia, on August 27, 1822. Appointed from Wisconsin, he was a non-graduating member of the Class of 1843 at the U.S. Military Academy.

He was appointed a commissary captain in the Confederate Army as of July 17, 1861. He was also nominated for a second lieutenancy in the Marine Corps from Virginia on July 30, 1861, but was not confirmed and does not seem to have performed any service as a Confederate Marine officer. Lloyd apparently served the entire war as a commissary captain.

He died, unmarried, on October 1, 1889, in Alexandria, and was buried in the Christ Church Cemetery on Wilkes Street, Alexandria.

HYAMS, ISAAC SMITH. Isaac S. Hyams, a son of Henry M. Hyams, one-time lieutenant-governor of Louisiana, was born in Louisiana on July 29, 1837. He attended the University of Louisiana in New Orleans for two years before being admitted to West Point on July 1, 1854. He attended West Point for two years with the Class of 1858. On the outbreak of the war, he was commissioned a first lieutenant of infantry, Louisiana State Army.

He was ordered on May 1, 1861, as a second lieutenant of infantry, C.S.A., to report to General Bragg at Pensacola. Shortly afterwards, he was attached to Marine Company B and served with this unit at Pensacola and Norfolk until detached on March 24, 1862.

Hyams then went on Army duty, serving as a drillmaster with the 39th North Carolina Infantry, with conscripts in Alabama, with Wharton's Cavalry, and other Army assignments. He took parole #68 at Millican, Texas, on July 5, 1865, as a captain, P.A.C.S.

Hyams married Lelia A. Smith on April 8, 1876. His service with the Marine Corps was a little over 10 months.

FOWLER, JOHN D. John D. Fowler was born in Virginia but was a resident of Uniontown, Perry County, Alabama, when he enlisted as a private in Capt. Richard Clarke's Company D, 4th Alabama Infantry (the "Cane Brake Rifle Guards") on April 25, 1861. He was 30 years old, single, and by occupation a brick mason.

He was severely wounded at Manassas on July 21, 1861, and was discharged on October 13, 1861, on account of his wounds. He was promised a promotion by President Davis who visited him while wounded and the promise was re-deemed by a Presidential appointment as a second lieutenant of Marines effective October 26, 1861. Assigned to Company B, Fowler was on recruiting duty in Norfolk as of May 1, 1862. He died at his mother's home in Goochland County, Virginia, on August 31, 1862.

Fowler was a Marine officer for just 10 months and 5 days. He was the only Marine officer to die while on active duty.

VAN de GRAAFF, JOHN S. John S. Van de Graaff was the son of John and Eliza Jane (Brooks) Van de Graaff. He was born in Woodford County, Kentucky, on January 22, 1832.

He enlisted on August 1, 1861, at Galveston, Texas, in an infantry company finally designated as Company E, 1st Texas Infantry. He accepted a commission as a second lieutenant of Marines effective March 17, 1863.

In the Corps, he served on the C.S. schooner *Gallego* on the James River which included service in the Navy Yard opposite Rocketts, Richmond, until August 7, 1863, and at Drewry's Bluff until he resigned effective September 11, 1863.

He then returned to Texas but does not seem to have performed any additional military service. He gave his personal parole as "late of the C.S. Service" on or about March 13, 1865, at New Orleans, intending to avail himself of Presidential Amnesty so he could return to his home in Kentucky. His brief Marine Corps service was just 5 months and 24 days.

THE NEW BREED

Among the unit histories of the U.S. Marine Corps is one by George McMillan titled, *The Old Breed, A History of the First Marine Division in World War II*, published in 1949. Just three years later, Andrew Geer produced *The New Breed: The Story of the U.S. Marines in Korea*. From this background of titles I have borrowed the expression, "The New Breed," to represent the officers of the Confederate States Marine Corps who were commissioned during the war without any prior Marine Corps service.

For convenience, these officers are grouped by the year in which they were commissioned. "The New Breed: 1861" included Lieutenants David G. Raney, James R. Y. Fendall, Thomas P. Gwynn, James Thurston, Francis H. Cameron, Fergus MacRee, and David Bradshaw. All of these officers had been promoted to first lieutenants by the end of 1863.

"The New Breed: 1862" was a small group of just three officers: Nathaniel E. Venable, Henry L. Graves, and H. Melville Doak. Both Venable and Graves received promotions to first lieutenant while Doak was the senior second lieutenant in the Corps from February 1863 to the end of the war.

"The New Breed: 1863" consisted of six second lieutenants: Albert S. Berry, Edward F. Neufville, Daniel G. Brent, J. Campbell Murdoch, Samuel M. Roberts, and John L. Rapier.

"The New Breed: 1864" consisted of nine second lieutenants: Lloyd B. Stephenson, Ruffin Thomson, Thomas St. G. Pratt, Henry H. McCune, Edward Crenshaw, Everard T. Eggleston, John DeB. Roberts, Eugene R. Smith, and John A. Pearson.

There were 25 of the "New Breed" who were being trained to be Marine officers.

In the text that follows, the biographical sketches are grouped according to the year of appointment under the heading "The New Breed: 1861," or 1862, 1863, or 1864 as their year might be.

THE NEW BREED: 1861

RANEY, DAVID GREENWAY, JR. David G. Raney, a son of David G. Raney and Francis H. Jordan, was born in Apalachicola on October 29, 1838. His parents were from Petersburg, Virginia, but moved to Florida in 1826, settling in Apalachicola in 1834.

He enlisted on April 4, 1861, at Apalachicola as a corporal in Captain Cropp's company, 1st Florida Infantry. He was on the company roll until May 3 when discharged because of his promotion to second lieutenant in the Marine Corps from Florida on April 22, 1861. He seems to have served first as an officer with Captain George Holmes' company ("A") at Pensacola. On or about June 19, 1861, he was detailed with twelve Marines to command the Steamer *Time* in Pensacola harbor. On September 18, 1861, his company was transferred to Savannah for duty. He landed on Hilton Head Island with Captain Holmes' company on November 7, 1861, to try to reinforce Fort Walker during the battle of Port Royal. Raney was promoted to first lieutenant on December 10, taking rank from November 22, 1861.

In March 1862 he was sent from the C.S.S. *Savannah* at Savannah to Apalachicola, where he "shipped" (recruited) seamen for service at Savannah. Shortly after May 22, 1862, he accompanied his company to Drewry's Bluff, but was transferred to Mobile later that year, being paid at Mobile from November 1, 1862. When the C.S.S. *Tennessee* was placed in commission, Raney was put in command of her Marine guard on March 1, 1864, and remained in command until captured in the battle of Mobile Bay on August 5, 1864.

After her capture, he was imprisoned in New Orleans but managed to escape on the night of October 13-14, 1864, and reported back for duty with the Mobile squadron. He remained with the squadron through the battles around Mobile and was the senior Marine officer present when the squadron was surrendered on May 5, 1865. He was paroled at Nanna Hubba Bluff, Alabama, on May 10, 1865, giving his residence as Apalachicola. He was described as 25 years old [?], having hazel eyes, dark hair, a dark complexion, and being 5 ′11 ″ tall.

Raney never married. He died in the house of his birth in Apalachicola on February 26, 1903.

FENDALL, JAMES ROBERT YOUNG. Fendall, born in 1838 or 1839 in either the District of Columbia or Maryland (both are given in various sources), was a son of Philip Richard Fendall (1794-1868) and Elizabeth Mary Young (1804-1859), and a cousin of the Lees of Virginia. His older brother was Major Philip R. Fendall, Jr., U.S.M.C. Other brothers were William Y., Arthur, Stratford, Reginald, and Clarence (who served in the U.S. Coast Survey during the Civil War). There were also three sisters. He was a nephew of Governor Albert G. Brown, of Mississippi, and was named for his maternal grandfather, Robert Young.

He first enlisted at Terry, Mississippi, on May 20, 1861, giving his residence as Georgetown, D. C., occupation as student, and age 22 years. He enlisted as a private in Capt. A. G. Brown's company of Mississippi Volunteers, the "Brown Rebels," later known as Company H, 18th Mississippi Infantry. This unit was mustered into Confederate service on June 4, 1861, at Corinth, and was sent to Virginia where it participated in the first battle of Manassas (Bull Run).

He was nominated as a second lieutenant of Marines from Mississippi on July 30, 1861, and confirmed on August 13, 1861. On September 29, 1861, Fendall left the regiment for Pensacola where he had been ordered as a Marine lieutenant. He was formally discharged from the Army on October 2, 1861, by Special Order 294/1.

After brief service at Pensacola, he was transferred to Virginia in charge of the Marine Guard on board the C.S.S. *Jamestown*, apparently on this duty from December 1, 1861, through April 30, 1862. In the meantime, his promotion to first lieutenant, *vice* First Lieutenant Henry B. Tyler, Jr., dismissed, was confirmed. He was nominated to the Congress on February 13, 1862, and confirmed on February 15, taking rank from December 10, 1861.

Fendall was transferred to Mobile in mid-1862, and by July 8 was on duty on that station. Here he had the usual duties with the recruiting and training of recruits. Immediately prior to January 5, 1864, he was appointed Acting Assistant Quartermaster and Commissary of the Marine Corps for the Mobile station by Colonel Commandant Beall in addition to his company duties.

On August 8, 1864, Fendall was captured at the surrender of Fort Gaines, Alabama, and imprisoned at New Orleans. He escaped from prison, and, with Lieutenant Rapier, made his way north to Brookhaven, Mississippi, and back to Mobile, returning for duty on November 10, 1864.

Fendall was then assigned to the command of the Marine Guard of the C.S.S. *Nashville*. In the operations against the enemy near Spanish Fort and at Fort Blakely in March and April 1865, his commanding officer reported he was "under special obligations" for Fendall's "intelligent assistance and cordial cooperation." He was surrendered and paroled at Nanna Hubba Bluff along with the crew of the *Nashville* on May 10, 1865.

After the war, he returned briefly (June to October 1865) to his uncle's home in Terry, but went to New Orleans where he secured a position as a depot clerk for the Jackson Railroad Company. His health deteriorated, and he died August 11, 1867, in New Orleans after collapsing on the street. He was buried originally in the Girod Street Cemetery but was reinterred at the Hope Mausoleum in 1957 when the Girod Street was demolished. He was not married.

GWYNN, THOMAS PETER. Thomas Peter Gwynn was born at Prairie du Chien, Wisconsin, and was 25 years old when he enlisted as a private on April 19, 1861, at Norfolk, in Captain E. Bradford's Company G, 6th Virginia Infantry. He was discharged at Craney Island (near Norfolk), on October 4, 1861, having received a commission as second lieutenant in the Marine Corps dated September 20, 1861.

He was assigned to the Marine Guard on board the Receiving Ship *United States* in the Gosport Navy Yard on December 9, 1861. He does not seem to have served with the Marine Battalion at Pensacola.

Gwynn was promoted to first lieutenant as of February 15, 1862. He was detached from the *United States* on March 15, 1862, to take temporary command of the Marine Guard at the Gosport Navy Yard during the leave of absence of Captain A. C. Van Benthuysen. There is a brief notation that on April 29, 1862, he was on board the C.S.S. *Jamestown* as a second lieutenant, but this assignment was apparently of short duration. Various records during 1863 indicate he was serving on shore, probably at Drewry's Bluff. From about March 7, 1864, until May 24, 1864, Gwynn was in command of the Marine Guard on board the

C.S.S. *Richmond.* He was transferred on May 24, 1864, to command the guard of the C.S.S. *Virginia, II,* staying on this assignment until Colonel Beall ordered him on February 9, 1865, to Drewry's Bluff, effective February 13.

On several occasions in June 1864, Gwynn commanded Marines of the James River Squadron on shore. He was on board *Virginia* January 23-24, 1865, when the James River Squadron failed to pass Trent's Reach on its effort to go down river.

Gwynn was apparently sick and hospitalized on board C.S.S. *Beaufort* as of October 1, 1864. He was furloughed February 1, 1865, for seven days to visit his sick brother in Petersburg.

He participated in the retreat from Richmond and was captured at Sayler's Creek on April 6, 1865. After his capture, he was sent first to Old Capitol Prison in Washington, D.C., and then to Johnson's Island, being released on taking the oath of allegiance on June 20, 1865. He gave his residence as Burlington, New Jersey, at the time of taking the oath, and his age as 33 (which doesn't agree with his age upon enlistment in 1861). He was described as having a dark complexion, hair, and eyes, and being 5 '6 " tall.

THURSTON, JAMES. James Thurston, the son of Robert Thurston and Eliza Emily North, was born October 25, 1840, in South Carolina and graduated in 1861 from the South Carolina Military Academy (The Citadel) in Charleston.

While at the Citadel, he was a member of the Cadet battery which fired upon the *Star of the West* and served later as an instructor of artillery in the Charleston Harbor batteries. He enlisted on June 26, 1861, in Captain A. H. Boykin's company of South Carolina cavalry (later Company A, 2nd South Carolina Cavalry) and served as a private and a corporal. On September 17, 1861, he was ordered to duty with Captain Sterrett, C.S.N., at the entrenched camp, Manassas, for duty with recruits. He was discharged by General Beauregard's order of November 1, 1861, to accept a commission as a second lieutenant of Marines. Marine Corps records show he accepted his commission on October 21, 1861, and it was back dated to September 20, 1861. At the time of accepting his commission, he was convalescent from typhoid fever at Charlottesville, Virginia.

He was ordered from Charleston to Savannah on November 25 to join Captain George Holmes' Company A. Here he was assigned to the C.S.S. *Sampson* of Tattnall's "Mosquito Fleet" which was then engaged in provisioning Fort Pulaski. Thurston was promoted to first lieutenant as of July 4, 1862.

Thurston was requested by Captain James H. North for transfer to Europe in 1862 for Marine duty on board ship, but he was assigned instead to the command of the Marine Guard of the illfated C.S.S. *Atlanta* at Savannah. He was captured in the engagement with the U.S.S. *Weehawken* on June 17, 1863.

Thurston was sent to Fort Lafayette and then to Fort Warren arriving on July 4, 1863. He made a prison escape with Naval Lieutenant Joseph W. Alexander on August 19, 1863, but was recaptured, confined in the Portland, Maine, jail, and then returned to Fort Warren on September 7, 1863.

After considerable delay, Thurston was paroled on September 28, 1864, and sent South for exchange on October 1, 1864, finally arriving at Richmond on or about October 22, 1864. He was exchanged at Cox's Wharf, Virginia, on October 18.

He apparently remained on duty at Drewry's Bluff the rest of the war. As of January 2, 1865, he was commanding Company C of the Marines as senior officer present. In February 1865, he accompanied Lieutenant C. W. Read's unsuccessful torpedo boat expedition around and behind Federal lines.

No record has been located of his capture, surrender, or parole.

He went into sawmilling for a year after the war, living in his old home in Charleston, then moving to his uncle's farm in Farquier County, Virginia. Thurston went into the storage business in Baltimore in 1872. He died of apoplexy in Catonsville, Maryland, on April 13, 1904, at the age of 63 years and was buried in a marked grave in Area K, Lot 75, Greenmount Cemetery, Baltimore.

He married Mary Jane ("Mollie") Wilson who survived him, dying on November 1, 1911, at Catonsville.

CAMERON, FRANCIS HAWKES. Cameron was born in Hillsboro, N. C., June 1, 1838. He is reported to have entered the U.S. Coast Survey in 1855 and was stationed at Brooklyn, N. Y., at the outbreak of the war. Unofficial sources state he declined a commission in the U.S. Army, ran the blockade to Savannah, and offered his services to the Confederacy. A. W. Venable recommended him to President Davis in August 1861 for a commission, referring to him as lately in the Coast Survey and a master's mate in the Navy. He was commissioned a second lieutenant in the Marine Corps on September 20, 1861.

He joined Company A at Savannah on October 2, 1861, where he is reported to have served on the *Huntress*, the flagship *Savannah*, and the *Fingal* (*Atlanta*), and to have participated in the engagement at Port Royal in November 1861.

Cameron was serving on board the *Huntress* at Charleston when ordered back to Savannah on January 15, 1862, reporting three days later. He accompanied his company to Virginia in the spring of 1862. He was promoted to first

1st Lt. Francis Hawkes Cameron
A war-time photograph
Photograph by courtesy of Lee A. Wallace, Jr., and now Defense Dept. Photo (Marine Corps) #515827

lieutenant, October 10, 1862, and remained on duty at Drewry's Bluff until April 1865 as Acting Assistant Quartermaster and Acting Assistant Commissary of Subsistance for the Marine battalion. An unofficial report says that he participated actively in Butler's defeat at Drewry's Bluff in May 1864.

Cameron participated in the Appomattox Campaign, avoided capture at Sayler's Creek on April 6, but finally surrendered at Appomattox on April 9, 1865. He was paroled in Richmond on May 13, 1865.

He returned to North Carolina after the war where he became active in the State militia. He served as a captain, 1877-1878, as Inspector-General (colonel), 1879-91, and finally as State Adjutant-General (brigadier-general), 1893-97. He was back in Richmond in the insurance business during the last three years of his life.

He died March 30, 1900, in Richmond, and was buried in St. Matthew's (Episcopal) Church Cemetery in Hillsboro, Orange County, North Carolina.

MACREE, FERGUS. Fergus MacRee, the 6th child of Colonel Samuel MacRee, U.S.A., and Mary Urquehart, widow of Major Henry Wheaton and daughter of Henry Urquehart, of Wilmington, North Carolina, was born April 26, 1839, in the St. Francis Barracks, St. Augustine, East Florida. His paternal grandmother was Ann Fergus. The family finally made its home at what was known as the MacRee Farm, then about three miles from St. Louis, Missouri, but now a part of that city. Colonel Samuel MacRee (as he chose to spell his name) died there July 15, 1849. Of their eleven children, only two lived to maturity, Fergus and William Griffith.

Fergus MacRee entered the Confederate service from St. Louis as a lieutenant of artillery in either the 1st or 2nd Missouri, according to an unofficial source.

MacRee entered the Marine Corps as a second lieutenant on October 9, 1861, and was promoted to first lieutenant on October 10, 1862. Few records exist of his duty assignments in 1862-63 except witnessing a Clothing Receipt Roll for Company B on September 2, 1863, presumably at Drewry's Bluff. He apparently commanded a Marine Guard at Wilmington from February 18 to March 18, 1864, when relieved by Lieutenant J. Campbell Murdoch. MacRee arrived back at Richmond on March 25. He was identified as Adjutant of the Post at Drewry's Bluff on May 12 and June 2, 1864, during the repulse of Butler's attack. He participated in the Appomattox Campaign and was captured at Sayler's Creek on April 6, 1865. Committed first to Old Capitol Prison on April 17, 1865, he was sent to Johnson's Island, reaching there May 3, 1865, and was released on taking the oath on June 13, 1865.

At the time of taking the oath, his residence was given as St. Louis, his age as 26, having a light complexion, light hair, blue eyes, and was 6 feet tall.

He wrote a letter in February 1866 to former Lieutenant Ruffin Thomson telling how he went to Canada after the war with no intention of returning but finally returned to St. Louis at the urging of his aged mother.

He was in business in St. Louis as late as 1870-'71 and was a lawyer at the time of his death. He died at St. Vincent's Asylum in St. Louis on January 2, 1883, and was buried in Bellefontaine Cemetery. MacRee never married, but was survived by his mother (d. October 20, 1889 in St. Louis) and his brother, William Griffith, and his brother's five children. While his father spelled the family name "MacRee," it was ultimately shortened to "McRee."

BRADFORD, DAVID. David Bradford, born in Louisiana about 1832, was a nephew of President Jefferson Davis, being the son of Amanda and David Bradford, sister and brother-in-law of Davis.

He enlisted on May 7, 1861, in the unit that became Company I, 10th Mississippi Infantry (formerly known as Captain Joseph R. Davis' Company, the Madison Rifles, 6th Regiment, 3rd Brigade, Mississippi Militia). This company went to the Pensacola area in the spring of 1861. Bradford was assigned on September 30, 1861, to duty with the Provost Marshal at the Navy Yard, serving until, on November 22, 1861, he accepted a Marine Corps commission as a second lieutenant. He apparently reported for duty with Captain Van Benthuysen's Company B at the Gosport Navy Yard in March 1862. He was detached from the company on board the Frigate *States* and assigned to duty with Captain John D. Simms in the Gosport Navy Yard on March 19, 1862. Upon the evacuation of Norfolk, May 10, 1862, he accompanied the Marines to Drewry's Bluff. Promoted to first lieutenant on December 11, 1862, he commanded Company B the last quarter of 1862 and the first half of 1863. Bradford accompanied the Marine battalion sent to Charleston in the spring of 1863.

From October 1, 1863, to May 24, 1864, Bradford commanded the Marine Guard at the Rocketts' Navy Yard in Richmond. On being relieved from the Navy Yard, he was attached to the C.S.S. *Fredericksburg* of the James River Squadron, serving on this duty until relieved on August 29, 1864. He was immediately sent to Wilmington with a small detachment, reaching his new station September 3, 1864.

He served on the Wilmington Station several weeks until transferred to the command of the Marine Guard of the C.S.S. *Chickamauga* serving on board for her cruise from October 28 to November 19, 1864. He was detached when *Chickamauga* was decommissioned on December 15, 1864.

Bradford was wounded (contusion of left hip by a shell) and captured in the second battle for the defense of Fort Fisher on January 15, 1865. After confinement at Fort Monroe, he was transferred to Fort Delaware on February 9, 1865, but was soon paroled and sent to City Point for exchange on February 27, 1865.

He was back in the Richmond area by March 5, and he accompanied President Davis' party on its flight South in April. Under orders for the Trans-Mississippi Department, Bradford received $300 in gold from Confederate Treasury funds at Washington, Georgia, and apparently went on his way.

Bradford married Ada Eliza Pottenger, the ninth child of George Washington Pottenger and Margaret Adeliza Talbott, of Kentucky, on December 18, 1883, but she died less than a year later on September 11, 1884. He was killed by a train in New Hope, Nelson County, Ky., on July 10, 1903.

THE NEW BREED: 1862

VENABLE, NATHANIEL E. Nathaniel E. Venable was born at "Scott-Greene" in Prince Edward County, Virginia, on December 2, 1836. He entered the U.S. Military Academy on July 1, 1852, at the age of 15 years, 7 months. He was found deficient in mathematics at the end of his second year (June 1854) and dropped from the Academy. He then attended Hampden-Sydney College, graduating in 1856, and entered the teaching profession. He was living in Texas (Victoria County?) at the outbreak of the war.

Although several excellent recommendations for a commission were on file, Venable enlisted as first sergeant, Company I, 23rd Virginia Infantry, on September 23, 1861. He was captured at Winchester (Kernstown) on March 23, 1862, sent to Fort Delaware, and then exchanged at Aiken's Landing on August 5, 1862. He then enlisted in Company D, 25th Battalion Virginia Volunteers (the Richmond City Battalion) on September 1, 1862, was promoted to corporal on October 14, 1862, but was discharged on October 21 by an order dated October 17, having been appointed a second lieutenant in the Marine Corps, effective October 24, 1862.

Shortly after entering the Marine Corps, he was assigned to the Navy Yard opposite Rocketts in Richmond, but was relieved of this duty by May 26, 1863. On July 2, 1863, he was ordered to report to the Corps Quartermaster for duty. Promoted to first lieutenant on January 14, 1864 (ranking from January 11, 1863[?]), he served as acting assistant quartermaster of the Corps for the remainder of the war. He rejected an offer of a commission as a second lieutenant of Artillery for Ordnance duty on February 2, 1864. Unofficial reports say he accompanied the quartermaster's records to Danville at the end of the war, but they were destroyed there.

He married Emily Crenshaw Miller of Victoria, Texas, in 1870, and they had four children. He died on May 13, 1893, at Leesburg, Lake County, Florida, and was buried in the Lone Oak Cemetery of that town.

GRAVES, HENRY LEA. Henry Lea Graves, the son of Iverson Graves and Sarah Ward Dutton, was born January 7, 1842, at Mount Pleasant plantation, Newton County, Georgia. He attended a preparatory school for the University of North Carolina, Bingham School, at Oaks, Orange County. But he returned to Georgia and entered Emory University as a sophomore in the fall of 1860.

He enlisted August 7, 1861, at Sewell's Point, Virginia, as a private, Company D, 2nd Independent Battalion, later Company B, 2nd Battalion, Georgia Infantry. He was not in good health at this time and during the winter was sent back to Georgia to recover. He was finally discharged on January 22, 1862, at the Georgia Barracks, Norfolk, Virginia, on a certificate of disability. His discharge states he was born in Newton County, was 19 years of age, 5 '9 " in height, with a fair complexion, blue eyes, light hair, and by occupation a student.

He must have re-enlisted in Company B, 2nd Georgia Battalion, as a pay voucher exists for July 1 - October 24, 1862, when he was commissioned as a second lieutenant in the Marine Corps. His first duty assignment was with the Marine battalion at Camp Beall, Drewry's Bluff. In September and December 1862, he witnessed Clothing Receipt Rolls for Company C, C.S.M.C. On January 14, 1863, he witnessed a Clothing Receipt Roll for Company B, C.S.M.C.

After several months at Drewry's Bluff, he received orders sending him to Savannah, where he reported to Commodore Josiah Tattnall and to Marine Captain John R. F. Tattnall, on February 2, 1863. At various times over the next several months, he recruited men for the Marine Corps at the Conscript Camp at Decatur. He was ordered on July 20, 1863, to the newly commissioned C.S.S. *Savannah* in command of the Marine Guard of that ship. He served on the *Savannah* until February 1, 1864, when he was returned to shore duty. On 7 January 1864 he received notification of his promotion to first lieutenant with his commission dated back to February 1, 1863.

Graves participated in the defense of Savannah, serving with a portion of Marine Company E under Captain Tattnall in the trenches near King's Bridge. He retreated with his company to Charleston, and from there to Greensboro, where he was paroled on April 28, 1865.

He returned to Mount Pleasant after the war and married Miss Henrietta Milligan of Augusta on June 2, 1869. They had five children.

Graves served as a representative for Newton County in the Georgia State Legislature, 1890-91. He died on December 16, 1892.

DOAK, HENRY MELVILLE. Henry Melville Doak was born in Washington County, Tennessee, on August 3, 1841, the son of the Reverend Archibald Alex. Doak and his wife, Sarah Paxton Cowan. Doak attended Stewart College in 1859 and studied law in 1860 at Knoxville under William Swan, later a member of the Confederate House of Representatives from Tennessee for the 1st and 2nd Congresses.

Doak enlisted at Knoxville, as a private in Company E, 19th Tennessee Infantry, on June 11, 1861, and was appointed regimental sergeant-major the same day. (Doak said later he enlisted on April 9, 1861.) He was "Special Adjutant" to the regiment at the battle of Fishing Creek on January 19-20, 1862, and his colonel wrote he ". . . distinguished himself by personal courage & exertions during the engagement & the retreat. . . ." when recommending him for promotion to lieutenant. His father, however, expressed his preference for Henry's promotion to a cadetship only. He was wounded at the battle of Shiloh on April 6-7, 1862.

After recovering from his wound, he was appointed a second lieutenant in the Marine Corps as of November 12, 1862, and served first at Drewry's Bluff. He was sent to Charleston during the spring of 1863 to arrest and return deserters. During the summer of 1863, Doak returned to Charleston to command the broadside guns on board C.S.S. *Charleston*, participating in three naval engagements and one land attack, according to his Memoirs. After a disagreement with Captain Isaac N. Brown, commanding *Charleston*, Doak was transferred to Marine duty at Savannah where he was located by October 31, 1863.

Upon being relieved by fellow Lieutenant T. St. Geo. Pratt on March 1, 1864, Doak was transferred to Wilmington to take command of the Marine Guard of C.S.S. *Raleigh* when completed. While awaiting the completion of *Raleigh*, Doak was in temporary command of the guard at the Navy cotton yard on the south side of the Cape Fear River. He served on board *Raleigh* in her engagement with the Federal blockaders on May 6-7, 1864. *Raleigh* ran aground on May 7 and broke her back. Three days later, Doak was ordered to report to Lieutenant Richard H. Henderson in Wilmington for duty. In July 1864, he was commanding a Marine Guard at Smithville. Assigned for a time to the Receiving Ship *Arctic*, Doak was assigned on October 1, 1864, to command the Marine Guard on C.S.S. *Tallahassee* renamed *Olustee* (vice Lieutenant Edward Crenshaw) in time to be on board for her second cruise. He reported on board October 3, 1864. The guard was detached December 14, 1864.

Doak participated in the defense of Fort Fisher, December 24-25, 1864, and again on January 13-15, 1865. He was wounded in the leg by a piece of shell on January 15 while commanding a mortar battery in Fort Fisher. He was captured and taken first to Fort Monroe (Military Prison, Camp Hamilton), and then transferred to Fort Delaware on February 11, 1865, being paroled on February 27, 1865. He visited friends in Newcastle, Delaware, and Baltimore, while on parole. He was forwarded to City Point for exchange, and on March 5 Lieutenant Crenshaw wrote in his diary that Doak had returned from prison.

He was hospitalized in the Naval Hospital upon arriving in Richmond as his wound had broken open. He was discharged on the morning of the city's evacuation, joined the retreat, surrendered, and was paroled at Appomattox on April 10, 1865.

Doak married Margaret Lacy Lockert, of Clarksville, Tennessee, in 1866, and bought half interest in a newspaper. In 1875 he was Editor-in-Chief of the Nashville *American*. He was appointed Clerk of the U.S. District Court in Nashville in 1886, holding this post until his accidental death on September 28, 1928, at the age of 87 years.

THE NEW BREED: 1863

BERRY, ALBERT SEATON. Albert Seaton Berry, the son of Major James Taylor Berry and Elizabeth Wise, was born at Fairfield, Jamestown (now Dayton), Campbell County, Kentucky, on May 13, 1836. His grandfather was Washington Berry who married Alice Taylor of Caroline County, Virginia.

Berry graduated from Miami University of Oxford, Ohio, in 1855, and from the Cincinnati Law School in 1858. He was the City Attorney of Newport, Kentucky, at the outbreak of the war.

He enlisted as a private in Company A, Caudill's Regiment of Kentucky Mounted Infantry (later 13th Kentucky Cavalry), on March 24, 1862. In early 1863, he was serving as a private detailed to the Signal Corps. A descriptive list at this time describes him as age 26, blue eyed, with brown hair, fair complexion, 6'6" in height, and a lawyer by occupation.

He was discharged from the Army on or about February 14, 1863, because of his appointment as a second lieutenant in the Marine Corps. He was nominated on February 27, 1863, and confirmed by the Senate on March 6, 1863. His first duty assignment was at Drewry's Bluff. He was assigned to the command of the Marine Guard of the C.S.S. *Charleston* at Charleston, on October 21, 1863, and reported on board November 5, 1863.

As of February 10, 1865, he was in command of the Marines of the Charleston Squadron, but the arrival of Company E brought Captain Tattnall from Savannah who outranked him. After the evacuation of Charleston and Wilmington, Berry retreated to Drewry's Bluff as a part of Flag-Officer Tucker's command which was re-organized and drilled as an infantry command styled "Tucker's Naval Brigade."

He participated in the Appomattox Campaign and is reported to have surrendered at Sayler's Creek on April 6, 1865. After a brief confinement in Old Capitol Prison and Johnson's Island, he was released on June 5, 1865.

After the war, he held various public offices, including Mayor of Newport, member of the Kentucky State Senate, and a member of the U.S. House of Representatives from the 53rd through the 56th Congresses (1893-1901). At the time of his death on January 6, 1908, he was Judge of the 17th Kentucky Judicial District. He was buried in Evergreen Cemetery, Newport.

Berry married Anne Shaler, sister of Professor Nathaniel Shaler, of Harvard College. Their children were Alice, Dr. Shaler (M.D.), Albert S., Jr., Anne Elizabeth, and Captain Robert Lawrence, U.S.N. His nephew Brent Spence occupied Berry's former seat in the U.S. House of Representatives from 1931 to 1962.

NEUFVILLE, EDWARD FENWICK. Edward Fenwick Neufville, son of the Rev. Edward N. Neufville and Mary Fenwick Kollack, was born in Savannah on September 28, 1841. His father was the rector of Christ Church in that city for 25 years.

He enlisted as a private in Lieutenant J. F. Waring's company of Georgia Hussars in Savannah on or about June 1, 1861, for 30 days. This company apparently served just 30 days in Confederate service.

The next record of his service is his enlistment on January 2, 1862, as a private in Captain Joseph S. Claghorn's company, Chatham Artillery, 1st Georgia Volunteer Regiment. (This unit was later an independent company and then still later was known as Captain Wheaton's company, Chatham Artillery, Georgia.)

He was assigned to special duty with the Signal Corps on October 10, 1862, as a corporal. He continued to serve on signal duty until commissioned a second lieutenant of Marines on February 23, 1863. His appointment was confirmed by the Senate on March 6, 1863. Neufville apparently entered directly upon his Marine duties on the Savannah Station.

Neufville was detailed on January 14, 1864, as Provost of a Naval General Court Martial presided over by Flag-Officer W. W. Hunter, C.S.N. On February 1, 1864, Neufville was ordered to command the Marine Guard on board C.S.S. *Savannah*, relieving Lieutenant Henry L. Graves. Neufville and a Marine guard took over the guarding of the prisoners from the captured U.S.S. *Water Witch* and escorted them to Savannah. He was detached from *Savannah* on August 1, 1864, and returned to shore duty. On November 1, 1864, Neufville signed the Company E muster roll as commanding officer. No further record has been found of Neufville's service.

His second wife, Mary Drayton ("Hattie"), was the daughter of Commodore Josiah Tattnall and a sister of Captain John R. F. Tattnall, C.S.M.C. They were married October 22, 1863.

Neufville died on September 27, 1890, the day before his 49th birthday, at Savannah and was buried in Bonaventure Cemetery (Lot 41, Section E) in that city. He was survived by his wife and a daughter.

BRENT, DANIEL GONZALEZ. Daniel Gonzalez Brent was born in the District of Columbia on April 17, 1842, but was reared and educated in Pensacola, Florida. His father was U.S. Navy Captain Thomas W. Brent, later of the Confederate Navy, and his mother was Merced Gonzalez of Pensacola.

Brent stated in his Confederate pension application that he participated in the capture of the Navy Yard at Pensacola as a member of the "Rifle Rangers," E. A. Perry commanding (later Co. A, 2nd Florida Infantry). He then enlisted on May 31, 1861, at Pensacola, in Captain A. H. Bright's Company K, 1st Florida Infantry (the "Pensacola Guards"), being promoted later to corporal. His company was re-designated as Company A in McDonell's Florida Battalion early in 1862. Brent was ordered detailed on April 24, 1862, and for some months he served as a clerk on ordnance duty at Okolona and West Point. He was referred to as "Ordnance Sergeant, General Canty's command" in March 1863.

Brent was discharged from the Army on March 31, 1863, at Tullahoma, Tennessee, to accept his appointment as a Marine Corps second lieutenant, dated the previous day. He was described as age 21, 5 '8 " tall, having a fair complexion, blue eyes, auburn hair, and a clerk by occupation.

He was serving on the Savannah station, home of Company E, as Acting Assistant Quartermaster and Acting Assistant Commissary of Subsistence from at least May 25, 1863, through the second quarter of 1864.

On February 15, 1865, at Greenville, Alabama, he reported his inability to reach Charleston to join his company and requested Flag-Officer Hunter at Augusta to assign him to temporary duty. Hunter assigned him to temporary duty on March 1, 1865, with a detachment of Marines from Company E serving on board C.S.S. *Macon* and to command the Marines of the *Macon* and *Sampson*. He was still at Augusta when the war ended, and he was paroled there in May 1865. He applied for a Florida State Pension in January 1914, giving his residence as Escambia County.

He pursued a civilian career after the war at Mobile with the *Times* and *Register* newspapers. He returned to Pensacola in 1876, later becoming manager of the Brent Lumber Co. During President Cleveland's second administration (1893-1897), Brent was Collector of the Port at Pensacola. He served for ten years on the County Board of Health and was President of the Board of County Commissioners. Brent died in Pensacola on November 28, 1918, and was buried in Saint Michael's Cemetery.

MURDOCH, JAMES CAMPBELL. Murdoch, the son of Thomas Murdoch and Mary Campbell, was born about 1840 in Baltimore, Maryland. He may have been the "James C. Murdoch" who applied for a commission in the U.S. Marine Corps in October 1858, giving his address as California. He enlisted as a private in Captain Gaither's Company M, 1st Virginia Cavalry (a Maryland company) at Leesburg, Virginia, on June 24, 1861. This company was later known as Company K of the same regiment.

He was commissioned a second lieutenant, in the Confederate Marines as of April 8, 1863. He was reported to have served on board C.S.S. *Richmond* of the James River Squadron for a time in 1863-64. Murdoch was ordered to Wilmington on March 7, 1864, arrived on station March 12, and served under Captain A. C. Van Benthuysen in a provisional company of Marines organized for duty on that station. Murdoch was captured at Fort Fisher on January 15, 1865, but he was back in the Richmond area by March 7, 1865.

He was reported to have been one of the leaders of the party which captured the schooner *St. Mary's* and the *J.B. Spafford* in Chesapeake Bay on March 31, 1865. Murdoch was paroled at Society Hill, Darlington District, South Carolina, on May 27, 1865.

He returned to Baltimore after the war where he died of tuberculosis at the age of 49 years on September 10, 1889. He was buried in St. Paul's Yard, Baltimore, on September 12, 1889.

2nd Lt. James Campbell Murdoch.
Commissioned a Marine officer April 8, 1863.
Photograph courtesy of Eleanor S. Brockenbrough Library,
The Museum of the Confederacy, Richmond, Virginia.

ROBERTS, SAMUEL M. Samuel M. Roberts was born in Philadelphia about 1840, but was a resident of Louisiana in 1861. He enlisted April 15, 1861, at New Orleans as a private in Captain S. W. Fisk's company, Crescent Rifles, Dreux's Battalion Louisiana Infantry (later Company B, 1st Special Battalion, Righter's Louisiana Infantry).

On March 8, 1862, he transferred to Company D, 1st Virginia Artillery (3rd Company, Richmond Howitzers) at Suffolk, Virginia, and served until commissioned as a second lieutenant in the Marine Corps on April 8, 1863. His descriptive roll gave his age as 22 years, a clerk by occupation, 5 '9 " tall, with hazel eyes, light hair, and a fair complexion.

Upon being commissioned, he was assigned to Company B. On August 11, 1863, he relieved Second Lieutenant Van de Graaff as commander of the Marine Guard on board the schooner *Gallego* on the James River. This assignment seems to have included command of the Marine Guard at the Navy Yard opposite Rocketts' in Richmond. This assignment terminated on May 31, 1864, and he reported on board C.S.S. *Richmond* the next day to command the ship's Marine Guard.

On October 1, 1864, Roberts was detached from the *Richmond* to serve with the battery at Bishop's (Battery Semmes) on the James River, but by the 16th had been relieved on account of illness. He is reported to have been returned to *Richmond* on November 13, 1864, but it appears he was readmitted to the hospital at Camp Winder on November 25, 1864, returning to duty January 7, 1865. The next day he was granted a week's leave to visit Fredericksburg, Va. No further war record has been located.

Although identification is not clear, he is believed to have been the Marine Lieutenant Roberts who was surrendered and paroled at Greensboro, North Carolina, as belonging to Semmes' Naval Brigade.

RAPIER, JOHN LAWRENCE. John Lawrence Rapier was born in Spring Hill, a suburb of Mobile, on June 15, 1842. He was a second cousin of Angela S. (Mrs. Stephen R.) Mallory.

He was enlisted on April 22, 1861, at New Orleans by Captain J. M. Galt as a private in Captain Henri St. Paul's company (First Company), Louisiana Foot Rifles, later designated as the 7th Battalion, Louisiana Infantry. The unit went to the Virginia theatre after the Battle of Manassas and was assigned to Pryor's Brigade on the Peninsula. On January 2, 1862, Rapier was hospitalized at Danville and was later transferred to a Richmond hospital.

His unit participated in the Battle of Williamsburg and in the Seven Days' Battles shortly thereafter. Rapier, serving as sergeant-major of St. Paul's battalion, was wounded in this campaign. Shortly thereafter, he is mentioned as sergeant-major, Louisiana Zouaves, Coppen's Battalion. On or about August 12, 1862, his unit, along with five Louisiana regiments, was assigned to Major General "Stonewall" Jackson's command on Starke's (Stafford's) Brigade of Taliaferro's Division.

Rapier had been promoted to second lieutenant in Coppen's battalion when he was commissioned a second lieutenant in the Marine Corps. His appointment was signed by the Secretary of the Navy on July 13, 1863, and dated from July 11. Orders were issued by the Army on August 1, 1863, assigning him to duty with the Marine Corps and ordering him to report to the Secretary of the Navy. The Colonel Commandant of the Marine Corps ordered him on August 3 to report for duty to the Commandant of the Marine Camp near Drewry's Bluff. He was assigned the next day to Company A by Major George H. Terrett. Finally, on August 8, 1863, his resignation as a lieutenant, Company D, Zouave Battalion, was accepted.

Rapier was ordered from Drewry's Bluff to Mobile on December 17, 1863, where he was to report to Admiral Buchanan for duty with Captain J. E. Meiere's Marine Company D. He reported for duty on December 28, 1863.

His regular assignment was at the Mobile Marine Barracks. With the opening of the campaign in Mobile Bay, Rapier, along with the other Marines on shore in Mobile, was ordered at midnight, August 3, 1864, to reinforce the garrison of Fort Gaines on Dauphin Island. Major W. R. Browne, commanding a provisional battalion which included the Marines, appointed Rapier his Adjutant the next day.

Rapier was surrendered as a member of the garrison of Fort Gaines on August 8, 1864, and taken to New Orleans for imprisonment. Here, on the night of October 13, 1864, he broke jail successfully along with his brother officers, Captain Meiere and Lieutenants David G. Raney and James R. Y. Fendall.

Teaming up with Lieutenant Fendall, Rapier made his way back to Mobile via Lake Maurepas, Bear Island, Springfield, Tickfaw, Amite City, Summit, and Brookhaven, which he reached on November 5, 1864. On reaching Mobile on November 10, 1864, Rapier was ordered to report to Captain Thomas S. Wilson, C.S.M.C., commanding the Mobile Marines in the absence of Captain Meiere. Rapier was ordered to command the Marine Guard on board C.S.S. *Morgan* on November 30, 1864.

He presumably remained on *Morgan* through the battles of Spanish Fort and Blakely until the final surrender of the Mobile Squadron at Nanna Hubba Bluff on May 10, 1865, when he took his parole.

After the war he went into newspaper work with Major Henri St. Paul, his father-in-law, and ultimately became the proprietor of the Mobile *Register*. He died in Mobile on May 7, 1905, and was buried in the Catholic Cemetery.

THE NEW BREED: 1864

STEPHENSON, LLOYD BEALL. Lloyd Beall Stephenson, the son of James Stephenson of Loudoun County, Virginia, and Elizabeth C. Beall, daughter of Major Lloyd Beall of Georgetown, D. C., was born at Middleburg, Virginia, on November 5, 1838. His pre-war home was in Leesburg. He served as a private and sergeant in a Loudoun County company at Charles Town during the John Brown raid.

He attended the University of Virginia as a law student during the session of 1860-61. Stephenson belonged to the Southern Guard of the University of Virginia at the outbreak of the war and was threatened with dismissal because of absences while with his company at Harper's Ferry.

In connection with a recommendation for a commission in the Virginia State Forces, mention was made of his being a nephew of two distinguished Army officers who had resigned. Presumably one was Lloyd J. Beall, soon to be Colonel Commandant of the Marine Corps.

Stephenson served as a second lieutenant in Company F, 8th Virginia Infantry, from at least September 1861 through March 1862 (probably until the reorganization elections in April 1862). He then served with 'Lige White's Independent Company of Cavalry. He was captured on or about October 1, 1862, and paroled from Old Capitol Prison on November 14, 1862, being delivered at City Point for exchange on November 18. After his return to duty, he served as sergeant-major February 28, 1863, through January 31, 1864.

Stephenson was nominated as a second lieutenant in the Marine Corps on February 9, 1864, and was confirmed by the Senate on February 11. He was first assigned to Company B at Drewry's Bluff. In mid-April, Stephenson was sent to Staunton to secure men for the Marine Corps, but his results are not a matter of record. He was ordered on May 24, 1864, to command the Marine Guard at the Navy Yard at Rocketts, Richmond.

He commanded Company B on the projected expedition from Wilmington to release the prisoners at Point Lookout in July 1864. After this project was abandoned, he returned to the Navy Yard at Rocketts.

Stephenson is reported to have been paroled at Conrad's Ferry, Richmond. (This was probably Conrad's Ferry over the Potomac near Leesburg in Loudoun County, now known as White's Ferry after 'Lige White who bought and operated the ferry after the war.)

He reported to Federal authorities in Washington, D. C., on June 2, 1865, with the expressed intention of remaining in Washington. Stephenson was reported as practicing law and serving as a prosecuting attorney at Shelbyville, Illinois, about 1878.

He died December 29, 1913, in San Antonio, Texas, and was buried in the Union Cemetery in Leesburg. His wife, Kate B. Gray (4/8/1844 - 5/26/1906), whom he married in Loudoun County on September 22, 1864, is buried in the same plot.

THOMSON, RUFFIN. Thomson was born in Hinds County, Mississippi, on August 4, 1841, and was a student at the University of North Carolina from 1859 to 1861.

He enlisted in Company H, the "Brown Rifles," 18th Mississippi Infantry, and served with this unit in the Army of Northern Virginia. He was captured at Fredericksburg on May 3, 1863, and sent first to Old Capitol Prison in Washington and then to Fort Delaware on May 7, 1863. As he stated in one of his letters, hard marching just prior to the Peninsula Campaign created a never dying desire to get into the Navy, but he was too old to enter the Navy as a midshipman. Offered a chance to be examined for a commission in the Marine Corps on December 26, 1863, he was appointed a second lieutenant on February 11, 1864.

Thomson was first ordered on February 22, 1864, to report to the Marine Camp "near Drewry's Bluff" for duty and instruction. Here he was assigned to Company C. Around April 1, 1864, he was appointed Ordnance Officer of the post. He obtained 40 days leave to visit his home in Mississippi, leaving on December 24, 1864, and returning to Drewry's Bluff on March 5, 1865. He was ordered on March 16, 1865, to report to Captain John R. F. Tattnall at Greensboro, for the purpose of obtaining provisions for Tatnall's command and for the Marine Guard at Charlotte. He was then to collect supplies for the Marines at Drewry's Bluff and store them at Greensboro. He remained at Greensboro until paroled on April 26, 1865, as belonging to Captain Tattnall's command.

Thomson went to Washington Territory as a clerk to the U.S. Indian Agency but died soon after his arrival in 1888. In 1911 the University of North Carolina posthumously awarded an A.B. degree to Thomson dated as of 1863.

PRATT, THOMAS ST. GEORGE. Thomas St. George Pratt, son of a former Governor of Maryland, Thomas George Pratt (1804-1869), and Adeline Kent, was a graduate in law from the University of Virginia. He served as a private in Company A, 2nd Battalion Maryland Infantry, from at least October 8, 1862, until February 11, 1864.

Pratt was nominated a second lieutenant of Marines on February 9, 1864, and was confirmed by the Senate two days later. He was ordered to Savannah on February 22, 1864, for duty with Captain Tattnall's company "E," and he reported on March 1, 1864.

After a period of shore duty, he was ordered to C.S.S. *Savannah* on August 1, 1864, relieving Lieutenant Edward F. Neufville. Pratt and his Marine Guard were temporarily assigned to help guard Federal prisoners in Savannah from September 10 until October 14, 1864.

The Marines of the *Savannah* under Pratt joined the evacuation of the city of Savannah on December 21. They arrived in Charleston in time to be sent as part of the reinforcements to Fort Johnson in Charleston Harbor on Christmas Day 1864.

Shortly thereafter, Pratt and his men were sent to reinforce Fort Fisher where he was wounded in the foot and captured on January 15, 1865. He was taken to Fort Monroe (Military Prison, Camp Hamilton) where he was confined until released on parole by order of President Lincoln on February 10. There is no record of Pratt being exchanged, and he was released on taking the oath of allegiance at Fort Monroe on May 26, 1865.

He died at the age of 58 years in Baltimore on January 7, 1895, and was buried from St. Anne's Episcopal Church, Annapolis, on January 10, 1895, in the church cemetery.

McCUNE, HENRY HARRISON. McCune was born in Pike County, Missouri, about 1841. He served in the Missouri State Guard as a quartermaster sergeant, 1st Regiment Cavalry, 2nd Division, before enlisting on December 8, 1861, at Sac River (Osceola) as a private in Company A, 2nd Missouri Regiment, giving his occupation as a machinist and his residence as St. Louis.

On January 16, 1862, he was appointed assistant quartermaster of his regiment. Upon the reorganization of his regiment, he resigned his commission on July 7. Colonel Burbridge asked McCune to join him, but while on his way, McCune was captured near Holly Springs, Mississippi, on August 10 [?], 1862, being identified as a captain on Burbridge's Missouri staff. Although paroled for a time, he refused to take the oath, his parole was revoked, and he was sent to the Alton, Illinois, Military Prison where he was imprisoned March 3-16, 1863. He was received at Camp Chase, Ohio, on March 17. He was described as 5 '8 ", age 22, with hazel eyes, dark hair, and a light complexion. He was transferred to City Point on March 28 for exchange, arriving there on April 2. He arrived at the Ballard House in Richmond on April 6, 1863. On the 16th, he participated in a testimonial to the Hon. Thomas A. Harris, a member of Congress from Missouri.

McCune was commissioned a second lieutenant in the Marine Corps, dating from March 14, 1864. He is reported to have served first at Camp Beall, Drewry's Bluff, assigned to Company A. He was then assigned to the command of the Marine Guard at the Navy Yard opposite Rocketts in Richmond on May 24, 1864, relieving Lieutenant Samuel M. Roberts. He commanded 40 men from the two Richmond Navy Yards sent to Wilmington with the Marines from Drewry's Bluff in July 1864 for the planned expedition to Point Lookout. After the expedition was called off, McCune returned to his Richmond Assignment.

McCune participated in the Appomattox Campaign. He was in command of the last organized body of Confederate Marines surrendered at Appomattox. His parole was dated April 10, 1865.

CRENSHAW, EDWARD. Edward Crenshaw, a son of Walter Henry Crenshaw (Speaker of the Alabama House of Representatives, 1861-1865) and Sarah Anderson, was born August 29, 1842, in Butler County, Alabama. He was graduated from the University of Alabama and in 1861 from the Law School of the University of Virginia. He entered the Confederate Army as a second lieutenant of Company F, 17th Alabama Volunteer Infantry.

His father, Judge Walter H. Crenshaw, wrote Secretary of War Leroy Pope Walker on May 15, 1861, requesting his son's commission as a lieutenant in the Regular Confederate Army. He remarked that Edward, age 19, was at the University of Virginia where he was a member of Professor Bledsoe's volunteer company.

Crenshaw was elected captain of Company B, 9th Alabama Battalion of Infantry, on March 2, 1863. In July, the battalion had several companies added to it, and it was reconstituted as the 58th Alabama Infantry Regiment.

Crenshaw received a severe face wound on September 19, 1863, while participating in a charge which resulted in the capture of a Federal battery during the battle of Chickamauga. Brigadier General H. D. Clayton, his brigade commander, referred to him as a "gallant officer." In January-February 1864 he was acting as Adjutant and Inspector General for General Clayton.

On April 25, 1864, Crenshaw submitted his resignation as an Army captain in order to accept a commission in the Confederate States Marine Corps. His colonel, Bush Jones, regretfully approved his resignation on account of Crenshaw's strong personal application. Although his resignation was disapproved by Generals W. D. Clayton, Alexander P. Stewart, and John B. Hood, General Joseph E. Johnston was of the opinion that the acceptance of the Marine commission vacated the earlier Army one. Various unsuccessful efforts were made to get him to return to his regiment, but he, at first, preferred to retain his Marine commission. He later regretted his decision and initiated the steps to retract his resignation from the Army and to return to his regiment.

Army orders dated May 3, 1864, announced his appointment as a Marine second lieutenant and ordered him to report to Richmond, Va., where he was assigned to Company B. He was ordered to Mobile on May 23 to take command of a detachment of Marines being transferred to Drewry's Bluff. He left Mobile on the return trip on June 8, having been detained on the trip South due to illness.

In July he accompanied the Marine battalion to Wilmington for a contemplated expedition. When the expedition was abandoned, he was ordered to the command of the Marine Guard which went on board the C.S.S. *Tallahassee* on July 29, 1864. The cruiser left Wilmington on August 6 and returned on the 16th, capturing 33 ships on its cruise that extended as far as Halifax, Nova Scotia.

When Crenshaw returned to port, he found that efforts had been made to revoke his resignation as an Army officer. He wrote to Secretary of the Navy Mallory on September 18 expressing his earnest desire to remain in the Marine service and his intention of ignoring further orders from the War Department. His apparent tardiness in writing was due to an illness which came upon him shortly after his return from the cruise and confined him to his room for several weeks. As a result of his illness, he was relieved of the command of the *Tallahassee's* guard on September 22, 1864, and ordered to Drewry's Bluff upon his recovery.

Crenshaw reported to Drewry's Bluff by October 3, 1864. On February 12, 1865, he was ordered to take command of the Marine Guard attached to the C.S. Ironclad *Virginia, II*, where he reported on the 13th.

As an officer of the James River Squadron, he belonged to the Naval contingent commanded by Admiral Raphael Semmes which took the train from Richmond to Danville, after destroying their vessels and evacuating Richmond. They leap-frogged Lee's Army of Northern Virginia. Crenshaw served as adjutant of the 1st Regiment of Semmes' provisional brigade and was surrendered at Greensboro, North Carolina, on April 26, as part of the surrender of Johnston's army. He received his parole on May 1, 1865, and started immediately for his home in Alabama as a member of Admiral Semmes' party.

After the war, he returned to Greenville, Alabama, to practice law. He was elected clerk of the circuit court for Butler County in 1869, serving five years. From 1879 to 1883, he was County Solicitor and served later as City Attorney of Greenville.

Crenshaw was married to Sara Edith Brittain in May 1872 at Greenville, and they had two children, Arthur (later captain in the U.S. Navy, #2259, U.S. Naval Academy Class of 1896), and Edith Crenshaw Tatum. He died on September 9, 1911, and was buried at Greenville.

EGGLESTON, EVERARD T. Everard T. Eggleston, a member of a distinguished Virginia family, was born in Amelia County, Virginia, March 3, 1841. At age 24, he enlisted for 12 months as a private in Captain S. W. Fisk's company, "Crescent Rifles," on April 15, 1861, at New Orleans. This company became Company B, 1st (Rightor's) Special Battalion Louisiana Infantry. During December 1861 and January 1862, Eggleston was employed in the Commissary Department at Yorktown, Virginia.

Fenner's Louisiana Battery was organized on May 16, 1862, composed principally of former members of Rightor's Battalion. A "J. T. Eggleston" (E. T. Eggleston) enlisted May 16, 1862, as a private at Jackson, Miss. He was present for duty until December 1863 when absent on furlough. Under date of June 30, 1864, he was listed on a clothing receipt roll which might have been covering the second quarter of 1864.

Eggleston was appointed a second lieutenant in the Marine Corps from Texas on May 30, 1864, and was assigned to duty at Drewry's Bluff with Company A. On August 8, 1864, Eggleston was sent to Wilmington to bring back to Drewry's Bluff those Marines not required by Colonel J. T. Wood for his Point Lookout expedition. He was ordered to C.S.S. *Fredericksburg* of the James River Squadron on August 29, 1864. Upon the destruction of the vessels of the Squadron, he left the Richmond area as a member of Semmes' Naval Brigade, serving as first lieutenant, Company F, 2nd Regiment. He was paroled at Greensboro, on April 28, 1865, as a member of Johnston's command.

He married Miss Kate Bremond on December 29, 1874. He died October 10, 1885, in Austin, Texas.

ROBERTS, JOHN DE BERNIERE. John de Berniere Roberts was born July 4, 1843, in Craven County, North Carolina, the son of the Rev. John Jones Roberts, of New Bern, and Louisa Hooper, the daughter of Archibald Maclaine Hooper (1775-1853) and Charlotte de Berniere (1786-1854). His father was Professor of Modern Languages at the University of North Carolina 1841-42, but became an Episcopal minister in 1846. He was rector of the Church of the Holy Cross at Stateburg, South Carolina, from 1853 through 1865.

Roberts enlisted as a private at Columbia, South Carolina, on July 15, 1861, and was mustered in on August 19, at the age of 18 in Captain James G. Spann's Company G of the infantry of Hampton's Legion. In September-October 1861, he was a corporal, and he was promoted to sergeant on February 28, 1863. He was hospitalized for a wounded arm and shoulder in September 1862.

He was nominated to the Confederate Senate as a second lieutenant in the Marine Corps as "J. DuBose Roberts" on June 7, 1864, was confirmed on June 9, and accepted his appointment on June 16. His descriptive list prepared at the time of his Army discharge gave his age as 20 years and his occupation as a student. He was 6′2″ tall with dark eyes and hair and a fair complexion.

Roberts was assigned to Company C at Drewry's Bluff upon appointment. On July 3, 1864, he accompanied the Marine battalion to Wilmington for the projected expedition to release the Confederate prisoners at Point Lookout, but on July 9, he fell down a hatchway on the *Let-Her-B* and had to drop out of the expedition. Roberts was ordered to Wilmington, on September 22, 1864, "for assignment to the command of one of the Marine Guards attached to the Cape Fear River Squadron." He reported to Captain A. C. Van Benthuysen on September 30. Beginning November 4, 1864, he was in command of a Marine detachment sent to the Naval Battery known as Battery Buchanan. He participated in the defense of Fort Fisher and was captured on January 15, 1865. Sent first to Fort Monroe, he was transferred to Fort Columbus in New York Harbor, reaching there on January 26. He was treated in the prison hospital February 15-20 for an injury caused by a pocket knife. He was paroled and transferred to City Point for exchange on February 25. He was back in Virginia on March 5, 1865, and presumably exchanged about the same date. Definite information concerning his final capture, parole, and postwar activities has not been located.

He died on April 28, 1880, at Charleston and was buried the next day in St. Philip's Churchyard, lot 3078, West Cemetery. He was survived by his father and his wife, Mary Lapham Roberts, and a son, John Lapham Roberts, who married Elizabeth Talbot, but they had no children. Roberts' sister, Mary Charlotte, (b. 11/13/1844), married Thomas McCrady of Charleston. They had five children.

His uncle, Johnson Jones Hooper, was editor of the Montgomery *Mail* until elected secretary of the Provisional Confederate Congress in 1861. His father, the Rev. John Jones Roberts, died in New York City on May 20, 1908.

SMITH, EUGENE ROBINETT. Smith, a son of Granville P. Smith and Leanora Cheney, was born December 9, 1843, at Nashville, Davidson County, Tennessee. He was a graduate of the Tennessee Military Academy at Nashville. He is reported to have enlisted in Company C, 2nd (Robinson's) Tennessee Infantry, Walker Legion, on April 10, 1861, and served with this unit until December 1, 1862, when he was assigned to General Bushrod R. Johnson's staff in the Assistant Adjutant General's office. He was transferred in the spring of 1863 to Company I, 44th (Consolidated) Tennessee Infantry. On May 11, 1863, he was elected second lieutenant of Company B, 25th Tennessee Regiment, and on the next day he was promoted to captain.

An active Army career took him through the battles of First Manassas, Shiloh, Red-House, Richmond, Big Hill, Perryville, and Murfreesboro as a private. He was commended by then-Brigadier General Bushrod R. Johnson for his services at Chickamauga, September 19-20, 1863, "... for the zeal and intelligence with which [he] performed [his] respective duties," for "conspicuous gallantry and zeal" in the affair at Bean Station on December 14, 1863, and again for his services as acting aide-de-camp at the explosion of the Petersburg Crater, July 30, 1864.

Smith hoped for a professional military career after the war and applied for a regular Marine Corps commission to avoid being dropped from the volunteer service at the end of the war. The Navy Department notified him on August 20, 1864, that upon the acceptance of his resignation as an Army officer, he would receive his appointment as a second lieutenant of Marines. He submitted his resignation on September 1, and it was accepted in orders dated September 13, 1864. He was nominated to the Senate on November 10, 1864, and was confirmed on November 23, his commission dating from September 13, 1864.

He was first assigned to duty with Company A at Drewry's Bluff but was ordered to Charleston on December 16, 1864. He left Drewry's Bluff on December 20, 1864, to assume command of the Marine Guard of the new C.S.S. *Columbia*. He reported on board *Columbia* on January 1, 1865, but after the failure to launch *Columbia* successfully and the loss of Charleston, Smith and his detachment returned to the Richmond area and Drewry's Bluff, participating in the evacuation of that post and joining the retreat of Lee's Army. He was captured at Sayler's Creek on April 6, 1865.

First confined in Old Capitol Prison in Washington, D. C., he was transferred to Johnson's Island for a short confinement, taking the oath of allegiance and being released on June 20, 1865. He was described as age 21, having a dark complexion, dark hair, dark eyes, and being 5'10" tall.

Smith returned to school after the war and graduated from the Medical Department of the University of Nashville in 1867. He married Minnie (Amelia) Woods Vanleer on July 26, 1870, while living in Nashville. They had six children, four sons and two daughters.

Smith and his family moved to the Hodge Community, Jackson County, Alabama, in 1879, where Mrs. Smith died in 1886 [?]. Dr. Smith later married Miss Cecilia Stringer, of Section, Alabama, on January 4, 1893, and they had three sons: Dixie, Pelham, and Gordon. In 1909, the Smiths moved to Section where he continued his practice of medicine until a few years before his death in 1929.

He practiced medicine in Jackson County for almost 50 years and was well-known in the area, having delivered over 2,400 babies. Dr. Smith was president of the Jackson County Medical Association for a number of years.

During the Reconstruction Period, he was a charter member of the original KKK. He was a member of the Methodist Church, a Mason, and a Shriner.

He applied for an Alabama Confederate pension on September 22, 1923. At this time, his wife was living as were three children: Mrs. Nettie Allen (age 40), Dixie Smith (age 29), and Gordon Smith (age 19). Dr. Smith suffered a stroke and died at his home in Section, March 28, 1929, and was buried with a Masonic ceremony in the Section Methodist Cemetery. Smith was apparently the last Marine Corps officer to die, surviving Henry M. Doak by about six months.

PEARSON, JOHN A. John A. Pearson, son of John Pearson, of Fort Smith, Arkansas, was born November 5, 1845. His father was a Master Armorer for the Confederacy at Fort Smith and other places. He was credited with doing much early work on the gun designs of Samuel Colt. Young Pearson was only 15½ years old when he joined the Confederate service on May 21, 1861. He served under General Ben McCulloch in his Missouri campaign, and, according to one of his letters, was in every engagement of the Army of the West from Oak Hill to Iuka. In September 1862, he was with Acting Brigadier General Frank C. Armstong, commanding cavalry, Army of the West, in Northern Alabama. Pearson applied for an Army cadetship on September 26, 1862, and was endorsed by numerous officers, including a number from the 3rd Louisiana Infantry. A second application was dated December 22, 1862.

Pearson was appointed a second lieutenant in the Marine Corps, on October 8, 1864, and joined Company C at Drewry's Bluff the next day. A brother officer commented that "He seems to be a very clever young gentleman, and barely 20 years of age. He is very intelligent and will no doubt prove quite an acquisition to our Corps."

Pearson was the last Marine officer to be nominated and confirmed in his rank by the Confederate Senate. He was nominated on November 10, 1864, and confirmed on November 23, taking rank from October 8, 1864.

He was hospitalized in Richmond on April 3, 1865, when captured. Available records show him hospitalized for "debilitas" in the Jackson Hospital between April 8 and 19 when he was reported as "deserting" the hospital. Pearson is reported to have died shortly after the war (1865) in his home town of Fort Smith.

THE "BILGERS"

Students at the United States Naval Academy apply a special term to those whose academic failures force them to drop out of the Academy. They are said to have "bilged." The Confederate Marine Corps had a group of eight officers who didn't measure up for one reason or another and were dropped from the Corps. Included in this group were Captains Jacob Read, Jabez C. Rich, and George P. Turner; First Lieutenants Adam N. Baker, James F. Claiborne, and Henry B. Tyler, Jr., and Second Lieutenants Robert McG. Ramsey and Edward C. Stockton. Five of these officers were former U.S. Marine officers and one had been a naval lieutenant.

READ, JACOB. Jacob Read was born at Drakies Plantation, Chatham County, Georgia, on December 9, 1825. His grandfather, also Jacob Read, had been a member of the Continental Congress, 1783-85, U.S. Senator from South Carolina, 1795-1802, and appointed by President John Adams a judge of the U.S. District Court for South Carolina in 1801.

Read was commissioned a second lieutenant in the U.S. Marine Corps from Georgia on March 3, 1847. In 1852, Read instructed the troops of King Kamehameha III, of Hawaii. He was promoted to first lieutenant on August 19, 1855.

On February 17, 1861, Read was announced as captain #9 of twenty appointed for two regular Georgia regiments being organized. He then resigned his United States commission after almost 14 years of service. He was the commanding officer of Oglethorpe Barracks in Savannah during the fall of 1861 as well as serving as battery commander of his own field artillery battery also known as Company D, 1st Georgia Regiment, and later as Maxwell's Regular Georgia Light Battery.

Although his battery rendered "brave and valuable aid" in the Port Royal, South Carolina, area in November 1861, his personal shortcomings led to his court-martial in late 1862. He was found guilty of flagrant neglect of duty, incompetency, conduct highly prejudicial to good order and military discipline, and conduct unbecoming an officer and a gentleman. Intemperance was a contributory factor.

The court-martial sentence that Read be dismissed from the service was approved by President Davis on July 17, 1863. The Marine Corps followed suit, and he was dismissed from the Corps effective February 1, 1863, the date of the court-martial decision.

Read died at Luray, Page County, Virginia, on May 13, 1864, of heart disease, and he was buried in the Cathedral (Catholic) Cemetery, Savannah. Read never served on duty with the Confederate States Marine Corps.

RICH, JABEZ CUSHMAN. Jabez Cushman Rich, the son of John Woodman Rich and Polly Cushman, was born at North Yarmouth, Maine, on February 22, 1812, and graduated with a B.A. degree from Bowdoin College in 1832. He was a lawyer at Yarmouth when commissioned a second lieutenant in the U.S. Marine Corps on June 13, 1834. He was promoted to first lieutenant on February 24, 1839. He married Miss Elizabeth Hudson in Philadelphia on May 2, 1839.

Rich served with the Marines attached to the Army in Mexico from May 24, 1847, until July 4, 1848, including the storming of Chapultepec Palace on September 13. He was unfortunate enough to become involved in a dispute and possible duel between two Marine officers in Mexico City. Rich was, as a result, court-martialed, found guilty, and sentenced to be "cashiered" (dismissed) from the Marine Corps. After admitting his error and apologizing, Rich's sentence was remitted by the Commanding General, and he retained his commission.

Following the Mexican War, an attempt was made to reduce the officer strength of the Marine Corps, and twelve officers (four in each company grade rank) were selected to be dropped. Rich was one of the four first lieutenants selected "out." However, public sympathy was so in favor of these 12 officers that Congress, on March 3, 1849, voted to retain all of them in the Corps at their former rank.

Rich was promoted to captain on November 27, 1853. He ran into trouble again in 1856 when he was court-martialed and found guilty of disobeying a lawful order of his superior officer and of treating with contempt his superior when in the execution of his office. He was again sentenced to be dismissed from the U.S. Marine Corps, but President Franklin Pierce reduced the sentence to suspension for two months from rank, pay, and emoluments.

Rich was on board the Receiving Ship *Pennsylvania* at the Gosport (Norfolk) Navy Yard in April 1861. He was reported to have deserted *Pennsylvania* on the night of April 20, 1861, although he said later that his resignation had been left on board the ship. He went immediately to Richmond to offer his services to the Governor of Virginia. His dismissal from the U.S. Marine Corps was dated May 22, 1861.

He served first as a captain in the Marine Corps of Virginia in the Norfolk/Portsmouth area, but his services were not satisfactory, and his Virginia Marine commission was revoked. However, Rich was tendered and accepted a Confederate Marine Corps commission on October 26, 1861. No record of duty assignments during the next year has been located.

Rich began a bizarre adventure in October 1862. Motivated by the death of his mother in Maine in June and by other important interests connected with his father, Rich surrendered to Federal authorities at Norfolk as a prisoner, took his parole, and went to Maine.

He stopped off in New York City where he was arrested and confined until late December 1862 when he returned to his parents' home in Maine. In March 1863, he was again arrested and confined in Fort Preble. Rich died March 25, 1865, at his father's home in Gorham. He seems to have abandoned his wife and children after "going South." There is no record of Capt. Rich actually having served on duty with the Confederate States Marine Corps.

TURNER, GEORGE PENDLETON. George Pendleton Turner, the son of George P. Turner, of Caroline County, Virginia, and Isabel Magruder, was born in March 1837. He was a nephew of Captain George A. Magruder, U.S.N., and Major General John B. Magruder, C.S.A. He was commissioned a second lieutenant in the U.S. Marine Corps on September 27, 1856, and served on board U.S.S. *Vincennes* and *Cyane* before the outbreak of the war. His discharge from the U.S. Marine Corps was dated June 25, 1861.

Turner was first commissioned as a second lieutenant in the Virginia Marine Corps as of May 2, 1861, and then as a first lieutenant in the Confederate Marine Corps as of July 2, 1861. After recruiting duty at Wilmington, Mobile, and Richmond, he was promoted to captain on December 5, 1861.

Difficulties arising from an episode of intemperance led to a court-martial and dismissal from the Corps on December 11, 1862. He then enlisted as a private in Company B, 1st Kentucky Cavalry, on January 1, 1863. His ability was soon recognized, and he was commissioned as a captain and assistant adjutant-general on May 28, 1863, ranking from May 2. In June 1864 both Generals Joseph Wheeler and John H. Kelly wrote recommendations for Turner to be commissioned in the Regular Army or the Marine Corps. The war ended before this could be done. He is reported to have surrendered at Decatur in April 1865.

He lived near Madison, Alabama, after the war until his death on June 29, 1905. He was buried in the Maple Hill Cemetery, Huntsville, Alabama. His wife, the former Anna Keller (1842-1914), was a cousin of the world famous Helen Keller.

BAKER, ADAM NEILL. Adam Neill Baker, the son of Capt. Daniel D. Baker, U.S.M.C., was born in Pennsylvania about 1835 and was appointed a second lieutenant in the U.S. Marine Corps from Florida on September 12, 1853, following the death of his father on August 31, 1853, at Pensacola of "Black Vomit" [Yellow Fever].

He was court-martialed on February 8, 1860, but was found "not guilty" although the Flag-Officer was instructed to admonish him privately "for borrowing money from the ship's corporal." He was promoted to first lieutenant effective August 1, 1860.

Baker was serving on the Norfolk Naval Station on April 20, 1861, when he resigned. Two days later, as a captain in the Virginia Marine Corps, he was ordered to open a rendezvous for men for that organization at the Gosport Navy Yard.

Baker was appointed a first lieutenant in the Confederate Marine Corps as of June 6, 1861, and was sent to the Marine battalion being assembled at Pensacola. He was detailed as Acting Quartermaster for the Marines as of November 6, 1861, upon the resignation of Major Gonzalez.

A week later, on November 13, 1861, he deserted by turning himself in at Fort Pickens. He was shipped north as a prisoner to Fort Lafayette, being released on February 21, 1862. He was dropped from the Confederate Marine Corps on October 10, 1862. No further record of Baker has been found.

CLAIBORNE, JAMES FRANCIS. James Francis Claiborne, born about 1833 in Mississippi, was a son of Colonel F. L. Claiborne, of Pointe Coupee. He originally enlisted on April 15, 1861, at New Orleans as a private in Captain Stuart W. Fisk's company of "Crescent Rifles" (later Co. B, 1st Special, or Rightor's, Battalion Louisiana Infantry). He was discharged as of October 28, 1861, having been appointed a second lieutenant in the Confederate Marine Corps by President Jefferson Davis, an old friend of the Claiborne family.

Assigned to Company B at Pensacola, he was transferred to the Nor-folk/Richmond area where he commanded the Marine Guard on board *Patrick Henry* from April 25, 1862, until the guard was sent ashore to Drewry's Bluff. He was promoted to first lieutenant on October 10, 1862. He was dismissed from the Marine Corps on January 14, 1863, but details have not been located.

Moving to the Western Department, Claiborne became a first lieutenant of the 1st Choctaw Regiment and served as adjutant to Brigadier General Douglas H. Cooper. Captured on February 19, 1865, at the mouth of the Red River, he was imprisoned briefly at Rock Island but exchanged on March 4, 1865. He took parole #915 at Shreveport, Louisiana, June 19, 1865, as lieuten-ant and adjutant, 1st Choctaw Mounted Regiment. Claiborne died in New Orleans on May 16, 1867.

TYLER, HENRY BALL, JR. Henry B. Tyler, Jr., was a son of Henry Ball Tyler, Sr., the lieutenant-colonel of the Confederate Marine Corps, and Eliza-beth Browne Tyler. He was born May 7, 1829, in the District of Columbia, and entered the U.S. Marine Corps as a second lieutenant on January 2, 1855.

At the outbreak of the war, Tyler was on board U.S.S. *Saratoga* of the African Squadron at the time the slaver *Nightingale*, of Boston, was captured with a cargo of 961 slaves. Tyler returned to the United States on board *Nightingale*, reaching port on June 15, 1861.

On the night of June 16, 1861, Tyler was arrested in New York City on a charge of being drunk and disorderly and using seditious language. As a result, he tendered his resignation from the Corps but it was not accepted, and he was dismissed as of June 21, 1861.

He went South and was commissioned a first lieutenant in the Confederate Marine Corps, accepting as of August 20, 1861. Before long he was court-martialed at Pensacola for conduct unbecoming to an officer and sentenced to be dismissed from the service on December 10, 1861. Intemperance was again a contributing factor. He seems to have remained South for the remainder of the war as a civilian.

He died in Washington, D.C., on January 22, 1896, and was buried in the family plot in the Fairfax Cemetery, Fairfax Court House, Virginia. Obituaries fail to mention any surviving immediate family members.

RAMSEY, ROBERT McGREADY. Robert Ramsey, the fourth son of Dr. James Gettye McGready Ramsey and Peggy Barton Crozier, was born c. 1832. His father was a well-known historian and public figure of East Tennessee.

Robert Ramsey was an ardent Southerner and anticipated the secession of Tennessee by enlisting as a private in Company L, 1st Georgia Regulars, at Atlanta on April 20, 1861, and served until discharged October 26, 1861, to accept a second lieutenancy in the Confederate Marine Corps two days later.

He reported for duty with Company B at Pensacola in December. At the end of February 1862, he rejoined his company at Mobile and went north with it to the Norfolk Navy Yard in early March and on the evacuation of Norfolk went with his company to Drewry's Bluff where they assisted in turning back the Federal ships on May 15, 1862.

According to his father, Robert obtained leave to participate in the battle of Malvern Hill, but overstayed his leave, was court-martialed, and dismissed from the Corps as of July 9, 1862.

Ramsey led a devious and checkered career from July until the close of the war marked by a trail of three dead bodies. On March 1, 1864, he enlisted as a private in Co. E, 12th (Day's) Battalion of Tennessee Cavalry and was shown as "present" on the January-February 1865 muster roll.

A Federal officer wrote Brigadier General John C. Vaughn, C.S.A., from Knoxville, on February 8, 1865, that a "Ramsey gave his parole as first lieutenant and aide-de-camp on your staff." This could have been Robert McG. Ramsey. Ramsey's war history as told by his father is difficult to confirm and makes extensive unproved claims.

Ramsey, as a citizen of Mecklenburg County, North Carolina, married Miss Mollie N. Atwell, daughter of W. B. Atwell, of Rowan County, on July 3, 1866, in Rowan County. He died June 4, 1890, at age 58, and was buried in Lot #64 in the Huntersville Presbyterian Church Cemetery in a marked grave.

STOCKTON, EDWARD CANTEY. Edward Cantey Stockton, born January 7, 1835 in New Jersey, was the second son of Lt. Philip Augustus Stockton, U.S.N., and Sally [Sarah] Cantey (12/19/1813 - 3/23/1835), of Camden, South Carolina, daughter of Brigadier General Zachariah Cantey and Sarah Boykin.

He entered the U.S. Naval Academy from New Jersey on October 16, 1849, at the age of 14, graduating #277. He accompanied Perry's expedition to Japan in 1853. He was promoted to passed midshipman on June 12, 1855, to master on September 16, 1855, and to lieutenant on February 7, 1857. He was dismissed from the Navy on June 30, 1858, for several incidents involving an altercation with another officer and neglect of duty with intemperance as a basic cause.

With the outbreak of the war, Stockton offered his services to the State of South Carolina, was appointed a second lieutenant and assigned to the command of the steam gunboat *Lady Davis*.

The officers of the South Carolina Navy being dismissed the last of May 1861, Stockton accepted an appointment as a second lieutenant in the Confederate Marine Corps and reported for duty with the Marine battalion at Pensacola.

His nomination was presented to the Confederate Congress on July 30, 1861, was tabled on August 13, rejected on August 16, and reconsideration moved on August 19, but was apparently defeated. The 1864 Navy Register gives September 30, 1861, as the termination date of his commission.

Returning to South Carolina, he enlisted his own company, Co. G, 21st South Carolina, on January 13, 1862, and was mustered in at Georgetown on January 16. He resigned his Army commission on or about April 15, 1862. He then accepted a commission as a master not in line of promotion in the Navy dating from March 6, 1862. He was later promoted to lieutenant for the war (2/26/63) and first lieutenant, Provisional Navy (1/6/64), serving on board C.S.S. *Gaines* and C.S.S. *Chicora*. His service was unique in that he was an officer in all three services, the Marines, Army, and Navy.

His first marriage in late 1857 was to Emma Smith, daughter of Newberry Allen Smith. They had one son, Newberry Allen Stockton. He was married a second time to Nellie Eliza Mitchell, daughter of James Mitchell, D. D., and Letitia Burwell, in Houston County, Texas, on April 26, 1866. There were three daughters by this marriage, Nellie, Berenice, and Maude.

Stockton and his family moved to St. Louis about 1878 where he represented the *United States Trade Journal* of Boston. Suffering financial reverses and having been treated for melancholia, he took his life by an overdose of morphine on February 29, 1880. He was buried in St. Louis. Stockton's service with the Confederate Marine Corps was between three and four months.

The sources of information on these officers are varied and many relatively obscure. The service records have been checked in the Confederate Marine Corps and applicable Navy records at the National Archives, in the "ZB" file in the U.S. Navy History Division, the Confederate Navy Registers, and both the Navy and Army *Official Records*. The Biographical Files in the Reference Section, Division of History and Museums, HQ, USMC, have been used for officers with prior service in the U.S. Marine Corps. More detail on sources is given in my *Biographical Sketches of the Commissioned Officers of the Confederate States Marine Corps* (Washington, N. C.: by the author, 1983), 60-67. Material on two Virginia State Marine Officers (James Otey Bradford and Cowles Myles Collier) are also found in the 1983 edition on pages 55-57, and brief notes on four individuals erroneously reported as Marine officers are given on pages 58 and 59.

As interest in the officers of the Corps has increased and material has come to light, individual sketches have been published. For additional sketches on particular officers, see the following:

Cameron, Francis Hawkes.
> Lee A. Wallace, Jr., "Lieutenant Francis Hawkes Cameron, Confederate States Marine Corps," *Military Collector & Historian*, v. VI, no. 3 (Sept. 1954), 79.

Fendall, James Robert Young.
> David M. Sullivan, "Brothers and enemise in Civil War," *Marine Corps Gazette*, v. LXI, no. 8 (August 1977), 20-21.

Fowler, John Douglas.
> David M. Sullivan, "Fowler the Soldier Fowler the Marine," *Civil War Times Illustrated*, v. 26, no. 10 (February 1988), 28-35, 44-45.

Graves, Henry Lea.
> Richard Harwell (ed.), *A Confederate Marine: A Sketch of Henry Lea Graves with Excerpts from the Graves Family Correspondence, 1861-1865* (Tuscaloosa, Ala.: Confederate Publishing Company, Inc., 1963).

Ramsey, Robert McGready.
> David M. Sullivan, "Confederate Marine Officer Robert M. Ramsey," *Military Collector & Historian*, v. XXXI, no. 4 (Winter 1979), 158-159; and "Robert Ramsey, C.S.M.C.," *Military Images*, v. II, no. 6 (May-June 1981), 3.

Rich, Jabez Cushman.
> See expanded sketch in Ralph W. Donnelly, *Biographical Sketches of the Commissioned Officers of the Confederate States Marine Corps* (Washington, N.C.: by the Author, 1983), 30-33.

Simms, John Douglas.
> Ralph W. Donnelly, "Formosa Spy." *Marine Corps Gazette*, v. 52, no. 11 (November 1968), 91-94.

Stockton, Edward Cantey.
     David M. Sullivan, "Vignette: Lt. Edward C. Stockton," *Military Images*, v. VI, no. 5 (March-April 1985), 14-15.

Tansill, Robert.
     Ralph W. Donnelly, "Robert Tansill, Captain, USMC, and Colonel, PACS, An Officer of Positive Convictions," scheduled for *Confederate Veteran*, Winter, 1989-1990.

Terrett, George Hunter.
     Ralph W. Donnelly, "George Hunter Terrett," *Yearbook. The Historical Society of Fairfax County, Virginia, Inc.*, v. 13 (1973-1975), 47-57.

Newspaper obituary for Everard T. Eggleston from David M. Sullivan has been helpful in clarifying his biographical sketch.

Chapter XII

CONCLUSIONS

For many years prior to the American Civil War, the major roles for Marines in naval combat had been to act with boarding parties, or to repel boarding parties, and to take post in the rigging or fighting tops of the sailing vessels so as to use musketry to deprive the enemy of his control of his own weather deck. The loss of this control affected the steering of the ship, the firing of the deck guns, the handling of sails and rigging, and, finally, the top command of the entire vessel.

The part played by the Irish/French/American Marines and the small arms men aloft on board the *Bon Homme Richard* in her victory over H.M.S. *Serapis* during the Revolutionary War has long been considered a classic example of the use of Marines in sea fights. Their shooting of the English seamen trying to sever the grappling lines that bound the ships together, the clearing of officers and men off the main deck (the *Serapis* lost eleven helmsmen, one after another shot down at his post), and the final blow of dropping hand grenades on the deck batteries and down the open deck hatches where they exploded exposed ammunition, were the actions which tipped the delicate balance of battle to John Paul Jones.[1]

Another outstanding example of the successful performance of Marines was during the battle between the U.S.S. *Constitution* and H.M.S. *Guerriere* during the War of 1812 when small arms fire from the *Constitution* was so effective that no one remained topside on the *Guerriere* to man her deck guns or even to strike her colors at the end of the battle.

These roles belonged to a pattern of naval warfare which was virtually outmoded during the Civil War for several reasons. First, there were no engagements of the style of the American Revolution, the Napoleonic Wars, or the War of 1812 in which full-rigged ships fought on the open sea in direct contact with boarding parties brought into action. Second, the development of the casemated ironclad river and harbor defense craft of the Confederate Navy and the matching monitors of the Union Navy eliminated the picturesque and deadly sharpshooting of Marines at close quarters which had been so characteristic of naval engagements prior to the Civil War. The steering wheel disappeared within the casemate or an armored pilot house. Armor protected all guns and their crews while sails and rigging were discarded as motive power and replaced by the steam engine shielded by the outer shell of the vessel.

Neither type of iron warship made provision for portholes for small arms firing, and, indeed, there was little need to do so since enemy personnel inside opposing ironclads presented no real target. The gun ports of the Confederate casemated ships did provide some small openings when their shutters were opened, but their openings were low to the water (just five feet, for instance, on the *Merrimack* or *Virginia*) and were largely blocked by the guns of the ship.

The Confederate casemated ships offered a boarding party little footing except on the narrow deck atop the casemate, at best a dangerous place with its iron gratings permitting an exchange of fire, or on the exposed flat deck fore or aft of the casemate with nothing visible to attack. There is only one report, which may have been a rumor, of a boarding attempt. The report is that when the *Cumberland* was rammed on March 8, 1862, "a part of her crew leaped on the roofing of the *Merrimack*, but they slid off the incline plane and the greater part were drowned."[2] In anticipation of such a maneuver, the slanted sides of the *Merrimack* had been sloshed with pork fat to cause shot to ricochet and, presumably, to prevent a foothold.

Yet the Confederates gave serious consideration to the possibility of boarding the flat decks of the Union monitors to bring about either their capture or neutralization. Secretary of the Navy Mallory and Flag-Officer Josiah Tattnall discussed detailed plans in April 1862 concerning the original *Monitor* in Hampton Roads. Boarding parties, one composed of Confederate Marines, were organized later for service against monitors in Charleston Harbor.

The function of Marines in boarding and in resisting boarders, and in maintaining small arms musketry upon an enemy ship became passé with the introduction of the Civil War ironclads.

On June 7, 1859, a General Order of Secretary of the Navy Isaac Toucey applying to the U.S. Marines provided that:

> As occasions may arise when it may become necessary to employ Marines at the great guns, they shall be instructed as full guns' crews by their own officers, and may also be assigned as parts of ordinary guns' crews under other officers of division. But the Commanding Officer will be careful not so to assign Marines except in cases of necessity.[3]

This same wording was carried over into the regulations for Confederate Marines as Article 13 of Chapter XXV.[4] The Civil War brought increased importance to this function, particularly in the Confederate Marine Corps. The big guns at Drewry's Bluff were useful in training both the junior officers and the enlisted Marines, and on board ship Marine officers were frequently used to command gun divisions while the enlisted Marines were manning the guns.

The practice of using Marines on gun crews was continued on the ships of the Federal Navy, but only on the larger sailing ships. Marines were not assigned to monitors with their small crews and low ranking officers.

The Confederate Navy, without large sailing ships-of-the-line, had room for large crews on their casemated vessels commanded by high ranking officers and assigned Marines to their new ironclads.

The Confederate Navy was perpetually short of experienced sailors and made frequent demands upon the Army for men to serve as landsmen. Whenever possible, the substitution of the regular Marines would bring better trained and disciplined men under their own officers to the ships — men enlisted to serve on board ship and ready-trained on the big guns.

Marines or Marine guards were assigned to practically all the larger vessels of the Confederate river and inland water Navy. At one time or another Marines were assigned to each of the following vessels:

C.S.S. *Atlanta*	C.S.S. *Morgan*
C.S.S. *Baltic*	C.S.S. *Nashville* (Ironclad)
C.S.S. *Charleston*	C.S.S. *North Carolina*
C.S.S. *Chicora**	C.S.S. *Palmetto State**
C.S.S. *Columbia*	C.S.S. *Patrick Henry*
C.S.R.S. *Dalman*	C.S.S. *Raleigh*
C.S.S. *Drewry*	C.S.S. *Resolute*
C.S.S. *Fredericksburg*	C.S.S. *Richmond*
C.S.S. *Gaines*	C.S.S. *Sampson*
C.S.Schr. *Gallego*	C.S.S. *Savannah* (Steamer)
C.S.S. *Huntress*	C.S.S. *Savannah* (Ironclad)
C.S.R.S. *Indian Chief*	C.S.S. *Tennessee*
C.S.S. *Isondiga*	C.S. Guard Ship *Time*
C.S.S. *Jamestown*	C.S.R.S. *United States*
C.S.S. *Macon*	C.S.S. *Virginia* (*Merrimack*)
C.S.S. *McRae*	C.S.S. *Virginia, II*

* Individual Marines assigned.

To the impressive list given above should be added three cruisers which sailed from Confederate ports: the C.S.S. *Chickamauga*, C.S.S. *Sumter*, and

C.S.S. *Tallahassee* (later *Olustee*). A full guard was enlisted at sea on the C.S. Cruiser *Shenandoah* while Marine sergeants served on board the C.S. Cruisers *Georgia, Rappahannock*, and *Stonewall*. Marines also served on the floating batteries C.S.S. *Arctic*, at Wilmington, and C.S.S. *Georgia*, at Savannah, and at the land batteries including *Buchanan* and Fort Fisher, in the Wilmington defenses, *Semmes*, on the James River, and *Shell Bluff*, on the Savannah River below Augusta.

Shore stations included the two Navy Yards at Richmond, Drewry's Bluff, Gosport (Norfolk) Navy Yard, Wilmington, Savannah, Pensacola, Mobile, and possibly the Navy Ordnance Works at Charlotte, North Carolina. Service at these stations was not continuous nor at all stations at the same time.

It was apparently planned to assign a Marine Guard to the C.S.S. *Pedee* which was being completed near Mars Bluff on the Pedee River during late 1864 as Second Lieutenant Ruffin Thomson wrote home that he understood he would "probably be ordered" to that ship.[5]

A major concept of the role of Marines as developed by U.S. Marine Commandant Archibald Henderson was that they should be ready instantly for any emergency. To implement his concept, Henderson maintained at least a skeletonized battalion at Headquarters, thoroughly trained in the latest developments in military weapons and tactics, to be used to assist in the training of new officers, and as a nucleus of a landing force (i.e., a mobile striking force.)[6] This concept was put into execution in the Creek and Seminole Wars and in the War with Mexico.

The Federal Marine Corps drifted away from this basic principle, and suffered accordingly. In attempting to please everyone Commandant John Harris almost lost the U.S. Marine Corps completely in a war-time move to disband the organization.

The Confederate Marine Corps, in contrast, and in spite of its small size, maintained a battalion organization within reach of Headquarters for almost the entire war, and it was always available to perform the very functions that Archibald Henderson visualized. Just who kept the Confederate Corps operating on these principles is not clear from the surviving records. The leadership probably came from the experienced Marine officers constituting the regimental staff (Lieutenant Colonel Henry B. Tyler, Major George H. Terrett, Adjutant Israel Greene, and Quartermaster Algernon S. Taylor) rather than from Colonel Beall himself. It is to Beall's credit that the Corps was permitted to follow Marine principles rather than develop into a regiment of sea-going infantry split into small units and scattered everywhere.

In the area of field operations, a precedent had been set and confirmed by an Act of Congress for the U.S. Marine Corps to furnish a detachment for service with the Army when the small Regular Army needed to be supplemented.

The basic conditions for field operations with the Army were present on the Confederate side at the outbreak of war — the lack of Navy ships on which to serve, operations basically on land, and an immediate need for trained and disciplined troops under experienced officers to supplement the available Army forces. In the absence of a Navy, the first companies of Confederate Marines were sent immediately to the nearest scene of action where troops might be required, Pensacola. They were not better trained or disciplined than the volunteers in the Army, but they did have experienced officers to lead and train them. But Pensacola remained a siege type operation, permitting the Marines to get practice on the big guns, but the battalion's infantry training was not put to use. The organization of a Navy of sorts brought the reassignment of most of the Marines to duty with the Navy where they remained until the Appomattox Campaign. Even so, they participated in numerous land engagements and campaigns:

1. Engagement of Ship Island, Mississippi, July 9, 1861. (Marine Guard of C.S.S. *McRae* and unassigned Marine recruits, Captain Reuben Thom, commanding.)

2. Port Royal, South Carolina, November 7, 1861. (Holmes' company later Co. A, Captain George Holmes, commanding.)

3. Bombardment of Pensacola, Florida, November 22-23, 1861. (Van Benthuysen's company, later Company B, Captain Alfred C. Van Benthuysen, commanding, actively engaged, and Thom's company, later Company C, Captain Reuben Thom, commanding, in reserve.)

4. Drewry's Bluff, Virginia, May 15, 1862. (Provisional battalion, Captain John D. Simms, commanding, consisting of Co. B, Captain Alfred C. Van Benthuysen, commanding, and Co. C, Captain Julius E. Meiere, commanding.)

5. Defense of Charleston, South Carolina, 1863-1865, including, in particular, the defense of Battery Simkins and Fort Johnson, July 10, 1864. (Various provisional units and guards. Officers included Lieutenants Albert S. Berry and Thomas St. George Pratt.)

6. Drewry's Bluff, May 9-16, 1864. (Battalion composed of Companies A, B, and C, less detachments, Major George H. Terrett, commanding.)

7. Defense of Fort Gaines, Alabama, August 4-8, 1864. (Detachments from Companies D and F stationed at Mobile, Captain Julius E. Meiere, commanding.)

8. Siege of Savannah, Georgia, December 1864. (Company E, less detachments, Captain John R. F. Tattnall, commanding.)

9. Defense of Fort Fisher, North Carolina, December 24-25, 1864, and January 13-15, 1865. (Provisional Guard Company stationed at Wilmington, Captain Alfred C. Van Benthuysen, commanding, a detachment from Co. E, Lieutenant Thomas St. George Pratt, commanding, and a few Marines from the cruisers *Tallahassee* and *Chickamauga*.)

10. Appomattox Campaign, including Sayler's Creek, Virginia, April 2-9, 1865. (Battalion composed of Companies A, B, and C, less detachments, Major George H. Terrett, Captain John D. Simms, and Second Lieutenant H. H. McCune, commanding at different times.)

11. Defense of Fort Blakely, Alabama, April 9, 1865. (Detachment of Company D, Sergeant Edmund N. Gardien, commanding.)

The Confederate Marine Corps was held available for special assignment for most of the war in the form of the battalion at Drewry's Bluff. It was not again placed under Army command and thus avoided being chewed up and decimated in combat beyond any hope of ever serving as a Marine unit.

One also looks for examples of amphibious operations by either Marine Corps during the American Civil War. A truly amphibious operation may be defined as the landing from small craft of armed forces on a contested hostile shore, usually under the protection of naval gunfire, after transportation from a distant base. Modernization does little beyond adding air control and helicopters to the landing. They are "ship to shore" operations with permanent intentions.

There was little American experience (or world experience either, for that matter) to set a pattern for such operations. The Colonial period furnished an example in the landing of Wolfe's British forces up-river from Quebec, leading to the defeat of Montcalm on the Plains of Abraham.[7] The unsuccessful American operations in the Penobscot Bay during the Revolutionary War contained the basic elements of an amphibious operation.[8] The American landings at Vera Cruz in March 1847 during the War with Mexico were perhaps the best example and were within the personal knowledge of many of the Marine officers on both sides during the Civil War.[9]

Yet the Confederacy with over 3,000 miles of shoreline to defend had little trouble from sea-borne offensive operations. Four which come to mind are the attack on Hatteras Inlet, the capture of Roanoke Island, the landings at Port Royal, and the capture of Fort Fisher. Only the last led to any penetration in depth of Confederate territory, and this was only incidental to other more successful Army land operations by Sherman and took place late in the war. Obviously the Marine arm of the Federal Navy was not performing one of its most important functions.

Amphibious operations depend upon the control of the sea adjacent to the landing point. The Federal Navy with its almost complete control of the sea and with miles of relatively easy shoreline made little effort to develop amphibious operations. The reliance was mainly upon the overland operations of the Army. Yet, time and again, the Army found the waterways invaluable in making its movements possible and in maintaining communications and lines of supplies.

Amphibious raids contain the same essential operational elements as amphibious operations. They differ in having limited objectives, and in withdrawing the forces once the immediate objectives have been achieved. Such raids have definite aims: punitive, reconnaissance, feint, the destruction or neutralization of a military objective, the release of prisoners, or the like.

The Confederate Marines had little opportunity to participate in amphibious raids since their Navy never had control of the offshore waters adjacent to the Northern States. One raid of real magnitude was planned, that to release the prisoners at Point Lookout, Maryland, but it was called off at the last minute.

On board ship, or at least on the water, the Confederate Marines participated actively and honorably in the following engagements or campaigns:

1. Attack upon Federal vessels at Head of Passes, Mississippi River, October 12, 1861. (Marine Guard on board C.S.S. *McRae*, Sergeant John Morgan, commanding.)

2. Engagements with Federal vessels on Mississippi River at Columbus, Kentucky, New Madrid, and Island #10, November 1861-April 1862. (Marine Guard on board C.S.S. *McRae*, Sergeant John Morgan and/or Sergeant John W. Seymour, commanding.)

3. Battles in Hampton Roads, Virginia. (Including *Monitor-Merrimack* fight), March 8-9, 1862. (Marine Guards on board C.S.S *Virginia*, Captain Reuben Thom, commanding; C.S.S. *Jamestown*, First Lieutenant James R. Y. Fendall, commanding; and C.S.S. *Patrick Henry*, First Lieutenant Richard H. Henderson, commanding.)

4. Battle for New Orleans, April 24, 1862. (Marine Guard on board C.S.S. *McRae*, Sergeant John W. Seymour, commanding.)

5. Battle in Wassaw Sound, Georgia, June 17, 1863. (Marine Guard on board C.S.S. *Atlanta*, First Lieutenant James Thurston, commanding.)

6. Cutting out the U.S.S. *Underwriter*, near New Bern, Neuse River, North Carolina, February 2, 1864. (Detachment of Co. C, Captain Thomas S. Wilson, commanding.)

7. Attack of C.S.S. *Raleigh* upon blockading fleet off New Inlet, North Carolina, May 6-7, 1864. (Marine Guard on board C.S.S. *Raleigh*, Second Lieutenant Henry M. Doak, commanding.)

8. Capture of U.S.S. *Water Witch*, Ossabaw Sound, Georgia, June 3, 1864. (Detachment from Savannah Squadron, probably from C.S. Ironclad *Savannah* and the Floating Battery *Georgia*, Marine commander unidentified.)

9. Battle of Mobile Bay, August 5, 1864. (Marine Guards on board C.S.S. *Tennessee*, First Lieutenant David G. Raney, commanding; C.S.S. *Morgan*, Sergeant John M. Bennett, commanding; and C.S.S. *Gaines*, Sergeant Charles Jenner, commanding.)

10. Engagement on Savannah River, near Argyle Island, December 12, 1864, with Captain Charles E. Winegar's Battery I, 1st N. Y. Light Artillery. (Marine Guard on board C.S.S. *Macon*, Sergeant N. J. Harness, commanding. [?])

11. Battles for Spanish Fort and Fort Blakely, Alabama, March 27-April 9, 1865. (Marine Guards on board C.S.S. *Nashville*, First Lieutenant James R. Y. Fendall, commanding; and C.S.S. *Morgan*, Second Lieutenant John L. Rapier, commanding. Senior Marine Officer with Mobile Squadron was First Lieutenant David G. Raney.)

From time to time the Confederate Marines were called upon for special operations, continually proving their worth, readiness, and versatility. Two of the more successful special operations were the "cutting out" of the U.S.S. *Underwriter* and the capture of the U.S.S. *Water Witch*. The third special operation, which unfortunately failed of its purpose through no fault of the Marines involved, was Lieutenant Charles W. Read's attempt to flank Grant's Army with small boats carried on the running gear of wagons, to mount torpedos on captured river tugs, and to start operations on the James River against the Federal Army's base at City Point.[10]

The Confederate States Marine Corps utilized the battalion at Drewry's Bluff as a training ground for new officers in much the same manner as Archibald Henderson visualized the use of his headquarters battalion. Once appointed and sworn in, the new second lieutenant was sent to Camp Beall at Drewry's Bluff for Marine training and indoctrination with the field battalion and under the observant eyes of the senior officers — the "old timers" from the U.S. Marine Corps. After several months of indoctrination, the new officer was transferred to company duty at Mobile or Savannah, to a Navy station or yard, or to the command of the Marine Guard on a ship. Assignments to ships were rotated every six months. The education of the new Marine officer was not considered complete at the end of his initial training and indoctrination period. He was expected to continue his studies under the watchful eyes of senior Marine officers.

The customary duties of maintaining order as ship's police continued to be a function of Marine Guards on board ships of the Confederate Navy. This was probably more important in the Confederate Navy than was usual since the crews usually had such a small percentage of real Navy seamen in them, and the control and discipline to which the officers of the "Old Navy" were accustomed was largely lacking. The security of Navy shore stations and installations was also a police function of a Marine Corps. In the performance of this function, the Confederate Marines served at the Gosport (Norfolk), Manchester (Richmond), and Rockett's (Richmond) Navy Yards, for a brief time at the Charlotte, North Carolina, Naval Ordnance Works, and on the Navy Stations of Charleston, South Carolina, Mobile, Alabama, Savannah, Georgia, and Wilmington, North Carolina.

In view of this list of activities, it seems hardly justified to say that the Confederate Marine Corps was of little use. On the contrary, the demand for Marines was constant and widespread, and they were used whenever available. The major problem was that there were not enough of them to do all the jobs that had to be done.

At least four times Confederate Marine units or detachments were included among those receiving the thanks of the Confederate Congress. The first occasion was on March 12, 1862, for the command of Captain Franklin Buchanan for the "recent successful attack upon the naval forces of the enemy in Hampton Roads [March 8-9, 1862]."[11] Essentially the same commendation was repeated on April 12, 1862, for the "officers and crews of the Patrick Henry, Jamestown, Teaser and other vessels engaged, . . . in the naval . . . victory on . . . James River on the 8th and 9th of March, 1862."[12] The second occasion was on September 9, 1862, when Congressional thanks were voted to "Captain Raphael Semmes and the officers and crew of the steamer *Sumter* . . . ."[13] The third occasion was on September 16, 1862, for the defenders of Drewry's Bluff on May 15, 1862,[14] and the fourth was on February 15, 1864, for cutting out the U.S.S. *Underwriter* on February 2, 1864.[15]

Companies B and C were included in the Joint Resolution of Thanks from the Florida Legislature to "Major General Braxton Bragg, and his gallant Army" for their successful defense of Pensacola on November 22-23, 1861.[16]

In brief, the history of the Confederate States Marine Corps seems to lead to these conclusions:

1. The role of Marines as riflemen on board ship during combat became obsolete with the development of the casemated ironclad, being replaced by a former secondary role of serving as guns' crews taking on new and increased prominence.

2. The role of Marines in the maintenance of order and security on board ship and at shore stations was continued and strengthened by the war.

3. The developing role of Marines as a mobile striking force for special assignments (land, water, and amphibious) received recognition.

4. The role of the Marine Corps as the military arm of the Navy to supplement the control of the sea was reiterated and strengthened as much by the essential failure of the U.S. Navy and Marine Corps as by the difficulties which handicapped the Confederate Navy and Marine Corps in trying to carry out this role.

5. The value of constant training for the Corps, and the careful selection of officers and their Marine education under the supervision of experienced officers in developing a professional Corps received reconfirmation.

6. A numerically adequate, trained, and experienced set of professional officers enabled the small Confederate Marine Corps to perform essentially Marine functions more satisfactorily than the much larger U.S. Marine Corps, handicapped by unimaginative leadership and by a short supply of trained officers, many of its better ones having joined the Confederacy.

7. The Confederate States Marine Corps was designed from its very beginning to be a permanent Regular organization, and the inherent weaknesses of the Army volunteer organizations were deliberately avoided.

8. In many ways, the Confederate States Marine Corps was the true connecting link between the Marine philosophy of Commandant Archibald Henderson and the U.S. Marine Corps of today.

NOTES AND REFERENCES

Chapter XII — Conclusions

1. Charles R. Smith, *Marines in the Revolution: A History of the Continental Marines in the American Revolution 1775-1783* (Washington, D.C.: History and Museums Division, Headquarters, U.S. Marine Corps, 1975), 232-234.

2. *N.O.R.* 7, 73: report of the Commanding Officer [Capt. Gautier] of H.M.S. *Gassendi* [French Navy] as translated.

3. *Register . . . of the Navy of the United States . . . for the year 1860* (Washington, 1860), 162.

4. See Appendix A.

5. Lt. Ruffin Thomson, C.S.M.C., to "Dear Pa," Augusta, Feb. 14, 1865, *Thomson Pp., SHC, UNC.*

6. Philip N. Pierce and Frank O. Hough, *The Compact History of the United States Marine Corps* (New York, 1960), 63.

7. Admiral of the Fleet, The Lord Keyes, *Amphibious Warfare and Combined Operations* (New York, 1943), Chap. I, "Combined Operations in the St. Lawrence River, 1759," *passim.* The almost forgotten British operation against Martinique and Guadeloupe, also in 1759, has been characterized by Samuel Eliot Morison as "perhaps the most successful amphibious landing in history, between Agamemnon's at Troy and General Eisenhower's in Normandy." See Marshall Smelser, *The Campaign for the Sugar Islands, 1759: A Study of Amphibious Warfare* (Chapel Hill, N.C.: The University of North Carolina Press, 1955).

8. Henry I. Shaw, Jr., "Penobscot Assault — 1779," *Military Affairs*, vol. 17, no. 2 (Summer 1953), 83-94.

9. K. Jack Bauer, "The Vera Cruz Expedition of 1847," *Military Affairs*, vol. 20, no. 3 (Fall 1956), 162-169.

10. Ralph W. Donnelly, "A Confederate Navy Forlorn Hope," *Military Affairs*, vol. 28, no. 2 (Summer 1964), 73-78.

11. II *N.O.R.* 3, 125.

12. *Ibid.*, 131, and *N.O.R.* 7, 57.

13. II *N.O.R.* 3, 136.

14. *Ibid.*, 136, and *N.O.R.* 7, 370.

15. II *N.O.R.* 3, 167.

16. G.O. 143, H.Q., Army of Pensacola (Bragg), Jan. 8, 1862, *Van B. Pp.*

Appendix A

CONFEDERATE MARINE CORPS REGULATIONS

(From *Regulations for the Navy of the Confederate States, 1862,* published in Richmond by MacFarlane & Fergusson, printer, 1862, pages 145-50, 221-25.)

CONFEDERATE MARINE CORPS REGULATIONS
CHAPTER XXV
MARINES
MARINES WHEN IN VESSELS

Article 1.
When a vessel is put in commission a guard to be sent on board.
When a vessel is to be put in commission the Secretary of the Navy will give the necessary instructions to the commandant of the marines to have the proper number of officers and marines prepared to go on board.

Article 2.
Commanding marine officer to be notified when the vessel is ready for their reception.
When a vessel is ready for the reception of the marines, the commanding officer of the station will notify the commanding marine officer, who duty it shall be to have sent to the designated place of embarkation the detachment which may have been previously ordered for such vessel.

Article 3.
They are to be entered separately on the ship's books.
When marines are received on board a vessel they are to be entered separately on her books as part of the complement, or as supernumeraries, as the case may require, and are to be, in all respects, upon the same footing as the seamen with regard to provisions and short allowances.

Article 4.
Senior marine officer will report daily in writing.
The senior marine officer shall report daily, in writing, to the commander of the vessel the state of the guard.

Article 5.
Locker for uniforms, &c.
A convenient locker shall be built, with shelves and pins arranged as a fixture on the berth deck, for the marines, where they may keep their uniform caps, pompoons, belts, &c.

Article 6.

Not to be diverted from appropriate duties, except.

They are not to be diverted from their appropriate duties, or called upon to coal ship or work as mechanics, except in case of emergency.

Article 7.

A musket-rack to be constructed.

A musket-rack shall be constructed against the cabin bulk-head, or other appropriate place, with a canvas screen to protect the muskets from the salt air and spray while at sea, where the arms will be in the most suitable place in case of any emergency.

Article 8.

They may be furnished with slop clothing.

They may be furnished by the paymaster with slop clothing and small stores when the commanding marine officer shall certify that they require them, and the commander of the vessel approves the issue.

Article 9.

Commanding marine officer to have charge of arms.

The commanding marine officer is to have charge of, and he will be accountable for, the arms, accoutrements, and clothing belonging to the marines, and he will be careful to have the whole preserved in the best possible manner. He will report any injury that may result to them from the neglect or misconduct of any person, that the amount may be recovered from him.

Article 10.

Officer to be allowed a store-room.

The marine officer will be allowed the exclusive use of a store-room, for the preservation of the clothing, accoutrements, and other articles belonging to the marines.

Article 11.

Detachments will be accompanies by one commissioned officer.

A detachment of marines, on joining a vessel-of-war for sea service, will always be accompanied by at least one of the commissioned officers who are attached to it.

Article 12.

They are to be frequently exercised.

They are to be frequently exercised by their own officers. A suitable place on deck will be assigned for that purpose, upon the application of the senior marine officer, when the other duties of the ship and the weather will, in the opinion of the commanding officer, permit.

Article 13.

Marines serving at great guns.

As occasions may arise when it may become necessary to employ marines at the great guns, they shall be instructed as full gun's crews by their own officers, and may also be assigned as parts of ordinary gun's crews under other officers of divisions. But the commanding officer will be careful not so to assign marines, except in cases of necessity.

Article 14.

When not on guard they are subject to orders of sea officers.

When not on guard, or on duty as sentinels, they are to be subject to the orders of the sea officers, in the same manner as the seamen.

Article 15.

General and special orders.

All "general orders" to sentinels shall pass through the marine officer. The sentinels on the spar-deck may receive "special orders" from the officer of the deck when an emergency may require it.

Article 16.

Reports of misbehavior to whom made.

Any misbehavior of the marines on guard duty, or on duty as sentinels, is to be reported to the officer of the deck, and by him reported to the senior marine officer on board, who will report the same to the commanding officer of the vessel for his decision.

Article 17.

No officer of inferior relative rank shall give orders to a marine officer.

No officer of the navy of inferior relative rank shall give orders to a marine officer unless such navy officer be at the time in command of the ship.

Article 18.

Detachments of marines and sailors, who shall command.

When detachments of sailors and marines are landed from a squadron or ship, the senior officer in rank shall command.

Article 19.

Precedence at courts martial, &c.

At courts martial, courts of inquiry, boards of officers, and upon all occasions of ceremony, the relative lineal rank between the officers of the navy and the marine corps shall be as now is, or may hereafter be established between the army and navy.

Article 20.

Commanding marine officer to attend to the comfort, &c., of his men.

The commanding marine officer will be particularly attentive to the comfort and cleanliness of his men, as well as their soldier-like appearance and efficiency. He will inspect the clothing at least once a month, and report to the commanding officer of the ship in case of any loss or abuse.

Article 21.

He will have charge of arm chest.

The commanding officer shall have charge of the arm chest intended for the use of the detachment.

Article 22.

Repairs of arms and accoutrements.

If repairs of the arms and accoutrements become necessary, the marine officer will apply to the commanding or executive officer of the ship for such assistance as can be afforded.

Article 23.

Non-commissioned officers may be reduced and promoted.

The marine officer, with the approval of the commander of the ship, may reduce non-commissioned officers and make promotions to supply vacancies.

Article 24.

Accounts that senior marine officers shall keep, and disposal thereof.

Such accounts are to be kept by the senior marine officer as may be directed or required by the commandant of the marine corps; and such reports and returns as he may require are to be forwarded through the senior marine officer, as directed in chapter on "Correspondence and Reports."

Article 25.

One officer shall be on board at all times, except.

When there shall be more than one marine officer attached to a vessel, one shall at all times be on board for duty, unless upon very particular occasions, to be judged of by the commanding officer of the vessel.

Article 26.

They shall remain on board until the vessel is turned over to officers of the yard.

On the return of a vessel from a foreign station, the marine officer, with the guard, shall remain on board until all the officers, seamen, &c, are detached, and the ship regularly turned over to the officers of the navy yard where they may arrive.

Article 27.

Liberty on shore.

He will regulate, under the control of the commander of the vessel, the permission of the marines to go on shore.

Article 28.

A citizen receiving an appointment, &c.

A citizen receiving an appointment in the marine corps, will be required to appear before a board of officers instituted by the Secretary of the Navy, for examination into his physical ability, moral character, attainments, and general fitness for the service, and he will only be deemed eligible for a commission upon the favorable report of the board.

Article 29.

No person from civil life shall be, &c.

No person from civil life shall be appointed a 2nd lieutenant of marines, who may be over twenty-five years of age.

Chapter XLVII
NAVY YARDS
MARINES IN NAVY YARDS

Article 1.

Detachment subject to orders of commandant of yard.

The marine detachment serving within a navy yard is to be subject to the orders of the commandant of the yard; but no part of the detachment shall be relieved or withdrawn therefrom except by order of the commandant of the marine corps, approved by the Secretary of the Navy. All such orders shall pass through the commandant of the yard.

Article 2.

Officer relieving the commanding marine officer to report to commandant of yard.

When a marine officer if ordered to relieve another officer commanding the marines within a navy yard, he shall on his arrival report himself to the commandant of the yard. Marine officers joining a navy yard will report to the commandant and commanding marine officer.

Article 3.

Commanding officer to post sentinels and report disposition of the force.

The commanding marine officer within a navy yard will cause to be posted such sentinels for the protection of the yard and vessels in ordinary as may be directed by the commandant of the yard. He will make to the commandant of the yard a daily report of the amount and disposition of the force under his command, specifying by name officers who may have joined in the previous twenty-four hours.

Article 4.

Countersign.

He will, unless the commandant shall think proper to issue it himself, transmit every morning, in writing, and under seal, to the commandant of the yard, and to such other officers and such only as he may designate, the countersign for the ensuing night.

Article 5.

During the absence of the commandant of the yard.

In the absence of the commandant of the yard, no navy officer temporarily in command shall give orders to a marine officer of superior relative lineal rank; but such navy officer may give to the marine officer of the day any orders in relation to the duties of the guard.

Article 6.

Police and internal government of the marine barracks.

The police and internal government of the marine barracks and the instruction of the marines within a navy yard shall be under the direction of the commanding marine officer, but must not conflict with the general police regulations of the commandant of the yard.

Article 7.

Non-commissioned officers may be reduced by commanding marine officer.

Non-commissioned officers serving within a navy yard or garrison, may be reduced by the commanding marine officer, he reporting the particulars of the case to the commandant of the corps; and he may promote to fill vacancies, with the sanction of the commandant of the corps.

Article 8.

Leaves of absence.

Marine officers belonging to a navy yard desiring leaves of absence will conform to the general rules of the navy on that subject. The customary liberty to non-commissioned officers, music, and privates may be granted at the discretion of the commanding marine officer.

Article 9.

Official communications.

All official communications to and from officers and enlisted men of the marine corps serving at navy yards shall be forwarded through their immediate commanding officer; but if such communications affect the commandant of the yard, or relate to any duties of the yard, they shall be forwarded by the commanding marine officer through the commandant of the yard.

Article 10.

Deficiences in the complements of marines in vessels may be supplied.

Deficiencies in the complements of marines in vessels on the eve of sailing may, by order of the commandant of the yard, be supplied by the commanding marine officer, and the circumstances of the case reported without delay to the commandant of the corps by the commanding officer of marines, and by the commandant of the navy yard to the Navy Department.

Article 11.

Offences by marines on post.

All offences or neglects which may be committed by marines as sentinels, or in violation of orders given by the commandant of the yard, must be reported to him. Other offences which may be committed by marines, either in barrack enclosures or elsewhere, may be punished by the commanding marine officer, as by law allowed, or be reported to the commandant of the marine corps.

Article 12.

They will conform to regulations.

Marines, when stationed at or employed within a navy yard, are to conform to all regulations which may be issued by the commandant thereof for its government and security.

Article 13.

Interior police and government of marines in barracks.

The interior police and government of marines when in barracks within or without a navy yard, and their military instruction, shall be under the immediate direction of the commanding marine officer.

Article 14.

Reviews and exercises.

The exercises and formation of marines at parades, reviews, inspections, escorts, guard mountings and funerals, challenges of persons, police and regulations for camp and garrison duties, and salutes, will be the same as those established, or which hereafter may be established for the army.

Article 15.

Transfer of marines from one station to another.

Where marines are transferred from one station to another, it shall be the duty of the officer transferring them to forward their returns forthwith to the officer to whom they are transferred.

Article 16.

Officers to assist in preparing rolls.

It is the duty of officers serving with detachments to assist their commander in making out rolls, reports, and returns; keeping the books of the detachment, attending to issues, and to everything connected with the welfare of the command. And the commander will see that their assistance is rendered.

Article 17.

Officer of the day. Inspection of meals.

The officer of the day will inspect the provisions daily issued to the troops, and if not of good quality, will report the same to the commanding officer. He will also inspect the different meals, to see that the rations are properly cooked and served.

Article 18.

Marines in garrison to wear prescribed uniform.

Officers and soldiers in garrison will wear the prescribed uniform of the corps.

Article 19.

Apprehension of a deserter.

When a deserter is apprehended, or surrenders himself, the officer in whose charge he is will immediately report the same to the headquarters of the corps, and to the commanding officer of the station or detachment from whence he deserted.

APPENDIX B

ORDNANCE INSTRUCTIONS APPLICABLE TO THE CONFEDERATE STATES MARINE CORPS

(From *Ordnance Instructions for the Confederate States Navy. . . .*, London: Saunders, Otley, & Co., 66 Brook Street, W., 1864, 3d Ed., in Rare Book Room, Library of Congress, VF 160.7.A3 - 1864, CSA.)

ORDNANCE INSTRUCTIONS

Article 71.

Division of Marines.

All the Marines who may not be distributed to other divisions for action, are to compose a Division of Marines, to be under the immediate command of the Superior or Senior Officer of Marines on board. He will form his division on such part or parts of the spar or upper deck as the Captain may direct.

Article 94.

Pikemen.

Pikemen are to be covered by the Marines with their bayonets fixed.

Article 164.

Calls for Assembling at Quarters.

Boarders, Pikemen, and *Sailtrimmers* of the *spar-deck guns,* or any portion of them, and of the Master's division, as well as the Marines, may be ordered from their quarters to perform a particular service, *without any call,* whenever the Captain may deem proper.

Article 260.

"Board the enemy."

Paragraph 2. In case the intention of boarding should be discovered by the enemy, and he should collect his men to repel the attack, the marines and small-arm men should take positions where they can best fire upon the men thus collected, ...

Article 261.

"Prepare to Repel Boarders!"

The Pikemen should arrange themselves in rear of those armed with swords, and in situations which will allow them to rest the points of their pikes on the hammocks or rail, and cover that part of the ship, and the ports where the assault is expected. The marines, with their muskets loaded and bayonets fixed, may be formed behind the Pikemen, or at any other place from which their fire on an assailing enemy may be most effective, and least dangerous to our own men.

Article 264.

Relating to 'Repel Boarders!'

Unless induced by circumstances to attempt to board the enemy first, the most favorable opportunity for attack will present itself when his men have been driven back; and to guard against the contingency of being repulsed, in all cases where the Boarders are called to attack the enemy, they are to be covered by the marines and all the available small-arm men on deck.

For the larger ships, the following was the usual provision for the distribution and use of the ship's Marines in action:

Marines. Officers, non-commissioned officers, musicians, and privates, to be stationed on [the spar] deck. When required, the marines may be stationed at the great guns, or howitzers. They may be distributed as the Captain of the ship may direct.

For smaller screw steamers, such as a 3d Class steamer armed with two XI inch guns and four 32 Pdrs. of 57 Cwt. each, the Marines ''. . . are to be distributed as the Captain of the vessel may direct. Their services, in action, will probably be most needed at the great Guns.'' On side wheel steamers the Marines were to be stationed on deck. They could be at the great Guns or as the Captain might direct.

Appendix C

CONFEDERATE MARINE CORPS PRISONERS

Fort Fisher, North Carolina,
January 15, 1865

CONFEDERATE MARINE CORPS PRISONERS, FORT FISHER, JANUARY 15,1865

Officers:

Bradford, David, 1st Lt., Co. B. Wdd., contusion of left hip by shell.
Doak, Henry M., 2d Lt., No Co. Wdd. in leg by shell fragment.
Murdoch, J. Campbell, 2d Lt., Co. C.
Pratt, Thomas St. Geo., 2d Lt., Co. E., Wdd. by "Minnie" ball in foot.
Roberts, J. DeBerniere, 2d Lt., Co., C.
Van Benthuysen, Alfred C., Capt., Co. B. Wdd. in head by shell.

Enlisted Men:

Ackey, John, Pvt., Co. C.
Adcock, Ransom J., Pvt., Co. B.
Barrett, James, Pvt., Co. E.
Bow, Michael, Pvt., Co. B., Wdd. in breast & bowels, DOW 1/17/65.
Bradley, Augustin, Pvt., No Co.
Bright, George F., Pvt., Co. A. Died 3/6/65 of pneumonia.
Broderick, John, Pvt., Co. E.
Brown, William, Pvt., Co. C. Died 4/4/65 of chronic diarrhoea.
Carroll, John, Pvt., Co. B.
Caul [Call], Stephen, Pvt., Co. C. Died 3/8/65 of pneumonia.
Clines, Patrick, Pvt., Co. B.
Collins, John, Pvt., Co. B.
Dean, A. F. [Frank B.], Pvt., Co. E. Wdd. Died 7/18/65 of diarrhoea.
Dillon, John, Pvt., Co. C. Wdd. slightly in hip.
Dobbs, Leonard W., Pvt., Co. E.
Drew, John [James], Pvt., Co. C. Died 2/27/65 of pneumonia.
Dunn, John, Pvt., Co. E.
Edwards, Jasper, Pvt., Co. B.
Fuller, Thomas, Pvt., Co. B.
Gafney, Dominick, Pvt., Co. B.
Gibson, Thomas P., Pvt., Co. A., Wdd. amp. at left thigh. DOW 1/17/65.
Green, George, Pvt., Co. A.
Haggerty, John, Pvt., Co. A.
Harris, Patrick, Corpl., Co. B.

Havens, Alfred, Pvt., Co. C.
Hickey, John, Pvt., Co. C.
Hogan, Joseph, Pvt., Co. A.
Huff, George B. G., Pvt., Co. E.
Jones, John P., Corpl., Co. B.
Jones, Joseph S., Pvt., Co. A.
Joyce, John, Corpl., Co. A.
Joyce, Patrick, Pvt., Co. C.
Keife, Frank, Pvt., Co. B.
Kirkland, John F., Pvt., Co. B.
Knight, Patrick, Pvt., Co. A.
Lawley, William H., Pvt., Co. B.
Lyons, Thomas J., Pvt., Co. E.
McCale, Patrick, Pvt., Co. E.
McCurdy, Samuel, Sgt., Co. E.
McDede, John, Pvt., Co. B.
McGinnis, Patrick, Pvt., Co. C.
McGuire, Edward, Pvt., Co. A.
McLaughlin, Joseph, Pvt., Co. B.
Martin, Allen A., Corpl., Co. E. Wdd.
Moore, William P. P., Pvt., Co. E. Wdd., shock & slight leg wound.
Muldoon, Arthur, Pvt., Co. A.
Mundine, John G., Pvt., Co. B.
Murphy, Thomas, Pvt., Co. C.
Nicholson, Richard J., Pvt., Co. E. Died 2/8/65 of pneumonia.
Nugent, James, Pvt., Co. B.
O'Keife, Robert, Pvt., Co. A. Wdd. GSW fracture, rt. arm.
Pierce, Richard, Pvt., Co. F.
Pittman, James M., Pvt., Co. B.
Quinn, William, Pvt., Co. A. Wdd. DOW 1/24/65, amp. left foot.
Russell, Calvin L., Pvt., Co. E. Died 4/16/65 of pneumonia.
Rutherford, George, Pvt., Co. E.
Sheehan, John D., Pvt., Co. B.
Smith, Philip C., Sgt., Co. C.
Sullivan, John, Pvt., Co. C.
Sullivan, John S., Pvt., Co. E.
Vickers, John C., Pvt., Co. E.
Walsh, Maurice, Corpl., Co. E.
Watson, Charles, Pvt., Co. B.
Williams, John, Pvt., Co. A.
Winslett, William F., Corpl., Co. C.
Wynne, Thomas, Pvt., Co. E.

SUMMARY

Company	Officers	Men	Total
A	0	13	13
B	2	20	22
C	2	13	15
E	1	18	19
F	0	1	1
None	1	1	2
	6	66	72

Appendix D

UNIFORMS, ARMS, AND ACCOUTREMENTS
OF
CONFEDERATE MARINES

UNIFORMS, ARMS, AND ACCOUTREMENTS
OF
CONFEDERATE MARINES

While a limited amount of manuscript material concerning the Corps still exists today, the fact remains that information concerning the uniforms and equipment of the Confederate Marine is quite sparse. No copies of Confederate Marine uniform regulations seem to be in existence, and the descriptions that have been found are indefinite and general.

As early as May 9, 1861, attempts were made by the Secretary of the Navy to procure articles of clothing for the Marines in Europe. His letter to James D. Bulloch referred to extracts at the end for a description of Marine clothing.[1] Unfortunately, these extracts were not printed in the Navy *Official Records*, and the Bulloch papers disappeared shortly after their return to England. All efforts to uncover the Bulloch papers today so these extracts could be inspected have been unsuccessful.

In attempting to reconstruct the Confederate Marine uniform, the fact that peaceful separation was to be accompanied by a virtual duplication of the old United States Government argues for a uniform similar to that established by the U.S. Marine Corps in 1859. This feeling is reinforced by General Order No. 2, General Headquarters, Navy Department [of the State of Virginia], Richmond, Va., April 25, 1861, which read:

> The uniform of the Officers, Seamen and Marines of the Virginia Navy shall correspond in all respects to that of the United States Navy, with the exception of the BUTTON, which shall be that of the Commonwealth of Virginia.[2]

The seizure of naval stores at Pensacola and Gosport (Norfolk) undoubtedly gave Florida and Virginia (and, indirectly, the Confederate Government) some supply of both Navy and Marine uniforms and equipment items. An English visitor commented early in 1862 on the Confederate seamen "dressed as they were in the neat blue uniforms captured at Norfolk,"[3] and it may not be without significance to note that U.S. Naval Storekeeper Samuel Z. Gonzalez became the first quartermaster of the Confederate States Marine Corps at Pensacola.

292

An undated clothing receipt roll, but apparently from the initial recruiting stage of the Marine Corps (March-April 1861), furnished certain interesting information concerning the initial issues made to the Marines. All men on this roll were listed as "privates," even those who were rated as sergeants and corporals on a roll dated July 25, 1861, indicating it was a recruit roll. Every one of the 115 men on this roll received at least one flannel shirt and a blanket. All but one man received a tin cup, tin pan, and an iron spoon. There were 109 pairs of cottonade pantaloons issued to 89 men, and 36 were issued canteens. Some 72 pairs of shoes were issued to 68 men.

Captain Van Benthuysen's company received various items up to May 6, 1861, from Captain Holmes, Major Gonzalez, and a "McMeen." Uniform items included 47 pairs of blue pants, 109 pairs of white pants, 124 gray flannel shirts, 52 blue flannel shirts, and 65 white shirts or jumpers.

Two clothing receipt rolls, one dated July 11, 1861, and the other July 19, 1861, and both presumably for issues made at the Warrington Navy Yard (Pensacola), refer to the issue of socks, white pants, blue pants, "satne" [blue satin?] pants, shoes, drawers, jackets, and Navy caps.

On a roll dated July 25, 1861, for Captain George Holmes' Company A, some 72 men received issued articles. There were 60 flannel shirts and 40 blankets issued in addition to those issued earlier. Apparently a uniform jacket had been prepared since each man was issued a jacket. An issue of white pants was made, some 82 being issued, with each man receiving at least one pair. In addition, 18 men were issued blue pants.

On the basis of these early clothing issues, it seems that the Marine enlisted man in 1861 was issued Navy caps, both blue and gray flannel shirts, both white and blue pants, and a jacket. The white trousers were apparently for summer fatigue wear in hot climate while the blues were a dress or cold weather proposition. Gray flannel shirts were probably for fatigue dress while the jackets (probably gray also) were a dress item to be worn with the blue pants. The blue flannel shirts could have been U.S. Marine Corps shirts captured at Pensacola and were used for fatigue or work until used up. The U.S. Marine Corps had just changed the uniform color of its flannel shirts from red to blue with the adoption of the 1859 Uniform Regulations.

The Confederate Marine was entitled to receive a rather complete set of clothing during his four years enlistment. Of course, it is entirely true that he didn't receive all of the listed items, but the intentions of the Government were honorable.

As might be expected, some of these items (e.g., pompoms and epaulettes) do not seem to have been issued while others were issued in quantities beyond normal expectations. Stocks are referred to only in 1861 when we find an issue of 100 to Captain Van Benthuysen's Company B at Pensacola on October 20, 1861. Shortly afterwards, Second Lieutenant Wilbur F. Johnson in his capacity as Acting Assistant Quartermaster receipted for 100 leather stocks. Presumably these were in storage for issue. It seems fair to assume that the quality of the goods produced and issued in the South was sufficiently below peace-time standards to upset any quartermaster's planned issue.

For comparative purposes, the U.S. Marine Corps clothing allowance by the 1859 Uniform Regulations is shown parallel to the Confederate allowance.

Comparative Allowances of Clothing for Federal and Confederate Marine Corps for a 4-year Enlistment.

1859 Federal Regulations[4]	1861 Confederate Receipt Roll[5]
1 Uniform Cap	1 Uniform Cap
2 Uniform Coats	2 Uniform Coats
2 Sets of epaulette bullion	1 Pair epaulettes or counter straps
7 Pairs linen trowsers	8 Pair linen overalls
8 Pairs woolen trowsers	4 Pairs woolen overalls
12 Shirts	16 Shirts
2 Stocks	2 Stocks
16 Pairs shoes	24 Pairs brogans
1 Blanket	2 Blankets
8 Pairs socks	8 Pairs socks
8 Pairs drawers	
4 Fatigue caps	3 Fatigue caps
4 Fatigue coats	4 Fatigue jackets
8 Blue flannel shirts	8 Flannel shirts
1 Great coat	1 Great coat
	3 Pompons
	2 Knapsacks
	6 Fatigue overalls
	5 Linen jackets

At least two items attract special attention today. The Confederate allowance of 24 pairs of brogans during four years indicates a life expectancy of only two months a pair. The other extreme is illustrated by an allowance of just eight pairs of socks for four years, or six months per pair. The shoes may have reflected the poor grade available yet 16 pairs in four years for the Federal Marine was hardly much better. Just eight pairs of socks per enlistment was the same allowance for both the Federal Marine and his Southern counterpart.

The Secretary of the Navy's letter of May 9, 1861, to James D. Bulloch in England requested him to purchase 2000 pairs of pants, 2000 jackets, 1000 overcoats and watch coats, 1000 pairs of shoes (brogans), 2000 flannel shirts, 2000 canton flannel drawers, 2000 pairs of woolen socks, 1000 blankets, 1000 fatigue caps, and 1000 shirts, both linen and cotton.[6]

In September 1861, Mallory again wrote to Bulloch suggesting that certain articles be shipped over from Europe for the Marine Corps. He now requested 800 overcoats (watch coats), 1000 waist belts of black leather, such as used in the British service, with cartridge box, cap box, and bayonet scabbard attached by means of slides. Also requested were 1000 knapsacks, such as used in the British service, with straps to connect with the waist belt, 20 bugles with extra mouth pieces, and 20 swords for noncommissioned officers with shoulder belts.[7] Again in March 1863, Mallory wrote Bulloch that supplies and Marine clothing and shoes for 1000 men for twelve months were urgently required. He reminded Bullock, "Marine cloth is gray."[8]

In a dispatch dated November 5, 1864, Captain Bullock at Liverpool, England, was sent an order for caps for the Marines. Bullock stated in his reply that he had requested Major Ferguson to determine the time needed to fill the order and to get cost estimates. Bullock expressed his intention of using funds derived from the sale of some of the Confederate ships to pay for the Marine clothing which he feared must be greatly needed.

An early mention of Marine uniforms is to be found in the papers of the C.S.S. *Sumter* in the itemized bill paid G. Samson of New Orleans on June 8, 1861, for uniforming the Marine Guard of that ship.[9] Lieutenant Becket K. Howell, commanding the Guard, signed for receiving and issuing the following items at the prices shown:

21 Undress uniforms for Marines	9.70	$203.70
3 Trimmings for Non-Comm'd Officers		1.50
20 Full dress suit[s] for Marines	11.50	230.00
20 Cap[s] & Cover	2.50	50.00
4 Gross Bell Buttons	8.00	32.00
		$517.20

In the fall of 1861, Van Benthuysen's company was apparently issued its regular uniform clothing. The company received at that time five pairs of jean pants and "satinett" frock coats for sergeants, four of the same uniforms for corporals, and 91 of the same uniforms for privates. Also of a uniform nature were 100 leather stocks and 100 forage caps. Of a more general nature were the 50 pairs of blankets, 100 pairs of drawers made from drilling, and 100 pairs of shoes.

Little published or manuscript material has been found that helps clarify either the cut or the color of the enlisted Marine's uniform. We do know that the Navy uniform as prescribed was gray, and there is the one mention in Secretary Mallory's correspondence that Marine cloth was gray. A possible description can be found in a deserter's notice in January 1863 which stated that "When this man ran off he was dressed in a *grey coat* and *black pants.*"[10] [Italics added.] Later in the year, a Savannah newspaper carried another deserter's advertisement which gave a slightly different version of an enlisted man's uniform: "Corp'l McDaniels, C.S.M. Corps aged 24 years, black eyes, 5 feet 7 inches high, black moustache, no beard, dressed in *grey coat trimmed with black* and blue pants.[11] [Italics added.]

On December 13, 1862, Captain George Holmes turned over various Quartermaster's Stores to Major A. S. Taylor, Corps Quartermaster. Among them was a parcel of 60 grey cloth uniform coats in good condition. There were also other uniforms coats on the list, but only the term "Tweed" is used to describe them.

Further confirmation of the details of an enlisted man's uniform is in a letter written by Captain J. E. Meiere on June 9, 1863, from Mobile to the Corps Quartermaster in which he said he could obtain ". . . about Eighty or ninety yards of *Blue Cloth such as the Marines' Pantaloons are made of* . . . ." [Italics added.] from the Naval Store House if the proper arrangements were made.[12]

Captain James Waddell of the C.S.S. *Shenandoah*, commenting on the capture of two dozen infantry pants and coats, said, "The pants would answer for the Marine guard which I hoped to be able to recruit for the steamer."[13] It is significant that the coats were not judged useful, and the assumption is that they were blue in color — blue being satisfactory for Confederate Marines' pants, but not their coats.

Uniform requisitions submitted from the Mobile Station in January 1864 reveal that a new pattern of uniform coats and caps had been authorized as 100 of each were ordered by Captain Meiere. The next month, after learning that some fatigue uniform coats and shirts were in the Quartermaster's stores, Captain Meiere ordered 150 of each. The fatigue uniform coats were particularly desired for wear in the coming summer as Captain Meiere considered the ones his Marines had were entirely too heavy for the summer climate. However, for the remainder of the winter a separate requisition was made for 100 watch coats. A new clothing requisition was made in April 1864 for 200 uniform coats and pantaloons, 144 uniform caps, 100 fatigue coats, and 200 cotton shirts, as well as drawers, sock, and brogans.

In November 1864, Navy Storekeeper D. R. Lindsay at Mobile received 324 gray flannel shirts which he distributed among the vessels of the Mobile

Squadron, Battery Buchanan, and the "Barracks." This last, which could only have been the Marine Barracks as the term was never used in reference to sailors' quarters, received some 36 of these shirts.[14]

We still have in existence today a considerable number of clothing receipt rolls for the years 1863 and 1864 for several of the Marine companies as well as scattered rolls for other years. A compilation of the items issued to the men of Company C, for instance, during the period of January 1863 through September 1864 is revealing as to the items and the quantity issued over this twenty-one month period. Of the basic uniform, there were 178 caps, 129 coats, and 227 pairs of trousers or pants issued as well as 38 greatcoats or overcoats. Probably uniform items, although not so specified, were 16 tunics and 12 blouses. In the line of general clothing, 277 pairs of brogans or infantry bootees, 297 pairs of under drawers (cotton, woolen, and unspecified), 302 shirts (flannel, cotton, and unspecified), 121 pairs of stockings (and 29 pairs of woolen sox in the winter) were issued. The only equipment issued was 101 blankets. The enlisted strength of Company C at this time was approximately 100 enlisted men so that the amount of clothing issued was a respectable *quantity* whatever the *quality* might have been.

The list value of various uniform items as late as 1864 is of more than passing interest and compares favorably with civilian prices for comparable items. The records show a transfer from the Corps Quartermaster to Captain John D. Simms at Camp Beall, Drewry's Bluff, of these articles:

90 cotton shirts @ $2.75
45 uniform caps @ $2.60
45 fatigue blouses @ $8.00
10 pairs uniform pants @ $8.00
15 pairs shoes @ $10.00
20 pairs shoes @ $10.00
 6 tunics @ $8.00
 4 uniform caps @ $2.60
 4 uniform coats @ $20.00
 4 blankets @ $6.90
10 pairs cotton pants @ $12.00[15]

The use of white clothing at Pensacola, on the Mobile station, and at New Orleans in the Deep South seems to have been uniform. There are references to white pants and shirts or jumpers being issued at Pensacola. The use of whites at Mobile is suggested by records showing that female laundresses were employed for the Marine Barracks. They were even authorized to draw rations. The Marines paid for their services, and the Paymaster was instructed on occasion to pay the laundresses the amounts due them before settling and transferring the pay accounts of transferred Marines.

Early concerns about the color scheme for uniforms worn by the field musicians of the Corps were satisfied by the location of a voucher dated September 10, 1864, for "One & a quarter yards of Blue Cloth to make pants for Drummer Boy." Since both blue and gray cloth is known to have been issued to make uniforms for Marine drummers, the identification of blue cloth for pants indicates that gray cloth was used for their coats.

Even the determination of the type, design, and color of the uniform headgear is a problem. Clothing Receipt Rolls of July 1861 show that "Navy caps" were issued at Pensacola. Efforts were made in May 1861 to secure 1000 fatigue caps in England. Fatigue caps were issued at both Pensacola and Savannah in October 1861. There was an issue of "caps" in November 1861 to Marines at Pensacola. Nothing definite showed up until a brief notation in "Police Matters" in a Richmond paper gave a hint concerning Marines' headgear. As a result of an altercation between a soldier and a Marine, it developed that upon searching the arrested soldier the city watchmen (police officer) found a Marine's *blue cloth cap* in his bosom.[16] On May 17, 1864, First Lieutenant T. P. Gwynn, commanding the Marine Guard on C.S.S. *Richmond*, requisitioned and received "1 Blue Cap" which was also referred to as "one uniform cap." This agrees with and confirms the assumption made from the earlier news story that Marine caps were blue.

The printed Receipt Roll for Regular Issues used in 1864 prescribed both a uniform cap with a pompon and a fatigue cap. The only visual representation of headgear that we have is in the sketch of the Marine Camp at Drewry's Bluff, Va., by the English artist-reporter, Frank Vizetelly, which shows both officers and men wearing a forage or fatigue cap normally identified as the French kepi. Published in November 1862, the drawing was made in the summer of 1862 following Vizetelly's arrival in the South in June. No representation of the dress cap has been located. It is assumed that the Navy caps issued at Pensacola in 1861 were a temporary expedient.

No cap ornament or Corps insignia has been located. The closest suggestion has been a reference to "Eagles and rings" printed on a clothing receipt roll dated June 1864 for Marines on the Wilmington, N. C., station.

Even when clothing was available, it was difficult to get the Marines to keep it. One problem was the selling of clothing to obtain cash. Captain Meiere found it necessary to write Colonel Beall on December 1, 1862, for pay to be sent for his men as they were "entirely without money, in consequence of which they sell their clothes and report them stolen."[17] The situation had not improved a year later, and Corps Quartermaster A. S. Taylor found it necessary to issue the following general notice on December 7, 1863:

Notice is hereby given that Marine clothing, found in the possession of any person not of the Corps, will be seized and such person,
if belonging to any military organization, will be reported to his commanding officer for infraction of regulation, and if a citizen, he will
be prosecuted for violation of the law. Marine clothing is readily
known by its material and style.[18]

Too bad we have not yet discovered the details of this distinctive material
and style!

The supply of regulation Marine clothing must have been scarce for about
this same time the Commandant was expressing his indebtedness to various
departments of the Army for their aid in supplying clothing and subsistence.

The problem continued during the war and as late as November 5, 1864,
Colonel Beall issued a general order calling for strict economy in the use of
Marine clothing because of the difficulty of obtaining it and the reduced supply on hand. He called for stringent measures to prevent Marine clothing being
sold or disposed of improperly. Commanding officers were ordered to report
to the Corps Adjutant the names of any Marines who should improperly part
with the clothing drawn from the Government. One culprit was named in orders
as being forbidden any further issue of clothing except by special order from
Headquarters because of "having repeatedly lost, sold or otherwise improperly disposed of his clothing."[19]

Curiosity is aroused by the mention under date of January 25, 1864, of
a new pattern of uniform coats and caps being prescribed for Confederate
Marines, and one wonders whether there was a change in the color of the uniform
at the same time.

On the same day, Captain O. F. Weisiger, C.S.A., Assistant Quartermaster,
receipted for 992¾ yards of "Blue Grey Army Cloth" and 30 gross gilt buttons for uniform coats for the C.S. Marine Corps. A reference to making pants
from the same material was stricken from the receipt. This last may have been
particularly significant as it suggests that both Marine uniform pants and coats
could have been made of the same "Blue Grey Army Cloth." Just how dark
this "Blue Grey Army Cloth" was is not known.

Two months later, Marine Quartermaster Taylor paid Captain Weisiger
$5,146.67 for making and trimming 485 Marine coats, presumably using some
of the cloth and buttons turned over to Weisiger on January 25, 1864. The
itemized bill for the 485 coats follows:

300 yds. Canvass .... @ .50	$	150.00
672 yds. Blue Jeans .... @ 1.25		840.00
1102 yds. Cotton Sleeves ..... @ .86		947.72
14 gross "A" Buttons ..... @ 7.50		105.00
15 lbs. Black Thread .... @ 4.00		60.00
122 Spools Cotton .... @ 1.25 pr doz.		12.70
Cutting & Trimming 485 F. Coats @ .25		121.25
Making 485 F. Coats .... @ 6.00		2910.00
		$5146.67

(Each coat took an average of 1 yd., 4 in., of Blue Jean cloth.)
(14 gross of buttons averages 4 buttons per coat plus 76 over.)
(Average cost per coat was $10.62.)

"F. Coats" probably meant field or fatigue coats. With only four buttons each, they were probably short, sack coats. Just four buttons per coat indicates only one size button was used, and that there were no trim buttons. The use of 15 lbs. of black thread suggests the color of the cloth was more dark blue than gray.

If the materials used for these 485 coats were a portion of the materials turned over to Captain Weisiger on January 25, there remained 320¾ yards of "Blue Grey Army Cloth" and 16 gross of "A" buttons available for further uniform manufacturing.[20]

At least one Marine Corps officer's uniform has survived to date and is currently on display in Atlanta, at McElreath Hall, headquarters of the Atlanta Historical Society. It is the uniform worn by First Lieutenant Henry Lea Graves. The uniform is quite similar to the regulation dress uniform of the Confederate Army, consisting of sky-blue trousers with a black welt down the outer seams topped with a bluish-gray double-breasted tunic with black edging on the cuffs. It appears to conform to the 1859 U.S.M.C. regulations as to length, the skirt extending three-fourths of the distance from the top of the hip to the bend of the knee. The Confederate Army coat skirt was to extend halfway between the hip and the knee. The tunic has a stand-up collar marked with rank bars of gold braid sown on horizontally, Army style, and gold braid shoulder knots. A double row of brass buttons, seven to a row, adorns the front of the tunic. A crimson sash was worn around the waist under the sword belt. There is no sleeve braid ("galloons") to designate rank.

A close observer reports that the buttons are not Army buttons but are those manufactured for the pre-war U.S. Marine Corps by A. N. Horstmann & Allien, carrying an eagle and a fouled anchor surmounted by a semi-circle of thirteen stars.[21]

There is no hat with the uniform today. Shortly after reporting to the Savannah Station, Graves had his gray cloth cap stolen from the rack at the house where he was taking his meals. He wrote home that common gray caps cost twelve or fourteen dollars so he purchased as a replacement a simple glazed cap, ordinarily worth 30¢, and had to pay $2.50 for it.[22]

A recent article compared Graves' uniform with that shown in a picture of Second Lieutenant Henry M. Doak, C.S.M.C. Doak's picture appeared to be a face superimposed on a drawing of a uniform. I would say the uniform coat was the product of a woman artist as the flap is from the right over the left, the way a woman's coat is buttoned. Men's coats flap over the other way, theoretically permitting the right (sword) hand to be inserted under the coat flap. This reversal is not the result of reversing the picture negative as the sword slings on the belt are pictured properly on the left side.

The pursuit of photographs of Confederate Marine Corps officers led to an interesting find on February 2, 1973, in the library of the Museum of the Confederacy in Richmond. In checking a list of Marine officers against the Museum's card index of photograph holdings, a promising listing was that of "Private Campbell Murdoch" in an album of Maryland men. This had to be James Campbell Murdoch who entered the war as a private in Company M (later Company K), a Maryland company serving in the 1st Virginia Cavalry, on June 14, 1861. He remained with this company through its transfer to the 1st Maryland Cavalry and until he was commissioned a second lieutenant, C.S. Marine Corps, as of April 8, 1863.

Inspection of this photograph instantly revealed the presence of shoulder knots as well as braided sleeve insignia of rank indicating that the subject was pictured in an officer's uniform. While the Confederate Army regulations prescribed braided sleeve insignia of rank, they did not provide for shoulder knots. The shoulder knots agree with those on the uniform of Lieutenant Graves mentioned above and conform to those prescribed in the 1859 uniform regulations of the U.S. Marine Corps.

The 1859 U.S. Marine Corps uniform regulations provided that,

All officers shall wear on each shoulder of the undress coat, and undress white linen coat, a shoulder knot of *fine gold cord* three sixteenths of an inch in diameter, the shoulder knot to consist of a twisted strap [of three cords for company officers and four cords for field grade officers], and an end of a clover leaf shape; the clover leaf end to be lined with scarlet cloth, to show through the openings; the twisted strap to be also lined *only* so as to show through the *openings*; there will be no cushion under the end which rests on the shoulder and the twisted strap extending from thence up to the coat collar; the knot to be fastened by a small Marine button, and tags at the collar, and at the shoulder two tags; tags to pass through the cloth of the coat and tie on the inside.[23]

Whether the Confederate Marine officer wore rank bars or other symbols on his shoulder is problematical. The surviving knot (Graves') and those in Lieutenant Murdoch's picture do not appear to have any.

The point of significance is that Murdoch was an officer in just one organization, the Confederate States Marine Corps, and this picture, in spite of the caption "Private Campbell Murdoch" actually pictures Murdoch in the uniform of the Confederate States Marine Corps.

This picture is also unique in that it shows the subject wearing headgear, a kepi-style cap, probably gray in color. There is just sufficient tilt to show a dark crown and just the faintest suggestion of some markings on the crown, possibly braid or a quatre-foil. No other picture of a Confederate Marine officer shows his headgear.

While the 1859 USMC Uniform Regulations prescribed a four-cord strap for field grade officers and a three-cord strap for company officers, war-time photographs of Second Lieutenant Frank L. Church, USMC,* of Second Lieutenant J. Campbell Murdoch, and the uniform of Second Lieutenant Henry L. Graves, CSMC, show that all three wore the double fancy cord knot shown above.

Possible system for shoulder knots and rank insignia for CSMC officers based on the 1859 USMC uniform regulations, the C.S. army system of rank designations, and the inspections of photos.

---

* James P. Jones and Edward F. Keuchel, *A Civil War Marine: A Diary of The Red River Expedition, 1864* (Washington, D.C.: History and Museums Divisions, HQ, USMC, 1975), 15.

Second lieutenants probably wore the strap without a rank bar. (The Atlanta Historical Society says there is no bar, nor evidence of there having been one, on Graves' shoulder knots.) The other officers probably wore the insignia of their rank as was done in the U.S. Marine Corps. (Major and Paymaster Richard T. Allison, CSMC, left two five-pointed plain gold or brass stars as mementos of his service according to Miss Margaret W. Worthington to the author, March 3, 1956. They could have been either collar or shoulder knot insignia.)

Shoulder knots would have been worn by officers on their undress coat and on their undress white linen coat (if any). The clover leaf end was to be lined with scarlet cloth to show through the circular openings. They were probably attached by a small Marine button with two tags at the shoulder to pass through the cloth of the coat and tie on the inside. There is no indication in C.S. Army or C.S. Navy Regulations that shoulder knots were worn by either of those services.

Various other photographs of Confederate Marine Corps officers exist, but they tend to illustrate differences more than similarities. Pictures made early in the war of Confederate Marine officers who had been in the U.S. Marine Corps are quite likely to be of their uniforms in the old service with possible adaptation by slight changes in ornaments, insignia, etc. The picture of Lieutenant Howell in the group of officers of the *Sumter* is an example.

Three photographs of Lieutenant Becket K. Howell exist. *The Photographic History of the Civil War* contains a small and somewhat poor picture of Howell taken in England just before joining the C.S.S. *Alabama*. He appears to be wearing a knee-length, double-breasted, gray frock coat with a high, rolled collar. In appearance it looks much the same as those worn by Navy officers pictured on the same page and presumably photographed in the same studio at the same time.

A steel engraving of Howell is to be found in Raphael Semmes' *Service Afloat* . . . . The picture shows nothing distinctive or unusual in uniform cut or design except for insignia. Although Navy-style shoulder straps were worn, the rank insignia is the Army bar for a lieutenant instead of the Navy star.

Another is in a group of the officers of C.S.S. *Sumter* taken in 1861 or 1862. Howell, standing to the viewer's right, is pictured in what appears to be a dark blue, full dress, frock coat, with gold apaulets, and wearing white gloves. It is probably his old Federal Marine Corps uniform. His coat has a double row of eight (8) buttons each, not the Navy nine, a standing collar, and two buttons on his sleeve as prescribed for a lieutenant's full dress coat in the U.S. Marine Corps. Six others of the group appear to be wearing their "Old Navy" blue uniforms with Confederate-style rank marking on their sleeves; the seventh (seated to Semmes' left) is Chief Engineer Miles J. Freeman, while not having come from the U.S. Navy, is wearing a Navy blue uniform with rank shown on his shoulder straps.

There was a second photograph made of this same group at the same times with only Captain Semmes seated. However, the identification of the officers is faulty and has been continued so in various books and magazines. In this version, only Cdr. Semmes, Chf. Engr. Freeman, and Lts. Stribling, Kell, and Chapman are identified properly; the other three are incorrect.

These pictures showing Lt. Howell in his full dress uniform are the only time there is any indication of this particular uniform being used, and no indication has been found of any other former U.S. Marine officers using their Federal uniforms while in Confederate service.[24]

A photograph exists of Lieutenant Francis H. Cameron, C.S.M.C., that shows him wearing what appears to be a double-breasted, roll collar, frock coat of Navy pattern. Rank is indicated by woven sleeve braid, Army style, rather than the stripes and loops of gold lace of the Navy. The cloth, judging by its pictured sheen, appears to be silk broadcloth, satinette, or possibly alpaca.

Another photo of a Confederate Marine Corps officer is that of Second Lieutenant John L. Rapier dated November 1864. This date places it immediately after Rapier's return to Mobile after escaping from the Federal prison in New Orleans where he had been imprisoned following his capture at Fort Gaines, outside Mobile, on August 8, 1864. This photograph shows only his head and chest so that the length of the coat cannot be determined. Insignia of rank is not apparent on the collar, and the sleeves do not show sufficiently to determine any rank markings. The color of the coat is apparently gray, and the cloth appears to be flannel. It is double-breasted with a stand-up collar and has a double row of buttons. The buttons appear to be covered with gray cloth.

The letters of Lieutenant Henry L. Graves are another source of information on the uniform of the Marine officers. On one occasion he wrote, "I got me a coat & pr pants the other day, made out of a sort of blue flannel, which is light & will do for the weather for a while yet. The white vests made military I should like very much."[25] (C.S. Navy Regulations provided for a steel gray or white vest.) On April 29, 1864, he wrote that "there is no cloth on this station [Savannah]. That from which I obtained my suit was issued by the Marine Department at Richmond."[26] The same day he wrote his mother for "some light material, jeans, or something else for a summer coat. . . I now have nothing but my heavy uniform coat.''[27] At the approach of winter, Graves sent home patterns for a duty coat and pants along with eighteen buttons for his overcoat. The overcoat he requested cut the same as a certain sack-looking, raglan style coat of his father's, only longer. The cape was to be cut so as to meet in front, under the throat, to be held up by buttons under the collar of the coat. Six buttons and eyelet holes at regular intervals were to run down the front of the cape making it so it could be buttoned up and worn at times by itself. He remarked that he had the cape buttons and requested that if enough cloth were available that a sack coat and a pair of pants be made also.[28]

Still, in view of the color scheme of gray coats and blue pants for the Corps as developed above, it is difficult to reconcile a letter from Lieutenant Thomas St. George Pratt, C.S.M.C., on duty at the Marine Barracks in Savannah, in April 1864 to a personal friend in which he queried, "Could you not draw a pair of Grey pants & dark jacket & let me have them [?]''[29]

During the second quarter of 1864, uniform cloth became available for the Navy and Marine officers on the Mobile station. Some six Marine officers (Captains Meiere, Thom, Sayre, and Van Benthuysen, and Lieutenants Fendall and Rapier) each received ten yards of gray flannel uniform cloth for complete suits. Each was charged at the rate of $3.56 a yard. This gray flannel was apparently the same as that sold to Navy officers as no distinction was made between Navy and Marine officers on the list of officers allocated cloth from the available bolts of material, officers from both services receiving cloth from the same bolt. The uniform worn by Lieutenant Rapier mentioned previously in the picture dated November 1864 might well be the one made up from this gray flannel uniform cloth. In this case, both the coat and the pantaloons would have been gray.

About the time these uniforms were made up, Admiral Franklin Buchanan issued an order that ''. . . in consequence of the hot weather from June 1 to October 1, officers attached to the Mobile Squadron may wear their gray flannel frock or sack coats with navy buttons, gray pantaloons, and vests.''[30]

Captain Meiere and Lieutenants Fendall and Rapier were then on Marine duty on the Mobile station, but Captains Thom and Sayre (major, P.A.C.S.) were serving with the Army. Capt. Van Benthuysen was in Mobile at this time awaiting orders after having been suspended from duty.

In the Richmond area, Lieutenant Ruffin Thomson was writing his father that he could get enough fine gray cloth from the Government to make one or two suits if he had some money. The cloth was double width and was selling at $16.00 per yard. Thomson expressed the hope that he would get enough for another uniform and a fine overcoat.[31]

306 The History of the Confederate States Marine Corps

During the third quarter of 1864, Navy Storekeeper D. R. Lindsay at Mobile received blue flannel, black alpaca, white flannel, and gray cloth for the making of clothing, but the invoice does not specify whether the cloth was for officers or enlisted men, or for Navy or Marine personnel. Perhaps it was for all.

In September 1864, Lieutenant Thomson wrote home that he thought he could get eight yards of very nice blue flannel, suitable for a summer outfit.[32] In February 1865, while passing through Columbus, Georgia, Thomson bought from the Quartermaster two yards of double-width blue cloth at $30.00 per yard. He considered this quite a bargain and valued it at between one and two hundred dollars on the open market.[33] Finally, in March of 1865, Thomson succeeded in getting enough gray cloth and trimmings for a new uniform coat and some English Tweed for pants.[34]

A feature that developed late in the war was the move to provide commissioned officers of the Army, Navy, and Marine Corps with clothing at Government expense. This culminated in the Act of January 16, 1865, which provided that officers of these services on active duty in the field, or service-connected disabled officers on duty, or officers of the Invalid Corps on duty (below the rank of Army brigadier-general or Navy captain) should receive one complete uniform a year. That act provided further that clothing for enlisted personnel should come first, and those officers on field duty should have preference over those on other duty.[35]

After considering for a number of years the question of the uniform for the Confederate States Marine Corps, available evidence indicates to me that the 1861 uniform basically followed the 1859 United States Marine Corps uniform substituting gray for blue in the prescribed color of the coat and cap with black trim in place of scarlet.

According to this theory, there would have been a full dress, an undress, and two fatigue uniforms, one gray and one white.

For officers, epaulets would be worn with full dress, both shoulder knots and collar rank insignia with the undress uniform, and collar rank insignia on the fatigue uniform. The scarlet sash would have been worn around the waist with the dress or undress uniform, but not with the fatigue uniform. The sash would have been worn by "Officers of the Day" across the body scarf fashion, from the right shoulder to the left side, instead of around the waist, tying behind the left hip.

Both the dress and undress uniform coats were probably double-breasted gray cloth frock coats, full skirted, with skirt extending three-fourths of the distance from the top of the hip to the bend of the knee. These coats would have had a double row of buttons, seven to a row, spaced evenly. Sleeve braid ("galloons") seems to have been worn, probably with the dress coat. The sleeve braid was probably in accordance with the Confederate Army style which provided for "gold braid extending around the seam of the cuff, and up the outside of the arm to bend of the elbow." There would have been one

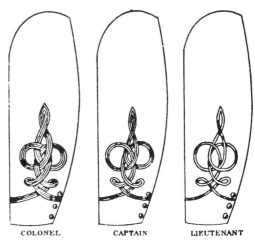

strand of braid for lieutenants, two for captains, and three for field officers. The normal width for braid was 1/8 inch.

Rank insignia was a single 3-inch long gold horizontal bar for a second lieutenant, two such bars for a first lieutenant, and three such bars for a captain. A major had one star on his collar, the lieutenant colonel two stars, arranged horizontally, and the colonel commandant probably three stars arranged in a horizontal line. This system of rank designation is the same as that used for the Confederate Army.

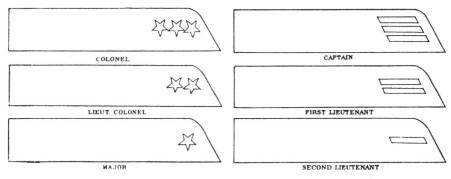

Lieutenant Murdoch's coat sleeve shows three small buttons at the end of the sleeve. This conforms to the U.S.M.C. undress coat regulations which prescribed "cuffs two and one-half inches deep, to go around the sleeve parallel with the lower edge, and *to button with three small buttons at the under seam*; . . . ."[36] [Italics mine.] Rapier's picture in his double-breasted coat shows three buttons on the under side of the right cuff. Graves' uniform coat today shows only one such button on each cuff, but the others could have been the casualties of time.

The coat flap and cuffs (and possibly the collar) were edged in black. In agreement with the black belts prescribed for enlisted men, it is supposed that the officers' sword belts were also black in color.

The cold-weather trousers for both company officers and enlisted men would have been sky-blue in color. The officers' trousers had a black welt let into each outer seam. The warm-weather trousers for both would have been white linen (or cotton duck).

The fatigue cap was probably most commonly used and was the commonplace kepi or French style. Indications are that Confederate enlisted Marine wore a *blue* cap. This conforms to Vizitelly's drawing as to design and to the Richmond news note of May 26, 1862, describing it as a "blue cloth cap." Lieutenant Murdoch's picture, while not in color, suggests a dark blue band, gray cloth sides, and a dark blue crown surmounted with a light colored knot or quatre-foil.

The enlisted man probably had a double-breasted gray frock dress coat, full-skirted, with skirt extending three-fourths of the distance from the hip to the bend of the knee. His undress coat was probably a single-breasted full-skirted gray frock coat, with stand-up collar, black welts in collar and down front seam, and buttoned with seven Marine buttons on the breast. The skirt was to extend from the top of the hip to the crotch of the trousers. His field or fatigue coat was probably a single-breasted gray sack coat, open half-way down the front, and buttoning with four small Marine buttons. Later in the war, the field or fatigue coat became a "shell jacket" or artillery jacket, a short jacket designed to fit close around the waist and extending just several inches (to the top of the hip?) below his equipment belt worn around his waist.

Chevrons for the enlisted noncommissioned officers were probably the same as in the U.S. Marine Corps, worn above the elbow, points up, probably of black material (or yellow on a black ground?). A corporal had two chevrons, a sergeant had three, and orderly (or first) sergeant had three with a lozenge below the inverted V's, the quartermaster sergeant had three chevrons with a single tie, and the sergeant major three chevrons and an arc.

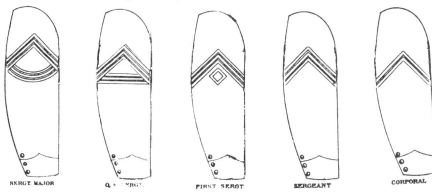

SERGT MAJOR   Q. M. SERGT.   FIRST SERGT   SERGEANT   CORPORAL

This belief is based upon an enlargement of Vizitelly's sketch showing a Marine corporal with his stripes pointed up. The use of black as trim is based on the fact that black trim (welt) was used on the one existing uniform (Graves'), Corporal McDaniel's desertion advertisement on June 2, 1863, which stated he was "dressed in grey coat trimmed with black . . . .", and the U.S. Marine Corps' 1859 Uniform Regulations as to chevrons.

OFFICERS' SWORDS

Over the years, a few notes have been accumulated on the swords carried by Confederate Marine officers.

Confederate Marine Corps officers with previous service in the U.S. Marine Corps were probably equipped with the sword prescribed in the 1859 Marine Corps Uniform Regulations. At this time, the Mameluke pattern swords were abandoned in favor of the Model 1850 foot officers' sword as used in the infantry of the U.S. Army. This sword was to have a 30 to 32 inch blade with a black leather scabbard with gilt bands and tips. Old-time officers probably had both this sword as well as one of the Mameluke pattern.

It seems reasonable to assume that former U.S. Marine Corps officers continued to use the swords they had carried in the former service. On one occasion, Lt. Edward Crenshaw wrote (October 3, 1864) in his diary, ". . . Borrowed a sword from Captain Simms today."[37] Apparently Capt. Simms, an old U.S. Marine Corps officer, had two or more military swords with him. Why Crenshaw had to borrow a sword is not clear when he had purchased an officer's sword from the Richmond Arsenal for $50 in May 1864.

Two Marine officers, Lts. Adam N. Baker and James R. Y. Fendall, received "Horse Artillery Sabres" from Capt. Oladowski at Pensacola, Fla., in the fall of 1861. While no price was mentioned for Baker's sabre, Fendall paid $5 for his.

There is a record of "1 Horse Arty. Sabre" issued to "Lieut. Tyler, C.S. Marine Corps" under date of October 15, 1862, by Lt. F. B. DuBarry, C.S. Artillery on Ordnance Duty. This is hard to acount for since Tyler had been dismissed from the Corps as of December 10, 1861, and was an unemployed civilian in October 1862. Since DuBarry had mislaid Tyler's signed receipt, it is possible this transaction had actually taken place months earlier.

As to these artillery sabres, L. Haiman, of Columbus, Ga., produced one with a 32-inch blade, a single strap guard, and a metal scabbard. James Conning, of Mobile, Ala., also produced a Confederate artillery sabre.

Newly appointed second lieutenants T. St. George Pratt and Lloyd B. Stephenson both received swords in early 1864 from Capt. O. W. Edwards, Military Storekeeper at the Richmond Arsenal, for which each paid $35, but no description is given. Although Lieutenant Edward Crenshaw had been an officer in the Army, he also purchased "1 Officer's Sword" from the Richmond Arsenal a few days after being commissioned a Marine officer. The price by this time (May 1864) had risen to $50. A picture of Lt. Crenshaw shows him holding a sword, but only the top of the hilt and guard show. The guard appears to have a disc on it, strongly suggestive of Plate 125 in Albaugh & Simmons, "Confederate Arms," page 110.

The best picture to have survived the years is one of Second Lieutenant Robert M. Ramsey who was an officer in the Marine Corps less than nine months (October 28, 1861 - July 9, 1862). Its general shape is that of an infantry officer's sword. Perhaps its unique feature is the attachment of the guard to the end of the hilt.

While some officers purchased their swords from Army Ordnance stores, others apparently carried the products of commercial suppliers. Relying on Col. Fred Todd's notes, an account of the capture of the C.S.S. *Atlanta* in Wassaw Sound, Ga., on June 17, 1863, in the Providence (R. I.) *Journal* stated, "Marine officer [James Thurston] has a sword and a fine one it is, with equipments, made by Firman & Sons, 153 Strand and 13 Conduit Street, London."[38]

In 1983, my attention was called to a sword owned by a gentleman in Texas which carried the inscription "Confederate States Marines" on the blade and "Hyde & Co New Orleans" on the back of the blade. Unfortunately, there was no *provenance* or trail of ownership.

The name of "Hyde & Co New Orleans" on the back of the blade appears to conflict with such information as we have on A. L. Hyde of New Orleans. He was a partner in the firm of Hyde & Goodrich, but withdrew from the firm on August 23, 1861. Hyde is not known to have been in business for himself, so we cannot verify the existence of "Hyde & Co."

The engraved title, "Confederate States Marines," was possible although the more formal "Marine Corps Confederate States" or "Confederate States Marine Corps" was more probable.

A sword collector friend, using just photographs, identified the sword as of French manufacture and its style as an 1850 Foot Officers Sword.

Assuming the sword was sold by "Hyde & Co New Orleans" to some Confederate Marine officer, it would have been done before April 1862 when the city was occupied by Federal forces. While the Marines did recruiting in New Orleans, the officers assigned to duty in New Orleans were probably all former U.S. Marine officers or had prior military service and therefore had their personal swords and did not need to purchase any. The public knowledge of a Confederate Marine Officer's sword not coming until the 1980's, one hundred and fifteen years after the end of the war, seems unlikely.

So much about this sword is "iffey" or "maybe", combined with faulty provenance, that a tentative conclusion is negative on its being a C.S. Marine officer's sword.

It is possible that the sword carried by Lt. Henry L. Graves may still be in the family. Richard Harwell, who edited the Graves' letters, has written that the swords of Henry and Dutton Graves (who had been an acting master's mate in the Navy) were tied with Henry's crimson uniform sash and hung in the hall of the family home in Georgia, Mount Pleasant, for many years. The swords may have descended to Mrs. John B. Reeves of Brevard, N.C., the youngest daughter of Henry Lea Graves.

The possibility of presentation swords must not be overlooked. Capt. Reuben Thom's grandson, J. Bernard Thom, wrote to the author in 1963, "you may have gotten on the trail of a handsome sword said to have been given to my grandfather by the ladies of Balto., Md. I can not get much of a line on it."[39] In a later letter Mr. Thom related how Gen. Joseph Wheeler, who had married a family cousin, wrote that the ladies of Baltimore had secured a handsome sword to present to Capt. Thom for his conduct on the *Merrimack* (*Virginia*). It seems most likely that such a presentation sword would have been inscribed with the name of the honored officer as well as several laudatory words, but the present existence of such a sword has not been made known publically.

A conclusion on the officers' swords is that while a certain degree of uniformity probably existed due to the securing of swords from Army Ordnance, there were probably a number of different styles used. Such evidence as exists suggests they carried Army swords, not Navy, and there was not a uniformity of style. Officers from the "Old Corps" probably carried the 1850 foot officers' sword while officers whose initial service was with the Confederacy probably used the so-called "Horse Artillery Sabre" as sold by the Confederate Army Ordnance Department.

Just as this revised edition was being prepared, information on the sword carried by 2nd Lt. J. Campbell Murdoch, has been revealed in an article by Daniel D. Hartzler. The sword, manufactured by Kraft, Goldsmith, and Kraft of Columbia, South Carolina, has a large brass hilt and is sheathed in a metal scabbard.

Sword carried by 2d Lt. James Campbell Murdoch, C.S.M.C.
It was made by Kraft, Goldsmith, and Kraft of Columbia, S.C. Note the silver cross
bottony bearing his name soldered to scabbard. The sword is privately owned.
Photograph by courtesy of Daniel D. Hartzler of New Windsor, Md.

The 32-inch blade is straight and basically single-edged, only the last nine inches being double-edged. Although the blade carries decorative etching, it does not carry a reference to the Confederate Marines. A silver cross has been soldered on the iron scabbard between the throat and the upper band. This "cross bottony was a symbol in the state of Maryland seal . . . and in form of a pin, adorned many uniforms of Maryland Confederates. . . ." It is engraved vertically, "Lt. Marines," and horizontally, "J. C. Murdoch."[40]

NON-COMMISSIONED OFFICERS SWORDS

Secretary of the Navy Mallory requested Capt. James D. Bulloch in England on September 26, 1861, to obtain, among other things, 20 swords for non-commissioned officers with shoulder belts, but there is no indication that they were ever received in the Confederacy or that substitutes were issued.

ARMS OF CONFEDERATE MARINES

The early Confederate Marines were promised their first arms when organized at Pensacola in the spring of 1861. A newspaper story in New Orleans reported Van Benthuysen's company was "to be armed with the Enfield rifles, as sharpshooters,"[41] but muster rolls and ordnance receipts show Van Benthuysen's company was first armed with 86 percussion smooth bore muskets (old pattern) received on May 16, 1861, from Capt. Hypolite Oladowski, Bragg's Chief of Ordnance. Accoutrements included 61 cartridge boxes and plates, 61 cartridge belts, 61 waist belts and plates, and 61 bayonet scabbards.

Captain George Holmes' Company A received an issue at the Warrington (Pensacola), Florida, Navy Yard on July 8, 1861, from Captain Oladowski consisting of:[42]

32 muskets	32 nipples
30 screw drivers	32 cartridge boxes
32 wipers	32 bayonet scabbards
3 spring vices	32 waist belts
3 ball screws	64 gunslings

When Captain Reuben Thom's Company C left Pensacola on November 29, 1861, for the Gosport Navy Yard at Norfolk, Virginia, they turned in their rifles. It is probable that the condition of these arms led to the following order issued by General Braxton Bragg:

> H Q Army of Pensacola
> Near Pensacola, Fla.
> December 1, 1861.

General Order 133.

The arms which have been turned in by the troops under a recent order, indicate a gross and unpardonable neglect by officers and men. Many are seriously damaged, some entirely ruined. The officer or soldier who by neglect or intention, thus destroys the efficiency of a gun, does his country as much harm as if he abandoned it to the enemy on the field of battle.

All commanders are called to see this evil, and correct it. Brave men are not wanting to use all arms we can procure, and the General will in future disarm any company which may be guilty of such an abuse, and turn over their guns to better men.[43]

On December 4, 1861, Flag-Officer French Forrest at the Gosport Navy Yard wrote Colonel Lloyd J. Beall, "The arms alluded to [by] you, some of those imported in the 'Fingal,' I presume have not arrived up to this date."[44] This must have been a reference to 1000 Enfield rifles (with ammunition) consigned to the Navy Department which were part of the 10,690 Enfields received from Europe on the *Fingal*.[45]

Van Benthuysen's Company B turned in their guns at Pensacola before coming north and were unarmed when they arrived at Norfolk on March 11, 1862. Arms for them were taken from local militiamen, but this must have been a stop-gap measure as the company received a new issue (probably *Fingal* imports) on April 22, 1862, of 94 Enfield rifles, rifle bayonets, bayonet slings, bayonet frogs, waist belts, and 1500 cartridges and caps approximately 16 per rifle).

But the three companies based at Drewry's Bluff do not seem to have retained these Enfields for in late 1864, their arms were variously reported to have been "indifferent," "in good condition but old pattern," "fair," or "percussion muskets."

The arms carried by Company E stationed at Savannah, Ga., were reported in July-October 1864 as "not good, but in good firing condition." In July 1863, the Marine Guard of C.S.S. *Savannah* was reported as having "15 muskets with bayonets." When *Atlanta* was captured in June 1863, the U.S. Navy inventory of small arms listed 22 Enfield rifles (caliber .58), 11 U.S. Muskets (caliber .69) and 30 breech loading Maynard rifles. Since the Marine Guard consisted of 22 privates and four non-commissioned officers, they were probably armed with either the Enfields or the Maynards. I suspect it was the Enfields because of the inherent difficulties of maintaining the ammunition supply of the Maynards.

There are some notes on the arms for Marines on the Mobile Station (Company D) for February-July 1863. Recruiting advertisements during February promised "Enfield Rifles with Sword Bayonets," and in March Captain Meiere requisitioned one hundred Enfields for his company. He remarked they were to replace the "very worthless Old Flint Lock Muskets altered" (caliber .69?) of which a very few would snap a cap — some with bayonets, some without.

It would make a good ending to say he received his Enfield rifles, but such was not the case. Meiere receipted for 150 Austrian rifles on June 6, 1863, and asked that suitable accoutrements be sent to him.[46] Bayonet scabbards were received two weeks later from the Army Military Storekeeper at Augusta, Georgia, Captain Isadore P. Girardy. The absence of the proper scabbards caused Captain Meiere to hold up the issue of the Austrian rifles, but once received, the issue of the rifles was again postponed by order of Admiral Buchanan on the grounds that the ammunition on hand for the Austrian rifles (45 rounds each) would not suffice should the Marines have to go into action to meet an expected attack. It was Captain Meiere's feeling that at least 250 rounds per rifle should be on hand. The altered flintlocks were usually caliber .69 while the typical Austrian rifles were caliber .58, so the ammunition was not interchangeable.

What arm was finally used at Mobile has not been clarified beyond the specific statement relating to Austrian rifles just discussed.

Two sets of small arms were on board the C.S.S. *Tennessee* when captured on August 5, 1864, in Mobile Bay, but which set belonged to the Marine Guard of the vessel is not clear. On board were "40 rifled muskets, with bayonets & scabbards" and "41 Springfield muskets, with bayonets & scabbards."[47] A 35-man Marine Guard could have used either set with the other for use by sailors.

The Marine Guard of the C.S.S. *Morgan* at Mobile was reported on December 1, 1864, as having a musket, cartridge box, cap box, belt, and bayonet scabbard for each man, but the type of musket is not indicated.[48]

Although the arms carried by the Marines of the James River Squadron surrendered as part of Semmes' Naval Brigade are not listed separately, the report of arms surrendered on April 30, 1865, shows that only one type was carried. The Naval Brigade, consisting of both sailors and Marines, surrendered just sixty .58 caliber, unspecified make, pieces.[49]

In conclusion, the Marines seem to have been armed with various weapons at various times and on various stations. There seems to have been no consistency or real uniformity, and one cannot point to a particular weapon and state positively, "The Confederate Marines were armed with that weapon."

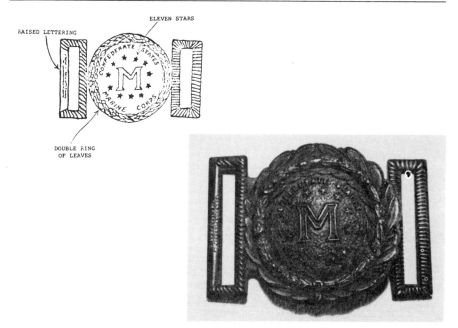

ELEVEN STARS

RAISED LETTERING

DOUBLE RING
OF LEAVES

A Pseudo Confederate Marine Belt Buckle.
Sketch by Ralph W. Donnelly. Photo by Karen L. Work and the North/South Trader.

ACCOUTREMENTS

In contrast with the U.S. Marine Corps accoutrements, white waist belts, and knapsack sliding slings of the French pattern, the Confederate Marine was prescribed black leather waist belts of the British style with cartridge box, cap box, and bayonet scabbard attached by means of slides. The knapsacks were to be the same as used in the British service with straps to connect with the waist belt.

Vizitelly's sketch shows enlisted men wearing belts over the right shoulder to the left hip, presumably for bayonets (which does not agree with the system above of attaching the bayonet scabbard to the waist belt by a slide).

Early in the 1970s, a belt buckle, purportedly a C. S. Marine Corps belt buckle, was introduced into the United States from England. Originally introduced as a curio with no pretense of authenticity, they sold in the $10-$15 range. At about the same time, they appeared in antique shops and flea markets in the D.C. area, priced in the $90-$100 range. These were sold without any guaranty or proof of authenticity, but purchasers were free to believe what they wanted to about the origin of the buckles.

The style of the buckle is not what might be expected. The questionable buckles have a circular belt plate with a single integral belt attachment for one end of the belt. A bent flat metal strap is soldered on the back as a hook in order to attach the plate to the "keeper." The more common style for the naval service at the time of the Civil War was a two-part buckle with a small interior circle interlocking within a larger outer circle, thus avoiding a soldered hook which could break easily.

Confused and improbable stories as to their origin, their failure to surface until more than a hundred years after the war; the absence of background information, and errors in names and addresses of military equipment firms combine to discredit these belt buckles as authentic Confederate Marine artifacts. The absence of an authentic buckle has complicated the evaluation of these recently surfaced items.

Even as late as 1864, rather complete equipment seems to have been issued to the enlisted Marines. Records of the Quartermaster, Major Algernon S. Taylor, show these items of equipment to have been issued commonly in the Richmond area; waist belts, bayonet scabbards for Enfield rifle bayonets, cap pouches, cartridge boxes, canteens and straps, haversacks, and sword bayonet frogs.[50]

On board ship the officer commanding the Marine guard was accountable for the arms, accoutrements, and clothing of his men and was charged with preserving them in the best possible manner. At least once a month he was required to make a clothing inspection and report loss or abuse to the ship's captain. The regulations provided that he was to be allowed the exclusive use of a storeroom. There was also a convenient locker to be built in each vessel as a fixture on the berth deck with shelves and pins where the Marines could keep their uniform caps, pompons, belts, etc. A musket rack was to be constructed against the cabin bulkhead or some other appropriate place considered the most suitable place in case of an emergency. It was to have a canvass screen to protect the arms from salt air and spray while at sea.[51] It seems fair to assume that newly constructed vessels complied with these regulations while the converted merchantmen should have approached compliance.

Appendices

319

NOTES AND REFERENCES

Appendix D — Uniforms, Arms, and Accoutrements of Confederate Marines.

1. II *N.O.R.* 2, 65.

2. Richmond *Enquirer*, Tues., May 7, 1861, 3:6 (published for one week from April 20).

3. An English Combatant, *Battle Fields of the South* (New York, 1864), 211.

4. *Regulations for the Uniform & Dress of the Marine Corps of the United States, October, 1859* (Philadelphia, 1859), 8.

5. Copied from a "Receipt Roll for Regular Issues" used in June 1864 by Maj. A. S. Taylor, Q.M., C.S.M.C., *Entry 426, R.G. 45,* U.S. National Archives.

6. II *N.O.R.* 2, 65.

7. *Ibid.*, 95.

8. *Ibid.*, 372.

9. Papers relating to the C.S.S. *Sumter*, Folder 501, Box 119, C.S.A., MSS. Div., Library of Congress. (Also on microfilm as "C.S.A. Pickett Pp., Vol. 119-120, Roll #69.")

10. Mobile *Advertiser and Register*, Jan. 24, 1863, 2:3.

11. Savannah *Republican*, June 2, 1863, 4:1

12. Capt. J. E. Meiere to Maj. A. S. Taylor, Q.M., C.S.M.C., Mobile, June 9, 1863, *Mobile C.O. Day Book*, 91.

13. *N.O.R.* 3, 819.

14. Naval Storekeeper D. R. Lindsey, C.S.N., to Paymaster Ware, C.S.N., Nov. 26, 1864, *Correspondence, October 1864-January 1865, Ware Pp.*

15. Invoice dated July 25, 1864, personal file of Major & Q.M. Algernon S. Taylor, C.S.M.C., *C.S.A. Carded Records, R.G. 109,* U.S. National Archives.

16. Richmond *Daily Examiner*, May 26, 1862, 2:2.

17. *Mobile C.O. Day Book*, 15: Capt. J. E. Meiere, C.S.M.C., to Col. Lloyd J. Beall, Mobile, Dec. 1, 1862.

18. Savannah *Republican*, Jan. 7, 1864, 1:1, and Mobile *Daily Advertiser and Register*, Jan. 1, 1864, 1:3.

19. G.O. 12, H.Q., C.S.M.C., Nov. 5, 1864, *Van B. Pp.*

20. Receipts in "OV" file (formerly Box 38), now Microfilm 1091, *Subject File of the Confederate States Navy 1861-1865,* U.S. National Archives.

21. This uniform was deposited with the Atlanta Historical Society by Mrs. John B. Reeves of Mt. Pleasant Plantation, Covington, Ga. It was first publicized by Richard Harwell in his "Introduction" to the reprint edition of *Uniform and Dress of the Army and Navy of the Confederate States of America* (New York, 1960), iv. Also see Lee A. Wallace, Jr., "Two C.S. Marine Corps Officers' Uniforms," *Military Collector & Historian*, v. 23, no. 2 (Summer 1974), 51-53.

22. Lt. Henry L. Graves, C.S.M.C., to "My Dear Mother," Savannah, Ga., Feb. 5, 1863, *Graves' Pp., SHC, UNC.*

23. *1859 U.S.M.C. Uniform Regs.*, 7.

24. Official U.S. Navy Photograph, NR&L (Old) #36. This picture is also reproduced in W. Adolphe Roberts, *Semmes of the Alabama* (New York, 1938). Curiously enough, another picture of the same group presumably taken at the same time exists. In this second version, the two officers seated with Semmes in the first picture are pictured as standing second from the end on either side.

In both pictures, the officer standing on the viewer's right is dressed in what appears to be a U.S. Marine Corps uniform — a double-breasted coat with a double row of buttons, *eight* to a row, and having two sleeve buttons without rank marking. The stand-up collar is also Marine rather than Navy. The eight coat buttons per row agree with the 1859 U.S.M.C. Uniform Regulations. By uniform alone, the man on the right has to be Marine Lt. Becket K. Howell as identified in the first picture. See p. 135.

25. Lt. Henry L. Graves, C.S.M.C., to "My Dear Mother," Savannah, Ga., April 22, 1863 (continuation of letter dated April 26), *Graves' Pp., SHC, UNC.*

26. *Loc. cit.*, Graves to "My Dear Sister," April 29, 1864.

27. *Loc. cit.*, Graves to "My Dear Mother," April 29, 1864.

28. *Loc. cit.*, Graves to "My Dear Mother," Nov. 3, 1864.

29. Lt. Thomas St. G. Pratt, C.S.M.C., to "Dear Ruck," Savannah, Ga., April 24, 1864, in personal file of Lt. Pratt, *Entry 198*, "Hospital and Prison Records . . . Navy and the Marine Corps," *R.G. 109*, U.S. National Archives. Also in Microcopy 260, Roll 3, U.S. National Archives.

30. *N.O.R.* 21, 899: G.O. 23, Naval Comdts. Office, Mobile, Ala., June 1, 1864.

31. Lt. Ruffin Thomson to "Dear Pa," Drewry's Bluff, Va., July 18, 1864, *Thomson, Pp., SHC, UNC.*

32. *Loc. cit.*, Lt. Ruffin Thomson to _____, Sept. 19 [1864].

33. *Loc. cit.*, Lt. Ruffin Thomson to "Dear Pa." Columbus, Ga., Feb. 9, 1865.

34. *Loc. cit.*, Lt. Ruffin Thomson to "Dear Pa," Drewry's Bluff. March 8, 1865.

35. C.S. Congress, *Journal*, IV, 443; Ramsdell, *op. cit.*, 16; and IV *O.R.* 3, 1033.

36. *1859 U.S.M.C. Uniform Regs.*, 6.

37. Entry dated Oct. 3, 1864, *Crenshaw's Diary.*

38. Providence [R.I.] *Journal,* Wed., June 17, 1863.

39. J. Bernard Thom to the author, May 28, 1963, and June 18, 1963.

40. Daniel D. Hartzler, "K.G&K. — The Other Side of the Crude Confederate Saber," *Military Collector & Historian,* vol. XXXIX, no. 3 (Fall 1987), 108-110.

41. New Orleans *Daily Picayune,* Wed., April 24, 1861, Supplement, 5:5.

42. Receipt for Ordnance Stores received from Capt. H. Oladowski, July 8, 1861, in personal file of Capt. George Holmes, C.S.M.C., *C.S.N. and C.S.M.C. Carded Records, R.G. 109,* U.S. National Archives.

43. G.O. 133, Dec. 1, 1861, Army of Pensacola (Bragg), *Entry 265, R.G. 109,* U.S. National Archives.

44. Letter Book, II, Gosport Dockyard, 107, *F. Forrest Pp., SHC, UNC:* Flag-Officer F. Forrest, C.S.N., to Comdt. L. J. Beall, C.S.M.C., Gosport, Dec. 4, 1861.

45. *O.R.* 53, 190: Gen. R. E. Lee to Secretary of War J. P. Benjamin. James D. Bulloch in his *The Secret Service of the Confederate States In Europe,* I, 112, says he brought over 1000 short rifles with cutlass bayonets for the Navy Department. There was a short model Enfield which carried a sword bayonet while the long model carried an angular bayonet, according to William A. Albaugh III, and Edward M. Simmons, *Confederate Arms* (New York: Bonanza Books, 1957), 62.

46. *Mobile C.O. Day Book,* 89: Capt. J. E. Meiere, C.S.M.C., to Major I. Greene, Adjt., C.S.M.C., Mobile, June 6, 1863.

47. *N.O.R.* 21, 553.

48. List of Clothing and Accoutrements of the Marine Guard of the C.S. Str. *Morgan,* Dec. 1, 1864, author's copy of an original in the papers of Lt. John L. Rapier, C.S.M.C., in the possession of Mrs. E. M. Trigg.

49. *O.R.* 47, pt. 3, 856.

50. Invoice of Ordnance Stores turned over to Capt. T. S. Wilson, C.S.M.C., March 28, 1864, in personal file of Major and Quartermaster Algernon S. Taylor, *C.S.A. Carded Records, R.G. 109,* U.S. National Archives.

51. *Regulations for the Navy of the Confederate States, 1862* (Richmond: Macfarlane & Fergusson, Printers, 1862), Chap. XXV, "Marines When in Vessels," 146 (Art. 9); 148-149 (Art. 20); 147 (Art. 10); 146 (Art. 5); 146 (Art. 7).

Letter from Lloyd J. Beall, formerly Colonel Commandant, C.S. Marine Corps, to Captain Henry Clay Cochrane, U.S.M.C., dated September 21st 1880, in which he states, "The books & papers appertaining to the C.S. Marine Corps were burnt by order of Mr. Mallory Sec. of the C.S. Navy.

This letter is photographically reproduced from a personal journal of Henry Clay Cochrane, U.S.M.C., in the holdings of the Personal Papers Collection (P.C. 1), History and Museums Division, H.Q., U.S.M.C.

SOURCES AND NOTES

The greatest problem in undertaking a study of the Confederate States Marine Corps is the paucity of existing documentary records, or at least, if they exist, the difficulty in locating them by the accepted procedures. It should not be overlooked that the entire organization was numerically small, being less than a full regiment, and the quantity of records would not be too great. On the other hand, the fact that the Marine Corps was a separate organization would lead one to expect certain headquarters records not customary with units as small as a regiment in Army service. The subdivision of the companies of the Corps into numerous detachments for service on Navy vessels and stations would result in additional records pertaining to these small units of the Corps within the records of the various naval commands.

There is evidence to show that within the Corps there was a feeling that the Navy appropriated all available credit to the exclusion of the Marines. Today, one can fairly say that the virtual absence of a mention of Marine activities in Navy reports tends to lend credence to this feeling. One Marine officer recorded this feeling in no uncertain terms in a letter to his father. His letter read, in part, as follows:

> If the chance is ever accorded to us of coming in conflict with the Enemy I think the Country will be Satisfied with our conduct. Our Corps has been represented in very many fights with the Yanks, but what they did was always appropriated by the Navy proper with whom they were acting. In Hampton Roads (the Merrimack fight) our Corps was largely represented — at Savannah — in Mobile Bay. On the famous "Alabama" & in fact in almost every action (naval) the Marines have played their part. But being Subordinate to the Navy — we got but little credit.[1].

Lt. Ruffin Thomson, who wrote the above letter, was apparently misinformed concerning Marines on the *Alabama*, and probably assumed the Marines on *Sumter* had been transferred to *Alabama*. But such had not been the case, and the sole Marine on board *Alabama* was 1st Lt. Becket K. Howell, a guard commander without a guard.

Ever since the publication of Scharf's *History of the Confederate States navy* in 1887, authors have replied upon his published report that many of the

323

most valuable records and books of the Corps were lost late in the war when the books and papers of the Colonel Commandant, Lloyd J. Beall, were destroyed by fire.[2] Only in July 1963 was a different version uncovered which goes far towards accounting for the paucity of official C.S. Marine Corps records. This was the discovery of a letter written on September 21, 1880, by the former Commandant in reply to an inquiry from the then Capt. Henry C. Cochrane, U.S.M.C., which modifies previous thinking about C.S. Marine Corps records. Beall wrote, in part:

> The books & papers appertaining to the C.S. Marine Corps were burnt by order of Mr. Mallory Sec. of the C.S. Navy, leaving me no record for reference, and I fear to trust a memory impaired by advancing age in making a statement such as you desire.
>
> I doubt whether there is any one living who could give you more reliable information in regard to the C.S. Marine Corps than my old friend Maj. [Simms?].[3]

Such an order could have been issued only upon the evacuation of Richmond or during the final retreat. The order could have caused the destruction of the records of the Adjutant, the Paymaster, and the Quartermaster, but we are not certain whether the order reached all the members of the Staff. In addition, there is always the possibility of a degree of disobedience sufficient to cause some records to become souvenirs.

The records of the Quartermaster's and Commissary's departments of the Corps, under the direction and supervision of Major Algernon S. Taylor, also are reported to have been destroyed. The story is that Lt. Nathaniel E. Venable, Taylor's assistant, acting under orders, accompanied all the books and papers of Taylor's departments from Richmond to Danville upon the evacuation of the former. Unfortunately, these records are reported to have been destroyed in Danville.[4]

The records which were presumed to be under the direct control of the Adjutant of the Corps, Major Israel Greene, and the headquarters clerk, John L. Adams, should have included the original manuscript copies of both the General Orders and Special Orders issued from Corps Headquarters, files of both in and out correspondence, applications for appointment as an officer of the Corps, and various personnel records. Among these last should have been the Adjutant's office file copies of the muster rolls of the companies and periodic reports from the commanders of Marine Guards on the various ships and stations. It is not clear from Col. Beall's letter whether these records were burned in Richmond or whether they were packed and carried out of town in the custody of the Adjutant who received orders to destroy them at some town or place along the line of retreat. Communications with members of Major Greene's family have not uncovered any of the records. Greene was paroled at Farmville, between April 11 and 21, 1865,[5] according to one record. Another says he was captured on April 14 which is not in conflict with the first record.[6] Assuming that he brought the various headquarter's records with him from Richmond, the question is raised, did he hide them between that fateful April 9 and April 14 when he was captured? Or did they get destroyed on the retreat from Richmond?

The second group of papers and records we should like to find are those of Major and Paymaster Richard T. Allison who surrendered with Capt. John R. F. Tattnall's Company E at Greensboro, North Carolina, as a part of Gen. Joseph E. Johnston's command. Here, again, we must presume they were destroyed as Allison apparently retained none of his official papers in his possession after the war. He left only a few mementos of his service in the Confederacy, including two stars and buttons, accompanied by a note stating his regret that he had nothing else to show for the four years, 1861-1865.[7]

One of the few items Allison left was a note giving his itinerary from Richmond south which read as follows:

April 2, 1865	Left Richmond.
" 3	At Mrs. Herrings.
" 4	George Scott's at Cumberland C.H.
" 5	Lentbanks, at Farmville.
" 6	Dr. Lewis' - Coles Ferry.
" 7	Jerry White's, Meadville.
" 8	Lamers, near Danville.
" 9	Danville.
" 10	Danville.
" 11	Left Danville.
Easter Sunday [April 16]	At Mr. Crowell's Stanley [Stanly] County, North Carolina.[8]

Allison's presence on April 16 so close to Charlotte, North Carolina, and its Naval Ordnance Works makes one wonder whether he went on to Charlotte following the President and Cabinet and returned later to Greensboro. The records of the Pay Office could have been destroyed in Richmond or destroyed or stored along the route of Allison's retreat, possibly even in Charlotte. The presumption is that they were in Richmond before April 2 and were not with Allison when he got home. What happened in between?

Confederate Marine material would normally be expected to be found both in the records of the Navy Department and in the records of the various naval vessels and stations. This complicates the search and makes it necessary to review many of the Confederate Navy records. But here again we have a problem. We are told that "of the records of the Navy Department practically none was captured [on the occupation of Richmond] except reports of investigations of the Navy Department."[9] Despite the story of "seven great boxes full of papers and instruments" belonging to the Confederate Navy at the home of Judge Garnett Andrews in Washington, Georgia, on April 27, 1865,[10] the best opinion today is that the "destruction of the Navy Department records at Charlotte fits into the whole picture of the collapse better than any other supposition."[11] This applies to those records which escaped destruction at Richmond.

There was some possibility that the history of the Confederate States Navy would have been written by Capt. William F. Lynch, C.S.N., as he was detailed by the Navy Department during the winter of 1864-65 to write reports on the battles and combats in which the C.S. Navy took part.[12] But how many documents he gathered is not known, nor do we know what happened to the ones he did collect. No documents used for the publication of the *Official Records of the Union and Confederate Navies . . .* are credited directly to Capt. Lynch although Scharf seems to have had access to some.

This paucity of Navy records was explained as long ago as 1867 by former Secretary of the Navy Stephen R. Mallory. In replying to the suggestion of a former Confederate Navy officer, James H. Rochelle, that he author a history of the Confederate Navy, Mallory wrote:

> Much, by far the largest and most important of the data important for such a work was destroyed, upon and soon after the evacuation of Richmond; and personal recollections must be relied upon, always a most unsatisfactory authority in matters touching the relative claims, merits, etc. . . . of men or military operations, — to make up history.[13]

In order to obtain the Confederate side of the war, some 2,232 different documents were borrowed by the U.S. Navy Department from private individuals or organizations of the South, of which 1,771 were returned to the owners. Of some 107 organizations and individuals loaning documents to the Office of Naval Records and Library, only one document (a personal letter) came from a former Confederate Marine, Lt. Everard T. Eggleston.[14]

There are three collections of war-time letters which have been most useful in preparing this history. These are the letters of Lts. Henry L. Graves, Ruffin

Thomson, and John L. Rapier. The Graves' letters, part of the holdings of the Southern Historical Collection of the University of North Carolina, have largely been published in 1963 as *A Confederate Marine: A Sketch of Henry Lea Graves with excerpts from the Graves Family Correspondence.* Edited by Richard Harwell, the book is Volume 24 of the Confederate Centennial Studies, W. Stanley Hoole, Editor-in-Chief.

The letters of Ruffin Thomson, of which some 120 are of the war period, include about 25 long letters written between February 11, 1864, and the end of the war, being the period when he was a Marine officer. Part of the holdings of the Southern Historical Collection, these letters are in holographic form and have not been published.

A collection of the war letters of Lt. John L. Rapier are in the possession of his granddaughter, Mrs. Edwin M. Trigg, of Mobile, Alabama. Not yet published, they should ultimately provide additional insight into the life and times of a Confederate Marine officer.

A small group of five war-time letters to, from, or about Lt. Edward Crenshaw during the war have been assembled by the Author. More important, however, is Crenshaw's war-time diary. It has been published (although poorly edited) in the *Alabama Historical Quarterly.* That portion dealing with his Marine Corps activities is to be found in No. 4 of Volume I and in the four numbers of Volume II.

These five installments are divided chronologically as follows:

July 1 - 17, 1864	Vol. I, no. 4, pp. 448-452.
July 18 - October 3, 1864	Vol. II, no. 1, pp 52-71.
October 4 - December 15, 1864	Vol. II, no. 2, pp. 221-238.
December 16, 1864 -	
March 30, 1865	Vol. II, no. 3, pp. 365-385.
March 31 - June 19, 1865	Vol. II, no. 4, pp. 465-482.

Of six letters written by Lt. John D. Fowler, C.S.M.C., and published just recently, just one has material relating to the Marine Corps history, that of April 23, 1862, to "My Dear Brother Theoph," and Fowler's appointment letter from President Jefferson Davis enclosed with his letter of October 27, 1861, to "My Dear Brother."[15]

The Manuscript Section of the Tennessee State Archives contains various writings of Lt. H. M. Doak. The major collection, Accession 266, consists of correspondence, clippings, various sketches written by Doak in later life, and a Confederate Questionnaire completed in 1921 at the request of the Tennessee State Archives. Of particular value to this history were pages 30-43 of an 81-page autobiography.

One of the largest private collections of Confederate Marine Corps papers is now located in the Archives Section of the Howard-Tilton Memorial Library of Tulane University in New Orleans, La. This collection consists of some 78 items which belonged at one time to Capt. Alfred C. Van Benthuysen. Included are various rolls and returns of Company B, documents relating to courts-martial, various General Orders from HQ, Marine Corps, letters from the Secretary of the Navy, orders from Army HQ in Pensacola, as well as various abstracts on disbursements, clothing issues, equipment issues, etc.

It would be illuminating to locate a similar collection of papers for Capts. John D. Simms, George Holmes, Reuben T. Thom, Thomas S. Wilson, or Julius Ernest Meiere, as well as for Col. Beall, Lt. Col. Tyler, or Major Terrett.

Efforts to locate the personal papers or letters of enlisted men have been more difficult than those of the officers. This revised history has been enriched by two post-war letters of Pvt. William McLeod and two war-time letters, one by Pvt. H. H. Bowen, and the second by W. J. Bowen, North Carolina conscripts.

Students who wish more documentation than given here should consult the original edition of *The History of the Confederate States Marine Corps* (Washington, N.C.: by the author, 1976), or, in the case of officers, consult the notes in *Biographical Sketches of the Commissioned Officers of the Confederate States Marine Corps* (Washington, N.C.: by the author, revised edition, 1983).

NOTES AND REFERENCES

Sources and Notes

1. Lt. Ruffin Thomson, C.S.M.C., to "Dear Pa," Drewry's Bluff, Va., Nov. 3, 1864, *Thomson Pp., SHC, UNC.*

2. Scharf, *History of the C.S.N.*, 770, note 2.

3. MS. Journal of Henry Clay Cochrane, U.S.M.C., Personal Papers Collections, Division of History and Museums, H.Q., U.S.M.C.

4. Scharf, *op. cit.*, 770, note 1. Contact with members of the Venable family has failed to confirm or deny the truth of this.

5. Papers of I. Greene, Major, C.S.M.C., in Hospital and Prison Records of Persons Serving in the Navy and the Marine Corps, 1862-1865, *Entry 198, R.G. 109*, U.S. National Archives.

6. *1931 C.S.N. Reg.*, 76.

7. Miss Margaret M. Worthington of Annapolis, Md., to the author, Jan. 30, 1956. Her mother was the last surviving legatee of Allison's estate.

8. Copy of item in papers of Richard T. Allison furnished to the author by Miss Margaret M. Worthington of Annapolis, Md., Jan. 30, 1956.

9. II *N.O.R.* 3, 15: remarks of Capt. C. C. Marsh, U.S.N., Ret., Officer in Charge, Naval Records and Library, U.S. Navy Dept., *circa* 1922.

10. Eliza Frances Andrews, *The War-Time Journal of a Georgia Girl 1864-1865* (Macon: The Ardivan Press, 1960), 187, 290-291. The records were seized by Capt. Lot Abraham, Co. D, 4th Iowa Cavalry, Acting Provost-Marshal at Washington, Ga., on June 7, 1865. These were probably records of the Confederate Naval Academy since they were brought to Washington by "Capt. Parker" [Lt. Wm. H. Parker, Supt.] and "Lieut. Peck" [Lt. George M. Peek, instructor in mathematics at the Academy].

11. Dallas D. Irvine, "The Fate of Confederate Archives," *American Historical Review*, vol. 44, no. 4 (July 1939), 833.

12. Scharf, *op. cit.*, 192.

13. Joseph T. Durkin, S.J., *Stephen R. Mallory* (Chapel Hill: The University of North Carolina Press, 1954), 409, and note 100: S. R. Mallory to James Henry Rochelle, Pensacola, Fla., May 21, 1867. The original letter is in the Rochelle Papers at Duke University.

14. II *N.O.R.* 3, 18-19.

15. David M. Sullivan (ed.), "Fowler the Soldier Fowler the Marine," *Civil War Times Illustrated*, v. 26, no. 10 (February 1988), 28-35, 44-45.

Roanoke Station, Va., 109.
Roberts, J. DeBerniere., 109, 111, 117, 119; bio sketch, 250-251.
Roberts, Samuel M., 57, 64; bio sketch, 242.
Robinson, William H., 8.
Roby, Francis M., 118.
Rochelle, James H., 127.
Rock Wharf, Va., 39.
Rocketts Navy Yard, Richmond, Va., 52, 53, 265.
Rodgers, John, 41.
Ryan, William, 134.
St. Mary's, Md., 111.
Sanders, George N., 190, 192; Mrs. George N. (Anna J.), 192.
Sanders, Reid, 190, 191, 192.
Santa Rosa Island, Fla., 23, 24.
Savannah, Ga., 22, 71, 72, 73, 98; marines at, Chapter V (89-100); marines from, 127, 128.
Sayler's Creek, Va., 60.
Sayre, Calvin L., 23, 68, 171, 172, 175; bio sketch, 222.
Scharf, J. Thomas, 32.
Scott, _____, conf spy, 195-196.
Scott, Charles, 15.
Seddon, James A., 106, 192.
Sellers, M.H., 126.
Sells, David Miles, 171.
Semmes, Raphael, 18, 55, 56, 62, 63, 64, 134, 136.
Serapis, 262.
Serial numbers: assigned by Paymaster Ware, 69.
Seymour, Truman, 60.
Shannon, William, 104.
Sharpsburg (Antietam), Md., 110.
Sheridan, Philip, 51.
Sherman, Thomas, 191.
Ship Island, Miss., 18, 19, 80, 95, 265.
Ships:**Confederate Navy:** Alabama, 136, 137, 175; Arctic, 107, 117, 265; Atlanta, (formerly Fingal), 72, 93, 94, 95, 115, 190, 263; Atlanta (later Tallahassee), 115, 127, 138, 139; Baltic, 72, 74, 79, 81, 85, 264; Beaufort, 56; Charleston, 126, 127, 264; Chickamauga, (formerly Edith), 115, 117, 141, 264; Chicora, 126, 264; Columbia, 127, 128, 129, 130, 264; Dolman, 28, 72, 264; Drewry, 264; Fredericksburg, 53, 56, 264; Gaines, 72, 73, 74, 79, 80, 264; Gallego, 53, 264; Georgia, 94, 95, 97, 98, 117, 128, 136, 265; Huntress, 89, 124, 264; Huntsville, 79, 83; Indian Chief, 128, 264; Isondiga, 95, 128, 264; Jamestown, 27, 36, 37, 40; Lady Davis, 89; McRae, 18, 19, 72, 264; Macon, 99, 100, 128, 264; Merrimack

(later Virginia), 27, 34, 36, 263; Morgan, 72, 74, 80, 81, 83, 84, 85, 196, 264; Nashville, 83, 84, 85, 196, 264; North Carolina, 104, 105, 106, 107, 115, 117, 264; Olustee, 139; Palmetto State, 127, 264; Patrick Henry, 27, 34, 36, 40, 48, 53, 264; Pedee, 265; Raleigh, 104, 105, 106, 107, 117, 264; Rappahannock, 138, 141, 265; Resolute, 89, 264; Richmond, 49, 56, 264; St. Philip (formerly Star of the West), 16, 18; Sampson, 89, 90, 93, 95, 100, 185, 264; Savannah (steamer), 73, 89, 90, 264; Savannah (ironclad), 93, 94, 95, 96, 97, 118 185, 264; Schultz (steamer), 49; Selma, 79, 80, 83; Shenandoah, 137; Stonewall, 137, 265; Stono, 125; Sumter, 18, 134, 136, 264; Tacony, 190, 192; Tallahassee (formerly Atlanta, later Olustee), 115, 117, 138, 139, 265; Teaser, ; Tennessee, 76, 79, 80, 83, 264; Tuscaloosa, 79, 83; United States, 27, 33, 34, 35, 264; Virginia (formerly Merrimack), 34, 36, 38, 39, 56, 57, 62, 91, 264;; Virginia II, 53, 264.
Confederate Private: Alice, 73, 106; Edith, 141; Fingal, 72, 93, 94, 95, 115, 190, 263; Florie, 110, 111, 113; Hansa, 106; Judah, 21, 23;Let-Her-B, 110, 111, 113; Mary Wilson, 72; St. Nicholas, 35; Time, 17, 24; Yorktown, 34, 53; **Federal Navy:** Aroostook, 41; Chocura, 38; Colorado, 26; Commodore, 196; Corwin, 38;Cumberland, 32, 263; Dobbin, 192; Galena, 41, 42; James Adger, 95; Monitor, 39, 263; Niphon, 105, 106; Pawnee, 32; Pennsylvania, 32; Pontoosuc, 118; Port Royal, 41; Saratoga, 186; Underwriter, 83, 98, 103-104; Vermont, 95; Wabash, 90; Water Witch, 98; Weehawken, 94, 95, 190; **Federal Private:** Abigail, 137; Ariel, 137; Cuba, 134;J. B. Spafford, 57; Machias, 134; Rhode Island, 28; St. Mary's, 57.
Signal Hill (James River), Va., 56.
Simms, John D., 5, 8, 35, 42, 60, 62, 108, 110, 125, 171, 172, 180, 181, 187, 188; bio sketch, 211-212; 260.
Skull Creek, S.C., 90.
Slaughter, Richard C., 103.
Smith, Eugene R., 62, 128; bio sketch, 251-252.
Smith Francis W., 49, 59.
Smith, Peter, 90.
Smith, Philip, 118.
Smithville (now Southport), N.C., 106, 111, 114, 117.
Society Hill, S.C., 120.
South, 3; Lower South, 172; Upper South, 3.
Southern Maryland, 108, 113.
Spencer, Henry, 134.

Spe - We

Spencer repeating rifles, 51.
Stark, Alexander W., 170, 171.
Staunton River Bridge, Va., 109.
Stephenson, George, 136.
Stephenson, Lloyd Beall, 53, 111; bio sketch, 244-245.
Stockton, Edward Cantey, bio sketch, 258-259; 261.
Stony Creek Bridge, Va., 50.
Stoney Creek Depot, Va., 109.
Stuart, James E.B., 51.
Surrender of C.S. Marines, at Appomattox, 57, 58, 59, 129; at Citronelle, 85; at Greensboro, N.C., 64, 131;at Nanna Hubba Bluff, Ala., 83, 85.
Sylvia, Emmanuel, 137.
Taliaferro, William B., 129.
Tansill, Robert, 7, 40, 171, 172, 180, 181; bio sketch, 221-222; 261.
Tattnall, John R. F., 7, 43, 64, 91, 93, 95, 97, 98, 99, 100, 128, 129, 131, 171, 172, 180, 181, 184; bio sketch, 212-213.
Tattnall, Josiah, 22, 39, 89, 91, 94, 96, 97, 263.
Taylor, Algernon S.,7, 8, 43, 62, 171, 172; bio sketch, 214-215.
Taylor, Richard, 85.
Terrett, George H., 7, 11, 21, 50, 51, 54, 58, 171, 172; bio sketch, 215-216; 261.
Thom, Reuben T., 14, 16, 19 20, 22, 23, 26-28, 32, 36, 40, 42, 43, 54, 62, 68, 71, 72, 172, 180; bio sketch, 202-203.
Thomason, H. I., 136.
Thomson, Ruffin, 11, 29, 99, 131, 182, 183; bio sketch, 245-246.
Thurston, James, 57, 71, 89, 92, 94, 95, 141, 190, 191, 192; bio sketch, 229-230.
Tickfaw, La., 196.
Tombigbee River, Ala., 85.
Tucker, John R., 35, 36, 53, 57, 60, 61, 62, 127, 129.
Turner, George P., 23, 43, 171, 172, 175, 189; sister, Henriette, 189; bio sketch, 255-256.
Twiggs, David E., 18, 19,20.
Tyler, Henry B., 8, 20, 22, 186, 187; bio sketch, 217.
Tyler, Henry B., Jr., 171, 172, 185, 186; bio sketch, 257-258.
Tyler, John, 112.
Union Press, New Orleans, La., 193.
United States Army, 15. Negro troops, 108.
UNITS: Sheridan's Cav, 51; Army of the James (Butler), 49; Army of the Potomac, 49; Grant's Army, 113 ; Sherman's Army, 98; 6th (Wright's) Corps, 60, 61; 3rd Div. 6th

AC, 60, 61 ; Custer's Cav. Div., 61; Merritt's Cav. Div., 61 ; REGULARS: 1st Arty, 15; 2d Arty, 15; Btry E, 5th Arty (Brincklé's), 60 ; 2d Cav, 15.; VOLUNTEERS: Massachusetts: 37th Inf, 60; New Hampshire: 3d, 51; New York: 6th Inf, 23; 100th Inf, 127; 121st Inf, 60; Pennsylvania: 55th Inf, at Drewry's Bluff, 51.
United States Government: Exec Doc No 3, 38th Cong, 1st Sess, 171; Consul at Gibraltar, 134; Marine Corps to serve with Army, 266;
United States Marine Corps,12, 21, 170, 174, 189, 265; Adj & Inspr, 1, 21; band, 165; destruction of Judah, 22, 23; not source of recruits for CSMC, 33, 137; pre-war strength, 1.
United States Military Academy, see West Point.
United States Navy, 2; Conf POWs enlist in, 82; destruction of Judah, 22, 23.
United States Navy Department, 12; Secretary of the Navy: Isaac Toucey (1859), 263; Gideon Welles (1861-1865), 111, 171.
Upper Marlboro, Md., 113.
Valley of Virginia, 108.
Van Benthuysen, Alfred C., 3, 14, 15, 16, 17, 22, 28, 38, 42, 107, 115, 117, 118, 119, 120, 172, 181, 187, 188; bio sketch, 203-205.
Vance, Zebulon, 115.
Van de Graaff, John S., bio sketch, 225.
Veitch, Thomas, 98.
Venable, Nathaniel E., 54, 188; bio sketch, 234-235.
Vicksburg, Miss., Conf Marines exchanged at, 85.
Vincent's Creek, S.C., 126, 127.
Virginia, 172; Conf Marines in Va., Chap III; Prov Army of, 21; State Ordinance of Apr. 27, 1861, 33.
Waddell, James I., 137.
Wagener, John A., 90.
Wallace Edwin, 8, 9.
War of 1812, 262.
Ware, Thomas R., 29, 68, 70, 74.
Warley, Alexander F., 19, 20, 126.
Warrington Navy Yard, Pensacola, Fla., 5, 17, 22, 265.
Washington, D.C., 108, 109, 111, 112 ; defenses of, 113.
Washington Marine Barracks, D.C., 70.
Watts, Thomas Hill, 181.
Webb, William A., 94, 124.
Weir Andrew, 33.
Weldon, N.C., 109.

Additional Books of Interest
published by

White Mane Publishing Company, Inc.

. . .

𝕻𝖚𝖇𝖑𝖎𝖘𝖍𝖊𝖗𝖘 𝖔𝖋 𝕬𝖒𝖊𝖗𝖎𝖈𝖆'𝖘 𝕮𝖎𝖛𝖎𝖑 𝖂𝖆𝖗 𝕳𝖊𝖗𝖎𝖙𝖆𝖌𝖊

SOUTHERN REVENGE
The Confederate Burning of Chambersburg, Pa.

Published By Greater Chambersburg Chamber of Commerce and White Mane Publishing Company, Inc.

ISBN 0-942597-14-1, hardcover, 200 pp.   **$28.95**

Southern Revenge is the Civil War history of Chambersburg, Pennsylvania, the only northern town burned by the Confederates. This pictorial history book to be released on the 125th anniversary of the burning is filled with rare photographs, diary accounts, period news paper articles and accurate historical text.

Chambersburg, Pennsylvania, a quiet farming community near the Maryland border, was truly the crossroads of destiny. The home of the Cumberland Valley Railroad, Chambersburg had much to offer the war effort. The railroad system provided a much needed supply route for the Union Army, as well as the Confederates.

For three long years Chambersburg residents endured an influx of both Union and Confederate troops, often outnumbered by them in their own community. As a staging area for the Union Army, thousands of soldiers prepared for war in the streets and outlining areas of the town. Confederate leaders such as Generals "JEB" Stuart and Robert E. Lee would come to Chambersburg.

Steeped in principle, Chambersburg residents refused the demands made upon them by Confederate troops. Thus the town was torched by General John McCausland on July 30, 1864. From the ashen pile of rubble the rebuilding began.

ANTIETAM: THE SOLDIERS' BATTLE

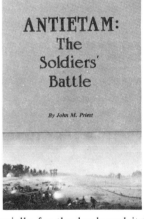

By John M. Priest

ISBN 0-942597-09-5, hardcover, 464 pp.   **$34.95**

Antietam is the most definitive study of the battle from the soldier's view. Anecdotes and vignettes take the reader back to September 16-18, 1862, providing an hour by hour account of the bloodiest day in American history. The careful weaving together of over 200 recollections, diaries, letters and regimental histories make it easy to visualize the battle as the average soldier experienced it.

This unique book is about individuals, their combat, and their heroism and death. Priest provides fact-filled drama, capturing the bravery, cowardice, pathos and humor of the soldiers and civilians caught up in the war. No student of Civil War combat, the enlisted men, or of the Civil War in Maryland can afford to miss this new study, with its 72 detailed maps created especially for the book and its illustrations rarely seen elsewhere.

As Jay Luvaas, Professor at the U.S. Army War College, wrote in his introduction, "The purpose of this book is . . . to weave a tapestry of individual experiences. The colors may not always be consistent or true, as in any battle, but in their separate detail the experiences of the participants come alive. It has been 40 years since Bruce Catton squeezed the human interest material out of shelves of neglected regimental histories to portray the Army of the Potomac and its campaigns and Bell Irvin Wiley reconstructed the wartime lives of Johnny Reb and Billy Yank. Here is a book that reaches deep into scattered manuscript sources to provide a similar service for the men who fought at Antietam."

Check with your local bookstore - OR - order directly from
WHITE MANE PUBLISHING COMPANY, INC., P.O. Box 152, Shippensburg, PA 17257

Civil War
Justice

Union Army Executions
under Lincoln

Robert I. Alotta

CIVIL WAR JUSTICE
Union Army Executions Under Lincoln
By Robert I. Alotta

ISBN 0-942597-10-9, hardcover, 234 pp. $24.95

This study brings to light a chapter of Civil War history that has been hidden in the archives. Dealing with the underside of the administration of the Union Army, Alotta shows us a different side of President Abraham Lincoln in this thorough study of the executions of Union soldiers. Alotta, the author of seven earlier books, provides not only a new interpretation of Union Army justice, but also extensive documentation revising upwards the number of known Union military executions. **Civil War Justice** is an examination of the administration of military justice, including an unusual chapter on the ritual of the executions themselves.

Civil War Justice's combination of interpretation and documentation offers double value. In his well-written book Alotta offers both new insights and reference materials.

Civil War Justice is the first book to deal with the court-martial system during the Civil War and the effect of this system on the common soldier. Alotta doesn't pull any punches, and his latest book is certain to generate controversy.

DEFENDER OF THE CHESAPEAKE
The Story of Fort Monroe
By Richard P. Weinert, Jr., and Robert Arthur

3rd Rev. Ed., ISBN 0-942597-12-5, hardcover, 373 pp. $19.95

Sited to guard the entrance to Virginia's Chesapeake Bay, Fort Monroe, the largest U.S. stone fort ever built, played a key role in the Civil War and is still used by the Army today. Peacetime garrison life, modernization of its ordnance, service in the Spanish-American war and World Wars I and II are described, documented, and well-illustrated in this history. Fort Monroe, where Jefferson Davis was imprisoned, appears on the National Register of Historic Places.

Fort Monroe's history is so rich that new information and photographs are constantly being discovered. This revised and updated edition includes the schools, commands, and soldiers stationed there through the last 166 years.

As *The Military Collector and Historian* said of the second edition, "This amply documented and well illustrated volume is a model for those who would write about other military posts." In Great Britain, the Newsletter of the Fortress Study Group, *Casemate*, said, "I recommend everybody interested in the fort, its armament, or U.S. military history in general to read this book."

THE TRAINING OF AN ARMY
Camp Curtin and the North's Civil War
By William J. Miller

ISBN 0-942597-15-X, hardcover, approx. 340 pp. $27.95

While the name of Camp Curtin will be recognized by most Civil War historians and buffs, the story of the Camp has remained unknown until the publication of **Training Of An Army**.

The Training Of An Army is a story of the education, supplying, and medical care of the North's soldiers. The author, William J. Miller, adds an important chapter to the story of the common soldier. The background, training, leisure time activities, all that made up the new recruits' introduction to military life, their wonder, amazement, accomplishments, and problems are reported and analyzed in this important new study.

These are the experiences of both the soldiers in the ranks and some of the future generals who passed through Camp Curtin on their way to Antietam, Gettysburg, the Wilderness and Petersburg. **The Training Of An Army** is a significant addition to our understanding of the Civil War's impact on town and family life in Pennsylvania, a large state where local and national history crossed in those years of 1861-1865.